Learning DevOps

Second Edition

A comprehensive guide to accelerating DevOps culture adoption with Terraform, Azure DevOps, Kubernetes, and Jenkins

Mikael Krief

BIRMINGHAM—MUMBAI

Learning DevOps
Second Edition

Group Product Manager: Rahul Nair
Publishing Product Manager: Preet Ahuja
Senior Editor: Shazeen Iqbal
Content Development Editor: Romy Dias
Technical Editor: Arjun Varma
Copy Editor: Safis Editing
Project Coordinator: Shagun Saini
Proofreader: Safis Editing
Indexer: Hemangini Bari
Production Designer: Jyoti Chauhan
Marketing Coordinator: Nimisha Dua

First published: October 2019
Second edition: February 2022

Production reference: 1240222

Published by Packt Publishing Ltd.
Livery Place
35 Livery Street
Birmingham
B3 2PB, UK.

ISBN 978-1-80181-896-4

www.packt.com

I would like to dedicate this book to my wife and children,
who are my source of happiness.

Contributors

About the author

Mikael Krief (born in 1980) lives in France and works as a DevOps engineer.

He loves to share his passion through various communities such as the HashiCorp User Group. In 2019, he wrote the first edition of this book, and in 2020, he wrote *Terraform Cookbook* (Packt Publishing), and also contributes to many public projects, writes blogs and books, and speaks at conferences.

He is interested in HashiCorp products and specializes in the use of Terraform in several company contexts.

For all his contributions and passion, he has received the Microsoft **Most Valuable Professional** (**MVP**) award, which Microsoft has awarded him for the last 6 years and he has been nominated and selected as a Hashicorp Ambassador since 2020.

I would like to extend my thanks to my family for accepting that I needed to work long hours on this book during family time. I would like to thank Meeta Rajani for giving me the opportunity to write this second edition of this book, which was a very enriching experience. Special thanks to Romy Dias and Vaidehi Sawant for their valuable input and time reviewing this book and to the entire Packt team for their support during the course of writing this book.

About the reviewers

Kevin Bridges is a senior DevOps engineer at Alegeus. Kevin's worked with a wide range of tools supporting stable releases and hotfixes. He's relatively new to the cloud space (Azure), is enjoying it so far, and just received Azure Fundamentals certification in June 2021.

Kevin spent 20 years in the Army in active and reserve capacities. He graduated from Granite State College with a Bachelor of Science in information technology in 2009 and graduated with an MBA from the University of New Hampshire (Manchester) in May 2015.

Kevin loves making complicated things simple.

I would like to thank all my family, friends, and colleagues
for all their support

Deb Bhattacharya applies Agile and DevOps to make organizations more successful. Over 20 years, Deb has helped over 50 teams across 4 countries to be more Agile and to be more DevOps. Deb is passionate about that.

Deb's other passion is sports. When Deb was younger, he used to play professional table tennis. He won many tournaments, but most importantly, he coached tournament-winning table tennis teams. Deb still enjoys playing table tennis.

Deb uses all his experience from his hands-on software development background and his sports background to develop high-performing Agile and DevOps teams. The two passions nicely come together here.

I am thankful to Anand Athani, the delivery manager I reported to some
20 years ago when I was an engineering lead. I was writing the thesis paper
for my master's and Anand suggested Rational Unified Process (RUP). That
started my Agile journey. The learning and contributing are still going on.

Table of Contents

5
Authoring the Development Environment with Vagrant

Section 2: DevOps CI/CD Pipeline

6
Managing Your Source Code with Git

7

Continuous Integration and Continuous Delivery

8

Deploying Infrastructure as Code with CI/CD Pipelines

Section 3: Containerized Microservices with Docker and Kubernetes

9
Containerizing Your Application with Docker

10
Managing Containers Effectively with Kubernetes

Section 4: Testing Your Application

11

Testing APIs with Postman

12
Static Code Analysis with SonarQube

13
Security and Performance Tests

Section 5: Taking DevOps Further/More on DevOps

14
Security in the DevOps Process with DevSecOps

15

Reducing Deployment Downtime

16

DevOps for Open Source Projects

17
DevOps Best Practices

Preface

Today, with the evolution of technologies and ever-increasing competition, companies are facing a real challenge to design and deliver products faster – all while maintaining user satisfaction.

One of the solutions to this challenge is to introduce (to companies) a culture of collaboration between different teams, such as development and operations, testers, and the security team. This culture, which has already been proven and is called a DevOps culture, can ensure that teams and certain practices reduce the time to market of companies through this collaboration – with shorter application deployment cycles and by bringing real value to the company's products and applications.

Moreover, with the major shift of companies toward the cloud, application infrastructures are evolving and the DevOps culture will allow better scalability and performance of applications, thus generating a financial gain for companies.

If you want to learn more about the DevOps culture and apply its practices to your projects, this book will introduce the basics of DevOps practices through different tools and labs.

In this book, we will discuss the fundamentals of the DevOps culture and practices, and then we will examine different labs used for the implementation of DevOps practices, such as IaC, using Git and CI/CD pipelines, test automation, code analysis, and DevSecOps, along with the addition of security to your processes.

A part of this book is also dedicated to the containerization of applications, with coverage of the simple use of Docker and the management of containers in Kubernetes. It includes downtime reduction topics during deployment and DevOps practices on open source projects.

This book ends with a chapter dedicated to some good DevOps practices that can be implemented throughout the life cycle of your projects.

In this second edition, all tools are upgraded and we will learn about Vagrant from HashiCorp and more on Kubernetes deployment.

The book aims to guide you through the step-by-step implementation of DevOps practices using different tools that are mostly open source or are leaders in the market.

In writing this book, my goal is to share my daily experience with you; I hope that it will be useful for you and be applied to your projects.

Who this book is for

This book is for anyone who wants to start implementing DevOps practices. No specific knowledge of development or system operations is required.

What this book covers

Chapter 1, The DevOps Culture and Infrastructure as Code Practices, explains the objectives of the DevOps culture and details the different DevOps practices – IaC and CI/CD pipelines – that will be seen throughout this book.

Chapter 2, Provisioning Cloud Infrastructure with Terraform, details provisioning cloud infrastructure with IaC using Terraform, including its installation, its command line, its life cycle, practical usage for provisioning a sample of Azure infrastructure, and the protection of Terraform state files with remote backends.

Chapter 3, Using Ansible for Configuring IaaS Infrastructure, concerns the configuration of VMs with Ansible, including Ansible's installation, command lines, setting up roles for an inventory and a playbook, its use in configuring VMs in Azure, data protection with Ansible Vault, and the use of a dynamic inventory.

Chapter 4, Optimizing Infrastructure Deployment with Packer, covers the use of Packer to create VM images, including its installation and how it is used for creating images in Azure.

Chapter 5, Authoring the Development Environment with Vagrant, explains how to build a local development environment using IaC and Vagrant.

Chapter 6, Managing Your Source Code with Git, explores the use of Git, including its installation, its principal command lines, its workflow, an overview of the branch system, and an example of a workflow with GitFlow.

Chapter 7, Continuous Integration and Continuous Delivery, shows the creation of an end-to-end CI/CD pipeline using three different tools: Jenkins, GitLab CI, and Azure Pipelines. For each of these tools, we will explain their characteristics in detail.

Chapter 8, Deploying Infrastructure as Code with a CI/CD Pipeline, discusses the usage of CI/CD pipelines with Azure Pipelines to automatically execute Packer, Terraform, and Ansible.

Chapter 9, Containerizing Your Application with Docker, covers the use of Docker, including its local installation, an overview of the Docker Hub registry, writing a Dockerfile, and a demonstration of how it can be used. An example of an application will be containerized, executed locally, and then deployed in an Azure container instance via a CI/CD pipeline.

Chapter 10, Managing Containers Effectively with Kubernetes, explains the basic use of Kubernetes, including its local installation and application deployment, and then an example of Kubernetes managed with Azure Kubernetes Services.

Chapter 11, Testing APIs with Postman, details the use of Postman to test an example of an API, including its local use and automation in a CI/CD pipeline with Newman and Azure Pipelines.

Chapter 12, Static Code Analysis with SonarQube, explains the use of SonarQube to analyze static code in an application, including its installation, real-time analysis with the SonarLint tool, and the integration of SonarQube into a CI pipeline in Azure Pipelines.

Chapter 13, Security and Performance Tests, discusses the security and performance of web applications, including demonstrations of how to use the ZAP tool to test OWASP rules and Postman to test API performance.

Chapter 14, Security in the DevOps Process with DevSecOps, explains how to use security integration in the DevOps process through testing compliance of the infrastructure with Inspec, and the usage of Vault for protecting sensitive data.

Chapter 15, Reducing Deployment Downtime, presents the reduction of deployment downtime with Terraform, the concepts and patterns of blue-green deployment, and how to apply them in Azure. Significant focus is also given to the use of feature flags within an application.

Chapter 16, DevOps for Open Source Projects, is dedicated to open source. It details the tools, processes, and practices for open source projects with collaboration in GitHub, pull requests, changelog files, binary sharing in GitHub releases, and an end-to-end example of a CI pipeline in Travis CI and in GitHub Actions. Open source code analysis and security are also discussed with SonarCloud and WhiteSource Bolt.

Chapter 17, DevOps Best Practices, reviews a DevOps list of good practices regarding automation, IaC, CI/CD pipelines, testing, security, monitoring, and project management.

To get the most out of this book

No development knowledge is required to understand this book. The only languages you will see are declarative languages such as JSON or YAML. In addition to this, no specific IDE is required. If you do not have one, you can use Visual Studio Code, which is free and cross-platform. It is available here: `https://code.visualstudio.com/`.

The cloud provider that serves as an example in this book is Microsoft Azure. If you don't have a subscription, you can create a free account here: `https://azure.microsoft.com/en-us/free/`.

As regards the operating systems you will need, there are no real prerequisites. Most of the tools we will use are cross-platform and compatible with Windows, Linux, and macOS. Their installations will be detailed in their respective chapters.

Software/hardware covered in the book	Operating system requirements
Terraform	Windows, macOS, or Linux
Ansible	Linux or macOs
Packer	Windows, macOS, or Linux
Vagrant	Windows, macOS, or Linux
Docker	Windows, macOS, or Linux
Azure CLI	Windows, macOS, or Linux
Helm	Windows, macOS, or Linux
Postman	Windows, macOS, or Linux
SonarLint	Windows, macOS, or Linux
Java Runtime	Windows, macOS, or Linux

If you are using the digital version of this book, we advise you to type the code yourself or access the code from the book's GitHub repository (a link is available in the next section). Doing so will help you avoid any potential errors related to the copying and pasting of code.

Download the example code files

You can download the example code files for this book from GitHub at `https://github.com/PacktPublishing/Learning-DevOps-Second-Edition`. If there's an update to the code, it will be updated in the GitHub repository.

We also have other code bundles from our rich catalog of books and videos available at `https://github.com/PacktPublishing/`. Check them out!

Code in Action

The Code in Action videos for this book can be viewed at `https://bit.ly/36xzV7u`.

Download the color images

We also provide a PDF file that has color images of the screenshots and diagrams used in this book. You can download it here: `https://static.packt-cdn.com/downloads/9781801818964_ColorImages.pdf`.

Conventions used

There are a number of text conventions used throughout this book.

`Code in text`: Indicates code words in text, database table names, folder names, filenames, file extensions, pathnames, dummy URLs, user input, and Twitter handles. Here is an example: "Navigate to the folder in which we created the `Vagrantfile` file."

A block of code is set as follows:

```
pool:
   vmImage: ubuntu-latest
steps:
- task: DotNetCoreCLI@2
   displayName: "Restore"
   inputs:
```

When we wish to draw your attention to a particular part of a code block, the relevant lines or items are set in bold:

```
[   inputs:
      command: 'test'
      projects: '**/tests/*.csproj'
      arguments: '--configuration Release'
- task: DotNetCoreCLI@2
```

Any command-line input or output is written as follows:

```
sudo apt-get update && sudo apt-get install -y gnupg software-
properties-common curl \
```

Bold: Indicates a new term, an important word, or words that you see onscreen. For instance, words in menus or dialog boxes appear in **bold**. Here is an example: "When choosing the **Adjusting your PATH environment** option, we can leave the default choice proposed by the installer."

> **Tips or Important Notes**
> Appear like this.

Get in touch

Feedback from our readers is always welcome.

General feedback: If you have questions about any aspect of this book, email us at customercare@packtpub.com and mention the book title in the subject of your message.

Errata: Although we have taken every care to ensure the accuracy of our content, mistakes do happen. If you have found a mistake in this book, we would be grateful if you would report this to us. Please visit www.packtpub.com/support/errata and fill in the form.

Piracy: If you come across any illegal copies of our works in any form on the internet, we would be grateful if you would provide us with the location address or website name. Please contact us at copyright@packt.com with a link to the material.

If you are interested in becoming an author: If there is a topic that you have expertise in and you are interested in either writing or contributing to a book, please visit authors.packtpub.com.

Share Your Thoughts

Once you've read *Learning DevOps - Second Edition*, we'd love to hear your thoughts! Scan the QR code below to go straight to the Amazon review page for this book and share your feedback.

https://packt.link/r/1801818967

Your review is important to us and the tech community and will help us make sure we're delivering excellent quality content.

Section 1: DevOps and Infrastructure as Code

The objectives of part one are to present the DevOps culture and to provide all the keys for the best infrastructure as code practices. This part explains the application of DevOps to cloud infrastructure, showing provisioning using Terraform and configuration with Ansible. Then, we improve on this by templating this infrastructure with Packer.

This section comprises the following chapters:

- *Chapter 1, The DevOps Culture and Infrastructure as Code Practices*
- *Chapter 2, Provisioning Cloud Infrastructure with Terraform*
- *Chapter 3, Using Ansible to Configure IaaS Infrastructure*
- *Chapter 4, Optimizing Infrastructure Deployment with Packer*
- *Chapter 5, Authoring the Development Environment with Vagrant*

1

The DevOps Culture and Infrastructure as Code Practices

DevOps, a term that we hear more and more in enterprises with phrases such as *We do DevOps* or *We use DevOps tools*, is the contraction of the words "Development" and "Operations."

DevOps is a culture that's different from traditional corporate cultures and requires a change in mindset, processes, and tools. It is often associated with **continuous integration (CI)** and **continuous delivery (CD)** practices, which are software engineering practices, but also with **Infrastructure as Code (IaC)**, which consists of *codifying* the structure and configuration of infrastructure.

In this chapter, we will see what DevOps culture is, what DevOps principles are, and the benefits they bring to a company. Then, we will explain CI/CD practices and, finally, we will detail IaC with its patterns and practices.

In this chapter, we will cover the following topics:

- Getting started with DevOps
- Implementing CI/CD and continuous deployment
- Understanding IaC practices

Check out the following video to view the Code in Action: `https://bit.ly/3JJAMAb`

Getting started with DevOps

The term *DevOps* was introduced in 2007-2009 by Patrick Debois, Gene Kim, and John Willis, and it represents the combination of **Development (Dev)** and **Operations (Ops)**. It has given rise to a movement that advocates bringing developers and operations together within teams. This delivers added business value to users more quickly, which makes it more competitive in the market.

DevOps culture is a set of practices that reduce the barriers between **developers**, who want to innovate and deliver faster, and **operations**, who want to guarantee the stability of production systems and the quality of the system changes they make.

DevOps culture is also the extension of agile processes (Scrum, XP, and so on), which makes it possible to reduce delivery times and already involves developers and business teams. However, they are often hindered because of the non-inclusion of Ops in the same teams.

The communication and this link between Dev and Ops allows a better follow-up of end-to-end production deployments and more frequent deployments that are of higher quality, saving money for the company.

To facilitate this collaboration and to improve communication between Dev and Ops, there are several key elements in the processes that must be put in place, as shown here:

- More frequent application deployments with integration and continuous delivery (called **CI/CD**).
- The implementation and automation of unitary and integration tests, with a process focused on **behavior-driven design (BDD)** or **test-driven design (TDD)**.
- The implementation of a means of collecting feedback from users.
- Monitoring applications and infrastructure.

The DevOps movement is based on three axes:

- **The culture of collaboration**: This is the very essence of DevOps – the fact that teams are no longer separated by silos specialization (one team of developers, one team of Ops, one team of testers, and so on). However, these people are brought together by making multidisciplinary teams that have the same objective: to deliver added value to the product as quickly as possible.

- **Processes**: To expect rapid deployment, these teams must follow development processes from agile methodologies with iterative phases that allow for better functionality, quality, and rapid feedback. These processes should not only be integrated into the development workflow with continuous integration, but also into the deployment workflow with continuous delivery and deployment. The DevOps process is divided into several phases:

  A. Planning and prioritizing functionalities

  B. Development

  C. Continuous integration and delivery

  D. Continuous deployment

  E. Continuous monitoring

  These phases are carried out cyclically and iteratively throughout the life of the project.

- **Tools**: The choice of tools and products used by teams is very important in DevOps. Indeed, when teams were separated into Dev and Ops, each team used their specific tools – deployment tools for developers and infrastructure tools for Ops – which further widened communication gaps.

With teams that bring development and operations together, and with this culture of unity, the tools that are used must be usable and exploitable by all members.

Developers need to integrate with the monitoring tools that are used by Ops teams to detect performance problems as early as possible, and with security tools provided by Ops to protect access to various resources.

Ops, on the other hand, must automate the process of creating and updating the infrastructure and integrate the code into a code manager. This is called IaC, but this can only be done in collaboration with developers who know the infrastructure that's needed for applications. Ops must also be integrated into application release processes and tools.

The following diagram illustrates the three axes of DevOps culture – the collaboration between Dev and Ops, the processes, and the use of tools:

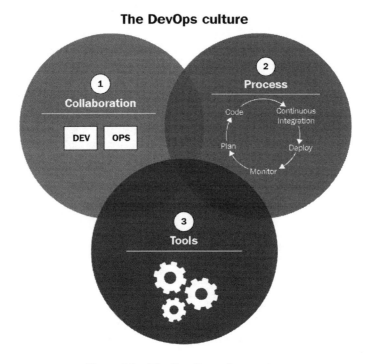

Figure 1.1 – The DevOps culture union

So, we can go back to DevOps culture with Donovan Brown's definition (http://donovanbrown.com/post/what-is-devops):

> *"DevOps is the union of people, processes, and products to enable continuous delivery of value to our end users."*

The benefits of establishing a DevOps culture within an enterprise are as follows:

- Better collaboration and communication in teams, which has a human and social impact within the company

- Shorter lead times to production, resulting in better performance and end user satisfaction

- Reduced infrastructure costs with IaC

- Significant time saved with iterative cycles that reduce application errors and automation tools that reduce manual tasks, so teams focus more on developing new functionalities with added business value.

> **Note**
>
> For more information about DevOps culture and its impact on, and transformation of, enterprises, read the book *The Phoenix Project: A Novel about IT, DevOps, and Helping Your Business Win*, by Gene Kim and Kevin Behr, and *The DevOps Handbook: How to Create World-Class Agility, Reliability, and Security in Technology Organizations*, by Gene Kim, Jez Humble, Patrick Debois, and John Willis.

In this section, we learned about the essential notions of the DevOps culture. Now, let's look at the first practice of the DevOps culture: the implementation of CI/CD and continuous deployment.

Implementing CI/CD and continuous deployment

Earlier, we learned that one of the key DevOps practices is the process of continuous integration and continuous delivery, also known as **CI/CD**. In fact, behind the acronyms of CI/CD, there are three practices:

- **Continuous integration (CI)**
- **Continuous delivery (CD)**
- **Continuous deployment**

What does each of these practices correspond to? What are their prerequisites and best practices? Where are they applicable?

Let's look at each of these practices in detail, starting with continuous integration.

Continuous integration (CI)

In the following definition given by Martin Fowler, three key things are mentioned – *members of a team*, *integrate*, and *as quickly as possible*:

> *"Continuous integration is a software development practice where members of a team integrate their work frequently... Each integration is verified by an automated build (including test) to detect integration errors as quickly as possible."*

That is, CI is an automatic process that allows you to check the completeness of an application's code every time a team member makes a change. This verification must be done as quickly as possible.

We see DevOps culture in CI very clearly, with the spirit of collaboration and communication, because the execution of CI impacts all members in terms of work methodology and therefore collaboration; moreover, CI requires the implementation of processes (branch, commit, pull request, code review, and so on) with automation that is done with tools that have been adapted to the whole team (Git, Jenkins, Azure DevOps, and so on). Finally, CI must run quickly to collect feedback on code integration as soon as possible and hence be able to deliver new features more quickly to users.

Implementing CI

Therefore, to set up CI, it is necessary to have a **Source Code Manager** (**SCM**) that will centralize the code of all members. This code manager can be of any type: Git, SVN, or **Team Foundation Version Control** (**TFVC**). It's also important to have an automatic *build manager* (CI server) that supports continuous integration, such as Jenkins, GitLab CI, TeamCity, Azure Pipelines, GitHub Actions, Travis CI, and Circle CI.

> **Note**
> In this book, we will use Git as an SCM, and we will look a little more deeply into its concrete uses.

Each team member will work on the application code daily, iteratively, and incrementally (such as in agile and scrum methods). Each task or feature must be partitioned from other developments with the use of branches.

Regularly, even several times a day, members archive or commit their code and preferably with small commits (trunks) that can easily be fixed in the event of an error. This will be integrated into the rest of the code of the application, with the rest of the commits of the other members.

Integrating all the commits is the starting point of the CI process.

This process, which is executed by the CI server, needs to be automated and triggered at each commit. The server will retrieve the code and then do the following:

- Build the application package – compilation, file transformation, and so on
- Perform unit tests (with code coverage)

> **Note**
>
> It is also possible to enrich this process with static code and vulnerability analysis, which we will look at in *Chapter 12, Static Code Analysis with SonarQube*, which is dedicated to testing.

This CI process must be optimized as soon as possible so that it can run fast, and so that developers can gather quick feedback on the integration of their code. For example, code that has been archived and does not compile or whose test execution fails can impact and block the entire team.

Sometimes, bad practices can cause tests to fail during CI. To deactivate this test's execution, you must take *it is not serious, it is necessary to deliver quickly,* or *the code that compiles it is essential* as an argument.

On the contrary, this practice can have serious consequences when the errors that are detected by the tests are revealed in production. The time that's saved during CI will be lost on fixing errors with hotfixes and redeploying them quickly, which can cause stress. This is the opposite of DevOps culture as there's poor application quality for end users and no real feedback; instead of developing new features, we spend time correcting errors.

With an optimized and complete CI process, the developer can quickly fix their problems and improve their code or discuss it with the rest of the team and commit their code for a new integration. Let's look at the following diagram:

The continuous integration (CI) pipeline

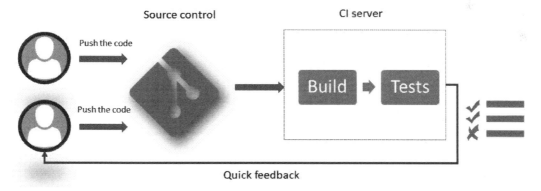

Figure 1.2 – The continuous integration workflow

This diagram shows the cyclical steps of continuous integration. This includes the code being pushed into the SCM by the team members and the build and test being executed by the CI server. The purpose of this process is to provide rapid feedback to members.

Now that we've seen what continuous integration is, let's look at continuous delivery.

Continuous delivery (CD)

Once continuous integration has been completed, the next step is to deploy the application automatically in one or more non-production environments, which is called **staging**. This process is called **continuous delivery (CD)**.

CD often starts with an application package being prepared by CI, which will be installed based on a list of automated tasks. These tasks can be of any type: unzip, stop and restart service, copy files, replace configuration, and so on. The execution of functional and acceptance tests can also be performed during the CD process.

Unlike CI, CD aims to test the entire application with all of its dependencies. This is very visible in microservice applications composed of several services and APIs; CI will only test the microservice under development, while once deployed in a staging environment, it will be possible to test and validate the entire application, as well as the APIs and microservices that it is composed of.

In practice, today, it is very common to link CI to CD in an *integration* environment; that is, CI deploys at the same time in an environment. This is necessary so that developers can not only execute unit tests but also verify the application as a whole (UI and functional) at each commit, along with the integration of the developments of the other team members.

It is important that the package that's generated during CI, which will also be deployed during CD, is the same one that will be installed on all environments, and this should be the case until production. However, there may be configuration file transformations that differ, depending on the environment, but the application code (binaries, DLL, Docker images, and JAR) must remain unchanged.

This immutable, unchangeable character of the code is the only guarantee that the application that's verified in an environment will be of the same quality as the version that was deployed in the previous environment, and also the same one that will be deployed in the next environment. If changes (improvements or bug fixes) are to be made to the code following verification in one of these environments, once done, the modifications will have to go through the CI and CD cycle again.

The tools that are set up for CI/CD are often used with other solutions, as follows:

- **A package manager**: This constitutes the storage space of the packages generated by CI and recovered by CD. These managers must support feeds, versioning, and different types of packages. There are several on the market, such as Nexus, ProGet, Artifactory, and Azure Artifacts.

- **A configuration manager**: This allows you to manage configuration changes during CD; most CD tools include a configuration mechanism with a system of variables.

In CD, deploying the application in each staging environment is triggered as follows:

- It can be triggered automatically, following a successful execution in a previous environment. For example, we can imagine a case where the deployment in the pre-production environment is automatically triggered when the integration tests have been successfully performed in a dedicated environment.

- It can be triggered manually, for sensitive environments such as the production environment, following manual approval by the person responsible for validating the proper functionality of the application in an environment.

What is important in a CD process is that the deployment to the production environment – that is, to the end user – is triggered manually by approved users.

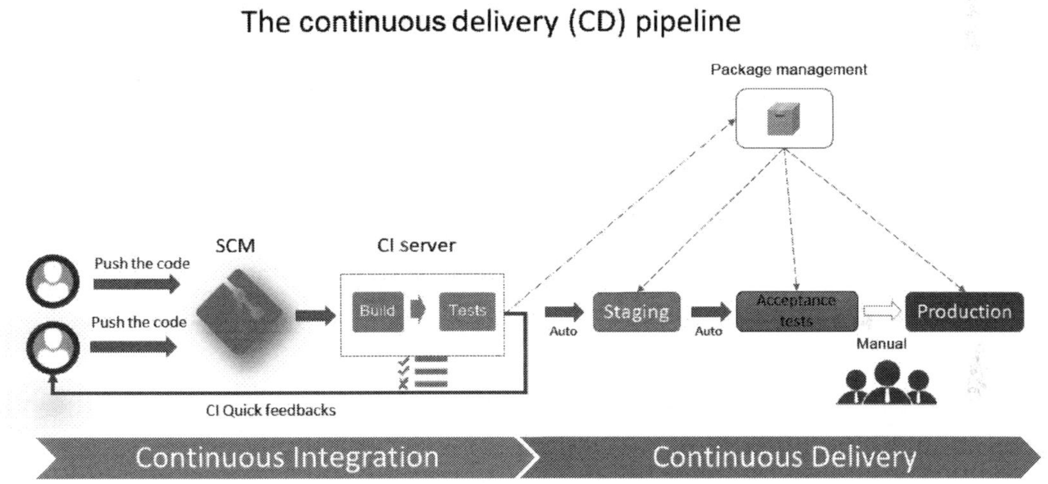

The continuous delivery (CD) pipeline

Figure 1.3 – The continuous delivery workflow

The preceding diagram clearly shows that the CD process is a continuation of the CI process. It represents the chain of CD steps, which are automatic for staging environments but manual for production deployments. It also shows that the package is generated by CI and stored in a package manager, and that it is the same package that is deployed in different environments.

Now that we've looked at CD, let's look at continuous deployment practices.

Continuous deployment

Continuous deployment is an extension of CD, but this time, with a process that automates the entire CI/CD pipeline from the moment the developer commits their code to deployment in production through all of the verification steps.

This practice is rarely implemented in enterprises because it requires a variety of tests (unit, functional, integration, performance, and so on) to be covered for the application. Successfully executing these tests is sufficient to validate the proper functionality of the application regarding all of these dependencies. However, it also allows you to automatically deploy to a production environment without any approval action required.

The continuous deployment process must also take into account all of the steps to restore the application in the event of a production problem.

Continuous deployment can be implemented by using and implementing feature toggle techniques (or feature flags), which involves encapsulating the application's functionalities in features and activating its features on demand, directly in production, without having to redeploy the code of the application.

Another technique is to use a blue-green production infrastructure, which consists of two production environments, one blue and one green. First, we deploy to the blue environment, then to the green one; this will ensure that no downtime is required.

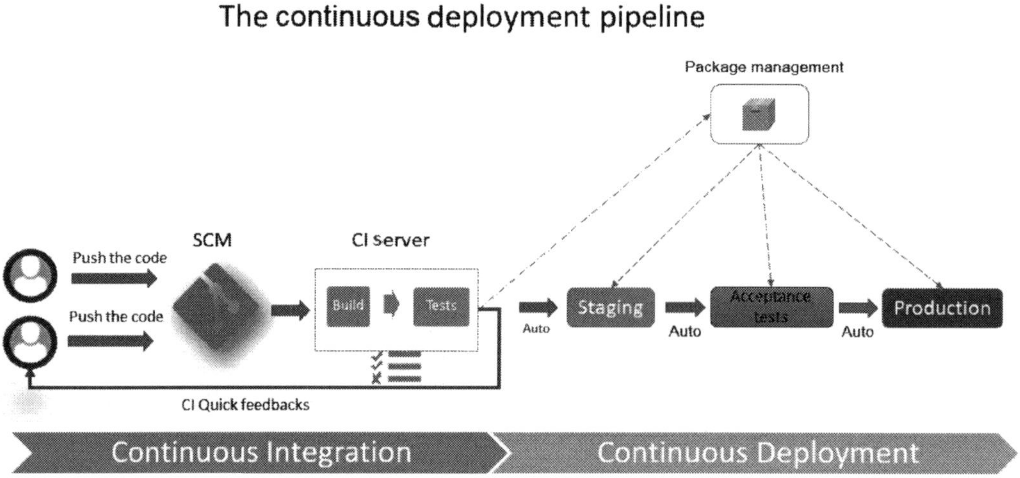

The continuous deployment pipeline

Figure 1.4 – The continuous deployment workflow

> **Note**
>
> We will look at the feature toggle and blue-green deployment usage in more detail in *Chapter 15, Reducing Deployment Downtime*.

The preceding diagram is almost the same as that of CD, but with the difference that it depicts automated end-to-end deployment.

CI/CD processes are therefore an essential part of DevOps culture, with CI allowing teams to integrate and test the coherence of its code and to obtain quick feedback regularly. CD automatically deploys on one or more staging environments and hence offers the possibility to test the entire application until it is deployed in production.

Finally, continuous deployment automates the ability to deploy the application from commit to the production environment.

> **Note**
>
> We will learn how to implement all of these processes in practice with Jenkins, Azure DevOps, and GitLab CI in *Chapter 7, Continuous Integration and Continuous Delivery*.

In this section, we discussed the practices that are essential to DevOps culture, which are continuous integration, continuous delivery, and continuous deployment.

In the next section, we will look at another DevOps practice, known as IaC.

Understanding IaC practices

IaC is a practice that consists of writing the code of the resources that make up an infrastructure.

This practice began to take effect with the rise of the DevOps culture and with the modernization of cloud infrastructure. Indeed, Ops teams that deploy infrastructures manually take the time to deliver infrastructure changes due to inconsistent handling and the risk of errors. Also, with the modernization of the cloud and its scalability, the way infrastructure is built requires reviewing the provisioning and change practices by adapting a more automated method.

IaC is the process of writing the code of the provisioning and configuration steps of infrastructure components, which helps automate its deployment in a repeatable and consistent manner.

Before we look at the use of IaC, we will see what the benefits of this practice are.

The benefits of IaC

The benefits of IaC are as follows:

- The standardization of infrastructure configuration reduces the risk of errors.
- The code that describes the infrastructure is versioned and controlled in a source code manager.
- The code is integrated into CI/CD pipelines.
- Deployments that make infrastructure changes are faster and more efficient.
- There's better management, control, and a reduction in infrastructure costs.

IaC also brings benefits to a DevOps team by allowing Ops to be more efficient in terms of infrastructure improvement tasks, rather than spending time on manual configuration. It also gives Dev the possibility to upgrade their infrastructures and make changes without having to ask for more Ops resources.

IaC also allows the creation of self-service, ephemeral environments that will give developers and testers more flexibility to test new features in isolation and independently of other environments.

IaC languages and tools

The languages and tools that are used to write the configuration of the infrastructure can be of different types; that is, **scripting**, **declarative**, and **programmatic**. We will explore them in the following sections.

Scripting types

These are scripts such as Bash, PowerShell, or others that use the different clients (SDKs) provided by the cloud provider; for example, you can script the provisioning of an Azure infrastructure with the Azure CLI or Azure PowerShell.

For example, here is the command that creates a resource group in Azure:

- Using the Azure CLI (the documentation is available at `https://bit.ly/2V1OfxJ`), we have the following:

```
az group create --location westeurope --resource-group
MyAppResourcegroup
```

- Using Azure PowerShell (the documentation is available at `https://bit.ly/2VcASeh`), we have the following:

```
New-AzResourceGroup -Name MyAppResourcegroup -Location
westeurope
```

The problem with these languages and tools is that they require a lot of lines of code. This is because we need to manage the different states of the manipulated resources, and it is necessary to write all the steps of creating or updating the desired infrastructure.

However, these languages and tools can be very useful for tasks that automate repetitive actions to be performed on a list of resources (selection and query), or that require complex processing with certain logic to be performed on infrastructure resources, such as a script that automates VMs that carry a certain tag being deleted.

Declarative types

These are languages in which it is sufficient to write the state of the desired system or infrastructure in the form of configuration and properties. This is the case, for example, for Terraform and Vagrant from HashiCorp, Ansible, the Azure ARM template, Azure Bicep (`https://docs.microsoft.com/en-us/azure/azure-resource-manager/templates/bicep-overview`), PowerShell DSC, Puppet, and Chef. All the user has to do is write the final state of the desired infrastructure; the tool will take care of applying it.

For example, the following Terraform code allows you to define the desired configuration of an Azure resource group:

```
resource "azurerm_resource_group" "myrg" {
    name = "MyAppResourceGroup"
    location = "West Europe"

    tags = {
        environment = "Bookdemo"
    }
}
```

In this example, if you want to add or modify a tag, just modify the `tags` property in the preceding code and Terraform will do the update itself.

Here is another example that allows you to install and restart nginx on a server using Ansible:

```
---
- hosts: all
  tasks:
  - name: install and check nginx latest version
    apt: name=nginx state=latest
  - name: start nginx
    service:
      name: nginx
      state: started
```

To ensure that the service is not installed, just change the preceding code, with service as an absent value and the state property with the stopped value:

```
---
- hosts: all
  tasks:
  - name: stop nginx
    service:
      name: nginx
      state: stopped
  - name: check nginx is not installed
    apt: name=nginx state=absent
```

In this example, it was enough to change the state property to indicate the desired state of the service.

> **Note**
>
> For details regarding the use of Terraform and Ansible, see *Chapter 2, Provisioning Cloud Infrastructure with Terraform*, and *Chapter 3, Using Ansible for Configuring IaaS Infrastructure*.

Programmatic types

For a few years now, an observation has been made that the two types of IaC code, which are of the scripting or declarative languages, are destined to be in the **operational** team. This does not commonly involve the developers in the IaC.

This is done to create more union between developers and operations so that we see the emergence of IaC tools that are based more on languages known by developers, such as TypeScript, Java, Python, and C#.

Among the IaC tools that allow us to provision infrastructure using a programming language, we have **Pulumi** (`https://www.pulumi.com/`) and **Terraform CDK** (`https://github.com/hashicorp/terraform-cdk`).

The following is an example of some *TypeScript* code written with the Terraform CDK:

```typescript
import { Construct } from 'constructs';
import { App, TerraformStack, TerraformOutput } from 'cdktf';
import {
   ResourceGroup,
} from './.gen/providers/azurerm';
class AzureRgCDK extends TerraformStack {
   constructor(scope: Construct, name: string) {
      super(scope, name);
      new AzurermProvider(this, 'azureFeature', {
         features: [{}],
      });
      const rg = new ResourceGroup(this, 'cdktf-rg', {
         name: 'MyAppResourceGroup',
         location: 'West Europe',
      });
   }
}
const app = new App();
new AzureRgCDK(app, 'azure-rg-demo');
app.synth();
```

In this example, which is written in Typescript, we are using two-tier libraries: the npm package and a Terraform CDK called `cdktf`. The npm package that's used to provision Azure resources is called `'gen/providers/azurerm'`.

Then, we declare a new class that initializes the Azure provider and we define the creation of the resource group with the `new ResourceGroup` method.

Finally, to create the resource group, we instantiate this class and call the `app.synth` method of the CDK.

> **Note**
>
> For more information about the Terraform CDK, I suggest reading the following blog posts and watching the following video:
>
> ```
> https://www.hashicorp.com/blog/cdk-for-terraform-
> enabling-python-and-typescript-support
> ```
>
> ```
> https://www.hashicorp.com/blog/announcing-cdk-for-
> terraform-0-1
> ```
>
> ```
> https://www.youtube.com/watch?v=5hSdb0nadRQ
> ```

The IaC topology

In a cloud infrastructure, IaC is divided into several typologies:

- Deploying and provisioning the infrastructure
- Server configuration and templating
- Containerization
- Configuration and deployment in Kubernetes

Let's deep dive into each topology.

Deploying and provisioning the infrastructure

Provisioning is the act of instantiating the resources that make up the infrastructure. They can be of the **Platform-as-a-Service (PaaS)** and serverless resource types, such as a web app, Azure function, or Event Hub, but also the entire network part that is managed, such as VNet, subnets, routing tables, or Azure Firewall. For virtual machine resources, the provisioning step only creates or updates the VM cloud resource, but not its content.

There are different provisioning tools we can use for this, such as Terraform, the ARM template, AWS Cloud training, the Azure CLI, Azure PowerShell, and also Google Cloud Deployment Manager. Of course, there are many more, but it is difficult to mention them all. In this book, we will look at, in detail, the use of Terraform to provide an infrastructure.

Server configuration

This step concerns configuring virtual machines, such as the hardening, directories, disk mounting, network configuration (firewall, proxy, and so on), and middleware installation.

There are different configuration tools, such as Ansible, PowerShell DSC, Chef, Puppet, and SaltStack. Of course, there are many more, but in this book, we will look in detail at the use of Ansible to configure a virtual machine.

To optimize server provisioning and configuration times, it is also possible to create and use server models, also called images, that contain all of the configuration (hardening, middleware, and so on) of the servers. While provisioning the server, we will indicate the template to use. So, in a few minutes, we will have a server that's been configured and is ready to be used.

There are also many IaC tools for creating server templates, such as **Aminator** (used by Netflix) and **HashiCorp Packer**.

Here is an example of some Packer file code for creating an Ubuntu image with package updates:

```
{
"builders": [{
    "type": "azure-arm",
    "os_type": "Linux",
    "image_publisher": "Canonical",
    "image_offer": "UbuntuServer",
    "image_sku": "16.04-LTS",
    "managed_image_resource_group_name": "demoBook",
    "managed_image_name": "SampleUbuntuImage",
    "location": "West Europe",
    "vm_size": "Standard_DS2_v2"
}],
 "provisioners": [{
    "execute_command": "chmod +x {{ .Path }}; {{ .Vars }} sudo
-E sh '{{ .Path }}'",
    "inline": [
    "apt-get update",
    "apt-get upgrade -y",
    "/usr/sbin/waagent -force -deprovision+user && export
HISTSIZE=0 && sync"
    ],
  "inline_shebang": "/bin/sh -x",
  "type": "shell"
```

```
    }]
    }
```

This script creates a template image for the `Standard_DS2_V2` virtual machine based on the Ubuntu OS (the `builders` section). Additionally, Packer will update all the packages during the creation of the image with the `apt-get update` command. Afterward, Packer will deprovision the image to delete all user information (the `provisioners` section).

> **Note**
>
> The Packer part will be discussed in detail in *Chapter 4, Optimizing Infrastructure Deployment with Packer.*

Immutable infrastructure with containers

Containerization consists of deploying applications in containers instead of deploying them in VMs.

Today, it is very clear that the container technology to be used is **Docker** and that a Docker image is configured with code in a *Dockerfile*. This file contains the declaration of the base image, which represents the operating system to be used, additional middleware to be installed on the image, only the files and binaries necessary for the application, and the network configuration of the ports. Unlike VMs, containers are said to be immutable; the configuration of a container cannot be modified during its execution.

Here is a simple example of a Dockerfile:

```
FROM ubuntu
RUN apt-get update
RUN apt-get install -y nginx
ENTRYPOINT ["/usr/sbin/nginx","-g","daemon off;"]
EXPOSE 80
```

In this Docker image, we are using a basic Ubuntu image, installing `nginx`, and exposing port `80`.

> **Note**
>
> The Docker part will be discussed in detail in *Chapter 9, Containerizing Your Application with Docker.*

Configuration and deployment in Kubernetes

Kubernetes is a container orchestrator – it is the technology that most embodies IaC (in my opinion) because of the way it deploys containers, the network architecture (load balancer, ports, and so on), and volume management, as well as how it protects sensitive information, all of which are described in the YAML specification files.

Here is a simple example of a YAML specification file:

```
apiVersion: apps/v1
kind: Deployment
metadata:
    name: nginx-demo
    labels:
        app: nginx
spec:
    replicas: 2
    selector:
      matchLabels:
          app: nginx
    template:
      metadata:
        labels:
            app: nginx
      spec:
        containers:
        - name: nginx
            image: nginx:1.7.9
          ports:
          - containerPort: 80
```

In the preceding specification file, we can see the name of the image to deploy (`ngnix`), the port to open (`80`), and the number of replicas (`2`).

> **Note**
> The Kubernetes part will be discussed in detail in *Chapter 10, Managing Containers Effectively with Kubernetes.*

IaC, like software development, requires that we implement practices and processes that allow the infrastructure code to evolve and be maintained.

Among these practices are those of software development, as follows:

- Have good principles of nomenclature.

- Do not overload the code with unnecessary comments.

- Use small functions.

- Implement error handling.

> **Note**
>
> To learn more about good software development practices, read the excellent book, which is, for my part, a reference on the subject, *Clean Code*, by Robert Martin.

However, there are more specific practices that I think deserve more attention:

- **Everything must be automated in the code**: When performing IaC, it is necessary to code and automate all of the provisioning steps and not leave the manual steps out of the code that distort the automation of the infrastructure, which can generate errors. And if necessary, do not hesitate to use several tools such as Terraform and Bash with the Azure CLI scripts.

- **The code must be in a source control manager**: The infrastructure code must also be in an SCM to be versioned, tracked, merged, and restored, and hence have better visibility of the code between Dev and Ops.

- **The infrastructure code must be with the application code**: In some cases, this may be difficult, but if possible, it is much better to place the infrastructure code in the same repository as the application code. This is to ensure we have better work organization between developers and operations, who will share the same workspace.

- **Separation of roles and directories**: It is good to separate the code from the infrastructure according to the role of the code. This allows you to create one directory for provisioning and configuring VMs and another that will contain the code for testing the integration of the complete infrastructure.

- **Integration into a CI/CD process**: One of the goals of IaC is to be able to automate the deployment of the infrastructure. So, from the beginning of its implementation, it is necessary to set up a CI/CD process that will integrate the code, test it, and deploy it in different environments. Some tools, such as Terratest, allow you to write tests on infrastructure code. One of the best practices is to integrate the CI/CD process of the infrastructure into the same pipeline as the application.

- **The code must be idempotent**: The execution of the infrastructure deployment code must be idempotent; that is, it should be automatically executable at will. This means that scripts must take into account the state of the infrastructure when running it and not generate an error if the resource to be created already exists, or if a resource to be deleted has already been deleted. We will see that declarative languages, such as Terraform, take on this aspect of idempotence natively. The code of the infrastructure, once fully automated, must allow the application's infrastructure to be constructed and destructed.

- **To be used as documentation**: The code of the infrastructure must be clear and must be able to serve as documentation. Infrastructure documentation takes a long time to write and, in many cases, it is not updated as the infrastructure evolves.

- **The code must be modular**: In infrastructure, the components often have the same code – the only difference is the value of their properties. Also, these components are used several times in the company's applications. Therefore, it is important to optimize the writing times of code by factoring it with modules (or roles, for Ansible) that will be called as functions. Another advantage of using modules is the ability to standardize resource nomenclature and compliance on some properties.

- **Having a development environment**: The problem with IaC is that it is difficult to test its infrastructure code under development in environments that are used for integration, as well as to test the application, because changing the infrastructure can have an impact. Therefore, it is important to have a development environment even for IaC that can be impacted or even destroyed at any time.

For local infrastructure tests, some tools simulate a local environment, such as Vagrant (from HashiCorp), so you should use them to test code scripts as much as possible.

Of course, the full list of good practices is longer than this; all the methods and processes of software engineering practices are also applicable.

Therefore, IaC, like CI/CD processes, is a key practice of **DevOps culture** that allows you to deploy and configure an infrastructure by writing code. However, IaC can only be effective with the use of appropriate tools and the implementation of good practices.

In this section, we covered an overview of some DevOps best practices. Next, we will present a brief overview of the evolution of the DevOps culture.

The evolution of the DevOps culture

With time and the experience that's been gained by using the DevOps culture, we can observe an evolution of the practices, as well as the teams that integrate with this movement.

This is, for example, the case of the **GitOps** practice, which is starting to emerge more and more in companies.

The GitOps workflow, which is commonly applied to Kubernetes, consists of using Git as the only source of truth; that is, the Git repository contains the code of the infrastructure state, as well as the code of the application to be deployed.

A controller will oversee retrieval of the Git source during a code commit, executing the tests, and redeploying the application.

> **Note**
> For more details about GitOps culture, practices, and workflows, read the official guide on the initiator of GitOps here: `https://www.weave.works/technologies/gitops/`.

Summary

In this chapter, we saw that the DevOps culture is a story of collaboration, processes, and tools. Then, we detailed the different steps of the CI/CD process and explained the difference between continuous integration, continuous delivery, and continuous deployment. Finally, the last part explained how to use IaC with its best practices, and we covered the evolution of the DevOps culture.

We learned about the basis of the DevOps culture and its practices, which sets the tone for the rest of the chapters in this book, where we will discuss how to apply this culture using tools and practices.

In the next chapter, we will begin by covering the implementation of *Infrastructure as Code* and how to provision infrastructure with Terraform.

Questions

1. Which words is DevOps a contraction of?

2. Is DevOps a term that represents the name of a tool, a culture or a society, or the title of a book?

3. What are the three axes of DevOps culture?

4. What is the objective of continuous integration?

5. What is the difference between continuous delivery and continuous deployment?

6. What is IaC?

Further reading

If you want to know more about DevOps culture, here are some resources:

*   *The DevOps Resource Center* (Microsoft resources): `https://docs.microsoft.com/en-us/azure/devops/learn/`

*   *2020 State of DevOps Report* (by Puppet): `https://puppet.com/resources/report/2020-state-of-devops-report`

2
Provisioning Cloud Infrastructure with Terraform

In the previous chapter, we introduced the tools, practices, and benefits of **Infrastructure as Code (IaC)** and its impact on DevOps culture. Out of all of the IaC tools that have been mentioned, one that is particularly popular and powerful is **Terraform**, which is part of the HashiCorp tools suite.

In this chapter, we will explore the basics of using Terraform to provision a cloud infrastructure, using Azure as an example. We will start with an overview of its strengths compared to other IaC tools. We will learn how to install it in both manual mode and automatic mode, and then we will create our first Terraform script to provision an Azure infrastructure with the use of best practices and its automation in a **Continuous Integration (CI)/Continuous Deployment (CD)** process. Finally, we will go a little deeper with the implementation of a remote backend for the Terraform state file.

In this chapter, we will cover the following topics:

- Installing Terraform
- Configuring Terraform for Azure
- Writing a Terraform script to deploy an Azure infrastructure
- Running Terraform for deployment
- Understanding the Terraform life cycle with different command-line options
- Protecting the state file with a remote backend

Technical requirements

This chapter will explain how you can use Terraform to provision an Azure infrastructure as an example of cloud infrastructure. Therefore, you will need an Azure subscription, which you can get, for free, at `https://azure.microsoft.com/en-us/free/`.

In addition, we will require a code editor to write the Terraform code. There are several editors out there, but I will be using **Visual Studio Code**. It is free, lightweight, multiplatform, and has several extensions for Terraform. You can download it at `https://code.visualstudio.com/`. The complete source code of this chapter is available at `https://github.com/PacktPublishing/Learning-DevOps-Second-Edition/tree/main/CHAP02`.

Check out the following video to view the Code in Action:

`https://bit.ly/3p7x63h`

Installing Terraform

Terraform is a command-line tool that, in its basic version, is open source, uses the **HashiCorp Configuration Language** (HCL), is declarative, and is relatively easy to read. Its main advantage is the use of the same language to deploy on a multitude of cloud providers such as Azure, AWS, and Google—the complete list is available at `https://www.terraform.io/docs/providers/`.

Terraform has other advantages:

- It's multiplatform, and it can be installed on Windows, Linux, and Mac.
- It allows a preview of infrastructure changes before they are implemented.

- It allows the parallelization of operations by considering resource dependencies.

- It integrates a very large number of providers.

Terraform can be installed onto your system in a number of ways. Let's begin by looking at the manual installation method.

Manual installation

To install Terraform manually, perform the following steps:

1. Go to the official download page at `https://www.terraform.io/downloads.html`. Then, download the package corresponding to your operating system.

2. After downloading, unzip and copy the binary into an execution directory (for example, inside `c:\Terraform`).

3. Then, the `PATH` environment variable must be completed with the path to the `binary` directory. For detailed instructions, please view the video at `https://learn.hashicorp.com/tutorials/terraform/install-cli`.

Now that we've learned how to install Terraform manually, let's take a look at the options available to us to install it using a script.

Installation by script

Script installation automates the installation or update of Terraform on a remote server that will be in charge of executing Terraform code, such as on a Jenkins slave or an Azure Pipelines agent.

Installing Terraform by script on Linux

To install the Terraform binary on Linux, we have two solutions. The first solution is to install Terraform using the following script:

```
TERRAFORM_VERSION="1.0.0" #Update with your desired version
curl -Os https://releases.hashicorp.com/terraform/${TERRAFORM_
VERSION}/terraform_${TERRAFORM_VERSION}_linux_amd64.zip \
&& curl -Os https://releases.hashicorp.com/
terraform/${TERRAFORM_VERSION}/terraform_${TERRAFORM_VERSION}_
SHA256SUMS \
&& curl https://keybase.io/hashicorp/pgp_keys.asc | gpg
```

```
--import \
```

```
&& curl -Os https://releases.hashicorp.com/
terraform/${TERRAFORM_VERSION}/terraform_${TERRAFORM_VERSION}_
SHA256SUMS.sig \
```

```
&& gpg --verify terraform_${TERRAFORM_VERSION}_SHA256SUMS.sig
terraform_${TERRAFORM_VERSION}_SHA256SUMS \
```

```
&& shasum -a 256 -c terraform_${TERRAFORM_VERSION}_SHA256SUMS
2>&1 | grep "${TERRAFORM_VERSION}_linux_amd64.zip:\sOK" \
```

```
&& unzip -o terraform_${TERRAFORM_VERSION}_linux_amd64.zip -d /
usr/local/bin
```

This script does the following:

- It sets the TERRAFORM_VERSION parameter with the version to download.
- It downloads the Terraform package by checking the checksum.
- It unzips the package in the user's local directory.

> **Important Note**
>
> This script is also available in the GitHub source for this book at https://
> github.com/PacktPublishing/Learning-DevOps-Second-
> Edition/blob/main/CHAP02/Terraform_install_Linux.
> sh.

To execute this script, follow these steps:

1. Open a command-line Terminal.
2. Copy and paste the preceding script.
3. Execute it by hitting *Enter* in the command-line Terminal.

The following screenshot displays an execution of the script to install Terraform on Linux:

```
root@ubuntu-bionic:/learningdevops/CHAP02# sh Terraform_install_Linux.sh
  % Total    % Received % Xferd  Average Speed   Time    Time     Time  Current
                                 Dload  Upload   Total   Spent    Left  Speed
100  7717  100  7717    0      0  20523      0 --:--:-- --:--:-- --:--:-- 20469
gpg: key 34365D9472D7468F: "HashiCorp Security (hashicorp.com/security) <security@hashicorp.com>" not changed
gpg: Total number processed: 1
gpg:              unchanged: 1
gpg: Signature made Tue Jun  8 11:21:42 2021 UTC
gpg:                using RSA key B36CBA91A2C0730C435FC280B0B441097685B676
gpg: Good signature from "HashiCorp Security (hashicorp.com/security) <security@hashicorp.com>" [unknown]
gpg: WARNING: This key is not certified with a trusted signature!
gpg:          There is no indication that the signature belongs to the owner.
Primary key fingerprint: C874 011F 0AB4 0511 0D02  1055 3436 5D94 72D7 468F
     Subkey fingerprint: B36C BA91 A2C0 730C 435F  C280 B0B4 4109 7685 B676
terraform_1.0.0_linux_amd64.zip: OK
Archive:  terraform_1.0.0_linux_amd64.zip
  inflating: /usr/local/bin/terraform
```

Figure 2.1 – The Terraform install script on Linux

In the execution of the preceding script, we can see the download of the Terraform ZIP package (using the `curl` tool) and the unzip operation of this package inside the `/usr/local/bin` folder.

The benefit of this solution is that we can choose the Terraform installation folder and that it is applicable on the various distributions of Linux. This is because it uses common tools, including `curl` and `unzip`.

The second solution for installing Terraform on Linux is to use the `apt` package manager. You can do so by using the following script for the Ubuntu distribution:

```
sudo apt-get update && sudo apt-get install -y gnupg software-
properties-common curl \
```

```
&& curl -fsSL https://apt.releases.hashicorp.com/gpg | sudo
apt-key add - \
```

```
&& sudo apt-add-repository "deb [arch=amd64] https://apt.
releases.hashicorp.com $(lsb_release -cs) main" \
```

```
&& sudo apt-get update && sudo apt-get install terraform
```

This script does the following:

- It adds the `apt` HashiCorp repository.
- It updates the local repository.
- It downloads the Terraform CLI.

> **Important Note**
>
> For additional details about this script and the installation of Terraform on other distributions, please refer to the documentation at `https://learn.hashicorp.com/tutorials/terraform/install-cli`, and navigate to the **Linux** tab.

The benefit of this solution is that you can use Linux package management, which can be integrated into popular configuration tools (for example, Ansible, Puppet, or Docker)

We have just discussed the installation of Terraform on Linux. Now, let's take a look at its installation on Windows.

Installing Terraform by script on Windows

If we use Windows, we can use **Chocolatey**, which is a free public package manager, such as **NuGet** or **npm**, but dedicated to software. It is widely used for the automation of software on Windows servers or even local machines.

> **Important Note**
>
> The Chocolatey official website can be found at `https://chocolatey.org/`, and its installation documentation can be located at `https://chocolatey.org/install`.

Once Chocolatey has been installed, we just need to run the following command in PowerShell or the CMD tool:

```
choco install terraform -y
```

The following is a screenshot of the Terraform installation for Windows with Chocolatey:

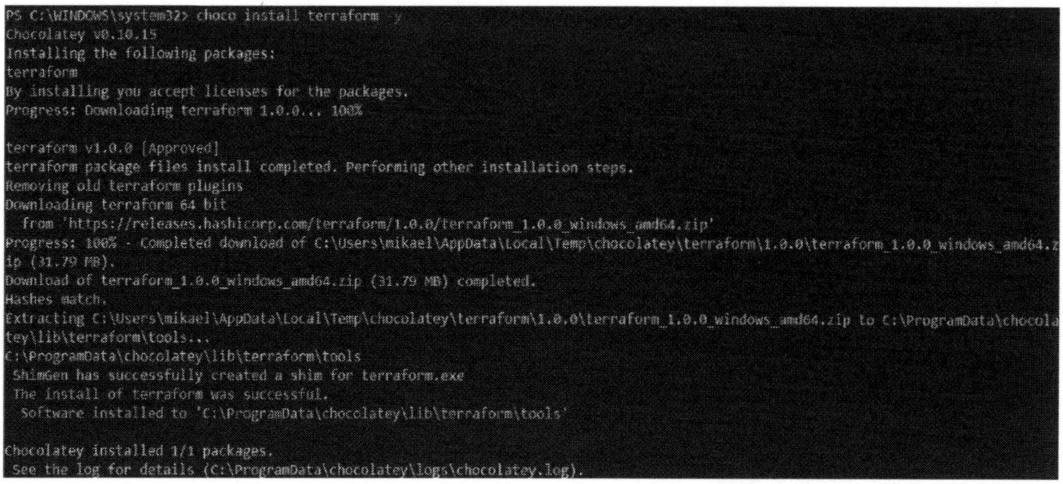

```
PS C:\WINDOWS\system32> choco install terraform -y
Chocolatey v0.10.15
Installing the following packages:
terraform
By installing you accept licenses for the packages.
Progress: Downloading terraform 1.0.0... 100%

terraform v1.0.0 [Approved]
terraform package files install completed. Performing other installation steps.
Removing old terraform plugins
Downloading terraform 64 bit
  from 'https://releases.hashicorp.com/terraform/1.0.0/terraform_1.0.0_windows_amd64.zip'
Progress: 100% - Completed download of C:\Users\mikael\AppData\Local\Temp\chocolatey\terraform\1.0.0\terraform_1.0.0_windows_amd64.z
ip (31.79 MB).
Download of terraform_1.0.0_windows_amd64.zip (31.79 MB) completed.
Hashes match.
Extracting C:\Users\mikael\AppData\Local\Temp\chocolatey\terraform\1.0.0\terraform_1.0.0_windows_amd64.zip to C:\ProgramData\chocola
tey\lib\terraform\tools...
C:\ProgramData\chocolatey\lib\terraform\tools
 ShimGen has successfully created a shim for terraform.exe
 The install of terraform was successful.
  Software installed to 'C:\ProgramData\chocolatey\lib\terraform\tools'

Chocolatey installed 1/1 packages.
 See the log for details (C:\ProgramData\chocolatey\logs\chocolatey.log).
```

Figure 2.2 – Terraform installation on Windows

Executing the `choco install terraform` command installs the latest version of Terraform from Chocolatey.

Once installed, we can check the Terraform version by running the following command:

```
terraform version
```

This command displays the installed Terraform version.

We can also check out the different commands that Terraform offers by running the following command:

```
terraform --help
```

The following screenshot lists the different commands and their functions:

```
                       :~$ terraform --help
Usage: terraform [-version] [-help] <command> [args]

The available commands for execution are listed below.
The most common, useful commands are shown first, followed by
less common or more advanced commands. If you're just getting
started with Terraform, stick with the common commands. For the
other commands, please read the help and docs before usage.

Common commands:
    apply              Builds or changes infrastructure
    console            Interactive console for Terraform interpolations
    destroy            Destroy Terraform-managed infrastructure
    env                Workspace management
    fmt                Rewrites config files to canonical format
    get                Download and install modules for the configuration
    graph              Create a visual graph of Terraform resources
    import             Import existing infrastructure into Terraform
    init               Initialize a Terraform working directory
    output             Read an output from a state file
    plan               Generate and show an execution plan
    providers          Prints a tree of the providers used in the configuration
    push               Upload this Terraform module to Atlas to run
    refresh            Update local state file against real resources
    show               Inspect Terraform state or plan
    taint              Manually mark a resource for recreation
    untaint            Manually unmark a resource as tainted
    validate           Validates the Terraform files
    version            Prints the Terraform version
    workspace          Workspace management

All other commands:
    debug              Debug output management (experimental)
    force-unlock       Manually unlock the terraform state
    state              Advanced state management
```

Figure 2.3 – Terraform's available commands

Now, let's take a look at the installation of Terraform on macOS.

Installing Terraform by script on macOS

On macOS, we can use **Homebrew**, the macOS package manager (`https://brew.sh/`), to install Terraform by executing the following command in your Terminal:

```
brew install terraform
```

That's all for the installation of Terraform by script. Let's take a look at another solution that uses Terraform in Azure without having to install it—**Azure Cloud Shell**.

Integrating Terraform with Azure Cloud Shell

If we are using Terraform to deploy a piece of infrastructure in Azure, we should also know that the Azure team has integrated Terraform into Azure Cloud Shell.

> **Important Note**
> To learn more about Azure Cloud Shell, please refer to its documentation at `https://azure.microsoft.com/en-us/features/cloud-shell/`.

To use it from the Azure Cloud Shell, follow these steps:

1. Connect to the Azure portal by opening `https://portal.azure.com`, and sign in with your Azure account:

Figure 2.4 – The Azure Sign in page

2. Open the Cloud Shell and choose the mode you want, that is, either Bash or PowerShell.

3. Then, we can run the Terraform command line in the shell.

The following is a screenshot of the execution of Terraform in Azure Cloud Shell:

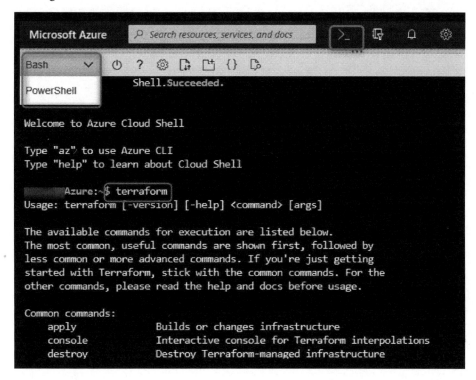

Figure 2.5 – Azure Cloud Shell

The advantage of using this solution is that we don't need any software to install; we can simply upload your Terraform files to Cloud Shell and run them in Cloud Shell. Additionally, we are already connected to Azure, so no configuration is required (please refer to the *Configuring Terraform for Azure* section).

However, this solution is only to be used in development mode and not for the local or automatic use of Terraform. For this reason, in this chapter, we will discuss the configuration of Terraform for Azure.

Now that we have installed Terraform, we can begin using it locally to provision an Azure infrastructure. We will start with the first step, which is to configure Terraform for Azure.

Configuring Terraform for Azure

Before writing the Terraform code in which to provision a cloud infrastructure such as Azure, we must configure Terraform to allow the manipulation of resources in an Azure subscription.

To do this, first, we will create a new Azure **Service Principal (SP)** in Azure **Active Directory (AD)**, which, in Azure, is an *application user* who has permission to manage Azure resources.

> **Important Note**
>
> For more details about the Azure SP, please read the documentation at https://docs.microsoft.com/en-us/azure/active-directory/develop/app-objects-and-service-principals.

For this Azure SP, we have to assign to it the contributing permissions on the subscription in which we will create resources.

Creating the Azure SP

This operation can be done either via the Azure portal (all steps are detailed within the official documentation at https://docs.microsoft.com/en-us/azure/active-directory/develop/howto-create-service-principal-portal) or via a script by executing the following az cli command (which we can launch in Azure Cloud Shell).

The following is a template az cli script that you have to run to create an SP. Here, you have to enter your SP name, role, and scope:

```
az ad sp create-for-rbac --name="<ServicePrincipal name>"
--role="Contributor" --scopes="/subscriptions/<subscription
Id>"
```

Take a look at the following example:

```
az ad sp create-for-rbac --name="SPForTerraform"
--role="Contributor" --scopes="/subscriptions/8921-1444-..."
```

This sample script creates a new SP, named SPForTerraform, and gives it the contributor permission on the subscription ID, that is, 8921....

> **Important Note**
>
> For more details about the Azure CLI command to create an Azure SP, please refer to the documentation at https://docs.microsoft.com/en-us/cli/azure/create-an-azure-service-principal-azure-cli?view=azure-cli-latest.

The following screenshot shows the execution of the script that creates an Azure SP:

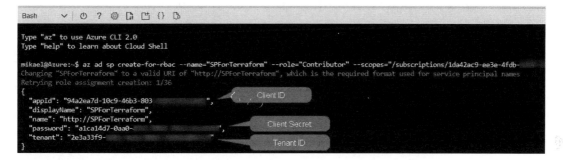

Figure 2.6 – Creating an Azure SP

The creation of this Azure SP returns three pieces of identification information:

- The application ID, which is also called the client ID
- The client secret
- The tenant ID

The SP is created in Azure AD. The following screenshot shows the Azure AD SP:

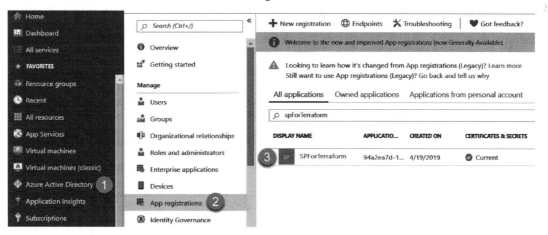

Figure 2.7 – The App registrations list in the Azure portal

Here, we have just discovered how to create an SP in Azure AD, and we have given it permissions to manipulate the resources of our Azure subscriptions.

Now, let's learn how to configure Terraform to use our Azure SP.

Configuring the Terraform provider

Once the Azure SP has been created, we will configure our Terraform configuration to connect to Azure using this SP. To do this, follow these steps:

1. In a directory of your choice, create a new filename, `provider.tf` (the extension `.tf` file corresponds to Terraform files), which contains the following code:

```
provider "azurerm" {
features {}
        subscription_id = "<subscription ID>"
        client_id = "<Client ID>"
        client_secret = "<Client Secret>"
        tenant_id = "<Tenant Id>"
}
```

In the preceding code, we indicate that the provider we are using is `azurerm`. The authentication information to Azure is the SP that has been created, and we add new block **features** that provide the possibility that we can customize the behavior of the Azure provider resources.

However, for security reasons, it is not advisable to put identification information in plain text inside your configuration, especially if you know that this code might be accessible by other people.

2. Therefore, we will improve the preceding code by replacing it with this one:

```
provider "azurerm" {
    features {}
}
```

3. So, we delete the credentials in the Terraform configuration, and we will pass the identification values to specific Terraform environment variables:

-   `ARM_SUBSCRIPTION_ID`
-   `ARM_CLIENT_ID`

- `ARM_CLIENT_SECRET`
- `ARM_TENANT_ID`

> **Important Note**
>
> For more information regarding the **azurerm** provider, please refer to the documentation at `https://registry.terraform.io/providers/hashicorp/azurerm/latest/docs`. We will learn how to set these environment variables later in this chapter, in the *Running Terraform form deployment* section.

As a result, the Terraform code no longer contains any identification information.

We have just learned how to configure Terraform for Azure authentication. Now, we will explain how to quickly configure Terraform to perform local development and testing.

The Terraform configuration for local development and testing

When you work locally and want to test the Terraform code quickly—for example, in a sandbox environment—it might be more convenient and faster to use your own Azure account instead of using an SP.

To do this, it is possible to connect to Azure beforehand using the `az login` command. Then, enter your identification information in the window that opens.

The following is a screenshot of the Azure login window:

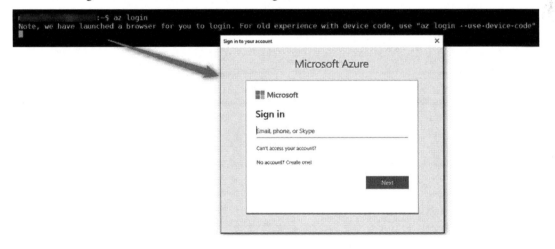

Figure 2.8 – The Azure Sign in page with Azure login

If several subscriptions are accessed, the desired one can be selected using the following command:

```
az account set --subscription="<Subscription ID>"
```

Then, we configure the Terraform provider as before using the *provider*, `"azurerm"` `{ }`.

Of course, this authentication method should not be done in the case of an execution on a remote server.

> **Important Note**
> For more information regarding the provider configuration, please refer to the documentation at `https://www.terraform.io/docs/providers/azurerm/index.html`.

Therefore, the Terraform configuration for Azure is defined by the configuration of the provider that uses the information from an Azure SP.

Once this configuration is complete, we can start writing the Terraform configuration to manage and provision Azure resources.

Writing a Terraform script to deploy an Azure infrastructure

To illustrate the use of Terraform to deploy resources in Azure, we will provide a simple Azure architecture with Terraform that is composed of the following components:

- There's an Azure resource group.
- There's also a network configuration that is composed of a virtual network and a subnet.
- In this subnet, we will create a virtual machine that has a public IP address in order to be publicly available.

To do this, in the same directory where we previously created the `provider.tf` file, we will create a `main.tf` file with the following code:

1. Let's start with the code that provides the `resource` group:

```
resource "azurerm_resource_group" "rg" {
    name = "bookRg"
    location = "West Europe"
```

```
    tags {
        environment = "Terraform Azure"
    }
}
```

Any piece of Terraform code is composed of the same syntax model, and the syntax of a Terraform object consists of four parts:

- A type of `resource` or `data` block

- A name of the resource to be managed (for example, `azurerm_resource_group`)

- An internal Terraform ID (for example, `rg`)

- A list of properties that correspond to the real properties of the resource (that is, `name` and `location`)

> **Important Note**
>
> More documentation regarding the Terraform syntax is available at `https://www.terraform.io/docs/configuration-0-11/resources.html`.

This code uses the `azurerm_resource_group` Terraform resource and will provision a resource group, named `bookRg`, that will be stored in the West Europe location.

2. Then, we will write the code for the network part:

```
resource "azurerm_virtual_network" "vnet" {
    name = "book-vnet"
    location = "West Europe"
    address_space = ["10.0.0.0/16"]
    resource_group_name = azurerm_resource_group.rg.name
}
resource "azurerm_subnet" "subnet" {
    name = "book-subnet"
    virtual_network_name = azurerm_virtual_network.vnet.name
    resource_group_name = azurerm_resource_group.rg.name
    address_prefix = "10.0.10.0/24"
}
```

In this Terraform code for the network part, we create the code for a VNet, `book-vnet`, and in it, we create a subnet called `book-subnet`.

If we look at this code carefully, we can see that, for the dependencies between the resources, we do not put in clear IDs, but we use pointers on the Terraform resources.

The VNet and subnet are the property of the resource group with `${azurerm_resource_group.rg.name}`, which tells Terraform that the VNet and subnet will be created just after the resource group. As for the subnet, it is dependent on its VNet with the use of the `${azurerm_virtual_network.vnet.name}` value; it's the explicit dependence concept.

Now, let's write the Terraform provisioning code of the virtual machine, which is composed of the following:

- A network interface
- A public IP address
- An Azure Storage object for the diagnostic boot (boot information logs)
- A virtual machine

The sample code for the **network interface** with the IP configuration is as follows:

```
resource "azurerm_network_interface" "nic" {
    name = "book-nic"
    location = "West Europe"
    resource_group_name = azurerm_resource_group.rg.name
    ip_configuration {
        name = "bookipconfig"
        subnet_id = azurerm_subnet.subnet.id
        private_ip_address_allocation = "Dynamic"
        public_ip_address_id = azurerm_public_ip.pip.id
    }
}
```

In this Terraform code, we use an `azurerm_network_interface` block (`https://www.terraform.io/docs/providers/azurerm/r/network_interface.html`). In it, we configure the name, region, resource group, and IP configuration with the dynamic IP address of the network interface.

The code for `public ip address`, which has an IP address in the subnet we just created, is as follows:

```
resource "azurerm_public_ip" "pip" {
  name = "book-ip"
  location = "West Europe"
  resource_group_name = "${azurerm_resource_group.rg.name}"
  public_ip_address_allocation = "Dynamic"
  domain_name_label = "bookdevops"
}
```

In this Terraform code, we use an `azurerm_public_ip` block at https://www.terraform.io/docs/providers/azurerm/r/public_ip.html. In it, we configure the dynamic allocation of the IP address and the DNS label.

The code for `storage account`, which we use for the boot diagnostic logs, is as follows:

```
resource "azurerm_storage_account" "stor" {
  name = "bookstor"
  location = "West Europe"
  resource_group_name = azurerm_resource_group.rg.name
  account_tier = "Standard"
  account_replication_type = "LRS"
}
```

In this Terraform code, we use an `azurerm_storage_account` block at https://www.terraform.io/docs/providers/azurerm/r/storage_account.html. In it, we configure the name, region, resource group, and type of storage, which, in our case, is Standard LRS.

> **Important Note**
>
> The documentation for the storage account can be found at https://docs.microsoft.com/en-us/azure/storage/common/storage-account-overview.

And the code for the Ubuntu virtual machine, which contains the ID of the network interface created earlier, is as follows:

```
resource "azurerm_linux_virtual_machine" "vm" {
  name = "bookvm"
  location = "West Europe"
  resource_group_name = azurerm_resource_group.rg.name
  vm_size = "Standard_DS1_v2"
  network_interface_ids = ["${azurerm_network_interface.nic.id}"]
  storage_image_reference {
      publisher = "Canonical"
      offer = "UbuntuServer"
      sku = "16.04-LTS"
      version = "latest"
  }
  ....
}
```

In this Terraform code, we use an `azurerm_linux_virtual_machine` block at `https://registry.terraform.io/providers/hashicorp/azurerm/latest/docs/resources/linux_virtual_machine`. In it, we configure the name, size (`Standard_DS1_V2`), reference to the `network_interface` Terraform object, and the type of virtual machine operating system (Ubuntu).

All of these code sections are exactly like the previous ones with the use of an explicit dependency to specify the relationships between the resources.

> **Important Note**
>
> This complete source code is available at `https://github.com/PacktPublishing/Learning-DevOps-Second-Edition/tree/main/CHAP02/terraform_simple_script`.

We have just created a complete Terraform script that allows us to provision a small Azure infrastructure. However, as in any language, there are good practices regarding file separation, applying a clear and readable code, and, finally, the use of built-in functions.

Following some Terraform good practices

We have just looked at an example of Terraform code to provision an Azure infrastructure, but it is also useful to look at some good practices for writing Terraform code.

Better visibility with the separation of files

When executing Terraform code, all of the configuration files in the `execution` directory that have the `.tf` extension are automatically executed; in our example, we have `provider.tf` and `main.tf`. It is good to separate the code into several files in order to improve the readability of the code and its evolution.

Using our example script, we can do better by separating it with the following:

- `Rg.tf`: This contains the code for the resource group.
- `Network.tf`: This contains the code for the VNet and subnet.
- `Compute.tf`: This contains the code for the network interface, public IP, storage, and virtual machine.

> **Important Note**
>
> The complete code with separate files can be located at `https://github.com/PacktPublishing/Learning-DevOps-Second-Edition/tree/main/CHAP02/terraform_separate_files`.

The protection of sensitive data

Care must be taken with sensitive data in the Terraform configuration, such as passwords and access permissions. We have already learned that, for access authentication to Azure, it is not necessary to leave them in the code. Additionally, in our example concerning the administrator account of the virtual machine, note that the password of the admin account of the virtual machine has been clearly specified in this Terraform configuration. To remedy this, we can use a strong secret manager to store passwords, such as Azure Key Vault or HashiCorp Vault, and get them via Terraform.

Dynamizing the configuration with variables and interpolation functions

When writing the Terraform configuration, it is important to take into account—from the beginning—that the infrastructure that will host an application is very often the same for all stages. However, only some information will vary from one stage to another, such as the name of the resources and the number of instances.

To give more flexibility to the code, we must use variables in the code with the following steps:

1. Declare the variables by adding the following sample code in the global Terraform code. Alternatively, we can add it within another file (such as `variables.tf`) for better readability of the code:

    ```
    variable "resource_group_name" {
        description ="Name of the resource group"
    }
    variable "location" {
        description ="Location of the resource"
        default ="West Europe"
    }
    variable "application_name" {
        description ="Name of the application"
    }
    ```

2. Instantiate their values in another `.tfvars` file, named `terraform.tfvars`, with the `variable_name=value` syntax, similar to the following:

    ```
    resource_group_name ="bookRg"
    application_name ="book"
    ```

3. Use these variables in code with `var.<name of the variable>`; for example, in the resource group Terraform code, we can write the following:

    ```
    resource "azurerm_resource_group" "rg" {
        name = var.resource_group_name
        location = var.location
        tags {
            environment = "Terraform Azure"
    ```

```
        }
    }
```

In addition to this, Terraform has a large list of built-in functions that can be used to manipulate data or variables. To learn more about these functions, please refer to the official documentation at `https://www.terraform.io/docs/configuration/functions.html`.

Of course, there are many other good practices, but these are to be applied from the first lines of code to ensure that your code is well maintained.

> **Important Note**
>
> The complete and final code of this example is available at `https://github.com/PacktPublishing/Learning-DevOps-Second-Edition/tree/main/CHAP02/terraform_vars_interp`.

We have written a Terraform configuration, using best practices, which allows us to create a simple cloud infrastructure in Azure that provides a network and a virtual machine. Now, let's take a look at how to run Terraform with our code in order to provision this infrastructure.

Running Terraform for deployment

With the Terraform configuration written, we now need to run Terraform to deploy our infrastructure.

However, before any execution, first, it is necessary to provide authentication with the Azure SP to ensure that Terraform can manage the Azure resources.

To do this, we can either set the environment variables specific to Terraform to contain the information of the SP created earlier in the *Configuring Terraform for Azure* section, or we can use the `az cli` script.

The following script exports the four Terraform environment variables in the Linux OS:

```
export ARM_SUBSCRIPTION_ID=xxxxx-xxxxx-xxxx-xxxx
export ARM_CLIENT_ID=xxxxx-xxxxx-xxxx-xxxx
export ARM_CLIENT_SECRET=xxxxxxxxxxxxxxxxxx
export ARM_TENANT_ID=xxxxx-xxxxx-xxxx-xxxx
```

Additionally, we can use the `az cli` script with the `login` command:

```
az login
```

Once authenticated, we can run the Terraform workflow.

In our scenario, we begin with an empty Azure subscription without any Azure resource groups; however, in the real world, our subscription might already contain a resource group.

Before running Terraform, in the Azure portal, check that you do not have a resource group in your subscription, as follows:

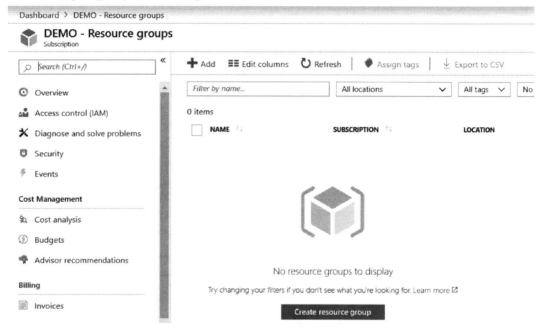

Figure 2.9 – No resource group on Azure

To run Terraform, we need to open a command-line Terminal such as CMD, PowerShell, or Bash and navigate to the directory where the Terraform configuration files we wrote earlier are located.

The Terraform configuration is executed in several steps, including initialization, the preview of changes, and the application of those changes.

Next, let's take a look, in detail, at the execution of these steps, starting with the initialization step.

Initialization

The initialization step allows Terraform to do the following:

- Initialize the Terraform context to check and make the connection between the Terraform provider and remote service—in our case, this is with Azure.

- Download the plugin(s) of the provider(s)—in our case, it will be the `azurerm` provider.

- Check the code variables.

To execute the initialization, run the `init` command:

```
terraform init
```

The following is a screenshot of `terraform init`:

```
root@ubuntu-bionic:/learningdevops/CHAP02/terraform_separate_files# terraform init

Initializing the backend...

Initializing provider plugins...
- Finding hashicorp/azurerm versions matching "2.63.0"...
- Installing hashicorp/azurerm v2.63.0...
- Installed hashicorp/azurerm v2.63.0 (signed by HashiCorp)

Terraform has created a lock file .terraform.lock.hcl to record the provider
selections it made above. Include this file in your version control repository
so that Terraform can guarantee to make the same selections by default when
you run "terraform init" in the future.

Terraform has been successfully initialized!

You may now begin working with Terraform. Try running "terraform plan" to see
any changes that are required for your infrastructure. All Terraform commands
should now work.

If you ever set or change modules or backend configuration for Terraform,
rerun this command to reinitialize your working directory. If you forget, other
commands will detect it and remind you to do so if necessary.
```

Figure 2.10 – Executing the terraform init command

As we have gathered during its execution of the preceding command, Terraform does the following:

- It downloads the latest version of the `azurerm` plugin.
- It creates a working `.terraform` directory.

The following is a screenshot of the `.terraform` directory:

Figure 2.11 – The Terraform configuration directory

> **Important Note**
>
> For more information about the `init` command line, please refer to the documentation at `https://www.terraform.io/docs/commands/init.html`.

Once the initialization step is complete, we can proceed to the next step, which is previewing the changes.

Previewing the changes

The next step is to preview the changes made to the infrastructure before applying them.

To do this, run Terraform with the `plan` command. When executed, the plan automatically uses the `terraform.tfvars` file to set the variables.

To execute it, launch the `plan` command:

```
terraform plan
```

The following output shows the execution of the `terraform plan` command:

```
                    :/mnt/d/DevOps/Learning-DevOps/CHAP02/terraform_separate_files$ terraform plan
Refreshing Terraform state in-memory prior to plan...
The refreshed state will be used to calculate this plan, but will not be
persisted to local or remote state storage.


..................................................................


An execution plan has been generated and is shown below.
Resource actions are indicated with the following symbols:
  + create

Terraform will perform the following actions:

  + azurerm_network_interface.nic
      id:                                                               <computed>
      applied_dns_servers.#:                                            <computed>
      dns_servers.#:                                                    <computed>
      enable_accelerated_networking:                                    "false"
      enable_ip_forwarding:                                             "false"
      internal_dns_name_label:                                          <computed>
      internal_fqdn:                                                    <computed>
      ip_configuration.#:                                               "1"
      ip_configuration.0.application_gateway_backend_address_pools_ids.#: <computed>
      ip_configuration.0.application_security_group_ids.#:              <computed>
      ip_configuration.0.load_balancer_backend_address_pools_ids.#:     <computed>
      ip_configuration.0.load_balancer_inbound_nat_rules_ids.#:         <computed>
      ip_configuration.0.name:                                          "bookipconfig"
      ip_configuration.0.primary:                                       <computed>
      ip_configuration.0.private_ip_address_allocation:                 "dynamic"
      ip_configuration.0.private_ip_address_version:                    "IPv4"
      ip_configuration.0.public_ip_address_id:                          "${azurerm_public_ip.pip.id}"
      ip_configuration.0.subnet_id:                                     "${azurerm_subnet.subnet.id}"
      location:                                                         "westeurope"

  + azurerm_virtual_network.vnet
      id:                                                               <computed>
      address_space.#:                                                  "1"
      address_space.0:                                                  "10.0.0.0/16"
      location:                                                         "westeurope"
      name:                                                             "book-vnet"
      resource_group_name:                                              "bookRg"
      subnet.#:                                                         <computed>
      tags.%:                                                           <computed>

Plan: 7 to add, 0 to change, 0 to destroy.

..................................................................

Note: You didn't specify an "-out" parameter to save this plan, so Terraform
can't guarantee that exactly these actions will be performed if
```

Figure 2.12 – Executing the terraform plan command

During the execution of the `plan` command, the command displays the name and properties of the resources that will be impacted by the change. It also displays the number of new resources and the number of resources that will be modified, along with the number of resources that will be deleted.

> **Important Note**
>
> For more information about the `plan` command line, please refer to the documentation at `https://www.terraform.io/docs/commands/plan.html`.

Therefore, we have just seen a prediction of the changes that will be applied to our infrastructure. Now, we will view how to apply them.

Applying the changes

After validating that the result of the `plan` command corresponds to our expectations, the final step is the application of the Terraform code in real time to provision and apply the changes to our infrastructure.

To do this, we will execute the `apply` command:

```
terraform apply
```

This command does the same operation as the `plan` command and interactively asks the user for confirmation that we want to implement the changes.

The following is a screenshot of the `terraform apply` confirmation:

```
                     :/mnt/d/DevOps/Learning-DevOps/CHAP02/terraform_separate_files$ terraform apply
An execution plan has been generated and is shown below.
Resource actions are indicated with the following symbols:
  + create

Terraform will perform the following actions:

  + azurerm_network_interface.nic
      id:                                                              <computed>
      applied_dns_servers.#:                                           <computed>

      tags.%:                                                          <computed>

Plan: 7 to add, 0 to change, 0 to destroy.

Do you want to perform these actions?
  Terraform will perform the actions described above.
  Only 'yes' will be accepted to approve.

  Enter a value:
```

Figure 2.13 – Confirmation of the changes to be applied in Terraform

The confirmation is given by inputting `yes` (or `no` to cancel), then Terraform applies the changes to the infrastructure.

The following is a screenshot of the `terraform apply` execution:

```
 Only 'yes' will be accepted to approve.

 Enter a value: yes

azurerm_resource_group.rg: Creating...
  location:            "" => "westeurope"
  name:                "" => "bookRg"
  tags.%:              "" => "1"
  tags.environment:    "" => "Terraform Azure"

azurerm_virtual_machine.vm: Still creating... (2m30s elapsed)
azurerm_virtual_machine.vm: Creation complete after 2m32s (ID: /subscriptions/1da42a

apply complete! Resources: 7 added, 0 changed, 0 destroyed.
```

Figure 2.14 – Executing the terraform apply command

The output of the `apply` command displays all actions executed by Terraform, along with all changes and the impacted resources. It ends with a summary line that displays the sum of all added, changed, or destroyed resources.

> **Important Note**
>
> For more information about the `apply` command line, please refer to the documentation at `https://www.terraform.io/docs/commands/apply.html`.

Since the Terraform `apply` command has been executed correctly, we can check in the Azure portal whether the resources described in the Terraform code are present.

The following is a screenshot of the Azure resources by Terraform:

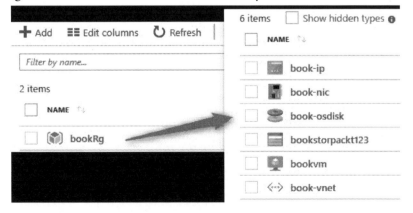

Figure 2.15 – A list of provisioned Azure resources

We can gather from the portal that the resources specified in the Terraform code have been provisioned successfully.

So, we have just learned how Terraform is useful for provisioning infrastructure using three main commands:

- The `init` command to initialize the context
- The `plan` command to preview the changes
- The `apply` command to apply the changes

In the next section, we will explore other Terraform commands and the Terraform life cycle.

Understanding the Terraform life cycle with different command-line options

We have just discovered that applying changes to a piece of infrastructure with Terraform is mainly done using three commands. They include the `init`, `plan`, and `apply` commands. However, Terraform has other very practical and important commands that can be used to best manage the life cycle of our infrastructure, and the question of how to execute Terraform in an automation context such as a CI/CD pipeline must also be considered.

Among the other operations that can be done on a piece of infrastructure is the cleaning up of resources by removing them. This is done to either better rebuild or remove temporary infrastructure.

Using destroy to better rebuild

One of the steps in the life cycle of infrastructure that is maintained by IaC is the removal of the infrastructure; do not forget that one of the objectives and benefits of IaC is to be able to make rapid changes to infrastructure but also create environments on demand. That is to say, we create and keep environments as long as we need them, and we will destroy them when they are no longer used, thereby allowing the company to make financial savings.

To accomplish this, it is necessary to automate the removal of the infrastructure in order to be able to rebuild it quickly.

To destroy infrastructure that has previously provisioned with Terraform, execute the following command:

```
terraform destroy
```

The execution of this command should give the following output:

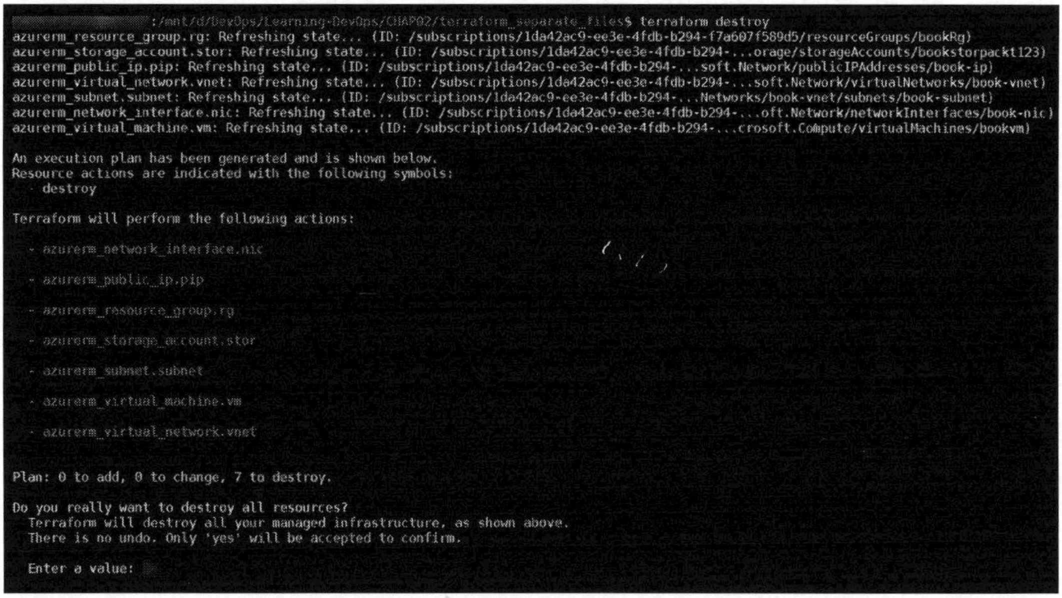

Figure 2.16 – Confirmation of the terraform destroy command

This command, as with `apply`, requires confirmation from the user before applying the destruction:

Figure 2.17 – Executing the terraform destroy command

Once validated, wait for the confirmation message that the infrastructure has been destroyed.

The `destroy` command only destroys the resources configured in the current Terraform configuration. Other resources (created manually or by another Terraform code) are not affected. However, if our Terraform code provides a resource group, it will destroy all of its content.

> **Important Note**
>
> For more information about the destroy command line, please refer to the documentation at https://www.terraform.io/docs/ commands/destroy.html.

We have just discovered that Terraform also allows you to destroy resources on the command line. Now, let's learn how to format and validate your Terraform code.

Formatting and validating the configuration

After learning how to destroy resources with Terraform, it is also important to emphasize the importance of having well-formatted code that meets Terraform's style rules and to validate that the code does not contain syntax or variable errors.

Formatting the code

Terraform has a command that allows the code to be properly aligned with Terraform's styles and conventions.

The following command automatically formats the code:

```
terraform fmt
```

The following is a screenshot of a Terraform-arranged file:

```
                          /d/Repos/Learning-DevOps/CHAP02/terraform_separate_files# terraform fmt
compute.tf
network.tf
provider.tf
rg.tf
```

Figure 2.18 – Executing the terraform fmt command

The command reformats the code and indicates the list of arranged files.

> **Important Note**
>
> For more information regarding the Terraform style guide, please refer to https://www.terraform.io/docs/configuration/ style.html. Additionally, for information about the terraform fmt command line, please refer to https://www.terraform.io/ docs/commands/fmt.html.

Validating the code

Along the same lines, Terraform has a command that validates the code and allows us to detect possible errors before executing the `plan` command or the `apply` command.

Let's consider the example of the following code extract:

```
resource "azurerm_public_ip" "pip" {
    name = var.ip-name
    location = var.location
    resource_group_name = "${azurerm_resource_group.rg.name}"
    allocation_method = "Dynamic"
    domain_name_label = "bookdevops"
}
```

In the `name` property, we use an `ip-name` variable that has not been declared or instantiated with any value.

Executing the `terraform plan` command should return an error:

```
:/d/Repos/Learning-DevOps/CHAP02/terraform_vars_interp# terraform plan
Error: resource 'azurerm_public_ip.pip' config: unknown variable referenced: 'ip-name'; define it with a 'variable' block
```

Figure 2.19 – The terraform plan command with an error

And because of this error, in a CI/CD process, it could delay the deployment of the infrastructure.

In order to detect errors in the Terraform code as early as possible in the development cycle, execute the following command. This validates all Terraform files in the directory:

```
terraform validate
```

The following screenshot shows the execution of this command:

```
:/d/Repos/Learning-DevOps/CHAP02/terraform_vars_interp# terraform validate
Error: resource 'azurerm_public_ip.pip' config: unknown variable referenced: 'ip-name'; define it with a 'variable' block
```

Figure 2.20 – Executing the terraform validate command

Here, we observe the same error as the one returned by the `plan` command.

We have just discovered Terraform's main command lines. Let's dive a little deeper with the integration of Terraform into a CI/CD process.

The Terraform life cycle within a CI/CD process

So far, we have seen and executed, *on the local machine*, the various Terraform commands that allow us to initialize, preview, apply, and destroy infrastructure and to format and validate Terraform code. When using Terraform locally, in a development context, the execution life cycle is as follows:

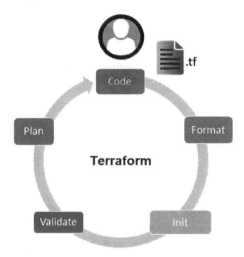

Figure 2.21 – The Terraform CICD process

The following steps explain the sequence in the preceding diagram:

1. Code development
2. Code formatting with `terraform fmt`
3. Initialization with `terraform init`
4. Code validation with `terraform validate`
5. Planning with `terraform plan`
6. Manual verification of Terraform changes on the infrastructure

However, IaC, similar to an application, must be deployed or executed in an **automatic CI/CD process**. This begins with the archiving of the Terraform code of the team members. Then, it triggers the CI and executes the Terraform commands that we have studied in this chapter.

The following is a screenshot of the Terraform life cycle in CI/CD automation:

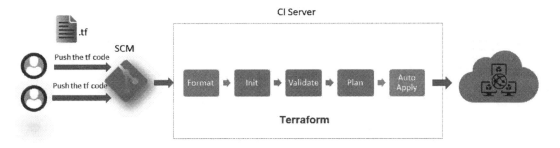

Figure 2.22 – The Terraform CICD workflow

The steps of CI/CD by the CI server (in which Terraform has been installed) for Terraform are as follows:

1. Retrieving the code from the SCM

2. Code formatting with `terraform fmt`

3. Initialization with `terraform init`

4. Code validation with `terraform validate`

5. Displaying a preview of the infrastructure changes with `terraform plan -out=out.tfplan`

6. Applying changes in automatic mode with `terraform apply --auto-approve out.tfplan`

By adding the `--auto-approve` option to the `apply` and `destroy` commands, Terraform can also be executed in automatic mode. This is to avoid asking for confirmation from the user to validate the changes that need to be applied. With this automation, Terraform can be integrated with CI/CD tools.

In the `plan` command, an `out` option is added to specify a file with the `.tfplan` format that corresponds to a file that contains the output of the `plan` command. This `out.tfplan` file is then used by the `apply` command. The advantage of this procedure is that it is possible to execute the application on a later plan, which can be used in a rollback case.

In this section, we have gathered that, aside from the usual Terraform commands of `init`, `plan`, `apply`, and `destroy`, Terraform also has options that will allow us to improve the readability of the code and validate the code syntax. Additionally, we explained that Terraform allows a perfect integration into a CI/CD pipeline with a life cycle and automation options.

In the next section, we will examine what the `tfstate` file is and how to protect it with a remote backend.

Protecting the state file with a remote backend

When Terraform handles resources, it writes the state of these resources in a Terraform state file. This file is in JSON format and preserves the resources and their properties throughout the execution of Terraform.

By default, this file, called `terraform.tfstate`, is created locally when the first execution of the `apply` command is executed. Then, it will be used by Terraform each time the `plan` command is executed in order to compare its state (written in the state file) with that of the target infrastructure. Finally, it will return a preview of what will be applied.

When using Terraform in an enterprise, this locally stored state file poses many problems:

- Knowing that this file contains the status of the infrastructure, it should not be deleted. If deleted, Terraform might not behave as expected when it is executed.

- It must be accessible at the same time by all members of the team who are handling resources on the same infrastructure.

- This file can contain sensitive data, so it must be secure.

- When provisioning multiple environments, it is necessary to be able to use multiple state files.

With all of these points, it is not possible to keep this state file locally or even to archive it in an SCM.

To solve this problem, Terraform allows this state file to be stored in a shared and secure storage called the **remote backend**.

> **Important Note**
> Terraform supports several types of remote backends; the full list is available at `https://www.terraform.io/docs/backends/types/remote.html`.

In our case, we will use an **azurerm remote backend** to store our state files with a storage account and a blob for the state file.

Therefore, we will implement and use a remote backend in three steps:

1. The creation of the storage account
2. The Terraform configuration for the remote backend
3. The execution of Terraform with the use of this remote backend

Let's take a look, in detail, at the execution of these steps:

1. To create an Azure storage account and a blob container, we can use either the
    Azure portal (https://docs.microsoft.com/en-gb/azure/storage/
    common/storage-quickstart-create-account?tabs=azure-portal)
    or an az cli script:

```
# 1-Create resource group

az group create --name MyRgRemoteBackend --location
westeurope

# 2-Create storage account

az storage account create --resource-group
MyRgRemoteBackend --name storageremotetf --sku Standard_
LRS --encryption-services blob

# 3-Get storage account key

ACCOUNT_KEY=$(az storage account keys list --resource-
group MyRgRemoteBackend --account-name storageremotetf
--query [0].value -o tsv)

# 4-Create blob container

az storage container create --name tfbackends --account-
name storageremotetf --account-key $ACCOUNT_KEY
```

This script creates a MyRgRemoteBackend resource group and a storage
account, called storageremotetf.

Then, the script retrieves the key account from the storage account and creates a
blob container, tfbackends, inside this storage account.

This script can be run in Azure Cloud Shell, and the advantage of using a script rather
than using the Azure portal is that this script can be integrated into a CI/CD process.

2. Then, to configure Terraform to use the previously created remote backend, we need
    to add the configuration section within the Terraform.tf file:

```
terraform {
    backend "azurerm" {
        storage_account_name  = "storageremotetfdemo"
        container_name        = "tfbackends"
        key                   = "myappli.tfstate"
snapshot              = true
    }
}
```

The storage_account_name property contains the name of the storage account, the container_name property contains the container name, the key property contains the name of the blob state object, and the snapshot property enables a snapshot of this blog object at each edition by Terraform execution.

However, there is still one more piece of configuration information to be provided to Terraform so that it can connect and have permissions on the storage account. This information is the access key, which is a private authentication and authorization key on the storage account. To provide the storage key to Terraform, as with the Azure SP information, set an ARM_STORAGE_KEY environment variable with the storage account access key value.

The following is a screenshot of the Azure storage access key:

Figure 2.23 – The Azure storage access key

> **Important Note**
>
> Terraform supports other types of authentications on the storage account such as the use of a SAS token or by using an SP. For more information on how to configure Terraform for an azurerm remote backend, please refer to the documentation at https://www.terraform.io/docs/backends/types/azurerm.html.

3. Finally, once the Terraform configuration is complete, Terraform can be run with this new remote backend. It is during `init` that Terraform initializes the context of the state file. By default, the `init` command remains unchanged with `terraform init`.

However, if multiple Terraform `states` are used to manage multiple environments, it's possible to create several remote backend configurations with the simplified code in the `.tf` file:

```
terraform {
    backend "azurerm" {}
}
```

Then, create several `backend.tfvars` files that only contain the properties of the backends.

These `backend` properties are the storage account name, the name of the blob container, and the blob name of the state file:

```
storage_account_name   = "storageremotetf"
container_name          = "tfbackends"
key                     = "myappli.tfstate"
snapshot                = true
```

In this scenario, when executing the `init` command, we can specify the `backend.tfvars` file to use with the following command:

```
terraform init -backend-config="backend.tfvars"
```

The `-backend-config` argument is the path to the backend configuration file.

Personally, I prefer this way of doing things as it allows me to decouple the code by externalizing the values of the backend properties for better readability of the code.

So, here is the execution of Terraform:

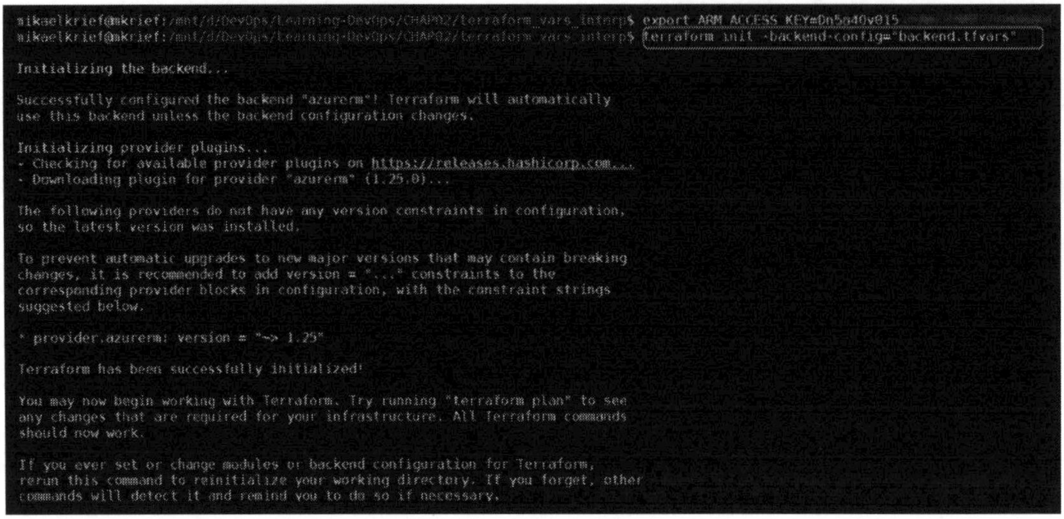

Figure 2.24 – The terraform init command with backend configuration

In this execution, we can view the export of the ARM_ACCESS_KEY environment variable, along with the Terraform init command that determines the backend configuration with the -backend-config option.

With this remote backend, the state file will no longer be stored locally but on a storage account, which is a shared space. Therefore, it can be used at the same time by several users. At the same time, this storage account offers security to protect the sensitive data of the state file and the possibility of any backups or restorations of the state files, which are both essential and critical elements of Terraform, too.

> **Note**
>
> The entire source code of this chapter is available at https://github.com/PacktPublishing/Learning-DevOps-Second-Edition/tree/main/CHAP02, and the final Terraform code is located inside the terraform_vars_interp folder.

Summary

In this chapter dedicated to Terraform, we learned that its installation can be done either manually or using scripts.

To apply Terraform, we detailed the different steps of its configuration to provision an Azure infrastructure using an Azure SP.

Additionally, we explained, step by step, its local execution with its main command lines, which are `init`, `plan`, `apply`, and `destroy`, along with its life cycle in a CI/CD process. Finally, we ended this chapter by looking at the protection of the state file in an Azure remote backend.

Therefore, Terraform is a tool that is in line with the principles of IaC. The Terraform code is readable and understandable to users, and its execution integrates very well into a CI/CD pipeline that allows you to automatically provision a cloud infrastructure.

Throughout this book, we will continue to discuss Terraform, with additions about its use with Packer, Azure Kubernetes Services, and downtime reduction.

In the next chapter, we will explore the next step of the IaC, which is configuration management by using Ansible. We will cover its installation, its usage for configuring our provisioned virtual machine, and how to protect secrets with Ansible Vault.

Questions

1. What is the language used by Terraform?
2. What is Terraform's role?
3. Is Terraform a scripting tool?
4. Which command allows you to display the installed version?
5. When using Terraform for Azure, what is the name of the Azure object that connects Terraform to Azure?
6. What are the three main commands of the Terraform workflow?
7. Which Terraform command allows you to destroy resources?
8. What is the option added to the `apply` command to automate the application of infrastructure changes?
9. What is the purpose of the Terraform state file?
10. Is it a good practice to leave the Terraform state file locally? If not, what should be done?

Further reading

If you want to know more about Terraform, here are some resources:

- The official Terraform documentation: `https://www.terraform.io/`

- Terraform download and installation information: `https://www.terraform.io/downloads.html`

- Terraform Azure provider: `https://www.terraform.io/docs/providers/azurerm/index.html`

- The official Azure documentation for Terraform: `https://docs.microsoft.com/en-us/azure/terraform/terraform-overview`

- Book: Terraform Cookbook: `https://www.packtpub.com/product/terraform-cookbook/9781800207554`

- *Getting Started with Terraform, Second Edition*: `https://www.packtpub.com/networking-and-servers/getting-started-terraform-second-edition`

- Online learning for Terraform: `https://learn.hashicorp.com/terraform`

3
Using Ansible for Configuring IaaS Infrastructure

In the previous chapter, we talked about provisioning an Azure cloud infrastructure with Terraform. If this infrastructure contains **virtual machines** (**VMs**), once they've been provisioned, it is necessary to configure their systems and install all the necessary middleware. This configuration will be necessary for the proper functionality of the applications that will be hosted on the VM.

There are several **Infrastructure as Code** (**IaC**) tools available for configuring VMs and the most well-known are Ansible, Puppet, Chef, SaltStack, and PowerShell DSC. Among them, Ansible from Red Hat (`https://www.ansible.com/overview/it-automation`) stands out for its many assets, as follows:

- It is declarative and uses the easy-to-read YAML language.
- Ansible only works with one executable.
- It does not require agents to be installed on the VMs to be configured.

- A simple SSL/WinRM connection is required for Ansible to connect to remote VMs.

- It has a template engine and a vault to encrypt/decrypt sensitive data.

- It is idempotent.

The main uses cases of Ansible are as follows:

- Configuring a VM with middleware and hardening, which we will learn about in this chapter

- Infrastructure provisioning, such as Terraform, but using YAML configuration

- Security compliance to test that the system or network configuration conforms to the enterprise requirements

In this chapter, we will learn how to install Ansible, and then use it to configure a VM with an inventory and a playbook. We will also learn how to protect sensitive data with Ansible Vault before discussing how to use a dynamic inventory in Azure.

The following topics will be covered in this chapter:

- Installing Ansible

- Creating an Ansible inventory

- Executing the first playbook

- Executing Ansible

- Protecting data with Ansible Vault

- Using a dynamic inventory for an Azure infrastructure

Technical requirements

To follow along with the chapter, you must meet the following technical requirements:

- To install Ansible, we need an OS such as Red Hat, Debian, CentOS, macOS, or any of the BSDs. For those who have Windows, you can install the **Windows Subsystem for Linux** (**WSL**); refer to the documentation at `https://docs.microsoft.com/en-us/windows/wsl/install-win10`.

- Python 2 (version 2.7) or Python 3 (version 3.5+) must be installed on the machine that runs Ansible. You can download it here: `https://www.python.org/downloads/`. For more information about the Ansible requirements, refer to the documentation here: `https://docs.ansible.com/ansible/latest/installation_guide/intro_installation.html#control-node-requirements`.

- An Ansible playbook uses YAML configuration files, so any code editor would work; however, we will be using Visual Studio Code as it is very suitable. You can download it here: `https://code.visualstudio.com/`.

- Most of this chapter will not focus on a particular cloud provider, except for the last section on Azure. We will need an Azure subscription for this, which we can get for free from here: `https://azure.microsoft.com/en-us/free/`.

- To run the Ansible dynamic inventory for Azure, we need to install the Azure Python SDK: `https://docs.microsoft.com/en-us/azure/python/python-sdk-azure-install?view=azure-python`.

- The complete source code for this chapter is available here: `https://github.com/PacktPublishing/Learning-DevOps-Second-Edition/tree/main/CHAP03`.

Check out the following video to see the Code in Action:

`https://bit.ly/3HdwbVc`.

Installing Ansible

Before we start using Ansible, we must know which OS we can use it on and how to install and configure it. Then, we must learn about some of the concepts surrounding the artifacts that it needs to operate.

In this section, we will look at how to install Ansible on a local or server machine and how to integrate Ansible in Azure Cloud Shell. Then, we will talk about the different elements or artifacts that make up Ansible. Finally, we will configure Ansible.

To get started, we will learn how to download and install Ansible with an automatic script.

Installing Ansible with a script

Unlike Terraform, Ansible is not multiplatform and can only be installed on Red Hat, Debian, CentOS, macOS, or any of the BSDs. You install it using a script that differs according to your OS.

For example, to install the latest version on Ubuntu, we must run the following script in a Bash Terminal:

```
sudo apt-get update
sudo apt-get install software-properties-common
sudo apt-add-repository --yes --update ppa:ansible/ansible
sudo apt-get install ansible
```

> **Important Note**
>
> This script is also available here: `https://github.com/` `PacktPublishing/Learning-DevOps-Second-Edition/` `blob/main/CHAP03/install_ansible_ubuntu.sh`.

This script updates the necessary packages, installs the `software-properties-common` dependency, adds the Ansible repository, and installs the latest version of Ansible.

> **Important Note**
>
> The Ansible installation scripts for all distribution types are available here: `https://docs.ansible.com/ansible/latest/` `installation_guide/intro_installation.` `html#installing-ansible-on-specific-operating-` `systems`.

To install Ansible locally on a Windows OS machine, there is no native solution, but it can be installed on a local VirtualBox VM or WSL. WSL allows developers who are on a Windows OS to test their scripts and applications directly on their workstations, without having to install a VM.

> **Important Note**
>
> Read this article to learn how to install Ansible on a local VirtualBox environment: `https://phoenixnap.com/kb/install-` `ansible-on-windows`. For more details about WSL, read the documentation here: `https://docs.microsoft.com/en-us/` `windows/wsl/about`.

To test whether it has been successfully installed, we can run the following command to check its installed version:

```
ansible --version
```

The result of executing this command provides some information on the installed version of Ansible, like this:

```
mikael@vmAnsible:~$ ansible --version
ansible 2.8.3
  config file = /etc/ansible/ansible.cfg
  configured module search path = [u'/home/mikael/.ansible/plugins/modules', u'/usr/share/ansible/plugins/modules']
  ansible python module location = /usr/lib/python2.7/dist-packages/ansible
  executable location = /usr/bin/ansible
  python version = 2.7.15+ (default, Oct  7 2019, 17:39:04) [GCC 7.4.0]
```

Figure 3.1 – The ansible --version command

To display a list of all Ansible commands and options, execute the `ansible` command with the `--help` argument:

```
ansible --help
```

The following screenshot shows the execution of this command:

```
                        :~$ ansible --help
Usage: ansible <host-pattern> [options]

Define and run a single task 'playbook' against a set of hosts

Options:
  -a MODULE_ARGS, --args=MODULE_ARGS
                        module arguments
  --ask-vault-pass      ask for vault password
  -B SECONDS, --background=SECONDS
                        run asynchronously, failing after X seconds
                        (default=N/A)
  -C, --check           don't make any changes; instead, try to predict some
                        of the changes that may occur
  -D, --diff            when changing (small) files and templates, show the
                        differences in those files; works great with --check
  -e EXTRA_VARS, --extra-vars=EXTRA_VARS
                        set additional variables as key=value or YAML/JSON, if
```

Figure 3.2 – The ansible --help command

As we can see, installing Ansible on a local or remote machine is quite simple and can be automated by a script. If we deploy infrastructure in Azure, we can also use Ansible as it is integrated into Azure Cloud Shell.

Now, let's look at how Ansible is integrated into Azure Cloud Shell.

Integrating Ansible into Azure Cloud Shell

As we learned in *Chapter 2, Provisioning Cloud Infrastructure with Terraform*, **Azure Cloud Shell** integrates third-party tools that can be used in Azure without having to install them on a VM. Among these tools is Terraform, which we saw in detail in the previous chapter, but there is also Ansible, which Microsoft has integrated to allow us to automatically configure the VMs that are hosted in Azure.

To use Ansible in Azure cloud, we must do the following:

1. Connect to the Azure portal at `https://portal.azure.com`.
2. Open Cloud Shell.
3. Choose Bash mode.
4. In the Terminal that opens, we now have access to all Ansible commands.

The following screenshot shows the `ansible` command in Azure Cloud Shell:

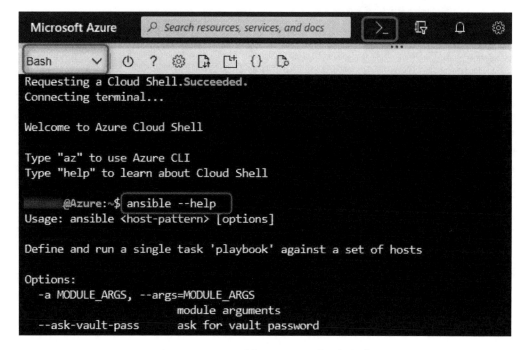

Figure 3.3 – Ansible in Azure Cloud Shell

This way, it will be possible to use Ansible for development and testing without installing any software.

Also, Ansible has modules that allow us to provision an Azure infrastructure (such as Terraform, but this aspect of Ansible will not be covered in this book), so its integration into Azure Cloud Shell allows for simplified authentication.

> **Important Note**
>
> Detailed documentation on integrating Ansible into Azure Cloud Shell is available here: https://docs.microsoft.com/en-us/azure/ansible/ansible-run-playbook-in-cloudshell.

Before we start using Ansible, we will review the important concepts (or artifacts) of Ansible that will serve us throughout this chapter.

Ansible artifacts

To configure a system, Ansible needs several main artifacts:

- **The hosts**: These are target systems that Ansible will configure; the host can also be a local system.

- **The inventory**: This is a file in INI or YAML format that contains the list of target hosts that Ansible will perform configuration actions on. This inventory can also be a script, which is the case with a dynamic inventory.

> **Important Note**
> We will look at how to implement an Ansible inventory in the *Creating an Ansible inventory* section, while we will look at how to implement a dynamic inventory in the *Using a dynamic inventory for Azure infrastructure* section.

- **The playbook**: This is the Ansible configuration script that will be executed to configure hosts.

> **Important Note**
> We will learn how to write playbooks in the *Executing the first playbook* section, later in this chapter.

After learning how to install Ansible, we looked at the essential elements of Ansible, which are hosts, inventory, and playbooks. Now, let's learn how to configure Ansible.

Configuring Ansible

By default, the Ansible configuration is in the /etc/ansible/ansible. cfg file, which is created while Ansible is being installed. This file contains several configuration keys, such as an SSL connection, a user, a protocol, transport, and many others.

As we mentioned previously, this file is created by default while Ansible is being installed. To help the user get started, initial content is placed in it. This content contains a multitude of configuration keys that are commented out so that they are not applied by Ansible but can be activated at any time by the user.

> **Note**
>
> If we use Ansible inside Azure Cloud Shell, we need to create this file
> (`ansible.cfg`) manually inside our Azure cloud drive and set the
> `ANSIBLE_CONFIG` environment variable with the path to the created
> file. The documentation for this environment variable is available here:
> `https://docs.ansible.com/ansible/latest/reference_`
> `appendices/config.html#envvar-ANSIBLE_CONFIG`.

The following screenshot shows an extract from this `/etc/ansible/ansible.`
`cfg` configuration file with some keys in the comments, as shown by the # symbol:

```
# config file for ansible -- https://ansible.com/
# ===============================================

# nearly all parameters can be overridden in ansible-playbook
# or with command line flags. ansible will read ANSIBLE_CONFIG,
# ansible.cfg in the current working directory, .ansible.cfg in
# the home directory or /etc/ansible/ansible.cfg, whichever it
# finds first

[defaults]

# some basic default values...

#inventory      = /etc/ansible/hosts
#library        = /usr/share/my_modules/
#module_utils   = /usr/share/my_module_utils/
#remote_tmp     = ~/.ansible/tmp
#local_tmp      = ~/.ansible/tmp
#plugin_filters_cfg = /etc/ansible/plugin_filters.yml
#forks          = 5
#poll_interval  = 15
#sudo_user      = root
#ask_sudo_pass  = True
#ask_pass       = True
#transport      = smart
#remote_port    = 22
#module_lang    = C
#module_set_locale = False
```

Figure 3.4 – Ansible configuration file

If we want to change the default Ansible configuration, we can modify this file.

> **Important Note**
>
> For more details about all Ansible configuration keys, see the official
> documentation: https://docs.ansible.com/ansible/
> latest/reference_appendices/config.html#ansible-
> configuration-settings.

We can also view and modify this configuration using the ansible-config command.
For example, to display the Ansible configuration file, we can execute the following
command:

```
ansible-config view
```

The following screenshot shows the execution of this command:

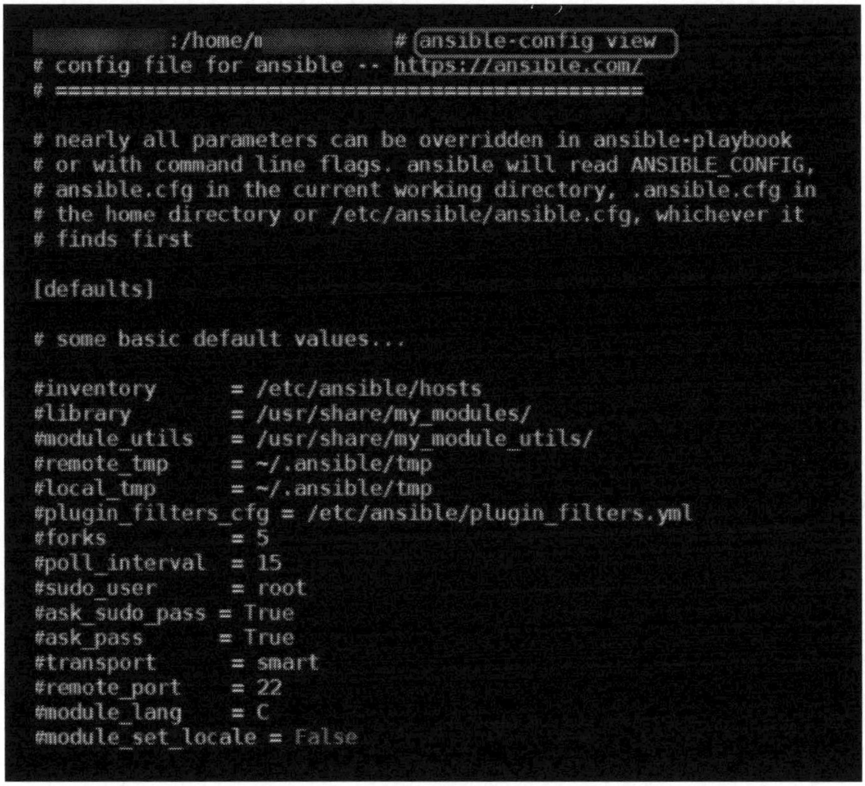

Figure 3.5 – Ansible view configuration with the CLI

In this section, we learned how to install Ansible and explored some of Ansible's artifacts.
Finally, we looked at different ways to configure Ansible.

In the next section, we will detail a static Ansible inventory and how to create it to target hosts.

Creating an Ansible inventory

The inventory contains the list of hosts that Ansible will perform administration and configuration actions on.

There are two types of inventories:

- **Static inventory**: Hosts are listed in a text file in INI (or YAML) format; this is the basic mode of Ansible inventory. The static inventory is used in cases where we know the host addresses (IP or FQDN).

- **Dynamic inventory**: The list of hosts is dynamically generated by an external script (for example, with a Python script). The dynamic inventory is used if we do not have the addresses of the hosts, for example, as with an infrastructure that is composed of on-demand environments.

In this section, we will learn how to create a static inventory in `init` format, starting with a basic example, and then we will look at the groups and host configuration.

Let's start by learning how to create a static inventory file.

The inventory file

For Ansible to configure hosts when running the playbook, it needs to have a file that contains the list of hosts; that is, the list of IP or **Fully Qualified Domain Name** (**FQDN**) addresses of the target machines. This list of hosts is noted in a static file called the **inventory file**.

By default, Ansible contains an inventory file that's created while it's being installed; this file is `/etc/ansible/hosts` and it contains several inventory configurations examples. In our case, we will manually create and fill this file in a directory of our choice, such as `devopsansible`.

Let's do this step by step:

1. First, we must create the directory with the following basic command:

```
mkdir devopsansible
cd devopsansible
```

2. Now, let's create a file named `myinventory` (without an extension) where we will write the IP addresses or the FQDN of the targets hosts, as shown in the following example:

```
192.10.14.10
mywebserver.entreprise.com
localhost
```

When Ansible is executed based on this inventory, it will execute all of the requested actions (playbook) on all the hosts mentioned in this inventory.

> **Important Note**
>
> For more information about the inventory file, read the documentation at https://docs.ansible.com/ansible/latest/user_guide/intro_inventory.html.

However, when you're using Ansible in an enterprise, the same Ansible code (or playbook) contains the configuration actions that are performed for all of the VMs of an application. Since these VMs have different roles within the application, such as an application that consists of one (or more) web server and one database server, we must divide our inventory to separate the VMs by functional roles.

To group VMs by role in the inventory, we will organize our VMs into groups that will be noted between [], which gives us the following inventory:

```
[webserver]
192.10.20.31
mywebserver.exemple.com
[database]
192.20.34.20
```

In this example, we have defined two groups, `webserver` and `database`. All the hosts are distributed into these groups.

As another example, we can also group the hosts by environments with this sample inventory:

```
[dev]
192.10.20.31
192.10.20.32
[qa]
```

```
192.20.34.20
192.20.34.21
[prod]
192.10.12.10
192.10.12.11
```

Later in this chapter, we will learn how these groups will be used in playbook writing.

Now, let's learn how to complete our inventory by configuring hosts.

Configuring hosts in the inventory

As we have seen, the entire Ansible configuration is in the `ansible.cfg` file. However, this configuration is generic and applies to all Ansible executions, as well as connectivity to hosts.

However, when using Ansible to configure VMs from different environments or roles with different permissions, it is important to have different connectivity configurations, such as different admin users and SSL keys per environment. For this reason, it is possible to override the default Ansible configuration in the inventory file by configuring specific parameters per host, as defined in this inventory.

The main configuration parameters that can be overridden are as follows:

- `ansible_user`: This is the user who connects to the remote host.
- `ansible_port`: It is possible to change the default value of the SSH port.
- `ansible_host`: This is an alias for the host.
- `ansible_connection`: This is the type of connection to the remote host and can be Paramiko, SSH, or local.
- `ansible_private_key_file`: This is the private key that's used to connect to the remote host.

> **Important Note**
> The complete list of parameters is available in the following documentation: `https://docs.ansible.com/ansible/latest/user_guide/intro_inventory.html#list-of-behavioral-inventory-parameters`.

Here is an example of an inventory where we have configured the connection of the hosts:

```
[webserver]
webserver1 ansible_host=192.10.20.31 ansible_port=2222
webserver2 ansible_host=192.10.20.31 ansible_port=2222
[database]
database1 ansible_host=192.20.34.20
ansible_user=databaseuser
database2 ansible_host=192.20.34.21
ansible_user=databaseuser
[dev]
webserver1
database1
[qa]
webserver2
database2
```

The following can be seen in this inventory example:

- The connection information has been specified beside each host.
- The alias implementation (such as webserver1 and webserver2) is used in another group (such as the qa group in this example).

Having implementing an Ansible inventory, we will now learn how to test this inventory.

Testing the inventory

Once the inventory has been written, it is possible to test whether all of the hosts mentioned can be accessed from Ansible. To do this, we can execute the following command:

```
ansible -i inventory all -u demobook -m ping
```

The -i argument is the path of the inventory file, the -u argument corresponds to the remote username that's used to connect to the remote machine, and -m is the command to execute. Here, we execute the ping command on all the machines in the inventory.

The following screenshot shows the execution of this command:

```
                                    /devopsansible# ansible -i inventory  all -u demobook -m ping
webserver2 | SUCCESS => {
    "changed": false,
    "ping": "pong"
}
database1 | SUCCESS => {
    "changed": false,
    "ping": "pong"
}
webserver1 | SUCCESS => {
    "changed": false,
    "ping": "pong"
}
```

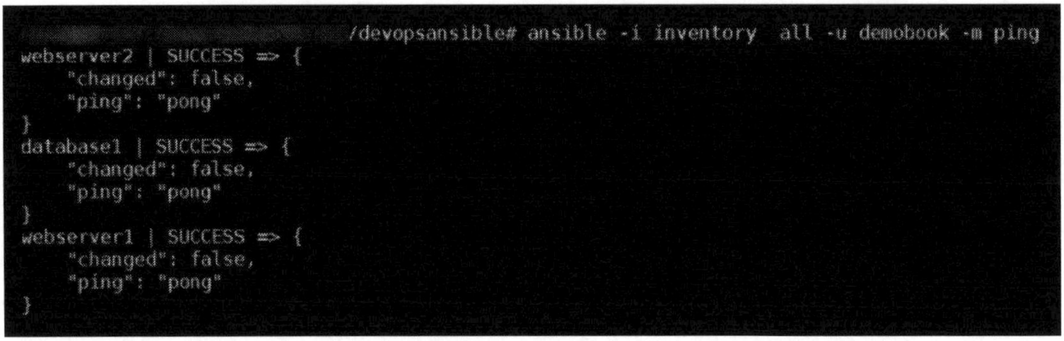

Figure 3.6 – Testing the ansible ping command with the all option

We can also test connectivity on the hosts of a particular group by calling this command with the group name instead of all. For example, in our case, we will execute this command:

```
ansible -i inventory webserver -u demobook -m ping
```

The following screenshot shows the execution of this command:

```
                                    /devopsansible# ansible -i inventory  webserver -u demobook -m ping
webserver1 | SUCCESS => {
    "changed": false,
    "ping": "pong"
}
webserver2 | SUCCESS => {
    "changed": false,
    "ping": "pong"
}
```

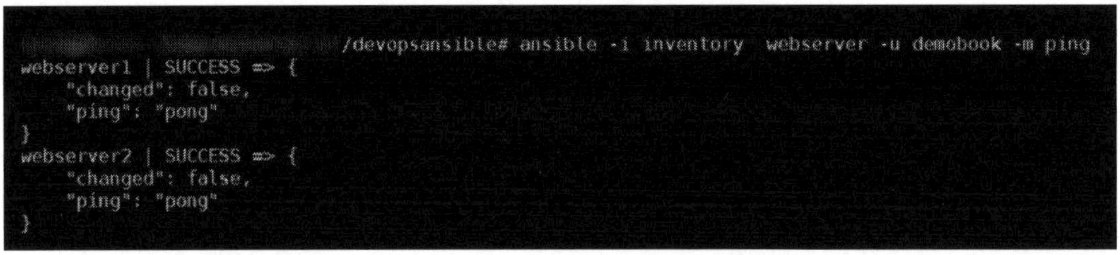

Figure 3.7 – Testing the ansible ping command for a specific host

In this section, we learned that Ansible needs an inventory file to configure hosts. Then, we created and tested our first inventory file before learning how to configure this file even further.

In the next section, we will learn how to set up and write the configuration action code in Ansible playbooks.

Executing the first playbook

One of the essential elements of Ansible is its playbooks because, as stipulated in the introduction, they contain the code of the actions or tasks that need to be performed to configure or administer a VM.

Indeed, once the VM has been provisioned, it must be configured, and all of the middleware needed to run the applications that will be hosted on this VM must be installed. Also, it is necessary to perform administrative tasks concerning the configuration of directories and their access.

In this section, we will see what a playbook is made up of, its modules, and how to improve our playbook with roles.

Now, let's start studying how to write a basic playbook.

Writing a basic playbook

The code of a playbook is written in YAML, a declarative language that allows us to easily visualize the configuration steps.

To understand what a playbook looks like, let's look at a simple and classic example; that is, installing an NGINX server on an Ubuntu VM. Previously, we created a working `devopsansible` directory, inside which we will create a `playbook.yml` file and insert the following content code:

```yaml
---
- hosts: all
  tasks:
  - name: install and check nginx latest version
      apt: name=nginx state=latest
  - name: start nginx
    service:
    name: nginx
    state: started
---
```

Let's take a look at this in detail:

- First of all, the YAML file starts and ends with the optional - - - characters.

- The - hosts property contains the list of hosts to configure. Here, we have written the value of this property as all to install NGINX on all of the VMs listed in our inventory. If we want to install it on only a particular group, for example, on the webserver group, we will note this as follows:

```yaml
---
- hosts: webserver
```

- Then, we indicate the list of tasks or actions to be performed on these VMs, with the property of the list of tasks.

- Under the `tasks` element, we describe the list of tasks and, for each of them, a name that serves as a label, in the `name` property. Under the name, we call the function to be executed using the *Ansible modules* and their properties. In our example, we have used two modules:

  - `apt`: This allows us to retrieve a package (the `apt-get` command) to get the latest version of the `nginx` package.

  - `service`: This allows us to start or stop a service – in this example, to start the NGINX service.

What we can see is that we do not require any knowledge of development or IT scripting to use Ansible; the important thing is to know the list of actions you can perform on VMs to configure them. The Ansible playbook is, therefore, a sequence of actions that are encoded in Ansible modules.

We have just seen that the tasks that are used in playbooks use modules. In the next section, we will provide a brief overview of modules and their use.

Understanding Ansible modules

In the previous section, we learned that, in Ansible playbooks, we use modules. This has made Ansible so popular today that there is a huge list of public modules provided by Ansible natively (+200). The complete list is available here: `https://docs.ansible.com/ansible/latest/collections/index_module.html`.

These modules allow us to perform all of the tasks and operations to be performed on a VM for its configuration and administration, without having to write any lines of code or scripts.

Within an enterprise, we can also create our custom modules and publish them in a private registry internally. More information can be found here: `https://docs.ansible.com/ansible/latest/dev_guide/developing_modules_general.html`.

Now that we've learned how to write a simple playbook and how to use modules, we will improve the playbook even further with roles.

Improving your playbooks with roles

Within an enterprise, when configuring a VM, we notice a certain repetition of tasks for each application. For example, several applications require the identical installation of NGINX, which must be performed in the same way.

With Ansible, this repetition will require duplicating the playbook code, as seen in our playbook example in the *Executing a basic playbook* section, between several playbooks (because each application contains a playbook). To avoid this duplication and, hence, save time, avoid errors, and homogenize installation and configuration actions, we can encapsulate the playbook code in a directory called `role` that can be used by several playbooks.

To create the `nginx` role corresponding to our example, we will create the following directory and file tree within our `devopsansible` directory:

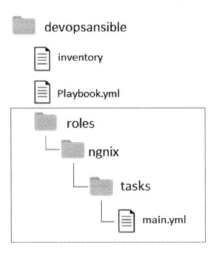

Figure 3.8 – The Ansible architecture folder

Then, in the `main.yml` file, which is located in `tasks`, we will copy and paste the following code from our playbook in the file that is created:

```
- name: install and check nginx latest version
    apt: name=nginx state=latest
- name: start nginx
    service:
      name: nginx
      state: started
```

Then, we will modify our playbook to use this role with the following content:

```
---
- hosts: webserver
  roles:
    - nginx
```

Following the node roles, we will provide a list of roles (the names of the role directories) to be used. So, this nginx role is now centralized and can be used in several playbooks without having to rewrite its code.

The following is the code of a playbook that configures a VM web server with Apache and another VM that contains a MySQL database:

```
---
- hosts: webserver
  roles:
    - php
    - apache
- hosts: database
  roles:
    - mysql
```

> **Important Note**
> For more information on role creation, read the official documentation at https://docs.ansible.com/ansible/latest/user_guide/playbooks_reuse_roles.html.

However, before we start creating a role, we can use Ansible Galaxy (https://galaxy.ansible.com/), which contains a large number of roles provided by the community and covers a high number of configuration and administration needs.

Within an enterprise, we can also create custom roles and publish them in a private galaxy within the company. More information can be found here: https://docs.ansible.com/ansible/latest/dev_guide/developing_modules_general.html.

In this section, we learned how to write a playbook, as well as how to improve one with roles. All of our artifacts are finally ready, so we will now be able to execute Ansible.

Executing Ansible

So far, we've learned how to install Ansible, listed the hosts in the inventory, and set up our Ansible playbook. Now, we can run Ansible to configure our VMs.

For this, we will run the Ansible tool with the `ansible-playbook` command, like this:

```
ansible-playbook -i inventory playbook.yml
```

The basic options for this command are as follows:

- The `-i` argument with the inventory file path
- The path of the playbook file

The following is the execution of this command:

```
                        /devopsansible# ansible-playbook -i inventory playbook.yml --check

PLAY [webserver] ***************************************************************

TASK [Gathering Facts] ********************************************************
ok: [webserver1]
ok: [webserver2]

TASK [nginx : install and check nginx latest version] ************************
changed: [webserver1]
changed: [webserver2]

TASK [nginx : start nginx] ***************************************************
changed: [webserver2]
changed: [webserver1]

PLAY RECAP *******************************************************************
webserver1                 : ok=3    changed=2    unreachable=0    failed=0
webserver2                 : ok=3    changed=2    unreachable=0    failed=0
```

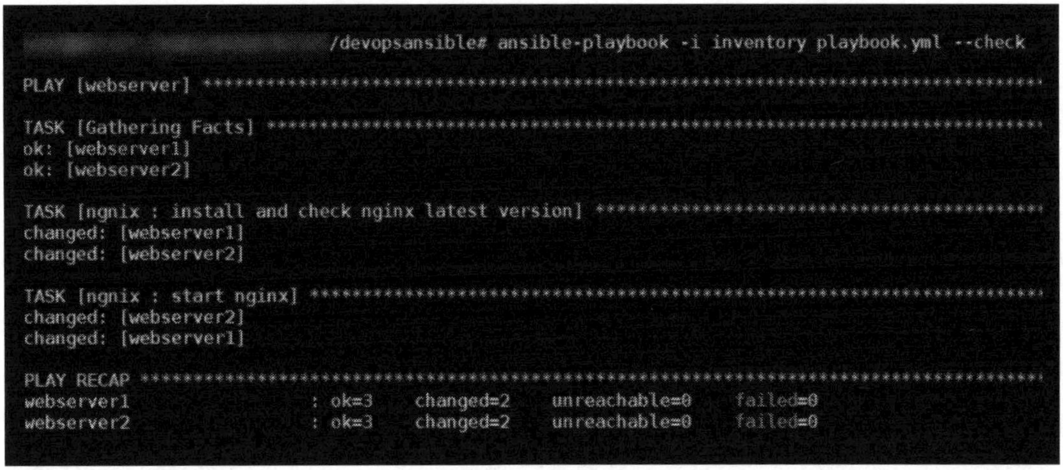

Figure 3.9 – Executing the Ansible playbook

The execution of this command applies the playbook to the hosts in the inventory in several steps:

1. Gathering facts: Ansible checks that the hosts can be reached.
2. The task's playbook is executed on hosts.

3.   PLAY Recap: This is the status of the changes that were executed on each host; the value of this status can be as follows:

ok	This is the number of playbook tasks that have been correctly applied to the host.
changed	This is the number of changes that have been applied.
unreachable	The host is unreachable.
failed	Execution failed on this host.

Table 3.1 – The values of PLAY Recap

If we need to upgrade our playbook to add or modify middleware on our VMs, during the second execution of Ansible with this upgraded playbook, we will see that Ansible did not reapply the complete configuration of the VMs; it only applied the differences.

The following screenshot shows the second execution of Ansible with no changes made to our playbook:

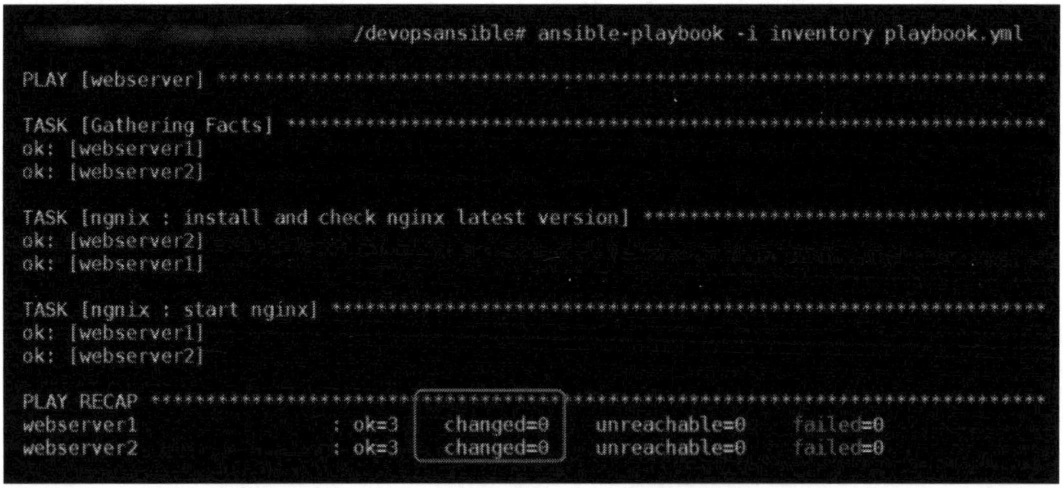

Figure 3.10 – The Ansible playbook's execution with changed information

Here, we can see that Ansible didn't change anything on the hosts (changed=0).

We can also add some useful options to this command to provide the following:

• A preview of Ansible changes before applying the changes

• More logs in the execution output

These options are not only important for the playbook development phase, but also for debugging them in case of errors during their execution.

Now, let's look at how to use these preview options.

Using the preview or dry run option

When coding an Ansible playbook, we often need to test different steps
without applying them directly to infrastructure. Hence, it is very useful, especially when
automating VM configuration with Ansible, to have a preview of its execution. This allows
us to check that the syntax of the playbook is maintaining good consistency with the
system configuration that already exists on the host.

With Ansible, it's possible to check the execution of a playbook on hosts by adding
the --check option to the command:

```
ansible-playbook -i inventory playbook.yml --check
```

Here is an example of this dry run execution:

```
                         /devopsansible# ansible-playbook -i inventory playbook.yml --check

PLAY [webserver] ***************************************************************************

TASK [Gathering Facts] ********************************************************************
ok: [webserver1]
ok: [webserver2]

TASK [ngnix : install and check nginx latest version] ***********************************
changed: [webserver1]
changed: [webserver2]

TASK [ngnix : start nginx] ***************************************************************
changed: [webserver2]
changed: [webserver1]

PLAY RECAP *******************************************************************************
webserver1                 : ok=3    changed=2    unreachable=0    failed=0
webserver2                 : ok=3    changed=2    unreachable=0    failed=0
```

Figure 3.11 – The Ansible playbook dry run execution

With this option, Ansible does not apply configuration changes to the host; it only checks
and previews the changes that have been made to the hosts.

> **Important Note**
>
> For more information on the --check option, please refer to the following
> documentation: https://docs.ansible.com/ansible/
> latest/user_guide/playbooks_checkmode.html.

We have just seen that Ansible allows us to check a playbook before applying it to a host; it is also necessary to know that there are other tools to test the functionality of a playbook (without having to simulate its execution), such as Vagrant by HashiCorp.

Vagrant allows us to locally create a test environment composed of VMs very quickly that we can run our playbooks on and see the results. For more information on the use of Ansible and Vagrant, refer to the following documentation: `https://docs.ansible.com/ansible/latest/scenario_guides/guide_vagrant.html`.

We have just learned how to preview the changes that will be applied by Ansible. Now, let's look at how to increase the log level output of Ansible's execution.

Increasing the log level output

In case of errors, it is possible to add more logs during the output by adding the -v, -vvv, or -vvvv option to the Ansible command.

The -v option enables basic verbose mode, the -vvv option enables verbose mode with more outputs, and the -vvvv option adds verbose mode and the connection debugging information.

Executing the following command applies a playbook and will display more log information using the -v option that has been added:

```
ansible-playbook -i inventory playbook.yml -v
```

This can be useful for debugging in case of Ansible errors.

> **Important Note**
>
> The complete documentation on the `ansible-playbook` command is available here: `https://docs.ansible.com/ansible/2.4/ansible-playbook.html`.

We have just learned how to execute Ansible with its inventory and playbook by exploring some options that allow for the following:

- Previewing the changes that will be made by Ansible
- Increasing the level of logs to make debugging easier

In the next section, we will talk about data security while using Ansible Vault.

Protecting data with Ansible Vault

So far, we've learned how to use Ansible with an inventory file that contains the list of hosts to configure, and with a playbook that contains the code of the host's configuration actions. But in all IaC tools, it will be necessary to extract some data that is specific to a context or environment inside variables.

In this section, we will look at how to use variables in Ansible and how to protect sensitive data with Ansible Vault.

To illustrate this use and protection of variables, we will complete our example by installing a MySQL server on the database server.

Let's begin by looking at the use and utility of variables in Ansible.

Using variables in Ansible for better configuration

When deploying infrastructure with IaC, the code that's used is often composed of two parts:

- A part that describes the elements or resources that make up the infrastructure.

- Another part that differentiates the properties of this infrastructure from one environment to another.

This second part of differentiation for each environment is done by using variables, and Ansible has a whole system that allows us to inject variables into playbooks.

To learn how to use variables in Ansible, we will complete our code and add a role called `mysql` to the `roles` directory with the following tree structure:

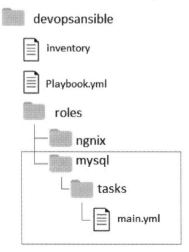

Figure 3.12 – The Ansible role folder structure

In the `main.yml` file of this role, we will write the following code:

```yaml
---
- name: Update apt cache
  apt: update_cache=yes cache_valid_time=3600
- name: Install required software
  apt: name="{{ packages }}" state=present
  vars:
    packages:
    - python-mysqldb
    - mysql-server
- name: Create mysql user
  mysql_user:
      name={{ mysql_user }}
      password={{ mysql_password }}
      priv=*.*:ALL
      state=present
```

In this code, some static information has been replaced by variables. They are as follows:

- packages: This contains a list of packages to install, and this list is defined in the following code.
- mysql_user: This contains the user admin of the MySQL database.
- mysql_password: This contains the admin password of the MySQL database.

The different tasks of this role are as follows:

- Updating packages
- Installing the MySQL server and Python MySQL packages
- Creating a MySQL user

> **Important Note**
>
> The complete source code for this role is available at https://github.com/PacktPublishing/Learning-DevOps-Second-Edition/tree/main/CHAP03/devopsansible/roles/mysql.

As we can see, in the user creation task, we have put the mysql_user and mysql_password variables in for the user name and password. Hence, this information may be different depending on the environment, or it may be instantiated dynamically when running Ansible.

To define the values of these variables, we will create a group_vars directory, which will contain all of the values of the variables for each group defined in our inventory.

Then, in this group_vars folder, we will create a database subdirectory corresponding to the database group defined in the inventory and a main.yml subfile.

In this main.yml file, we put the desired values of these variables, as follows:

```
---
mysql_user: mydbuserdef
mysql_password: mydbpassworddef
```

Finally, we will complete our playbook by calling the mysql role by adding the following code:

```
- hosts: database
become: true
roles:
  - mysql
```

We can execute Ansible with the same command as the previous one, `ansible-playbook -i inventory playbook.yml`. The following output is generated:

```
root@DESKTOP-9Q2U73J:/d/devopsansible# ansible-playbook -i inventory playbook.yml
PLAY [webserver] ***************************************************************

TASK [Gathering Facts] ********************************************************
ok: [webserver1]
ok: [webserver2]

TASK [ngnix : install and check nginx latest version] *************************
ok: [webserver1]
ok: [webserver2]

TASK [ngnix : start nginx] ****************************************************
ok: [webserver1]
ok: [webserver2]

PLAY [database] ***************************************************************

TASK [Gathering Facts] ********************************************************
ok: [database1]

TASK [mysql : Update apt cache] **********************************************
ok: [database1]

TASK [mysql : Install required software] *************************************
changed: [database1]

TASK [mysql : Create mysql user] ********************************************
changed: [database1]

PLAY RECAP ******************************************************************
database1                  : ok=4    changed=2    unreachable=0    failed=0
webserver1                 : ok=3    changed=0    unreachable=0    failed=0
webserver2                 : ok=3    changed=0    unreachable=0    failed=0
```

Figure 3.13 – The Ansible playbook's MySQL execution

Here, Ansible has updated the database server with two changes: the list of packages to be installed and the MySQL admin user. We have just learned how to use variables in Ansible, but this one is clear in the code, which raises security issues.

> **Important Note**
> For more information about Ansible variables, read the complete documentation here: `https://docs.ansible.com/ansible/latest/user_guide/playbooks_variables.html`.

Now, let's learn how to use Ansible Vault to protect playbook variables.

Protecting sensitive data with Ansible Vault

Configuring a system often requires sensitive information that should not be in the wrong hands. In the Ansible tool, there is a sub-tool called **Ansible Vault** that protects the data that's transmitted to Ansible through playbooks.

In this section, we'll learn how to manipulate Ansible Vault to encrypt and decrypt the information of the MySQL user.

The first step is to encrypt the `group_vars/database/main.yml` file, which contains the values of the variables, by executing the following command:

```
ansible-vault encrypt group_vars/database/main.yml
```

Ansible Vault requests that you include a password that will be required to decrypt the file and then shows the execution of this command to encrypt the content of a file:

```
                        /devopsansible# ansible-vault encrypt group_vars/database/main.yml
New Vault password:
Confirm New Vault password:
Encryption successful
```

Figure 3.14 – Ansible Vault encryption

After executing this command, the content of the file is encrypted, so the values are no longer clear. The following is a sample from it:

```
$ANSIBLE_VAULT;1.1;AES256
6231313630336362323534353031313939396232326464616661373133363335
3236313832323736373064353465353236665333638323166a6134653265
3434346639633066343438386133383930383038663934336633323323465
3336633033643735310a626134313164323933336313932343737373303161
3563316330356238316264626266653430383138363431393466326303137
3335633630373039376666666566653538363936656533836633396432613630 33
6262633032336263330323063363136653962
```

Figure 3.15 – Encrypted file

To decrypt the file to modify it, you must execute the `decrypt` command:

```
ansible-vault decrypt group_vars/database/main.yml
```

Ansible Vault requests the password that was used to encrypt the file, and the file becomes readable again.

In an Ansible usage automation process, it is preferable to store the password in a file in a protected location; for example, in the `~/.vault_pass.txt` file.

Then, to encrypt the variable file with this file, we must execute the `ansible-vault` command and add the `--vault-password-file` option:

```
ansible-vault encrypt group_vars/database/main.yml --vault-
password-file ~/.vault_pass.txt
```

Now that the file has been encrypted and the data is protected, we will run Ansible.

In **interactive mode**, we will run the following command:

```
ansible-playbook -i inventory playbook.yml --ask-vault-pass
```

Ansible asks the user to enter the password shown in the following screenshot:

```
                    /devopsansible# ansible-playbook -i inventory playbook.yml --ask-vault-pass
Vault password:
```

Figure 3.16 – Decrypted file with Ansible Vault

In **automatic mode** – that is, in a CI/CD pipeline – we can add the `--vault-password-file` parameter with the path of the file that contains the password to decrypt the data:

```
ansible-playbook -i inventory playbook.yml --vault-password-
file ~/.vault_pass.txt
```

With that, we've executed Ansible with data that is no longer clear in the code and with the use of the `ansible-vault` command.

> **Important Note**
>
> The entire source code for the inventory, playbook, and roles is available here: `https://github.com/PacktPublishing/Learning-DevOps-Second-Edition/tree/main/CHAP03/devopsansible`.

In this section, we learned how to protect sensitive data in our playbooks using the `ansible-vault` utility. We encrypted and decrypted variable files to protect them, and then re-ran Ansible with these encrypted files.

In the following section, we will learn how to use Ansible with a dynamic inventory.

Using a dynamic inventory for an Azure infrastructure

When configuring an infrastructure that is composed of several VMs, along with ephemeral environments that are built on demand, the observation that's often made is that maintaining a static inventory, as we saw in the *Creating an Ansible inventory* section, can quickly become complicated and its maintenance takes a lot of time to complete.

To overcome this problem, Ansible allows inventories to be obtained dynamically by calling a script (for example, in Python) that is either provided by cloud providers or a script that we can develop ourselves that returns the contents of the inventory.

In this section, we will look at the different ways to use Ansible to configure VMs in Azure using a dynamic inventory. Let's get started:

1. The first step is to configure Ansible to be able to access Azure resources. For this, we will create an Azure Service Principal in Azure AD, in exactly the same way as we did for Terraform (see the *Configuring Terraform for Azure* section of *Chapter 2, Provisioning Cloud Infrastructure with Terraform*). Then, we must export the information of the four service principal IDs to the following environment variables:

   ```
   export AZURE_SUBSCRIPTION_ID=<subscription_id>
   export AZURE_CLIENT_ID=<client ID>
   export AZURE_SECRET=<client Secret>
   export AZURE_TENANT=<tenant ID>
   ```

   > **Important Note**
   >
   > For more information on the Azure environment variables for Ansible, please refer to the Azure documentation here: `https://docs.ansible.com/ansible/latest/scenario_guides/guide_azure.html`.

2. Then, to be able to generate an inventory with groups and to filter VMs, it is better to add tags to the VMs. Tags can be added using Terraform, an `az cli` command line, or an Azure PowerShell script.

   Here is an example script with `az cli`:

   ```
   az resource tag --tags role=webserver -n VM01 -g
   demoAnsible --resource-type "Microsoft.Compute/
   virtualMachines"
   ```

The preceding script adds a `role` tag of the `webserver` value to the VM01 VM. Then, we must perform the same operation on the VM02 VM (just change the value of the `-n` parameter to VM02 in the preceding script).

The following screenshot shows the VM tag in the Azure portal:

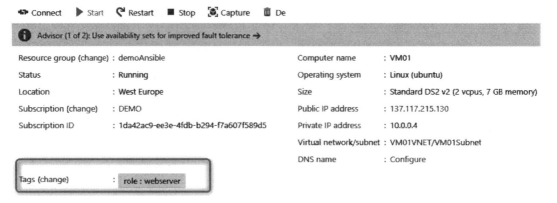

Figure 3.17 – Azure role tag

Now, we must add to our VM the tag that contains the database with this script:

```
az resource tag --tags role=database -n VM04 -g
demoAnsible --resource-type "Microsoft.Compute/
virtualMachines"
```

This script adds a `role` tag to VM04, which has a value of `database`.

> **Important Note**
>
> The `az cli` documentation for managing Azure tags can
> be found here: `https://docs.microsoft.com/`
> `fr-fr/cli/azure/resource?view=azure-cli-`
> `latest&viewFallbackFrom=azure-cli-latest.md#az-`
> `resource-tag`.

3. To use a dynamic inventory in Azure, we need to do the following actions:

   • Install the Ansible Azure module on the machine with the following script.

   ```
   wget -q https://raw.githubusercontent.com/ansible-
   collections/azure/dev/requirements-azure.txt;
   pip3 install -r requirements-azure.txt;
   ```

- We can also install the Azure module using Ansible Galaxy by executing the following command:

```
ansible-galaxy collection install azure.azcollection
```

> **Note**
>
> For more details about the **Azure collection**, read the documentation at
> `https://galaxy.ansible.com/azure/azcollection`.

Create a new file named `inv.azure_rm.yml` (the name of this file must finish with `azure_rm`) and write in this file the following configuration:

- Use the `azure_rm` plugin.
- Allow the returned VM list to be grouped by **role** tags.
- Filter only in the `demoAnsible` resource group.

The contents of this file will look as follows:

```
plugin: azure_rm
include_vm_resource_groups:
- demoAnsible
auth_source: auto
keyed_groups:
- key: tags.role
leading_separator : false
```

> **Important Note**
>
> The complete source code for the `inv.azure_rm.yml` file is
> available here: `https://github.com/PacktPublishing/`
> `Learning-DevOps-Second-Edition/tree/main/CHAP03/`
> `devopsansible/inventories`.

4. After setting up all of the artifacts for our Ansible dynamic inventory in Azure, it is good to test its functionality, which includes doing the following:

A. Ensuring there are no execution errors.

B. Ensuring the connection and authentication to our Azure environment are done correctly.

C. Ensuring its execution returns the Azure VMs from our infrastructure.

> **Important Note**
>
> As mentioned in the *Technical requirements* section, before running the
> following commands, we need to have the Azure Python module installed on
> the machine.

To perform this test, execute the following command:

```
ansible-inventory -i inv.azure_rm.yml --list
```

This command allows us to display as output the inventory script in list format.
Here is a small sample screen from this execution:

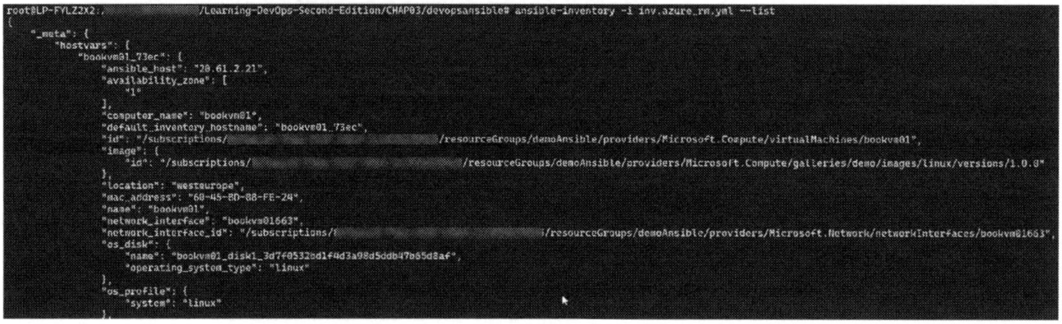

Figure 3.18 – Dynamic Ansible inventory list of VMs

We can also display this inventory in graph mode by running the same command
but with the --graph option, as follows:

Figure 3.19 – Dynamic Ansible inventory list of VMs grouped by role

With the --graph option, we get a better visualization of the VMs according to
their tags.

With the test concluded, we can proceed to the final step, which is executing Ansible
with a dynamic inventory.

5. Once we have tested our dynamic inventory in Azure, we just have to run Ansible
    on it, using the tags we applied to the VMs. For this, we must run our playbook with
    the following command:

```
ansible-playbook playbook.yaml -i inv.azurerm.yml -u
demobook —ask-pass
```

> **Note**
>
> In our lab we use a VM with a username and password, and it's because
> of this that in the preceding command, we use the -u parameter (for the
> VM username) and the —ask-pass parameter (to ask for the VM user
> password). But it's better and recommended to use SSH public/private keys
> instead of a password.

The following screenshot shows the execution of the Ansible playbook with the
dynamic inventory:

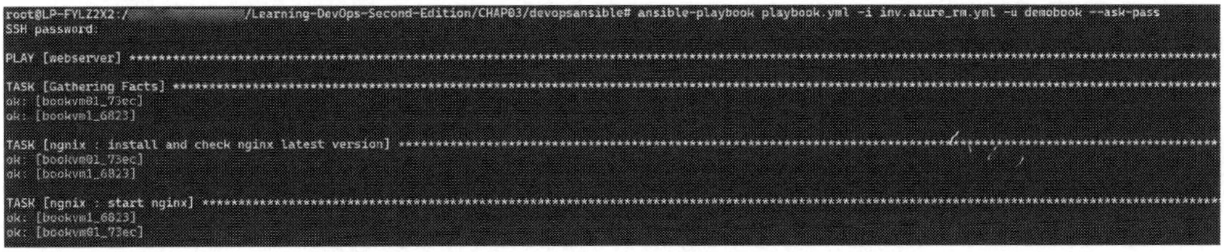

Figure 3.20 – Dynamic Ansible inventory execution

From now on, each time a VM on our Azure infrastructure has a role=webserver tag,
it will be automatically taken into account by the dynamic inventory, so no code
modifications will be necessary.

> **Important Note**
>
> For other ways to use dynamic inventories on Azure, you can consult the
> Azure documentation at https://docs.microsoft.com/en-
> us/azure/developer/ansible/dynamic-inventory-
> configure?tabs=azure-cli.

By using a dynamic inventory, we can take full advantage of the scalability of the cloud
with an automatic VM configuration and without having to make any code changes.

In this section, we learned how to use a dynamic inventory in Azure by implementing
its configuration and doing the necessary script recovery, before executing this dynamic
inventory with Ansible.

Summary

In this chapter, we saw that Ansible is a very powerful and complete tool that allows us
to automate server configuration and administration. To work, it uses an inventory that
contains the list of hosts to be configured and a playbook that the list of configuration
actions is coded in.

Roles, modules, and variables also allow for better management and centralization of playbook code. Ansible also has a vault that protects sensitive playbook data. Finally, for dynamic environments, inventory writing can be simplified by implementing dynamic inventories.

In the next chapter, we will learn how to optimize infrastructure deployment with the use of Packer to create server templates.

Questions

1.   What is the role of Ansible that was detailed in this chapter?

2.   Can we install Ansible on a Windows OS?

3.   What are the two artifacts that we studied in this chapter that Ansible needs to run?

4.   What is the name of the option that was added to the `ansible-playbook` command that is used to preview the changes that will be applied?

5.   What is the name of the utility used to encrypt and decrypt Ansible data?

6.   When using a dynamic inventory in Azure, on which properties of the VMs is the inventory script used to return the list of VMs?

Further reading

If you want to know more about Ansible, here are some resources:

- The Ansible documentation: `https://docs.ansible.com/ansible/latest/index.html`

- Quick Start video: `https://www.ansible.com/resources/videos/quick-start-video?extIdCarryOver=true&sc_cid=701f2000001OH6uAAG`

- Ansible on Azure documentation: `https://docs.microsoft.com/en-us/azure/ansible/`

- Visual Studio Code Ansible extension: `https://marketplace.visualstudio.com/items?itemName=vscoss.vscode-ansible`

- Mastering Ansible: `https://www.packtpub.com/virtualization-and-cloud/mastering-ansible-third-edition`

- Ansible Webinars Training: `https://www.ansible.com/resources/webinars-training`

4

Optimizing Infrastructure Deployment with Packer

In the previous chapters, we learned how to provision a cloud infrastructure using Terraform and then we continued with the automated configuration of VMs with Ansible. This automation allows us to benefit from a real improvement in productivity and very visible time-saving.

However, despite this automation, we notice the following:

- Configuring a VM can be very time-consuming because it depends on its hardening as well as the middleware that will be installed and configured on this VM.

- Between each environment or application, the middleware versions are not identical because their automation script is not necessarily identical or maintained over time. Hence, for example, the production environment, being more critical, will be more likely to have the latest version of packages, which is not the case in pre-production environments. And with this situation, we often encounter issues with the behavior of applications in production.

- Configuration and security compliance is not often applied or updated.

To address these issues, all cloud providers have integrated a service that allows them to create or generate custom VM images. These images contain all of the configurations of the VMs with their security administration and middleware configurations and can then be used as a basis to create VMs for applications.

The benefits of using these images are as follows:

- The provisioning of a VM from an image is very fast.

- Each VM is uniform in configuration and, above all, is safety compliant.

Among the **Infrastructure as Code (IaC)** tools, there is Packer from the HashiCorp tools, which allows us to create VM images from a file (or template).

In this chapter, we will learn how to install Packer in different modes. We will discuss the syntax of Packer templates to create custom VM images in Azure that use scripts or Ansible playbooks.

We will detail the execution of Packer with these templates using JSON and HCL format. Finally, we will see how Terraform uses the images created by Packer. Through this chapter, we'll understand that Packer is a simple tool that simplifies the creation of VMs in a DevOps process and integrates very well with Terraform.

In this chapter, we will cover the following:

- An overview of Packer

- Creating Packer templates using scripts

- Creating Packer templates using Ansible

- Executing Packer

- Writing Packer templates with HCL format
- Using images created by Packer with Terraform

Technical requirements

This chapter will explain how to use Packer to create a VM image in an Azure infrastructure as an example of cloud infrastructure. So, you will need an Azure subscription, which you can get here for free: `https://azure.microsoft.com/en-us/free/`.

In the *Using Ansible in a Packer template* section, we will learn how to write Packer templates that use Ansible, so you will need to install Ansible on your machine and understand how it works, which is detailed in *Chapter 3, Using Ansible for Configuring IaaS Infrastructure*.

The last section of this chapter will give an example of using Terraform with a Packer image; for its application, it will be necessary to install Terraform and understand its operation, which is detailed in *Chapter 2, Provisioning Cloud Infrastructure with Terraform*.

The entire source code of this chapter is available at `https://github.com/PacktPublishing/Learning-DevOps-Second-Edition/tree/main/CHAP04`.

Check out the following video to see the Code in Action: `https://bit.ly/35exxSo`.

An overview of Packer

Packer is part of the HashiCorp open source suite of tools, and this is the official Packer page: `https://www.packer.io/`. It's an open source command-line tool that allows us to create custom VM images of any OS (these images are also called **templates**) on several platforms from a JSON file.

Packer's operation is simple; it is based on the basic OS provided by the different cloud providers and configures a temporary VM by executing the scripts described in the JSON or HCL template. Then, from this temporary VM, Packer generates a custom image ready to be used to provision VMs.

Apart from VM images, Packer also provides other types of images such as Docker images or Vagrant images. After this brief overview of Packer, let's look at the different installation modes.

Installing Packer

Packer, like Terraform, is a cross-platform tool and can be installed on Windows, Linux, or macOS. The installation of Packer is almost identical to the Terraform installation (see *Chapter 2, Provisioning Cloud Infrastructure with Terraform*) and can be done in two ways: either manually or via a script.

Installing manually

To install Packer manually, use the followings steps:

1. Go to the official download page (`https://www.packer.io/downloads.html`) and download the package corresponding to your operating system.

2. After downloading, unzip and copy the binary into an execution directory (for example, inside `c:\Packer`).

3. Then, the `PATH` environment variable must be set with the path to the binary directory.

> **Tip**
>
> For detailed instructions on how to update the `PATH` environment variable on Windows, refer to this article: `https://www.architectryan.com/2018/03/17/add-to-the-path-on-windows-10/`, and for Linux, refer to this one: `https://www.techrepublic.com/article/how-to-add-directories-to-your-path-in-linux/`.

Now that we've learned how to install Packer manually, let's look at the options available to us to install it using a script.

Installing by script

It is also possible to install Packer with an automatic script that can be installed on a remote server and be used on a CI/CD process. Indeed, Packer can be used locally, as we will see in this chapter, but its real goal is to be integrated into a CI/CD pipeline. This automatic DevOps pipeline will allow the construction and publication of uniform VM images that will guarantee the integrity of middleware and VM security based on these images.

Let's see the structure of these scripts for the different OSes, that is, Linux, Windows, and macOS.

Installing Packer by script on Linux

For installing the Packer binary on Linux, we have two solutions:

- The first solution is to install Packer with the following script:

```
PACKER_VERSION="1.7.3" #Update with your desired version
curl -Os https://releases.hashicorp.com/packer/${PACKER_
VERSION}/packer_${PACKER_VERSION}_linux_amd64.zip \
&& curl -Os https://releases.hashicorp.com/
packer/${PACKER_VERSION}/packer_${PACKER_VERSION}_
SHA256SUMS \
&& curl https://keybase.io/hashicorp/pgp_keys.asc | gpg
--import \
&& curl -Os https://releases.hashicorp.com/
packer/${PACKER_VERSION}/packer_${PACKER_VERSION}_
SHA256SUMS.sig \
&& gpg --verify packer_${PACKER_VERSION}_SHA256SUMS.sig
packer_${PACKER_VERSION}_SHA256SUMS \
&& shasum -a 256 -c packer_${PACKER_VERSION}_SHA256SUMS
2>&1 | grep "${PACKER_VERSION}_linux_amd64.zip:\sOK" \
&& unzip -o packer_${PACKER_VERSION}_linux_amd64.zip -d /
usr/local/bin
```

> **Note**
>
> The code of this script is also available here: https://github.com/
> PacktPublishing/Learning-DevOps-Second-Edition/
> blob/main/CHAP04/install_packer.sh.

This script performs the following actions:

- Downloads the Packer version 1.7.3 package and checks the checksum

- Unzips and copies the package into a local directory, /usr/local/bin
  (by default, this folder is in the PATH environment variable)

The following is a screenshot of the execution of the script for installing Packer on Linux:

```
                                        ./CHAP04# sh install_packer.sh
                                    Speed   Time    Time    Time  Current
                            Dload  Upload  Total   Spent   Left  Speed
100  1696  100  1696     0      0   3981      0 --:--:-- --:--:-- --:--:--  3971
gpg: key 51852D87348FFC4C: "HashiCorp Security <security@hashicorp.com>" not changed
gpg: Total number processed: 1
gpg:              unchanged: 1
gpg: Signature made Thu Apr 11 20:30:03 2019 DST
gpg:              using RSA key 91A6E7F85D05C65630BEF18951852D87348FFC4C
gpg: Good signature from "HashiCorp Security <security@hashicorp.com>" [unknown]
gpg: WARNING: This key is not certified with a trusted signature!
gpg:          There is no indication that the signature belongs to the owner.
Primary key fingerprint: 91A6 E7F8 5D05 C656 30BE  F189 5185 2D87 348F FC4C
packer_1.4.0_linux_amd64.zip: OK
Archive:  packer_1.4.0_linux_amd64.zip
  inflating: /usr/local/bin/packer
```

Figure 4.1 – Install Packer script execution

The benefit of this solution is that we can choose the Packer installation folder and that it is applicable on the various distributions of Linux as it uses common tools, which are `curl` and `unzip`.

- The second solution for installing Packer on Linux is to use the `apt` package manager by using the following script for Ubuntu distribution:

```
sudo apt-get update && sudo apt-get install -y gnupg
software-properties-common curl \

&& curl -fsSL https://apt.releases.hashicorp.com/gpg |
sudo apt-key add - \

&& sudo apt-add-repository "deb [arch=amd64] https://apt.
releases.hashicorp.com $(lsb_release -cs) main" \

&& sudo apt-get update && sudo apt-get install packer
```

This script does the following:

- Adds the `apt` HashiCorp repositor

- Updates the local repositor

- Downloads the Packer CL

> **Important Note**
>
> For more details about this script and the installation of Packer on other distributions, read the documentation at `https://learn.hashicorp.com/tutorials/packer/get-started-install-cli?in=packer/docker-get-started`, and navigate to the **Linux** tab.

Installing Packer by script on Windows

On Windows, we can use **Chocolatey**, which is a software package manager. Chocolatey is a free public package manager, like NuGet or npm, but dedicated to software. It is widely used for the automation of software on Windows servers or even local machines. Chocolatey's official website is here: `https://chocolatey.org/`, and its installation documentation is here: `https://chocolatey.org/install`.

Once Chocolatey is installed, we just need to run the following command in PowerShell or in the CMD tool:

```
choco install packer -y
```

The following is a screenshot of the Packer installation for Windows with Chocolatey:

```
PS C:\Windows\system32> choco install packer -y
Chocolatey v0.10.11
Installing the following packages:
packer
By installing you accept licenses for the packages.
Progress: Downloading packer 1.4.0... 100%

packer v1.4.0 [Approved]
packer package files install completed. Performing other installation steps.
Removing old packer plugins
Downloading packer 64 bit
  from 'https://releases.hashicorp.com/packer/1.4.0/packer_1.4.0_windows_amd64.zip'
Progress: 100% - Completed download of C:\Users\MikaelKRIEF\AppData\Local\Temp\chocolatey\packer\1.4.0\packer_1.4.0_wind
ows_amd64.zip (33.61 MB).
Download of packer_1.4.0_windows_amd64.zip (33.61 MB) completed.
Hashes match.
Extracting C:\Users\MikaelKRIEF\AppData\Local\Temp\chocolatey\packer\1.4.0\packer_1.4.0_windows_amd64.zip to C:\ProgramD
ata\chocolatey\lib\packer\tools...
C:\ProgramData\chocolatey\lib\packer\tools
  ShimGen has successfully created a shim for packer.exe
  The install of packer was successful.
   Software installed to 'C:\ProgramData\chocolatey\lib\packer\tools'

Chocolatey installed 1/1 packages.
  See the log for details (C:\ProgramData\chocolatey\logs\chocolatey.log).
PS C:\Windows\system32>
```

Figure 4.2 – Installing Packer using Chocolatey

The execution of `choco install packer -y` installs the latest version of Packer from Chocolatey.

Installing Packer by script on macOS

On macOS, we can use **Homebrew**, the macOS package manager (`https://brew.sh/`), for installing Packer by executing the following command in our Terminal:

```
brew install packer
```

Integrating Packer with Azure Cloud Shell

Just as we learned in detail for Terraform in the *Integrating Terraform with Azure Cloud Shell* section in *Chapter 2, Provisioning Cloud Infrastructure with Terraform*, Packer is also integrated with Azure Cloud Shell, as shown in the following screenshot:

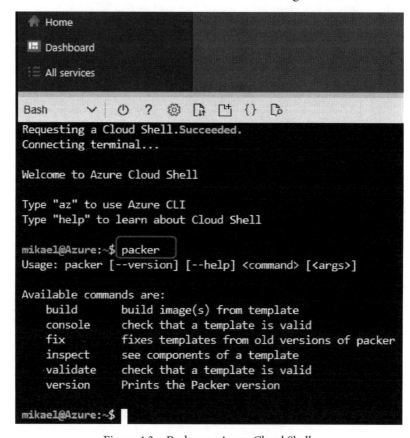

Figure 4.3 – Packer on Azure Cloud Shell

Now that we have seen the installation of Packer on different operating systems and its integration with Azure Cloud Shell, we will next check its installed version.

Checking the Packer installation

Once installed, we can check the installed version of Packer by running the following command:

```
packer --version
```

This command displays the installed Packer version:

```
PS C:\Users\mkrief> packer --version
1.7.3
```

Figure 4.4 – Packer version command

To see all of the Packer command-line options, we can execute the following command:

```
packer --help
```

After executing, we will see a list of available commands, as shown in the following screenshot:

```
PS C:\Users\mkrief> packer --help
Usage: packer [--version] [--help] <command> [<args>]

Available commands are:
    build          build image(s) from template
    console        creates a console for testing variable interpolation
    fix            fixes templates from old versions of packer
    fmt            Rewrites HCL2 config files to canonical format
    hcl2_upgrade   transform a JSON template into an HCL2 configuration
    init           Install missing plugins or upgrade plugins
    inspect        see components of a template
    validate       check that a template is valid
    version        Prints the Packer version
```

Figure 4.5 – Packer help command

We have just seen the manual installation procedure for Packer and installation with a script on different OSes, as well as its integration with Azure Cloud Shell.

We will now write a template to create a VM image in Azure with Packer using scripts.

Creating Packer templates for Azure VMs with scripts

As mentioned in the introduction, to create a VM image, Packer is based on a file (template) that is written in JSON format or in **HashiCorp Configuration Language** (**HCL**), which was introduced in Packer from version 1.5.0 (read the following blog post for more information: https://www.packer.io/guides/hcl). We will first see the structure and composition of this template, and then we will put into practice how to create a template that will create a VM image in Azure.

The structure of the Packer template

The Packer template is composed of several main sections, such as `builders`, `provisioners`, and `variables`. The JSON format of the template is as follows:

```
{
    "variables": {
    // list of variables
    ...
    },
    "builders": [
        {
        //builders properties
        ...
        }
    ],
    "provisioners": [
        {
        // list of scripts to execute for image provisionning
        ...
        }
    ]
}
```

Let's look at the details of each section.

The builders section

The `builders` section is mandatory and contains all of the properties that define the image and its location, such as its name, the type of image, the cloud provider on which the image will be generated, connection information to the cloud, the base image to use, and other properties that are specific to the image type.

Here is some example code of a `builders` section:

```
{
"builders": [{
    "type": "azure-rm",
    "client_id": "xxxxxxxx",
    "client_secret": "xxxxxxxx",
```

```
    "subscription_id": "xxxxxxxxxx",
    "tenant_id": "xxxxxx",
    "os_type": "Linux",
    "image_publisher": "Canonical",
    "image_offer": "UbuntuServer",
    "location": "westus"
.......
  }]
}
```

In this sample, the builders section defines an image that will be stored in the Azure cloud and is based on the Linux Ubuntu OS. We also configure the authentication keys for the cloud.

> **Note**
>
> The documentation on the builders section is here: https://www.packer.io/docs/builders.

If we want to create the same image but on several providers, we can indicate in the same template file multiple block builders that will contain the provider properties. For example, see the following code sample in JSON format:

```
{
"builders": [
    {
      "type": "azure-rm",
      "location": "westus",
      ....
    },
    {
      "type": "docker",
      "image": "alpine:latest",
      ...
    }
  ]
}
```

To translate the same block code in HCL format, we write first two `sources` block that define the different provider properties. And we call these `sources` in the `build` section as follows:

```
build {
    sources = ["sources.azure-arm.azurevm","sources.docker.
docker-img"]
    ...
}
```

In this code sample, we define in the Packer template the information for an image of an Azure VM, and the information for a Docker image based on Alpine. The advantage of this is to standardize the scripts that will be detailed in the provisioning section of these two images.

Just after the details of each section, we will see a concrete example with a `builders` section to create an image in Azure.

Let's move on to explaining the `provisioners` section.

The provisioners section

The `provisioners` section, which is optional, contains a list of scripts that will be executed by Packer on a temporary VM base image in order to build our custom VM image according to our needs.

If the Packer template does not contain a `provisioners` section, no configuration will be made on the base images.

The actions defined in this section are available for Windows as well as Linux images, and the actions can be of several types, such as executing a local or remote script, executing a command, or copying a file.

> **Note**
> The `provisioners` type proposed natively by Packer is detailed in the documentation: https://www.packer.io/docs/provisioners/index.html.

It is also possible to extend Packer by creating custom provisioning types. To learn more about custom `provisioners`, refer to the documentation here: https://www.packer.io/docs/extending/custom-provisioners.html.

The following is a sample of a `provisioners` section for JSON format:

```json
{
...
    "provisioners": [
        {
            "type": "shell",
            "script": "hardening-config.sh"
        },
        {
            "type": "file",
            "source": "scripts/installers",
            "destination": "/tmp/scripts"
        }
    ]
...
}
```

And the following is the same block code in HCL format:

```hcl
provisioner "shell" {
    scripts = ["hardening-config.sh"]
}
provisioner "file" {
    source = "scripts/installers"
    destination = "/tmp/scripts"
}
```

In this `provisioners` section, Packer will upload and execute the local script, `hardening-config.sh`, to apply the hardening configuration on the remote temporary VM base image, and copy the content of the `scripts/installers` local folder to the remote folder, `/tmp/scripts`, to configure the image.

So, in this section, we list all of the configuration actions for the image to be created.

However, when creating an image of a VM, it's necessary to generalize it – in other words, delete all of the personal user information that was used to create this image.

For example, for a Windows VM image, we will use the Sysprep tool as the last step of `provisioners` with the following code:

```
"provisioners": [
...
{
 "type": "powershell",
 "inline": ["& C:\\windows\\System32\\Sysprep\\Sysprep.exe /
oobe /generalize /shutdown /quiet"]}
]
```

Another example of Sysprep usage in Packer templates is available here: https://www.packer.io/docs/builders/azure.html.

And for deleting the personal user information on a Linux image, we will use the following code:

```
"provisioners": [
.....
{
 "type": "shell",
 "execute_command": "sudo sh -c '{{ .Vars }} {{ .Path }}'",
 "inline": [
     "/usr/sbin/waagent -force -deprovision+user && export
HISTSIZE=0 && sync"
 ]
}
]
```

> **Note**
>
> For more information about the `provisioners` section, refer to the documentation here: https://www.packer.io/docs/templates/provisioners.html, and the list of actions can be found here: https://www.packer.io/docs/provisioners/index.html.

After the `provisioners` section, let's talk about variables.

The variables section

In the Packer template, we may often need to use values that are not static in the code. This optional `variables` section is used to define variables that will be filled either as command-line arguments or as environment variables. These variables will then be used in the `builders` or `provisioners` sections.

Here is an example of a `variables` section:

```
{
  "variables": {
      "access_key": "{{env 'ACCESS_KEY'}}",
      "image_folder": "/image",
      "vm_size": "Standard_DS2_v2"
  },
  ....
}
```

In this example, we initialize the following:

- The `access_key` variable with the `ACCESS_KEY` environment variable
- The `image_folder` variable with the `/image` value
- The value of the VM image size, which is the `vm_size` variable

To use these so-called user variables, we use the `{{user 'variablename' }}` notation, and here is an example of using these variables in the `builders` section:

```
"builders": [
    {
        "type": "azure-arm",
        "access_key": "{{user 'access_key'}}",
        "vm_size": "{{user 'vm_size'}}",
        ...
    }
],
```

And in the `provisioners` section, we use the variables defined in the `variables` section, as follows:

```
"provisioners": [
    {
```

```
        "type": "shell",
        "inline": [
        "mkdir {{user 'image_folder'}}",
        "chmod 777 {{user 'image_folder'}}",
        ...
    ],
        "execute_command": "sudo sh -c '{{ .Vars }} {{ .Path
}}'"
    },
...
]
```

We, therefore, define the properties of the image with variables that will be provided when executing the Packer template. We can also use these variables in the `provisioners` section for centralizing these properties and not have to be redefined , here, the path of the images (`/image`) that will be repeated several times in the templates.

> **Note**
>
> Apart from the variables provided by the user, it is also possible to retrieve other variable sources, such as secrets stored in HashiCorp Vault or Consul. For more information about variables, refer to the documentation: `https://www.packer.io/docs/templates/legacy_json_ templates/user-variables`.

We have just seen the structure of the Packer template with the principal sections that compose it, which are `builders`, `provisioners`, and `variables`. Now let's look at a concrete example with the writing of a Packer template to create an image in Azure.

Building an Azure image with the Packer template

With all of the elements we saw earlier, we will now be able to create a Packer template that will create a VM image in Azure.

For this, we will need to first create an Azure AD **Service Principal (SP)** that will have the permissions to create resources in our subscription. The creation is exactly the same as we did for Terraform; for more details, see the *Configuring Terraform for Azure* section in *Chapter 2, Provisioning Cloud Infrastructure with Terraform*. Then, on the local disk, we will create a Packer template file.

If you want to use JSON template format, create an `azure_linux.json` file, which will be our Packer template. We will start writing to this file with the `builders` section, as follows:

```
..."builders": [{
    "type": "azure-arm",
    "client_id": "{{user 'clientid'}}",
    "client_secret": "{{user 'clientsecret'}}",
    "subscription_id": "{{user 'subscriptionid'}}",
    "tenant_id": "{{user 'tenantid'}}",

    "os_type": "Linux",
    "image_publisher": "Canonical",
    "image_offer": "UbuntuServer",
    "image_sku": "18.04-LTS",
    "location": "West Europe",
    "vm_size": "Standard_DS2_v3",

    "managed_image_resource_group_name": "{{user 'resource_
group'}}",
    "managed_image_name": "{{user 'image_name'}}-{{user 'image_
version'}}",
    "azure_tags": {
    "version": "{{user 'image_version'}}",
    "role": "WebServer"
    }
}],....
```

This section describes the following:

- It describes the `azure_rm` type, which indicates the provider.
- Also, it describes the `client_id`, `secret_client`, `subscription_id`, and `tenant_id` properties, which contain information from the previously created SP. For security reasons, these values are not written in plain text in the JSON template; they will be placed in variables (which we will see right after the details of the `builders` section).

- The `managed_image_resource_group_name` and `managed_image_name` properties indicate the resource group as well as the name of the image to be created. The name of the image is also placed into a variable with a name and a version number.

- The other properties correspond to the information of the OS type (Ubuntu 18), size (`Standard_DS2_v3`), region, and tag.

Now we will write the `variables` section that defines the elements that are not fixed:

```
..."variables": {
 "subscriptionid": "{{env 'AZURE_SUBSCRIPTION_ID'}}",
 "clientid": "{{env 'AZURE_CLIENT_ID'}}",
 "clientsecret": "{{env 'AZURE_CLIENT_SECRET'}}",
 "tenantid": "{{env 'AZURE_TENANT_ID'}}",

 "resource_group": "rg_images",
 "image_name": "linuxWeb",
 "image_version": "0.0.1"
 },...
```

We have defined the variables and their default values with the following:

- The four pieces of authentication information from the SP will be passed either in the Packer command line or as an environment variable.

- The resource group, name, size, and region of the image to be generated are also in `variables`.

- The `image_version` variable that contains the version of the image (used in the name of the image) is defined.

So, with these variables, we will be able to use the same JSON template file to generate several images with different names and sizes (we will see this when Packer is executed).

Finally, the last action is to write the steps of the `provisioners` image with the following code:

```
"provisioners": [
 {
    "type": "shell",
    "execute_command": "sudo sh -c '{{ .Vars }} {{ .Path }}'",
     "inline": [
```

```
        "apt-get update",
        "apt-get -y install nginx"
    ]
},
{
    "type": "shell",
    "execute_command": "sudo sh -c '{{ .Vars }} {{ .Path }}'",
    "inline": [
        "/usr/sbin/waagent -force -deprovision+user && export
HISTSIZE=0 && sync"
    ]
}
]
```

Here is what the preceding code block is doing:

- It updates packages with `apt-get update` and `upgrade`.

- It installs NGINX.

Then, in the last step before the image is created, the VM is deprovisioned to delete the user information that was used to install everything on the temporary VM using the following command:

```
/usr/sbin/waagent -force -deprovision+user && export HISTSIZE=0
&& sync
```

> **Note**
> The complete source code of this Packer template is available here:
> `https://github.com/PacktPublishing/Learning-DevOps-Second-Edition/blob/main/CHAP04/templates/azure_linux.json`.

We have just seen the structure of a Packer template, which is mainly composed of three sections, which are `variables`, `builders`, and `provisioners`, and from there we saw a concrete example with the writing of a Packer template to generate a custom VM image in Azure that uses scripts or provisioning commands.

We have our Packer template finished and ready to be run, but first we will see another type of `provisioners` using Ansible.

Using Ansible in a Packer template

We have just seen how to write a Packer template that uses command scripts (for example, `apt-get`), but it is also possible to use Ansible playbooks to create an image. Indeed, when we use IaC to configure VMs, we are often used to configuring the VMs directly using Ansible before thinking about making them into VM images.

What is interesting about Packer is that we can reuse the same playbook scripts that we used to configure VMs to create our VM images. So it's a huge time-saver because we don't have to rewrite the scripts.

To put this into practice, we will write the following:

- An Ansible playbook that installs NGINX

- A Packer template that uses Ansible with our playbook

Let's start with the writing of the Ansible playbook.

Writing the Ansible playbook

The playbook we are going to write is almost identical to the one we set up in *Chapter 3, Using Ansible for Configuring IaaS Infrastructure*, but with some changes.

The following code is the sample of the playbook:

```
---
- hosts: 127.0.0.1
  become: true
  connection: local
  tasks:
  - name: installing Ngnix latest version
    apt:
      name: nginx
      state: latest
  - name: starting Nginx service
    service:
      name: nginx
      state: started
```

The changes made are as follows:

- There is no inventory because it is Packer that manages the remote host, which is the temporary VM that will be used to create the image.

- The value of `hosts` is, therefore, the local IP address.

- We only keep the installation of NGINX in this playbook and we deleted the task that installed the MySQL database.

> **Note**
>
> The code of this playbook is available here: `https://github.com/PacktPublishing/Learning-DevOps-Second-Edition/blob/main/CHAP04/templates/ansible/playbookdemo.yml`.

Now that we have written our Ansible playbook, we will see how to integrate its execution into the Packer template.

Integrating an Ansible playbook in a Packer template

In terms of the Packer template, the JSON `builders` and `variables` sections are identical to one of the templates that uses scripts that we detailed earlier in the *Using Ansible in a Packer template* section. What is different is the JSON `provisioners` section, which we will write as follows:

```
provisioners": [
  {
    "type": "shell",
    "execute_command": "sudo sh -c '{{ .Vars }} {{ .Path }}'",
    "inline": [
      "add-apt-repository ppa:ansible/ansible", "apt-get update", "apt-get install ansible -y"
    ]
  },
  {
    "type": "ansible-local",
    "playbook_file": "ansible/playbookdemo.yml"
  },
  {
```

```
    "type": "shell",
    "execute_command": "sudo sh -c '{{ .Vars }} {{ .Path }}'",
    "script": "clean.sh"
  },
  .....//Deprovision the VM
  ]
```

The actions described in this `provisioners` section, which Packer will execute using this template, are as follows:

1. Installs Ansible on the temporary VM.

2. On this temporary VM, the `ansible-local` provisioner runs the playbook `playbookdemo.yaml` that installs and starts NGINX. The documentation of this provisioner is here: `https://www.packer.io/docs/provisioners/ansible/ansible-local`.

3. The `clean.sh` script deletes Ansible and its dependent packages that are no longer used.

4. Deprovisions the VM to delete the local user information.

> **Note**
>
> The complete Packer template is available here: `https://github.com/PacktPublishing/Learning-DevOps-Second-Edition/blob/main/CHAP04/templates/azure_linux_ansible.json`, and the source of the clean script, `clean.sh`, is available here: `https://github.com/PacktPublishing/Learning-DevOps-Second-Edition/blob/main/CHAP04/templates/clean.sh`.

As we can see here, Packer will execute Ansible on the temporary VM that will be used to create the image, but it is also possible to use Ansible remotely by using Packer's Ansible provisioner, the documentation of which is located here: `https://www.packer.io/docs/provisioners/ansible/ansible`.

We have seen up to this point how a Packer template is composed of the `builders`, `variables`, and `provisioners` sections, and we have seen that it is possible to use Ansible within a Packer template.

We will now run Packer with these JSON templates to create a VM image in Azure.

Executing Packer

Now that we have created the Packer templates, the next step is to run Packer to generate a custom VM image, which will be used to quickly provision VMs that are already configured and ready to use for your applications.

As a reminder, to generate this image, Packer will, from our JSON template, *create a temporary VM*, on which it will *perform all of the configuration actions* described in this template, and then it will *generate an image* from this image. Finally, at the end of its execution, it *removes the temporary VM* and all of its dependencies.

To generate our VM image in Azure, follow these steps:

1. Configure Packer to authenticate to Azure.
2. Check our Packer template.
3. Run Packer to generate our image.

Let's look in detail at the execution of each of its steps.

Configuring Packer to authenticate to Azure

To allow Packer to create resources in Azure, we will use the Azure AD SP that we created earlier in this chapter in the *Building an Azure image with the Packer template* section. To execute Packer in Azure, we will use the four pieces of authentication information (subscription_id, client_id, client_secret, and tenant_id) of this SP in the environment variables provided in our Packer template in the variables section.

In our following template, we have four variables (client_id, client_secret, subscription_id, and tenant_id), which take as their values four environment variables (ARM_CLIENT_ID, ARM_CLIENT_SECRET, ARM_SUBSCRIPTION_ID, and ARM_TENANT_ID):

```
"variables": {
    "client_id": "{{env `ARM_CLIENT_ID` }}",
    "client_secret": "{{env `ARM_CLIENT_SECRET` }}",
    "subscription_id": "{{env `ARM_SUBSCRIPTION_ID` }}",
    "tenant_id": "{{env `ARM_TENANT_ID` }}",
    "resource_group": "rg_images",
    "image_name": "linuxWeb",
    "image_version": "0.0.1",
    "location": "West Europe",
    "vm_size": "Standard_DS2_v2"
},
```

Figure 4.6 – Packer template variables

So we can set these environment variables as follows (this is a Linux example):

```
export ARM_SUBSCRIPTION_ID=<subscription_id>export ARM_CLIENT_
ID=<client ID>export ARM_SECRET_SECRET=<client Secret>export
ARM_TENANT_ID=<tenant ID>
```

> **Note**
>
> For Windows, we can use the PowerShell $env command to set an
> environment variable.

The first step of authentication is done, and we will now check the Packer template we
wrote.

Checking the validity of the Packer template

Before executing Packer to generate the image, we will execute the packer validate
command to check that our template is correct.

So, inside the folder that contains the Packer template, we execute the following command
on the template:

```
packer validate azure_linux.json
```

The output of the execution of this command returns the status of the check for whether
the template is valid, as shown in the following screenshot:

Figure 4.7 – Packer validate command

Our Packer template is correct in its syntax, so we can launch Packer to generate
our image.

Running Packer to generate our VM image

To generate our image with Packer, we will execute Packer with the build command
on the template file as follows:

```
packer build azure_linux.json
```

In the output of the Packer execution, we can see the different actions being performed by Packer. First is the creation of the temporary VM, as shown in the following screenshot:

```
                                        /CHAP04/templates# packer build azure_linux.json
azure-arm output will be in this color.

==> azure-arm: Running builder ...
==> azure-arm: Getting tokens using client secret
    azure-arm: Creating Azure Resource Manager (ARM) client ...
==> azure-arm: WARNING: Zone resiliency may not be supported in West Europe, checkout the docs at https:/
==> azure-arm: Creating resource group ...
==> azure-arm:  -> ResourceGroupName : 'packer-Resource-Group-xwzj9da4y4'
==> azure-arm:  -> Location          : 'West Europe'
==> azure-arm:  -> Tags              :
==> azure-arm:  ->> version : 0.0.1
==> azure-arm:  ->> role : WebServer
==> azure-arm: Validating deployment template ...
==> azure-arm:  -> ResourceGroupName : 'packer-Resource-Group-xwzj9da4y4'
==> azure-arm:  -> DeploymentName    : 'pkrdpxwzj9da4y4'
==> azure-arm: Deploying deployment template ...
==> azure-arm:  -> ResourceGroupName : 'packer-Resource-Group-xwzj9da4y4'
==> azure-arm:  -> DeploymentName    : 'pkrdpxwzj9da4y4'
```

Figure 4.8 – Packer creating temporary VM output

In the Azure portal, we see a temporary resource group and its resources created by Packer, as shown in the following screenshot:

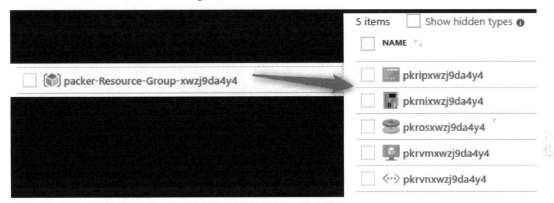

Figure 4.9 – Packer temporary resource group in the Azure portal

The execution time of Packer depends on the actions to be performed on the temporary VM. At the end of its execution, Packer indicates that it has generated the image and deletes the temporary resources.

The following screenshot is the end of the output of the Packer execution, which displays the deletion of the temporary resource group and the generation of the image:

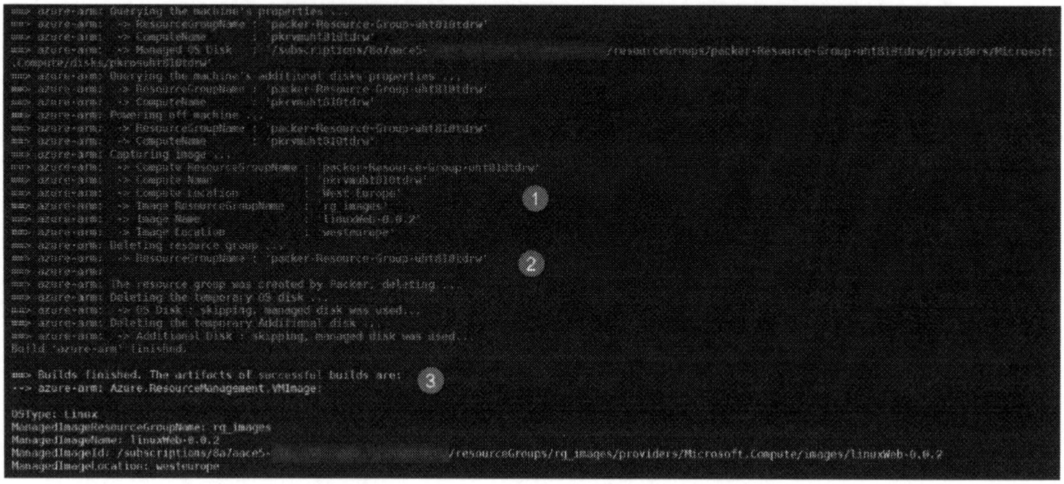

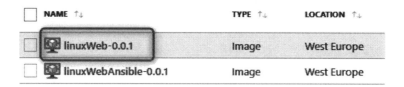

Figure 4.10 – Packer execution output

After the Packer execution, in the Azure portal, we check that the image is present. The following screenshot shows our generated image:

NAME ↑↓	TYPE ↑↓	LOCATION ↑↓
linuxWeb-0.0.1	Image	West Europe
linuxWebAnsible-0.0.1	Image	West Europe

Figure 4.11 – Azure VM image created by Packer

In this screen, we can see our image and the images that we generated with the Packer template, which uses Ansible.

It is also interesting to know that we can override the variables of our template when executing the `packer build` command, as in the following example:

```
packer build -var 'image_version=0.0.2' azure_linux.json
```

We can pass all variables with the `-var` options to the `build` command.

So, with this option, we can change the name of the image without changing the content of the template, and we can do this for all of the variables that are defined in our template.

> **Note**
>
> The complete documentation of the Packer `build` command is available here:
> `https://www.packer.io/docs/commands/build.html`.

We have just seen the Packer command lines to check the syntax of the JSON Packer template and then to run Packer on a template that generates a VM image in Azure.

Now we will learn about the basic elements for writing Packer templates using HCL format.

Writing Packer templates with HCL format

Since the release of version 1.5.0 of Packer, it's possible to write Packer templates using HCL format, which we learned in detail in *Chapter 2, Provisioning Cloud Infrastructure with Terraform*.

> **Note**
>
> The HCL integration in Packer is currently in Beta, and will be preferred by HashiCorp from version 1.7.0.

The HCL format of the template is very similar to the JSON format and it's composed of `variable`, `source`, `build`, and `provisioner` blocks. The following code shows the structure of the HCL Packer template.

For writing an HCL template, create a file, `.pkr.hcl`, that contains all the following code:

```
packer {
    required_plugins
    {
        azure =
        {
            version = ">= 1.0.0"
            source  = "github.com/hashicorp/azure"
        }
    }
}

Variable "var name"{
```

```
    ...
}
Source "name" {
    ...
}
Build {
    Source = []
    Provisionner "" {}
}
```

First, we start with the Packer plugin configuration that has been introduced from version 1.7.0. In this block, we list all plugins that will be used in the code.

> **Note**
>
> For more information about Packer plugins, read the documentation at
> `https://www.packer.io/docs/plugins`.

Then, in the `variable` block, we declare the user variables, for example Azure credentials, VM name, VM size, or other variables. The following code shows a sample `variable` block:

```
variable "image_folder" {
    default = "/image"
}
variable "vm_size" {
    default = "Standard_DS2_v2"
}
```

> **Note**
>
> For more information and details about HCL variables, read the
> documentation at `https://www.packer.io/guides/hcl/`
> `variables`.

The `source` block contains the properties of the target image to build an Azure image or Docker image. The following code show examples of two `source` blocks:

- The first `source` declaration is for an Azure VM:

```
source "azure-arm" "azurevm" {
    os_type = "Linux"
    location = "West Europe"
    vm_size = "Standard_DS2_V2"
    ....
}
```

- The second `source` declaration is for the Docker image:

```
source "docker" "docker-img"
{
    image = "ubuntu"
    export_path = "imagedocker.tar"
}
```

The `build` block contains the source list to use and the `provisioner` scripts for configuring the images. The following code show a sample `build` block:

```
build {
  sources = ["sources.azure-arm.azurevm","sources.docker.docker-img"]
provisioner "shell" {
  inline = [
  "apt-get update",
    "apt-get -y install nginx"
  ]
    execute_command  = "chmod +x {{ .Path }}; {{ .Vars }} sudo -E sh '{{ .Path }}'"
  inline_shebang = "/bin/sh -x"
}
provisioner "shell" {
  inline = [
    "sleep 30",
    "/usr/sbin/waagent -force -deprovision+user && export HISTSIZE=0 && sync"
```

```
    ]
    execute_command  = "chmod +x {{ .Path }}; {{ .Vars }} sudo -E
sh '{{ .Path }}'"
    inline_shebang = "/bin/sh -x"
  }
}
```

In the preceding code, the source property contains the list of sources declared just before in the source block details.

Then we use a list of provisioner blocks of shell type to install the NGINX package and clean the image with personal information – exactly the same operations that we did with the JSON format.

> **Note**
>
> The code source of this HCL template format is available at https://github.com/PacktPublishing/Learning-DevOps-Second-Edition/blob/main/CHAP04/templates/.pkr.hcl.

Finally, to execute Packer using an HCL template, we execute the following command to download plugins:

```
packer init .pkr.hcl
```

Then we check the template syntax by running the validate command:

```
packer validate .pkr.hcl
```

Finally, we build the desired image by running this following command:

```
packer build .pkr.hcl
```

After the execution of the preceding command, the image will be created, exactly as we have already seen with the JSON format.

> **Note**
>
> To migrate Packer templates from JSON format to HCL format, read this documentation: https://learn.hashicorp.com/tutorials/packer/hcl2-upgrade.

We have discussed how to write and execute Packer templates using the HCL format that will become the preferred format for HashiCorp. We will now learn how to provision, with Terraform, a VM based on this image that we have just generated.

Using a Packer image with Terraform

Now that we have generated a custom VM image, we will provision a new VM based on this new image. For the provisioning of this VM, we will continue to use IaC practices using Terraform from HashiCorp.

To do this, we will take the Terraform script created in *Chapter 2, Provisioning Cloud Infrastructure with Terraform,*, and modify it to use the custom image.

In the `compute.tf` script, add the following block of data, which will point to the VM image that we generated with Packer in the last section:

```
## GET THE CUSTOM IMAGE CREATED BY PACKER
data "azurerm_image" "customngnix" {
  name = "linuxWeb-0.0.1"
  resource_group_name = "rg_images"
}
```

In this code, we add a block of `azurerm_image` Terraform data that allows us to retrieve the properties of a VM image in Azure, in which we specify the `name` property with name of the custom image, and the `resource_group_name` property with the resource group of the image.

For more information about this `azurerm_image` data block and its properties, refer to the documentation: `https://www.terraform.io/docs/providers/azurerm/d/image.html`.

Then, in the VM Terraform code in the `azurerm_virtual_machine` resource code (still in the `compute.tf` file), the `storage_image_reference` section is modified with the following code:

```
resource "azurerm_virtual_machine" "vm" {
...
  ## USE THE CUSTOM IMAGE
  storage_image_reference {
  id = "${data.azurerm_image.customngnix.id}"
```

```
    }
    ...
}
```

In this code, the ID property uses the `id` of the image from the block data that we added earlier.

> **Note**
>
> The entire code for the `compute.tf` script is available here: `https://github.com/PacktPublishing/Learning-DevOps-Second-Edition/blob/main/CHAP04/terraform/compute.tf` and the full Terraform code is here: `https://github.com/PacktPublishing/Learning-DevOps-Second-Edition/tree/main/CHAP04/terraform`.

When executing this Terraform code, which is identical to a classic Terraform execution, as seen in *Chapter 2, Provisioning Cloud Infrastructure with Terraform*, the provisioned VM will be based on the custom image generated by Packer.

We have seen that by changing a little bit of our previous Terraform code, adding a data block that retrieves information from a VM image, and using the ID of that image, we can, in Terraform, use custom VM images generated by Packer.

Summary

In this chapter, we have seen how to install Packer and use it to create custom VM images. The VM image was made from two Packer templates: the first one using scripts and the second one using Ansible.

Then, we saw how to write Packer templates with HCL format. Finally, we modified our Terraform code to use our VM image.

This chapter ends the implementation of IaC practices, starting with **Terraform** to provision a cloud infrastructure, then using **Ansible** for server configuration, and, finally, finishing with **Packer** for VM image creation.

With these VM images created by Packer, we will be able to improve infrastructure provisioning times with faster deployment, ready-to-use VMs, and, therefore, a reduction in downtime.

Obviously, these are not the only IaC tools; there are many others on the marketplace, and you will have to do technology monitoring to find the ones that best suit your needs.

In the next chapter, we will start a new part, which is the implementation of CI/CD, and we will learn how to use Git for sourcing your code.

Questions

1. What are the two ways to install Packer?
2. What are the mandatory sections of a Packer template that are used to create a VM image in Azure?
3. Which command is used to validate a Packer template?
4. Which command is used to generate a Packer image?

Further reading

If you want to know more about Packer, here are some resources:

*   Packer documentation: `https://www.packer.io/docs/`
*   Packer Learning: `https://learn.hashicorp.com/packer`
*   Using Packer in Azure: `https://docs.microsoft.com/en-us/azure/virtual-machines/linux/build-image-with-packer`
*   Designing Immutable Infrastructure with Packer (Pluralsight Video): `https://www.pluralsight.com/courses/packer-designing-immutable-infrastructure`

5

Authoring the Development Environment with Vagrant

In the previous chapters, we learned how to provision a piece of infrastructure with Terraform, how to install middleware with Ansible, and, finally, how to create **Virtual Machine (VM)** images with Packer.

One problem that is frequently pointed out by operational teams is the fact that they need to be able to test all of the automation scripts on isolated environments, that is, environments that are not on the local machine. Indeed, writing scripts with Ansible under Linux, for example, is difficult to test on a local Windows machine.

To answer this problem, we can use virtualization systems such as Hyper-V or VirtualBox, which allow you to have VMs with different operating systems that run locally. However, to go even further, we can automate the creation and provisioning of these VMs using the tiers tool from HashiCorp, called **Vagrant**.

In this chapter, we will learn about the basics of using Vagrant. We will discuss its installation, how to write Vagrant files, and, finally, we will examine its execution to create and provision a Linux VM.

In this chapter, we're going to cover the following main topics:

- Installing Vagrant
- Writing a Vagrant configuration file
- Provisioning a local VM with the Vagrant CLI

Technical requirements

Vagrant can create a VM on any hypervisor. In this chapter, we will use VirtualBox as a local VM hypervisor. You can download and install it from `https://www.virtualbox.org/wiki/Downloads`.

On Windows, if you have already installed Hyper-V, to use VirtualBox, you need to disable Hyper-V. Please refer to the following documentation:

`https://www.vagrantup.com/docs/installation#windows-virtualbox-and-hyper-v`

All of the commands executed in this chapter will be executed in a terminal console such as PowerShell or Bash.

The complete source code for this chapter is available here:

`https://github.com/PacktPublishing/Learning-DevOps-Second-Edition/tree/main/CHAP05/`

Check out the following video to view the Code in Action: `https://bit.ly/3s5aO49`

Installing Vagrant

Vagrant is a cross-platform tool that can be installed on Windows, Linux, or macOS. Installation can be done in two ways: either manually or via a script in Windows.

Installing manually on Windows

To install Vagrant manually on Windows, perform the following steps:

1. Go to the official download page (`https://www.vagrantup.com/downloads`), click on the **Windows** tab, and download the MSI package corresponding to your operating system's CPU type (either 32 bits or 64 bits).

2. After downloading, click on the downloaded MSI file and select the installation directory (keep the default value):

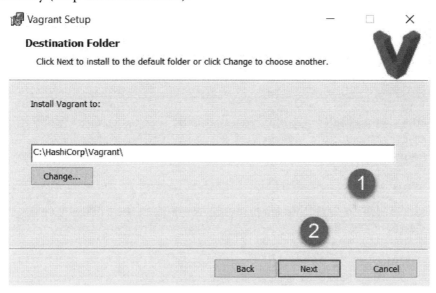

Figure 5.1 – Vagrant Setup folder choice

3. Then, click on the **Install** button:

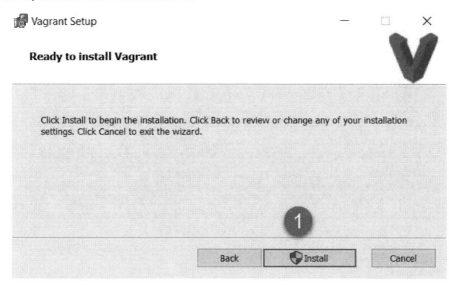

Figure 5.2 – The Vagrant Setup Install button

You have learned how to install Vagrant manually on a Windows system. In the next section, we will discuss the installation of Vagrant using Chocolatey or a script.

Installing Vagrant by script on Windows

On Windows, we can use **Chocolatey**, which is a software package manager.

> **Note**
>
> In this chapter, I will not reintroduce Chocolatey, as we have already introduced it in the previous chapters. For additional information about Chocolatey, please read the documentation at `https://chocolatey.org/`.

Once Chocolatey has been installed, we simply need to run the following command in PowerShell or the CMD tool:

```
choco install vagrant -y
```

The following is a screenshot of the Vagrant installation for Windows using Chocolatey:

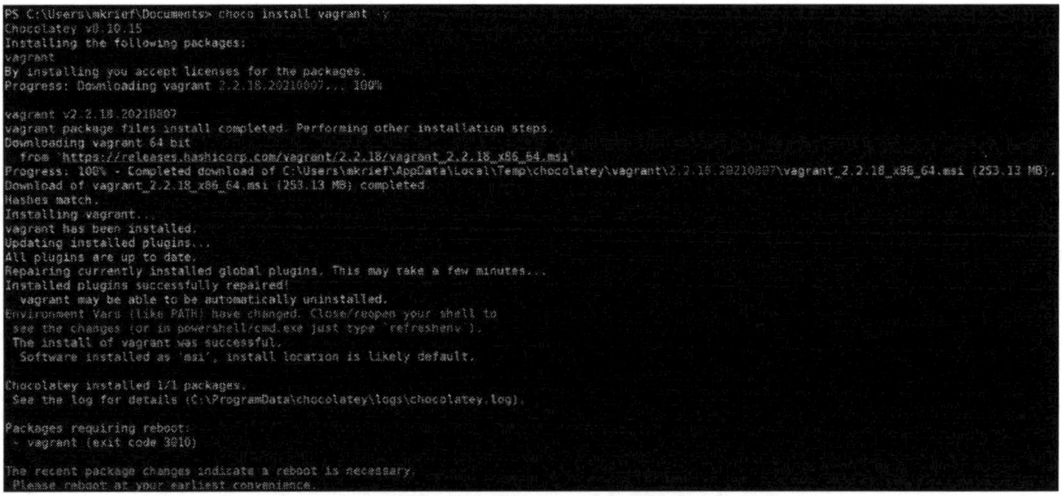

Figure 5.3 – Vagrant installation with Chocolatey

To finalize the installation of Vagrant, we need to reboot the machine.

Installing Vagrant by script on Linux

On Linux, we can execute the following script to install Vagrant automatically:

```
sudo apt-get update && sudo apt-get install -y gnupg software-
properties-common curl \
&& curl -fsSL https://apt.releases.hashicorp.com/gpg | sudo
apt-key add - \
&& sudo apt-add-repository "deb [arch=amd64] https://apt.
releases.hashicorp.com $(lsb_release -cs) main" \
&& sudo apt-get update && sudo apt-get install vagrant
```

This script does the following:

- It adds the apt HashiCorp repository.
- It updates the local repository.
- It downloads and installs the Vagrant CLI.

> **Note**
>
> For additional information about all installations of Vagrant on other operating systems, please refer to the documentation at https://www.vagrantup.com/downloads.

Once Vagrant has been installed, we can test the installation of the Vagrant CLI by running the following command:

```
vagrant --version
```

The preceding command displays the version of Vagrant that has been installed, and the following screenshot shows the execution of this command:

```
PS ·             \Learning-DevOps-Second-Edition\CHAP05\VagrantFiles> vagrant --version
Vagrant 2.2.18
```

Figure 5.4 – Displaying the installed version of Vagrant

We have just learned the manual installation procedure for Vagrant and how to install it using a script on Linux.

Now, we will expose some main Vagrant artifacts and write a Vagrant template configuration to create a basic Linux VM locally and configure it with Ansible to test Ansible scripts.

Writing a Vagrant configuration file

Before we discuss how to write the Vagrant configuration file, it is important to mention a few artifacts of Vagrant.

The important elements of Vagrant are the following:

- The Vagrant binary (CLI): We learned how to download and install this in the previous section, *Installing Vagrant*.

- The base image of the VM, called **Vagrant Boxes**, will be used and mentioned in the configuration file. This image can be either public, that is, published in the Vagrant cloud, or local on the machine.

- The configuration file defines the composition of our VM that we want to create locally.

Now that we have looked at the different elements of Vagrant, we are going to write the configuration file of our VM. To begin, we are going to check which base machine we are going to use.

Using Vagrant Cloud for Vagrant Boxes

To use basic Vagrant images, HashiCorp has set up a portal that allows you to publish and publicly share images of VMs that are compatible with Vagrant.

To gain access to these images, called boxes, you can navigate to the site at `https://app.vagrantup.com/boxes/search` and then perform a search on the specific box that interests you according to the following criteria:

- The operating system (Windows or Linux)
- The supported hypervisor
- The middleware that has already been installed
- The publisher

The following screenshot shows an example of how to search on Vagrant Cloud:

Figure 5.5 – The Vagrant Cloud search box

In this example, we are searching for a basic Bionic box. In the list of results, we find the official `ubuntu/bionic64` box, which is compatible with the VirtualBox hypervisor.

By clicking on the desired box, the portal displays more information, such as the configuration details and the changelog of the box:

Figure 5.6 – The Vagrant Cloud box details

> **Note**
>
> For more information about Vagrant Cloud and how to create and publish your custom boxes, I suggest you refer to the official documentation at `https://www.vagrantup.com/vagrant-cloud`.

Now that we have chosen our base box, we will write the Vagrant configuration file for our VM.

Writing the Vagrant configuration file

To create a local VM using Vagrant, we need to write the configuration of the VM in the configuration file.

This configuration will contain information about the VM, such as the following:

- The box to use
- The hardware configuration such as the RAM and CPU
- The network configuration
- The scripts to use to provision and configure the VM
- The local folder to share with the VM

In this section, we will learn how to create a basic Vagrant configuration file that creates a local VM that contains an Ansible binary already installed.

To create a Vagrant configuration, perform the following steps:

1. Create a folder called `VagrantFiles`.
2. Inside this folder, open a new terminal console and run the `vagrant init` command with the name of the box, as follows:

   ```
   vagrant init ubuntu/bionic64
   ```

   The following screenshot shows the execution of this command:

   ```
   PS               \Learning-DevOps-Second-Edition\CHAP05\VagrantFiles> vagrant init ubuntu/bionic64
   A `Vagrantfile` has been placed in this directory. You are now
   ready to `vagrant up` your first virtual environment! Please read
   the comments in the Vagrantfile as well as documentation on
   `vagrantup.com` for more information on using Vagrant.
   ```

   Figure 5.7 – The init Vagrant file

   The preceding command creates a new `Vagrantfile` file with the basic configuration for a bionic VM with the following code:

   ```
   Vagrant.configure("2") do |config|
       config.vm.box = "ubuntu/bionic64"
   end
   ```

   Next, we will add scripts to install Ansible during the provisioning of this VM.

3. In this `VagrantFiles` folder, create a new folder called `scripts` and then create a new file script, called `ansible.sh`, using the following content:

   ```
   apt-get update
   sudo apt-get --assume-yes install software-properties-
   common
   sudo apt-add-repository --yes --update ppa:ansible/
   ansible
   sudo apt-get --assume-yes install ansible
   ```

4. In the `Vagrantfile` file, update the configuration with the following lines:

```
Vagrant.configure("2") do |config|
  config.vm.box = "ubuntu/bionic64"
        config.vm.provision "shell", path: "scripts/
ansible.sh"
end
```

5. To test the local Ansible playbook, we can share the local directory with the VM by adding the following lines to the configuration file:

```
Vagrant.configure("2") do |config|
  config.vm.box = "ubuntu/bionic64"      config.vm.provision
  "shell", path: "scripts/ansible.sh"


  config.vm.synced_folder "C:\\<path>\\CHAP03\\
  devopsansible", "/learningdevops"
end
```

In the preceding configuration, we shared the local `c:\\...Chap03\` `devopsansible` folder (this is an example of a local folder) between the local machine and the `/learningdevops` folder in the VM.

> **Note**
>
> For more details about this Vagrant configuration file, please refer to the complete documentation at `https://www.vagrantup.com/docs/` `vagrantfile`.

6. The final step is to validate this configuration file by running the following command:

```
vagrant validate
```

The output of this command is shown in the following screenshot:

```
PS               \Learning-DevOps-Second-Edition\CHAP05\VagrantFiles> vagrant validate
Vagrantfile validated successfully.
```

Figure 5.8 – Validating the Vagrant configuration

> **Note**
>
> In this section, we learned how to create a VM using a Vagrant configuration file. If you wish to create multiple VMs in the same configuration file, please refer to the official documentation at `https://www.vagrantup.com/docs/multi-machine`.

We have just discussed how to choose a Vagrant box and how to write a Vagrant configuration file. Now, in the next section, we will learn how to use the Vagrant CLI and the configuration file to create a VM locally.

Creating a local VM using the Vagrant CLI

Now that we have written the configuration file, we can create our VM locally.

To perform this, we will use several Vagrant CLI commands. To display all of the available commands, we will run the `vagrant --help` command:

```
PS                \Learning-DevOps-Second-Edition\CHAP05\VagrantFiles> vagrant --help
Usage: vagrant [options] <command> [<args>]

    -h, --help                      Print this help.

Common commands:
    autocomplete    manages autocomplete installation on host
    box             manages boxes: installation, removal, etc.
    cloud           manages everything related to Vagrant Cloud
    destroy         stops and deletes all traces of the vagrant machine
    global-status   outputs status Vagrant environments for this user
    halt            stops the vagrant machine
    help            shows the help for a subcommand
    init            initializes a new Vagrant environment by creating a Vagrantfile
    login
    package         packages a running vagrant environment into a box
    plugin          manages plugins: install, uninstall, update, etc.
    port            displays information about guest port mappings
    powershell      connects to machine via powershell remoting
    provision       provisions the vagrant machine
    push            deploys code in this environment to a configured destination
    rdp             connects to machine via RDP
    reload          restarts vagrant machine, loads new Vagrantfile configuration
    resume          resume a suspended vagrant machine
    snapshot        manages snapshots: saving, restoring, etc.
    ssh             connects to machine via SSH
    ssh-config      outputs OpenSSH valid configuration to connect to the machine
    status          outputs status of the vagrant machine
    suspend         suspends the machine
    up              starts and provisions the vagrant environment
    upload          upload to machine via communicator
    validate        validates the Vagrantfile
    vbguest         plugin: vagrant-vbguest: install VirtualBox Guest Additions to the machine
    version         prints current and latest Vagrant version
    winrm           executes commands on a machine via WinRM
    winrm-config    outputs WinRM configuration to connect to the machine
```

Figure 5.9 – Displaying the Vagrant commands

> **Note**
>
> All details about the Vagrant CLI commands are documented at
> `https://www.vagrantup.com/docs/cli`.

In the next section we will learn how to create the VM, then we will connect to this VM, and finally we will perform some scripts.

Creating the VM

To create the VM, navigate to the folder in which we created the `Vagrantfile` file, and run the following command:

```
vagrant up
```

The output is shown in the following screenshot:

Figure 5.10 – The Vagrant up execution workflow

The execution of the preceding command performs the following steps:

1. Import the box from Vagrant Cloud.
2. Create a new VM in the hypervisor (in our case, this is VirtualBox).

3. Create an SSH connection with SSH keys (Vagrant creates private/public SSH keys).

4. Mount the shared folder.

5. Apply the provisioning Ansible script.

After the provisioning of the VM, we can view this VM in the hypervisor here in VirtualBox.

Now that the VM is up and has been provisioned, we can connect it.

Connecting to the VM

To connect the VM with SSH, we can use the default SSH command dedicated to Vagrant (in administrator mode):

```
vagrant ssh
```

The output is shown in the following screenshot:

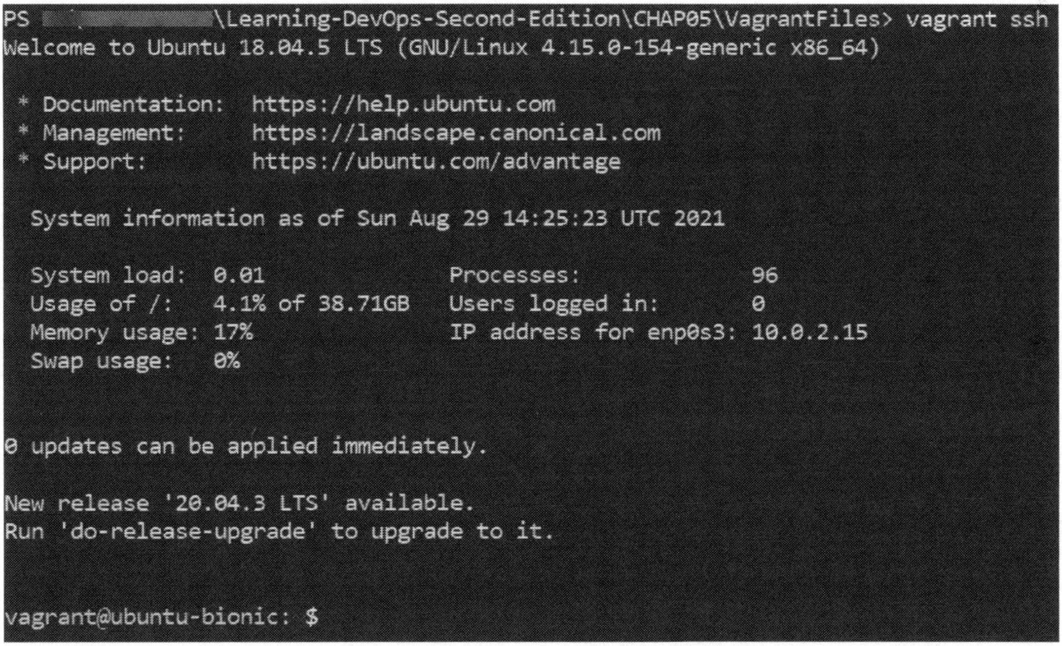

```
PS               \Learning-DevOps-Second-Edition\CHAP05\VagrantFiles> vagrant ssh
Welcome to Ubuntu 18.04.5 LTS (GNU/Linux 4.15.0-154-generic x86_64)

 * Documentation:  https://help.ubuntu.com
 * Management:     https://landscape.canonical.com
 * Support:        https://ubuntu.com/advantage

  System information as of Sun Aug 29 14:25:23 UTC 2021

  System load:  0.01              Processes:              96
  Usage of /:   4.1% of 38.71GB   Users logged in:        0
  Memory usage: 17%               IP address for enp0s3:  10.0.2.15
  Swap usage:   0%


0 updates can be applied immediately.

New release '20.04.3 LTS' available.
Run 'do-release-upgrade' to upgrade to it.


vagrant@ubuntu-bionic: $
```

Figure 5.11 – Connecting SSH to the Vagrant VM

The execution of this command means that Vagrant automatically connects the SSH credential to the VM, and we can run any commands or scripts inside the VM.

For example, we can run the `ansible -version` command to display the installed version of Ansible:

```
vagrant@ubuntu-bionic: $ ansible --version
ansible 2.9.24
  config file = /etc/ansible/ansible.cfg
  configured module search path = [u'/home/vagrant/.ansible/plugins/modules', u'/usr/share/ansible/plugins/modules']
  ansible python module location = /usr/lib/python2.7/dist-packages/ansible
  executable location = /usr/bin/ansible
  python version = 2.7.17 (default, Feb 27 2021, 15:10:58) [GCC 7.5.0]
vagrant@ubuntu-bionic: $
```

Figure 5.12 – Executing commands inside the VM

After running the desired tests, if we wish to destroy this VM to remake it, we can run the `vagrant destroy` command:

```
PS          \Learning-DevOps-Second-Edition\CHAP05\VagrantFiles> vagrant destroy
    default: Are you sure you want to destroy the 'default' VM? [y/N] y
==> default: Forcing shutdown of VM...
==> default: Destroying VM and associated drives...
```

Figure 5.13 – Destroying the Vagrant VM

In this section, we learned how to create a VM and connect to it using the Vagrant CLI.

Summary

In this chapter, we learned that it was possible to create VMs locally using Vagrant from HashiCorp in order to have an isolated development environment.

We discussed how to download and install it. Then, we learned how to write a Vagrant configuration file using a Bionic box, an `ansible install` script, and a locally shared folder.

Finally, we learned how to execute the Vagrant command lines in order to create this VM and connect to it for testing purposes.

In the next chapter, we will start a new topic, which is the implementation of CI/CD, and we will learn how to use Git to source your code.

Questions

1. What is the role of Vagrant?
2. What is the Vagrant command to create a VM?
3. What is the Vagrant command to connect SSH to a VM?

Further reading

If you want to know more about Vagrant, please take a look at the following resources:

- The official Vagrant documentation : `https://www.vagrantup.com/docs/index`
- The official Vagrant Cloud documentation: `https://www.vagrantup.com/vagrant-cloud`

Section 2: DevOps CI/CD Pipeline

This part covers the DevOps pipeline process, starting with the principles of continuous integration and continuous deployment. It will be illustrated through the use of different tools, including Jenkins, Azure Pipelines, and GitLab.

This section comprises the following chapters:

6
Managing Your Source Code with Git

A few years ago, when we were developers and writing code as part of a team, we encountered recurring problems that were for the most part as follows:

- How to share my code with my team members
- How to version the update of my code
- How to track changes to my code
- How to retrieve an old state of my code or part of it

Over time, these issues have been solved with the emergence of source code managers, also called a **version control system** (**VCS**) or noted more commonly as a **version control manager** (**VCM**).

The goals of these VCSs are mainly to do the following:

- Allow collaboration of developers' code
- Retrieve the code
- Version the code
- Track code changes

With the advent of agile methods and a **development-operations (DevOps)** culture, the use of a VCS in processes has become mandatory. Indeed, as mentioned in *Chapter 1, The DevOps Culture and Infrastructure as Code Practices*, the implementation of a **continuous integration/continuous deployment (CI/CD)** process can only be done with a VCS as a prerequisite.

In this chapter, we will see how to use one of the best-known VCSs, which is Git. We will start with an overview of Git and see how to install it. Then, we will see its main command lines to familiarize any developer with their uses. Finally, we will see the current process of using Git workflows and usage of Gitflow. The purpose of this chapter is to show the usage of Git daily with simple processes.

This chapter covers the following topics:

- Overviewing Git and its principal command lines
- Understanding the Git process and Gitflow pattern

This chapter does not cover the installation of a Git server, so if you want to know more about that, you can refer to the documentation at the following link: `https://git-scm.com/book/en/v2/Git-on-the-Server-The-Protocols`.

Technical requirements

The use of Git does not have any technical prerequisites; we just need a command-line Terminal.

To illustrate its usage in this chapter, we will use Azure Repos from the Azure DevOps platform (formerly **Visual Studio Team System (VSTS)**), which is a cloud platform that has a Git repository manager. You can register here for free: `https://visualstudio.microsoft.com/team-services/`.

Check out the following video to see the code in action: `https://bit.ly/3LTcoOi`.

Overviewing Git and its principal command lines

To understand the origin of Git, it is necessary to know that there are two types of VCSs: centralized and distributed systems.

The first type to emerge were **centralized systems**, such as **Subversion (SVN)**, **Concurrent Version System (CVS)**, and **Team Foundation Version Control (TFVC)** and Microsoft **Visual SourceSafe (VSS)**. These systems consist of a remote server that centralizes the code of all developers.

We can represent a centralized source control system like this:

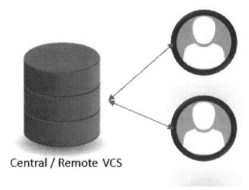

Central / Remote VCS

Figure 6.1 – Centralized source control

All developers can archive and retrieve their code on the remote server. The system allows better collaboration between teams and a guarantee of code backup. However, it has its drawbacks, such as the following:

- In case of no connection (for a network problem or internet disconnection) between the developers and the remote server, no more archiving or code recovery actions can be performed.

- If the remote server no longer works, the code, as well as the history, will be lost.

The second type of VCS, which appeared later, is a **distributed system**, such as Mercurial or Git. These systems consist of a remote repository and a local copy of this repository on each developer's local machine, as shown in the following screenshot:

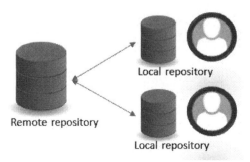

Remote repository

Local repository

Local repository

Figure 6.2 – Distributed source control

So, with this distributed system, even in the event of disconnection from the remote repository, developers can continue to work with the local repository, and synchronization will be done when the remote repository is accessible again. A copy of the code and its history is also present in the local repository.

Git is, therefore, a distributed VCS that was created in 2005 by Linus Torvalds and the Linux development community.

> **Note**
>
> To learn a little more about Git's history, read this page: `https://git-scm.com/book/en/v2/Getting-Started-A-Short-History-of-Git`.

Since its creation, Git has become a very powerful and mature tool that can be used by anyone for coding.

Git is a free, cross-platform tool, and it can be installed on a local machine for people who manipulate code—that is, in client mode—but can also be installed on servers to host and manage remote repositories.

Git is a command-line tool with a multitude of options. Nevertheless, there are many graphical tools today—such as Git GUI, GitKraken, GitHub Desktop, or Sourcetree—that allow you to interact with Git operations more easily and graphically without having to use command lines yourself. However, these graphical tools do not contain all of the operations and options available on the command line. Fortunately, many code editors such as **Visual Studio Code** (**VS Code**), Visual Studio, JetBrains, and Sublime Text allow direct code integration with Git and remote repositories.

For remote repositories, there are several cloud and free solutions such as GitHub, GitLab, Azure DevOps, or Bitbucket Cloud. Also, there are other solutions called on-premises solutions that can be installed in an enterprise, such as Azure DevOps Server, Bitbucket, or GitHub Enterprise.

In this chapter, we will see the usage of Git—for example, with Azure DevOps as a remote repository—and we will see the usage of GitLab and GitHub in future chapters.

In this section, we have introduced Git, and we will now see how to install it on a local machine to develop and version our sources.

Git installation

We will now detail the steps of installing and configuring Git on Windows, Linux, and macOS systems.

To install on a Windows machine manually, we must download the **Git for Windows tool** executable from `https://gitforwindows.org/`, and, once downloaded, we click on the executable file and follow the next different configuration steps during the installation:

1. Select an installation path for the Git binaries. We keep the default path, as illustrated in the following screenshot:

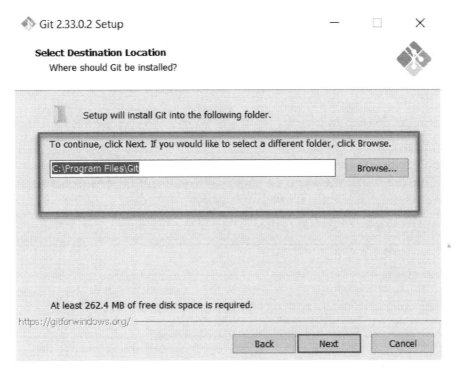

Figure 6.3 – Git installation path

2. Choose Git integration components in Windows Explorer by marking the **Windows Explorer integration** checkbox, as illustrated in the following screenshot:

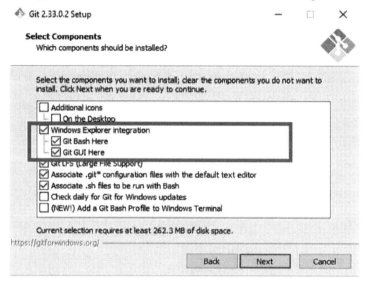

Figure 6.4 – Choosing Git installation components

3. Choose your code editor **integrated development environment (IDE)**; in our case, we use VS Code by selecting the **Use Visual Studio Code as Git's default editor** option, as illustrated in the following screenshot:

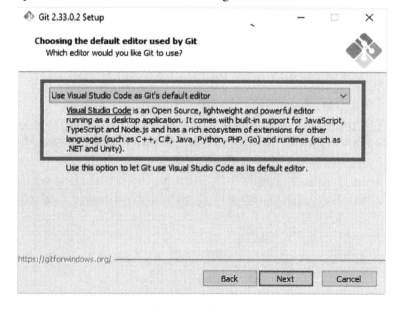

Figure 6.5 – Choosing Git installation editor

4. Configure the name of the default branch. We can keep the default option to use `master` as the default branch name, as illustrated in the following screenshot:

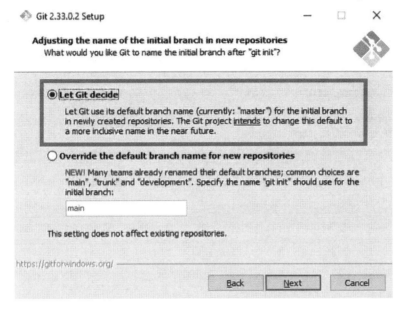

Figure 6.6 – Git configuration default branch name

5. When choosing an **Adjusting your PATH environment** option, we can leave the default choice proposed by the installer, as illustrated in the following screenshot:

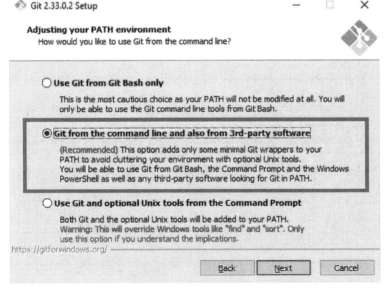

Figure 6.7 – Git installation PATH configuration

6. Choose a **Secure Shell (SSH)** client to use by keeping the default option to use the integrated ssh.exe client, as illustrated in the following screenshot:

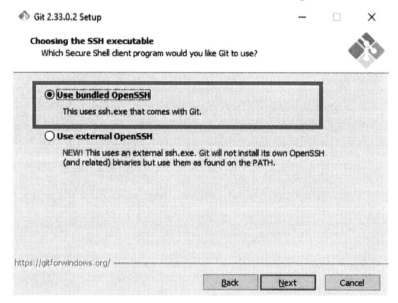

Figure 6.8 – Git installation SSH tool

7. Choose a type of **HyperText Transfer Protocol Secure (HTTPS)** transport, which we will also leave by default at the **Use the OpenSSL library** option, as illustrated in the following screenshot:

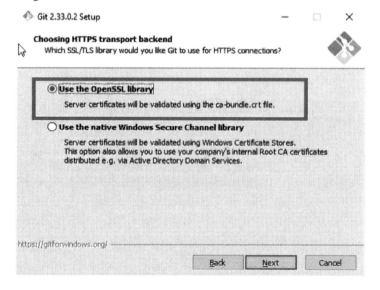

Figure 6.9 – Git installation using OpenSSL

8. Choose an option for the encoding of the end files. We will also select the default option, which archives in Unix format, as illustrated in the following screenshot:

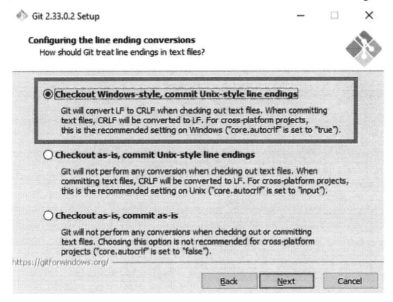

Figure 6.10 – Choosing encoding of Git installation files

9. Select a default terminal emulator for Git Bash. We choose MinTTy, as illustrated in the following screenshot:

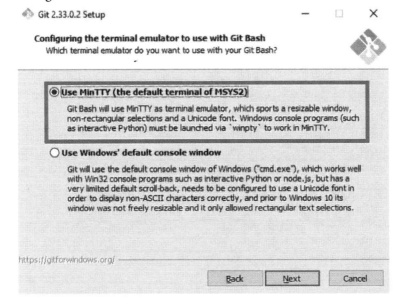

Figure 6.11 – Git installation terminal emulator

10. Choose the default behavior of the `git pull` command. We keep the default option, as illustrated in the following screenshot:

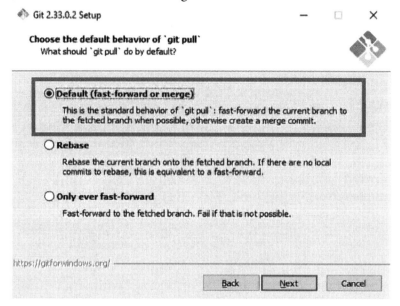

Figure 6.12 – Git installation default git pull command

11. Choose a credential manager helper by keeping the default option, as illustrated in the following screenshot:

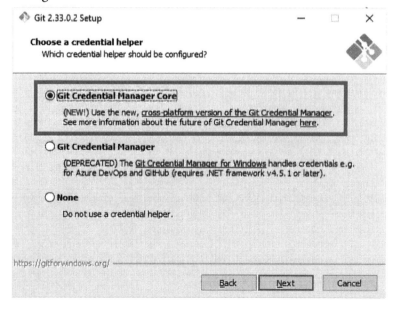

Figure 6.13 – Git installation credential manager

12. In the next screen, we enable file system caching, as follows:

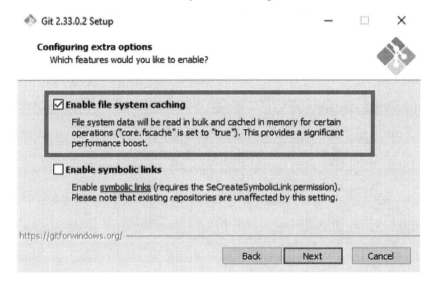

Figure 6.14 – Git installation file caching

13. Then, finish the installation configuration by clicking on the **Install** button, as illustrated in the following screenshot:

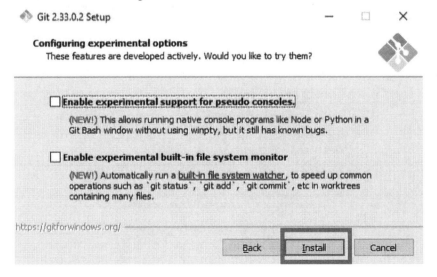

Figure 6.15 – Git installation last step

At the end of the installation, the installation utility proposes to open Git Bash, which is a command-line Terminal Linux emulator dedicated to Git commands, as illustrated in the following screenshot:

Figure 6.16 – End of Git installation

After the installation, we can immediately check the status of the Git installation directly in the Git Bash window by running the `git version` command, as follows:

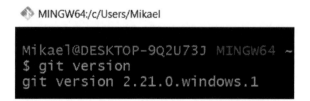

Figure 6.17 – Displaying Git version

We can also install Git using an automatic script with **Chocolatey**, the Windows software package manager, which we already used in the previous chapters on Terraform and Packer. (As a reminder, the Chocolatey documentation is available here: https://chocolatey.org/.)

To install Git for Windows with Chocolatey, we must execute the following command in an operating Terminal:

```
choco install -y git
```

And the result of this execution is displayed in the following screenshot:

```
Administrator: Windows PowerShell
PS C:\WINDOWS\system32> choco install -y git
Chocolatey v0.10.15
Installing the following packages:
git
By installing you accept licenses for the packages.
Progress: Downloading git.install 2.33.0.2... 100%
Progress: Downloading git 2.33.0.2... 100%

git.install v2.33.0.2 [Approved]
git.install package files install completed. Performing other installation steps.
Using Git LFS
Installing 64-bit git.install...
git.install has been installed.
WARNING: Can't find git.install install location
  git.install can be automatically uninstalled.
Environment Vars (like PATH) have changed. Close/reopen your shell to
see the changes (or in powershell/cmd.exe just type `refreshenv`).
 The install of git.install was successful.
  Software installed to 'C:\Program Files\Git\'

git v2.33.0.2 [Approved]
git package files install completed. Performing other installation steps.
 The install of git was successful.
  Software install location not explicitly set, could be in package or
  default install location if installer.

Chocolatey installed 2/2 packages.
 See the log for details (C:\ProgramData\chocolatey\logs\chocolatey.log).
```

Figure 6.18 – Git installation with Chocolatey

To install Git on a **Linux** machine, for Debian systems such as Ubuntu, we run the apt-get command as follows:

```
apt-get install git
```

Or for **CentOS** or **Fedora**, install Git with the yum command, like this:

```
yum install git
```

For a **macOS** system, we can download and install Git using Homebrew (https://brew.sh/), which is a package manager dedicated to macOS, by executing this command in the Terminal:

```
brew install git
```

The installation of Git is finished, and we will now proceed to its configuration.

Git configuration

Git configuration requires us to configure our username and email, which will be used during code commit. To perform this configuration, we execute the following commands in a Terminal—either the one that is native to your **operating system (OS)** or Git Bash for Windows:

```
git config --global user.name "<your username>"
git config --global user.email "<your email>"
```

Then, we can check the configuration values by executing the following command:

```
git config --global --list
```

Refer to the following screenshot:

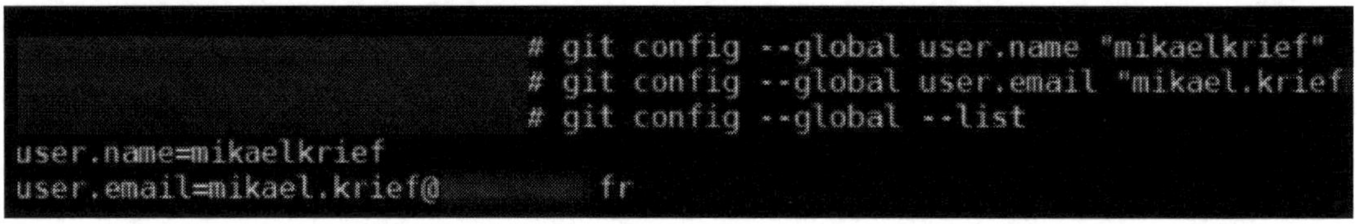

Figure 6.19 – Git configuration

Git is now configured and ready to use, but before using it, we will provide an overview of its vocabulary.

Useful Git vocabulary

Git is a tool that is very rich in objects and terminology and has its own concepts. Before using it, it is important to have some knowledge of its artifacts and the terms that compose it. Here is a brief list of this vocabulary:

- **Repository**: A repository is the basic element of Git; it is the storage space where the sources are tracked and versioned. There are **remote repositories** that centralize a team's code and allow team collaboration. There is also the **local repository**, which is a copy of the local repository on the local machine.

- **Clone**: Cloning is the act of making a local copy of a remote repository.

- **Commit**: A commit is a change made to one or more files, and the change is saved to the local repository. Each commit is unique and is identified by a unique number called **SHA-1**, by which code changes can be tracked.

- **Branch**: The code that is in the repository is stored by default in a `master` branch. A branch can create other branches that will be a replica of the master on which developers make changes, and that will allow us to work in isolation without affecting the master branch. At any time, we can merge one branch with another.

- **Merge**: This is an action that consists of merging the code of one branch with another.

- **Checkout**: This is an action that allows us to switch from one branch to another.

- **Fetch**: This is an action of retrieving the code from the remote repository without merging it with the local repository.

- **Pull**: This is an action that consists of updating your local repository from the remote repository. A pull is equivalent to a fetch and merge operation.

- **Push**: A push is the reverse action of a pull—it allows us to update the remote repository from the local repository.

- **Pull request (PR)**: A PR is a Git feature (initiated by GitHub) that provides a **graphical user interface (GUI)** client or web interface for discussing proposed changes, between teams' users, before integrating them into the main branch. If you want more information about PRs, read the GitHub documentation at `https://docs.github.com/en/github/collaborating-with-pull-requests/proposing-changes-to-your-work-with-pull-requests/about-pull-requests`.

These are the concepts to know when using Git and its workflow. Of course, this list is not exhaustive, and there are other important terms and notions; we can find information on several sites. Here is a small list:

- **GitHub vocabulary**: `https://help.github.com/en/articles/github-glossary`

- **Atlassian glossary**: `https://www.atlassian.com/git/glossary/terminology`

- **Linux Academy**: `https://linuxacademy.com/blog/linux/git-terms-explained/`

With these concepts explained, we can now see how to use Git with its command lines.

Git command lines

With everything we've seen so far on Git, we can now start manipulating it. The best way to do so is to first learn to use Git on the command line; then, once the process is assimilated, we can use the graphical tools better.

Here is a presentation of the main Git command lines that are now part of (or should be part of) developers' daily lives. We will see their application in practice in the next section, *Understanding the Git process and Gitflow pattern*.

The first command is the one that allows us to retrieve code from a remote repository.

Retrieving a remote repository

The first command line to know is the `clone` command, which makes a copy of a remote repository to create a local repository. The command to execute is shown here:

```
git clone <url of the remote repository>
```

The only mandatory parameter is the repository **Uniform Resource Locator** (**URL**) (any repository is identifiable by a unique URL). Once this command is executed, the content of the remote repository is downloaded to the local machine, and the local repository is automatically created and configured.

Initializing a local repository

Note that `init` is the Git command that allows you to create a local repository. To do this in the directory that will contain your local repository, run the following simple command:

```
git init
```

This command creates a `.git` directory that contains all of the folders and configuration files of the local repository.

Configuring a local repository

After the `init` command, the new local repository must be configured by setting up the linked remote repository. To make this setting, we will add `remote` with the following command:

```
git remote add <name> <url of the remote>
```

The name passed as a parameter allows this remote repository to be identified locally; it is the equivalent of an alias. It is also possible to configure several remote devices on our local repository.

Adding a file for the next commit

Making a commit (which we will see next) is to archive our changes in our local repository. When we edit files, we can choose which ones will be included in the next commit; it's a staged concept. The other files not selected will be set aside for a later commit.

To add files to the next commit, we execute the `add` command, as follows:

```
git add <files path to add>
```

So, for example, if we want all of the files modified at the next commit, execute the `git add .` command. We can also filter the files to be added with **regular expressions** (**RegEx**), such as `git add *.txt`.

Creating a commit

A commit is a Git entity that contains a list of changes made to files and that have been registered in the local repository. Making a commit, therefore, consists of archiving changes made to files that have been previously selected with the `add` command.

The command to create a commit is shown here:

```
git commit -m "<your commit message>"
```

The `-m` parameter corresponds to a message, or description, that we assign to this commit. The message is very important because we will be able to identify the reason for the changes in the files.

It is also possible to commit all files modified since the last commit, without having to execute the `add` command, by executing the `git commit -a -m "<message>"` command.

Once the commit is executed, the changes are archived in the local repository.

Updating the remote repository

When we make commits, they are stored in the local repository, and when we are ready to share them with the rest of the team for validation or deployment, we must publish them to the remote repository. To update a remote repository from commits made on a local repository, a `push` operation is performed with this command:

```
git push <alias> <branch>
```

The alias passed as a parameter corresponds to the alias of the remote repository configured in the Git configuration of the local repository (done by the `git remote add` command).

And the branch parameter is the branch to be updated—by default, it is the `master` branch.

Synchronizing the local repository from the remote

As we discussed previously, the Git command line is used to update the remote repository from the local repository. Now, to perform the reverse operation—that is, update the repository with all of the changes of the other members that have been pushed on the remote repository—we will perform a `pull` operation with this command:

```
git pull
```

The execution of this command leads to two operations:

1. Merging the local code with the remote code.
2. Committing to the local repository.

On the other hand, if we do not want to commit—to be able to make other changes, for example—instead of the `pull` command, we must execute `fetch` with this command:

```
git fetch
```

Its execution only merges the local code from the remote code, and to archive it, we will have to execute `commit` to update the local repository.

Managing branches

By default, when creating a repository, the code is placed in the main branch called `master`. In order to be able to isolate the developments of the `master` branch—for example, to develop a new feature, fix a bug, or even make technical experiments—we can create new branches from other branches and merge them together when we want to merge their code.

To create a branch from the current locally loaded branch, we execute the following command:

```
git branch <name of the desired branch>
```

To switch to another branch, we execute the following command:

```
git checkout <name of the branch>
```

This command changes the branch and loads the current working directory with the contents of that branch.

To merge a branch to the current branch, execute the `merge` command, as follows:

```
git merge <branch name>
```

With the name of the branch, we want to merge as a parameter.

Finally, to display a list of local branches, we execute the `branch` command, as follows:

```
git branch
```

Branch management is not easy to use from the command line. The graphical tools of Git, already mentioned, allow better visualization and management of the branches. We will see their uses in detail in the next section, which will deal with the Git process. That's all for the usual Git command lines, although there are many more to handle.

In the next section, we will put all of this into practice by applying the work and collaboration process with Git, and look at an overview of the Gitflow pattern.

Understanding the Git process and Gitflow pattern

So far, we have seen the fundamentals of a very powerful VCS, which is Git, with its installation, configuration, and some of its most common command lines. In this section, we will put all of this into practice with a case study that will show which Git process to apply throughout the life cycle of a project.

In this case study, for remote repositories, we will use **Azure Repos** (one of the Azure DevOps services), which is a free Git cloud platform that can be used for personal or even business projects. To learn more about Azure DevOps, consult the documentation here: https://azure.microsoft.com/en-us/services/devops/. We will often talk about it in this book.

Let's first look at how collaboration with Git is constituted, and then we will see how to isolate code using branches.

Starting with the Git process

In this lab, we will explain the Git collaboration process with a team of two developers who start a new application development project.

Here are the steps of the Git process that we will discuss in detail in this section:

1. The first developer commits the code on the local repository and pushes it to the remote repository.
2. Then, the second developer gets the pushed code from the remote repository.
3. The second developer updates this code, creates a commit, and pushes the new version of the code to the remote repository.
4. Finally, the first developer retrieves the last version of the code in the local repository.

The Gitflow data flow that we'll learn about is illustrated in the following diagram:

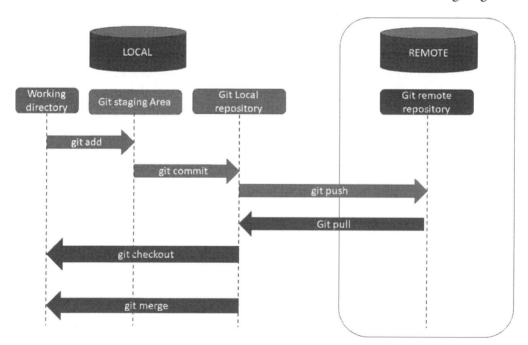

Figure 6.20 – Git data flow

However, before we start working with Git commands, we will have a look at the steps to create and configure a Git repository in Azure Repos.

Creating and configuring a Git repository

To start with, we will create a remote Git repository in Azure DevOps that will be used to collaborate with other team members. Follow these steps:

1. In Azure DevOps, we will create a new project, as follows:

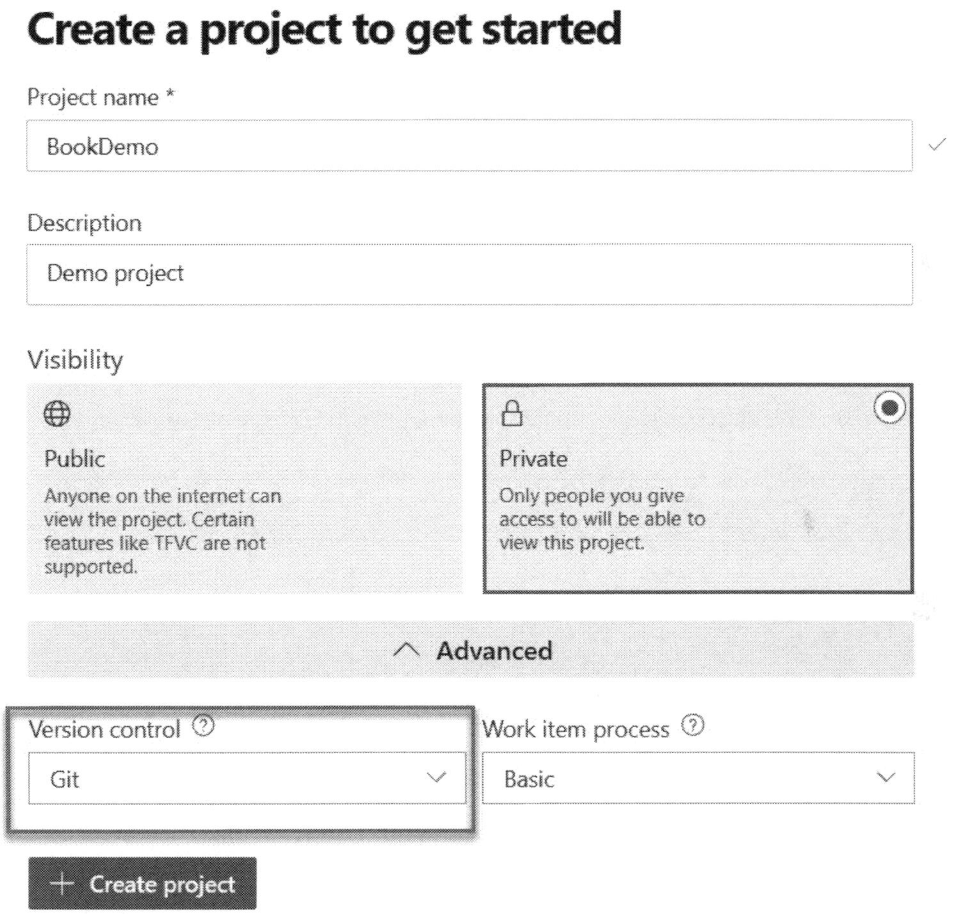

Create a project to get started

Project name *

> BookDemo

Description

> Demo project

Visibility

⊕	🔒 ⦿
Public	**Private**
Anyone on the internet can view the project. Certain features like TFVC are not supported.	Only people you give access to will be able to view this project.

︿ **Advanced**

Version control ⑦

> Git ⌄

Work item process ⑦

> Basic ⌄

+ Create project

Figure 6.21 – Creating an Azure DevOps project

2. Enter a name and description for the project, and as we can see from the preceding screenshot, the **Version control** type is **Git**. Then, on the left-side menu, we click on the Azure **Repos** service, as follows:

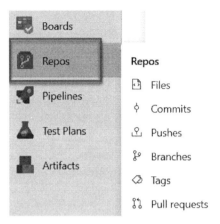

Figure 6.22 – Azure Repos menu

3. A default repository is already created, and it has the same name as the project, as we can see here:

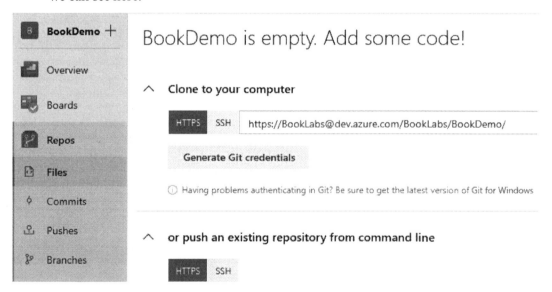

Figure 6.23 – Azure DevOps new repository

Now that the Git repository is created in Azure Repos, we will see how to initialize and configure our local working directory to work with this Git repository.

4. To initialize this repository, we will create a local directory and name it (for example, bookProject). This will contain the application code.

5. Once this directory is created, we will initialize a local Git repository by executing inside the bookProject folder the git init command, as follows:

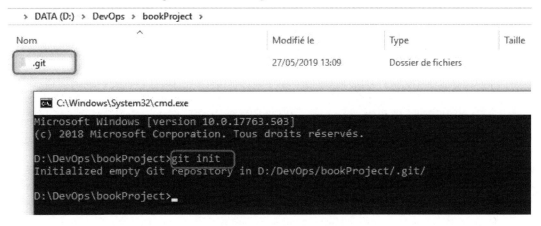

Figure 6.24 – git init command

The result of the preceding command is a confirmation message and a new .git directory. This new directory will contain all of the information and configuration of the local Git repository.

6. Then, we will configure this local repository to be linked to the Azure DevOps remote repository. This link will allow the synchronization of local and remote repositories. For this, in Azure DevOps, we get the URL of the repository, which is found in the repository information, as shown in the following screenshot:

BookDemo is empty. Add some code!

Figure 6.25 – Azure DevOps repository URL

7. Run the git remote add command inside the bookProject folder that we created in *Step 4*, as follows:

```
git remote add origin <url of the remote repository>
```

By executing the preceding command, we create an `origin` alias that will point to the remote repository URL.

> **Note**
>
> This whole initialization and configuration procedure also applies to an empty directory, as in our case, or to a directory that already contains code that we want to archive.

So, we now have a local Git repository that we will work on. After creating and configuring our repository, we will start developing code for our application and collaborate using the Git process by starting with a commit of the code.

Committing the code

The first step in the process is the code commit, which allows you to store your code changes in your local Git repository, by following these steps:

1. In our directory, we will create a `Readme.md` file that contains the following example text:

Figure 6.26 – Sample of README file

2. To make a commit of this file in our local repository, we must add it to the list of the next commit by executing the `git add .` command (the `.` character at the end indicates to include all of the files to modify, add, or delete).

3. We can also see the status of changes that will be made to the local repository by running the `git status` command, as shown in the following screenshot:

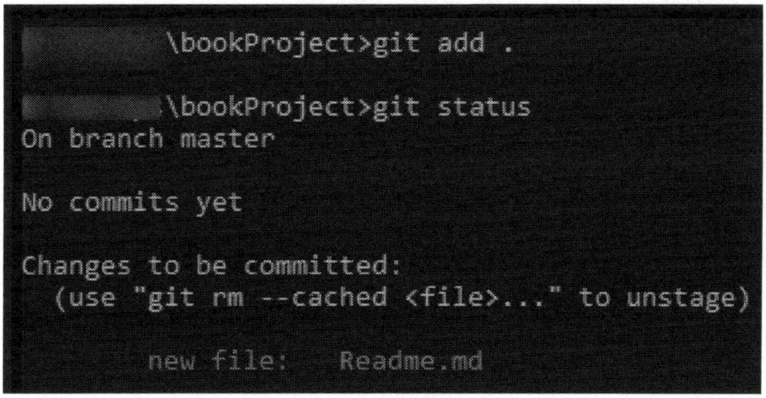

```
              \bookProject>git add .

              \bookProject>git status
On branch master

No commits yet

Changes to be committed:
  (use "git rm --cached <file>..." to unstage)

      new file:   Readme.md
```

Figure 6.27 – git add . command

From the preceding execution, we can see that a Readme.md file is created and it will also integrate to commit.

The last operation to do is validate the change by archiving it in the local repository, and for this, we execute the following command:

```
git commit -m "Add file readme.md"
```

We make a commit with a description, for keeping track of changes. Here is a screenshot of the preceding command:

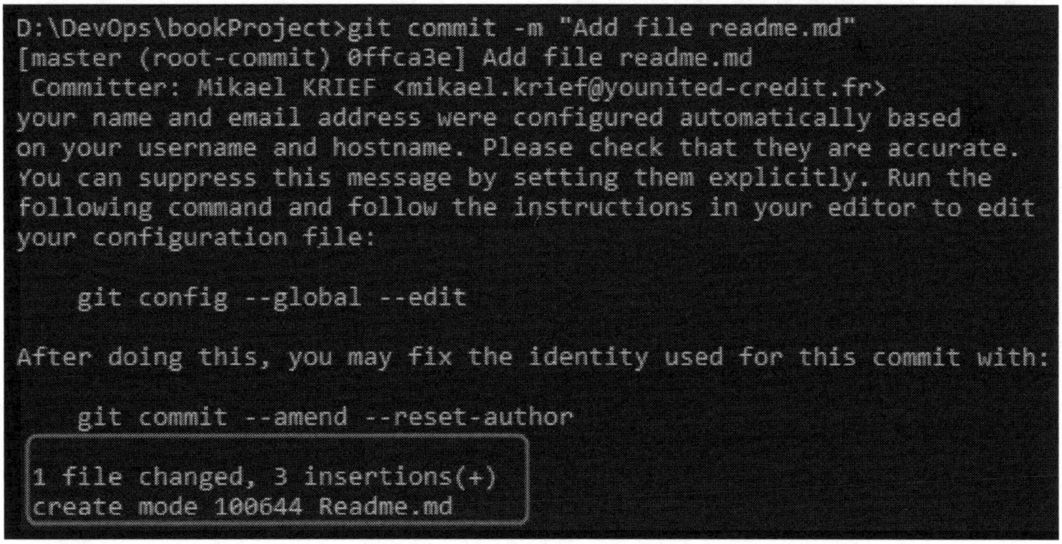

```
D:\DevOps\bookProject>git commit -m "Add file readme.md"
[master (root-commit) 0ffca3e] Add file readme.md
 Committer: Mikael KRIEF <mikael.krief@younited-credit.fr>
your name and email address were configured automatically based
on your username and hostname. Please check that they are accurate.
You can suppress this message by setting them explicitly. Run the
following command and follow the instructions in your editor to edit
your configuration file:

    git config --global --edit

After doing this, you may fix the identity used for this commit with:

    git commit --amend --reset-author

 1 file changed, 3 insertions(+)
 create mode 100644 Readme.md
```

Figure 6.28 – git commit command

> **Note**
>
> In this example, we also notice a Git message that gives information about the user's Git configuration.

Now that our local Git repository is up to date with our changes, we just have to archive them on the remote repository.

Archiving on the remote repository

To archive local changes and allow the team to work and collaborate on this code as well, we will push our commit in the remote repository by executing the following command:

```
git push origin master
```

We indicate to the `git push` command the alias and the branch of the remote repository. During the first execution of this command, we will be asked to authenticate to the Azure DevOps repository, as shown in the following screenshot:

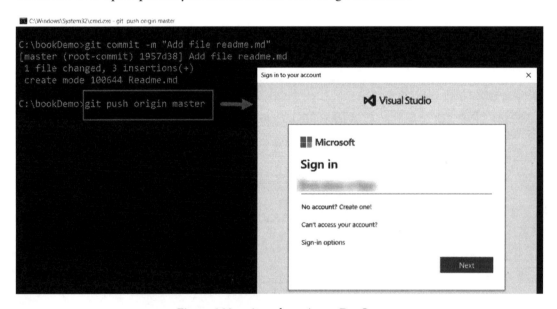

Figure 6.29 – git push on Azure DevOps

And after authentication, the push is executed, as follows:

```
          \bookProject>git push origin master
Enumerating objects: 3, done.
Counting objects: 100% (3/3), done.
Writing objects: 100% (3/3), 275 bytes | 275.00 KiB/s, done.
Total 3 (delta 0), reused 0 (delta 0)
remote: Analyzing objects... (3/3) (6 ms)
remote: Storing packfile... done (324 ms)
remote: Storing index... done (148 ms)
To https://dev.azure.com/BookLabs/BookDemo/_git/BookDemo
 * [new branch]      master -> master
```

Figure 6.30 – git push result

The remote repository is up to date with our changes, and in the Azure Repos interface, we can see the code of the remote repository. The following screenshot shows the directory in Azure Repos that contains the added file:

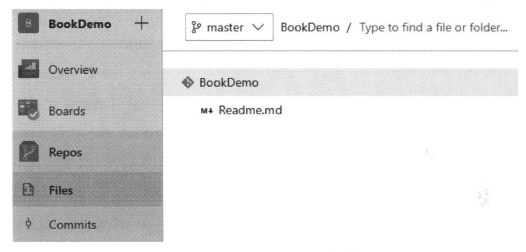

Figure 6.31 – Azure Repos new file added

That's it: we have performed the first major step of the Git process, which consists of initializing a repository and pushing code into a remote repository. The next step is to make changes to the code by another team member.

Cloning the repository

When another member wants to retrieve the entire remote repository code for the first time, they perform a clone operation, and to do so, they must execute this command:

```
git clone <repository url>
```

The execution of this command performs these actions, as follows:

1. Creates a new directory with the name of the repository.
2. Creates a local repository with its initialization and configuration.
3. Downloads the remote code.

The team member can therefore modify and make changes to the code.

Updating the code

When the code is modified and the developer updates their changes on the remote repository, they will perform exactly the same actions as when the remote repository was initialized, with the execution of the following commands:

```
git add .
git commit -m "update the code"
git push origin master
```

We added the files to the next commit, created a commit, and pushed the commit to the remote repository.

The last remaining step is the retrieval of updates by other members.

Retrieving updates

When one member updates the remote repository, it is possible to retrieve these updates and update our local repository with the changes by running the git pull command, as follows:

```
git pull origin master
```

The following screenshot shows the execution of this git pull command:

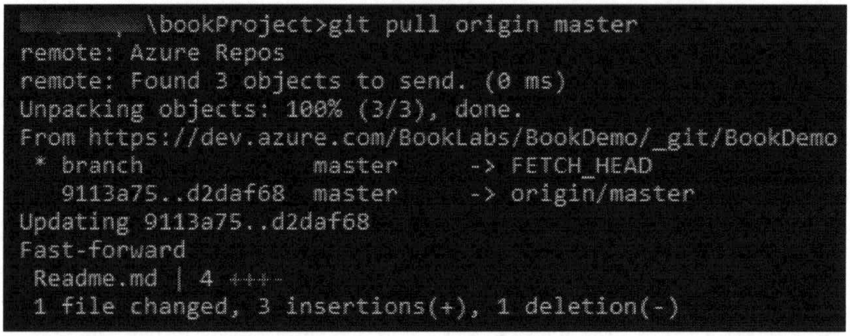

Figure 6.32 – git pull command

From the preceding execution, we indicate the `origin` alias and `master` branch to be updated in the local repository, and its execution displays the pushed commits. At the end of the execution of this command, our local repository is up to date.

For the rest of the process with the code update, this is the same as we saw earlier in the *Updating the code* section.

We have just seen the simple process of using Git, but it is also possible to isolate its development with the use of branches.

Isolating your code with branches

When developing an application, we often need to modify part of the code without wanting to impact the existing stable code of the application. For this, we will use a feature that exists in all VCSs that allows us to create and manage branches.

The mechanics of using the branches are quite simple, as outlined here:

1. From a branch, we create another branch.
2. We develop this new branch.
3. In case we work in teams, create a PR for a discussion about the code changes. If reviewers agree with these changes, they approve the changes' code.
4. To apply the changes made on this new branch to the original branch, a merge operation is performed.

Conceptually, a branch system is represented in this way:

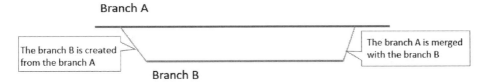

Figure 6.33 – Branch diagram

In this diagram, we see that branch **B** is created from branch **A**. These two branches will be modified by development teams for adding a new feature to our application. But in the end, branch **A** is merged with branch **B**, and hence the branch **B** code changes.

Now that we have seen the branch bases, let's look at how to use branches in Git by following these steps:

1. The purpose of this lab is to create a `Feature1` branch from the `master` branch. Then, after some changes on the `Feature1` branch, we will merge the code changes from the `Feature1` branch to the `master` branch. First, create a `Feature1` branch on the local repository, from `master`, with the help of the following command:

    ```
    git branch Feature1
    ```

    The execution of this command created a new branch, `Feature1`, which contains exactly the same code as the parent branch, `master`.

2. To load your working directory with the code of this branch, we execute the following command:

    ```
    git checkout Feature1
    ```

    From the following output, we can see the switch of the branch:

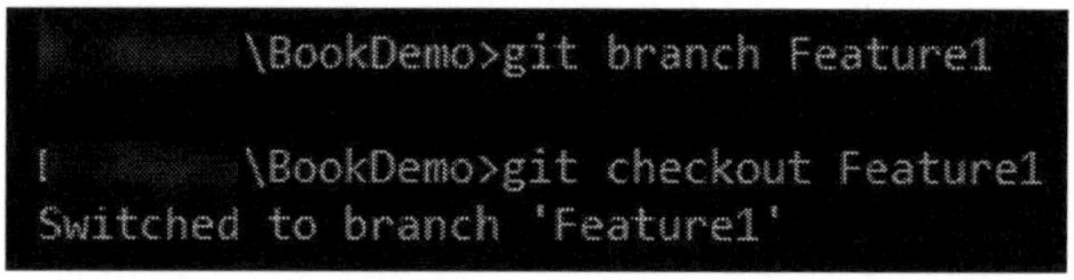

    Figure 6.34 – Git switch branch

3. We can also see a list of branches of our local repository with the following command:

    ```
    git branch
    ```

    The output of this command is shown here:

    Figure 6.35 – git branch command

    During execution, we can see two branches and the active branch as well.

4. Now, we will make changes to our code on this branch. The update mechanism is identical to everything we have already seen previously, so we will execute the following commands:

    ```
    git add .
    ```
    ```
    git commit -m "Add feature 1 code"
    ```

5. For the `push` operation, we will specify the name of the `Feature1` branch in the parameter with this command:

```
git push origin Feature1
```

The following screenshot shows the code execution that performs all of these steps:

```
\BookDemo>git add .

\BookDemo>git commit -m "Add feature 1 code"
[Feature1 0ed2a45] Add feature 1 code
 1 file changed, 3 insertions(+), 1 deletion(-)

\BookDemo>git push origin Feature1
Enumerating objects: 5, done.
Counting objects: 100% (5/5), done.
Delta compression using up to 4 threads
Compressing objects: 100% (2/2), done.
Writing objects: 100% (3/3), 306 bytes | 153.00 KiB/s, done.
Total 3 (delta 1), reused 0 (delta 0)
remote: Analyzing objects... (3/3) (97 ms)
remote: Storing packfile... done (188 ms)
remote: Storing index... done (92 ms)
To https://dev.azure.com/BookLabs/BookDemo/_git/BookDemo
 * [new branch]      Feature1 -> Feature1
```

Figure 6.36 – Adding a Git branch

6. With the preceding commands that we executed, we created a commit on the `Feature1` branch. We then executed the `push` command to publish the new branch as well as its commit in the remote repository. On the other hand, in the Azure Repos interface, we can see our two branches in the **Branches** section, as shown in the following screenshot:

Figure 6.37 – Azure Repos branches list

7. Before merging the code, we create a PR for a discussion about the changes. The following screenshots show PR creation and approval steps in Azure DevOps.

    We start by creating a PR, as follows:

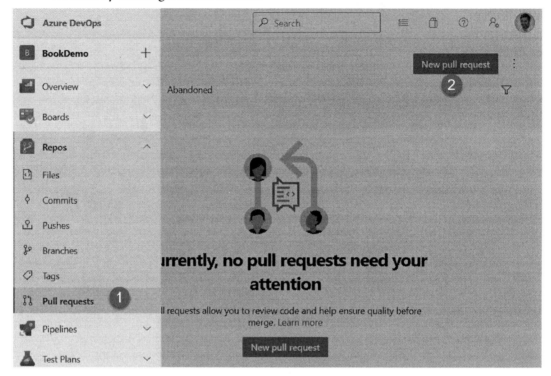

Figure 6.38 – Azure Repos: Creating a PR

Then, fill in the form of this PR by selecting the source and target branches, entering a title and description, and choosing reviewers. We can also view the difference in the code that will be merged. The process is illustrated in the following screenshot:

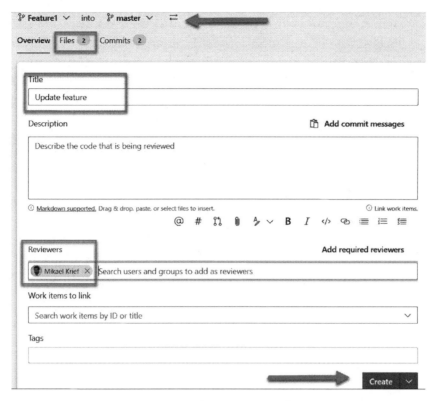

Figure 6.39 – Azure Repos PR form

Finally, the reviewers will review, approve, or reject the changes (they can also merge directly), as illustrated in the following screenshot:

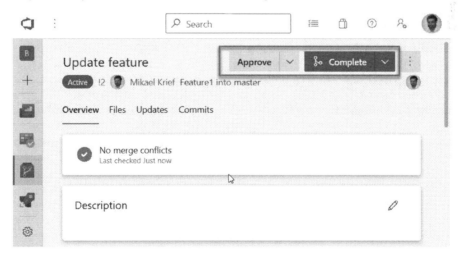

Figure 6.40 – Azure Repos PR approval

8. The last step in our process is to merge the code of the `Feature1` branch into that of the master branch, `master`. To perform this merge, we will first load our working directory with the `master` branch, then merge the `Feature1` branch to the current branch, which is `master`.

To do this, we will execute the following commands:

```
git checkout master
git merge Feature1
```

The execution of these commands is displayed as follows:

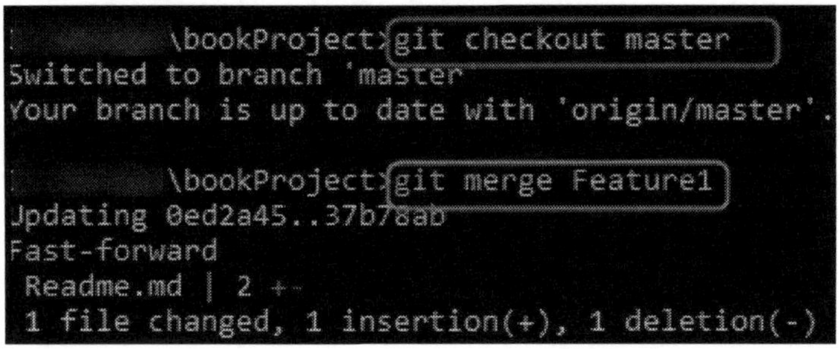

```
              \bookProject>git checkout master
Switched to branch 'master'
Your branch is up to date with 'origin/master'.

              \bookProject>git merge Feature1
Updating 0ed2a45..37b78ab
Fast-forward
 Readme.md | 2 +-
 1 file changed, 1 insertion(+), 1 deletion(-)
```

Figure 6.41 – git merge branch

At the end of its execution, the code of the `master` branch thus contains the changes made in the `Feature1` branch.

We have just seen the use of branches and their merges in Git; now, let's look at the Gitflow branch pattern and its utility.

Branching strategy with Gitflow

When we start using branches in Git, the question that often arises is: *Which is the right branch strategy to use?* In other words, what is the key that we need to isolate our code—is it by environment, functionality, theme, or release?

This question has no universal answer, and the management of branches within a project depends on the context of the project. However, there are branch strategy patterns that have been approved by several communities and a multitude of users that allow a better collaboration process in a project under Git.

I suggest we have a closer look at one of these branch patterns, which is Gitflow.

The Gitflow pattern

One of these patterns is **Gitflow**, developed by *nvie*, which is very popular and has a very easy-to-learn Git workflow.

A branch diagram of Gitflow is shown here:

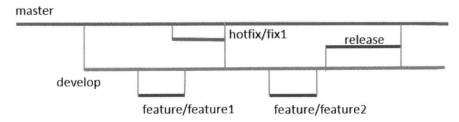

Figure 6.42 – Gitflow diagram

Let's look at the details of this workflow, as well as the purpose of each of these branches in their order of creation, as follows:

1. First of all, we have the master branch, which contains the code that is currently in production. No developer is working directly on it.

2. From this master branch, we create a develop branch, which is the branch that will contain the changes to be deployed in the next delivery of the application.

3. For each of the application's functionalities, a feature/<name of the feature> branch is created (/ will hence create a feature directory) from the develop branch.

4. As soon as a feature is finished being coded, the branch of the feature is merged into the develop branch.

5. Then, as soon as we want to deploy all of the latest features developed, we create a release branch from develop.

6. The release branch content is deployed in all environments successively.

7. As soon as the deployment in production has taken place, the release branch is merged with the master branch, and, with this merge operation, the master branch contains the production code. Hence, the code that is on the release branch and feature branch is no longer necessary, and these branches can be deleted.

8. If a bug is detected in production, we create a hotfix/<bug name> branch; then, once the bug is fixed, we merge this branch into the master and develop branches to propagate the fix on the next branches and deployments.

After seeing the workflow of the Gitflow pattern, we'll discuss the tools that facilitate its implementation.

Gitflow tools

To help teams and developers to use Gitflow, *nvie* created a Git override command-line tool that allows you to easily create branches according to the workflow step. This tool is available on the *nvie* GitHub page here: `https://github.com/nvie/gitflow`.

On the other hand, there are also Git graphical tools that support the Gitflow model, such as GitKraken (`https://www.gitkraken.com/`) and Sourcetree (`https://www.sourcetreeapp.com/`). These tools allow us to use the Gitflow process via a graphical interface, as shown in the following screenshot, with the use of Sourcetree with a `Git-flow` feature that allows us to create a branch using the Gitflow pattern.

The following screenshot shows the configuration of Sourcetree for Gitflow pattern branch naming:

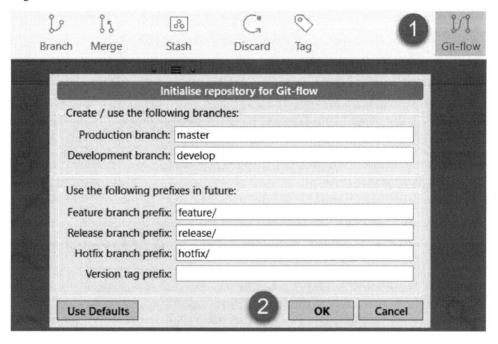

Figure 6.43 – Sourcetree Git-flow tool

Then, after this configuration, we can create a branch easily with this name, as shown in the following screenshot:

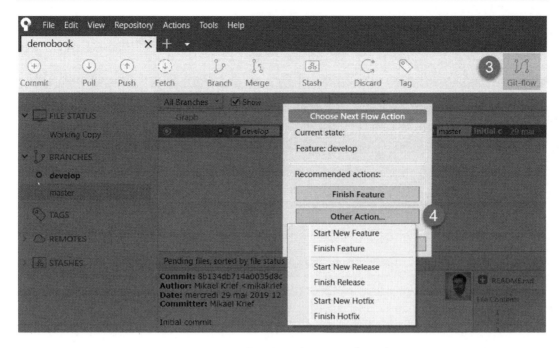

Figure 6.44 – Creating a Sourcetree branch

As shown in the preceding screenshots, we use Sourcetree and the graphical interface that allows us to create branches intuitively.

> **Note**
>
> For more documentation on Gitflow and its process, read this article: `https://jeffkreeftmeijer.com/git-flow/`.

To get started with Gitflow, I suggest you get used to small projects, then you will see that the mechanism is the same for larger projects. In this section, we saw the process of using Git's command lines with its workflow. Then, we talked about the management of development branches, and finally, we went a little further into branches with Gitflow, which allows the simple management of branches and a better development workflow with Git.

Summary

Git is today an essential tool for all developers; it allows us to use command lines or graphical tools and share and version code for better team collaboration.

In this chapter, we saw how to install Git on the different OSes and an overview of the main command lines. Then, through a small lab, we saw the Git workflow with the application of Git command lines. Finally, we presented the isolation of code with the implementation of branches and the use of the Gitflow pattern, which gives a simple model of branch strategy.

In the next chapter, we will talk about CI/CD, which is one of the key practices of the DevOps culture.

Questions

1. What is Git?

2. Which command is used to initialize a repository?

3. What is the name of the Git artifact for saving part of the code?

4. Which Git command allows you to save your code in the local repository?

5. Which Git command allows you to send your code to the remote repository?

6. Which Git command allows you to update your local repository from the remote repository?

7. Which Git mechanism is used for Git code isolation?

8. What is Gitflow?

Further reading

If you want to know more about Git, here are some resources:

- Git documentation: https://www.git-scm.com/doc

- *Pro Git* book: https://git-scm.com/book/en/v2

- *Mastering Git* book: https://www.packtpub.com/application-development/mastering-git

- *Set up Git*: https://try.github.io/

- *Learn Git Branching*: https://learngitbranching.js.org/

- Atlassian Git tutorials: https://www.atlassian.com/git/tutorials

- *git-flow cheat sheet*: https://danielkummer.github.io/git-flow-cheatsheet/

7
Continuous Integration and Continuous Delivery

One of the main pillars of **development-operations (DevOps)** culture is the implementation of **continuous integration (CI)** and deployment processes, as we explained in *Chapter 1, The DevOps Culture and Infrastructure as Code Practices.*

In the previous chapter, we looked at the use of Git with its command lines and usage workflow, and in this chapter, we will look at the important role Git has in the CI/CD workflow.

CI is a process that provides rapid feedback on the consistency and quality of code to all members of a team. It occurs when each user's code commit retrieves and merges the code from a remote repository, compiles it, and tests it.

Continuous delivery (CD) is the automation of the process that deploys an application in different stages (or environments).

In this chapter, we will learn the principles of the CI/CD process as well as its practical use with different tools such as **Jenkins**, **Azure Pipelines**, and **GitLab CI**. For each of these tools, we will present the advantages, disadvantages, and best practices, and look at a practical example of implementing a CI/CD pipeline.

You will learn about the concept of a CI/CD pipeline. After this, we will explore package managers and the role they play in the pipeline.

Then, you will learn how to install Jenkins and, finally, build a CI/CD pipeline on Jenkins, Azure Pipelines, and GitLab CI.

This chapter covers the following topics:

- CI/CD principles
- Using a package manager in the CI/CD process
- Using Jenkins for CI/CD implementation
- Using Azure Pipelines for CI/CD
- Using GitLab CI

Technical requirements

The only requirement for this chapter is to have Git installed on your system, as detailed in the previous chapter.

The source code for this chapter is available at `https://github.com/PacktPublishing/Learning-DevOps-Second-Edition/tree/main/CHAP07`.

Check out the following video to see the code in action: `https://bit.ly/3s9G8Pj`.

CI/CD principles

To implement a CI/CD pipeline, it is important to know the different elements that will be required to build an efficient and safe pipeline. In order to understand the principles of CI/CD, the following diagram shows the different steps of a CI/CD workflow, which we already saw in *Chapter 1, The DevOps Culture and Infrastructure as Code Practices*:

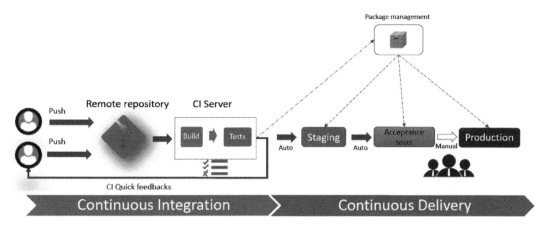

Figure 7.1 – CI/CD workflow

Let's look in detail at each of these steps in order to list the artifacts of the CI/CD process.

CI

The CI phase checks the code archived by the team members. It must be executed on each commit that has been pushed to the remote repository.

The setting up of a Git-type **source control version (SCV)** is a necessary prerequisite that makes it possible to centralize the code of all the members of a team.

The team will have to decide on a code branch that will be used for CI. For example, we can use the `master` branch, or the `develop` branch as part of GitFlow; it just needs to be an active branch that very regularly centralizes code changes.

In addition, CI is achieved by an automatic task suite that is executed on a server, following similar patterns executed on a developer's laptop that has the necessary tools for CI; this server is called the **CI server**.

The CI server can be either of the on-premises type, installed in the company data center, such as Jenkins or TeamCity, or perhaps a cloud type that we don't have to worry about installing and maintaining, such as Azure Pipelines or GitLab CI.

The tasks performed during the CI phase must be automated and take into account all the elements that are necessary for the verification of the code.

These tasks are generally the compilation of code and the execution of unit tests with code coverage. We can also add static code analysis with SonarQube (or SonarCloud), which we will look at in *Chapter 12, Static Code Analysis with SonarQube*.

At the end of the verification tasks, in many cases, the CI generates an application package that will be deployed on the different environments (also called **stages**).

To be able to host this package, we need a package manager, also called a **repository manager**, which can be on-premises (installed locally) such as Nexus, Artifactory, or ProGet, or a **software-as-a-service (SaaS)** solution such as Azure Pipelines, Azure Artifacts, or the GitHub Packages registry. This package must also be neutral in terms of environment configuration and *must* be versioned in order to deploy the application in a previous version if necessary.

CD

Once the application has been packaged and stored in a package manager during CI, the CD process is ready to retrieve the package and deploy it in different environments.

The deployment in each environment consists of a succession of automated tasks that are also executed on a remote server that has access to the different environments.

It is, therefore, necessary to involve Dev, Ops, and also the security team in the implementation of CI/CD tools and processes. It will, indeed, be this union of people with the tools and processes that will deploy applications on the different servers or cloud resources, respecting the network rules but also the company's security standards.

During the deployment phase, it is often necessary to modify the configuration of the application in the generated package in order for it to be adapted to the target environment. It is, therefore, necessary to integrate a **configuration manager** that is already present in common CI/CD tools such as Jenkins, Azure Pipelines, or Octopus Deploy. In addition, when there is a new configuration key, it is good practice for every environment, including production, to be entered with the involvement of the Ops team.

Finally, the triggering of a deployment can be done automatically, but for environments that are more critical (for example, production environments), heavily regulated companies may have gateways that require a manual trigger with checks on the people authorized to trigger the deployment.

The different tools for setting up a CI/CD pipeline are listed here:

- An SCV
- A package manager
- A CI server
- A configuration manager

But let's not forget that all these tools will only be really effective in delivering added value to the product if the Dev and Ops teams work together around them.

We have just looked at the principles of implementing a CI/CD pipeline. In the rest of the chapter, we will look at the practical implementation with different tools, starting with package managers.

Using a package manager in the CI/CD process

A package manager is a central repository to centralize and share packages, development libraries, tools, and software.

For consumer clients that use package managers, the benefit is the possibility to track, update, install, and remove installed packages.

There are many public package managers, such as NuGet, **Node Package Manager (npm)**, Maven, Bower, and Chocolatey, that provide frameworks or tools for developers in different languages and platforms.

The following screenshot is from the NuGet package manager, which publicly provides more than 150,000 .NET frameworks:

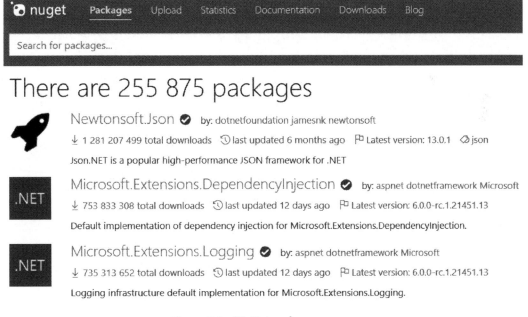

Figure 7.2 – NuGet package manager

One of the advantages for the developer of using this type of package manager is that they don't have to store the packages with the application sources but can make them a reference in a configuration file so that the packages will be automatically retrieved.

In an enterprise application, things are a little different because, although developers use packages from public managers, some elements that are generated in an enterprise must remain internal.

Indeed, it is often the case that frameworks (such as NuGet or npm libraries) are developed internally and cannot be exposed publicly. Moreover, as we have seen in the CI/CD pipeline, we need to make a package for our application and store it in a package manager that will be private to the company.

That's why looking at package managers such as NuGet and npm, which can be used within an enterprise or for personal needs, is suggested.

Private NuGet and npm repository

If you need to centralize your NuGet or npm packages, you can create your own local repository.

To create your **NuGet server** instance, here is the Microsoft documentation: `https://docs.microsoft.com/en-us/nuget/hosting-packages/overview`.

For npm, we can also install it locally with the `npm local-npm` package, whose documentation is available here: `https://www.npmjs.com/package/local-npm`.

The problem with installing one repository per package-type method is that we need to install and maintain a repository and its infrastructure for the different types of packages.

This is why it is preferable to switch to universal repository solutions such as Nexus (Sonatype), ProGet, and Artifactory for on-premises solutions, and Azure Artifacts, MyGet, or Artifactory for SaaS solutions.

To understand how a package manager works, we will look at Nexus Repository OSS and Azure Artifacts.

Nexus Repository OSS

Nexus Repository is a product of the Sonatype company (`https://www.sonatype.com/`), which specializes in **development-security-operations** (**DevSecOps**) tools that integrate security controls in the code of applications.

Nexus Repository exists in an open source/free version, and its documentation is available at `https://www.sonatype.com/nexus-repository-oss?smtNoRedir=1` and `https://help.sonatype.com/repomanager3`.

Before installing and using Nexus, please take into consideration the software and hardware requirements detailed in the requirements documentation here: `https://help.sonatype.com/repomanager3/installation/system-requirements`.

For the installation and configuration steps, refer to the installation procedure, which is available here: `https://help.sonatype.com/repomanager3/installation`.

You can also use it via a Docker container (we will look at Docker in detail in the next chapter), and here is the documentation regarding this: `https://hub.docker.com/r/sonatype/nexus3/`.

Once Nexus Repository is installed, we must create a repository by following these steps:

1. In the **Repositories** section, click on the **Create repository** button.
2. Then, choose the type of packages (for example, npm, NuGet, or Bower) that will be stored in the repository, as shown in the following screenshot:

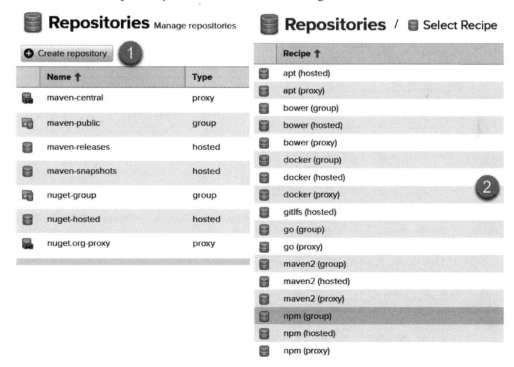

Figure 7.3 – Nexus package manager

Nexus is a high-performance and widely used enterprise repository, but it requires effort to install and maintain it. This is not the case for SaaS package managers such as Azure Artifacts, which we'll look at now.

Azure Artifacts

Azure Artifacts is one of the services provided by Azure DevOps. We already looked at it in the previous chapter, and we will also cover it again later, in the *Using Azure Pipelines for CI/CD* section of this chapter. It is hosted in the cloud, and therefore allows private package feeds to be managed.

The packages supported today are NuGet, npm, Maven, Gradle, Python, and also universal packages. The main difference compared with Nexus is that in Azure Artifacts, the feed is not by package type, and one feed can contain different types of packages.

One of the advantages of Azure Artifacts is that it is fully integrated with other Azure DevOps services such as Azure Pipelines, which allows for the management of CI/CD pipelines, as we will see shortly.

In Azure Artifacts, there is also a type of package called a **universal package** that allows the storing of all types of files (called a **package**) in a feed that can be consumed by other services or users.

Here is an example of an Azure Artifacts feed containing several types of packages, in which we can see one NuGet package, one npm package, one universal package, one Maven package, and one Python package:

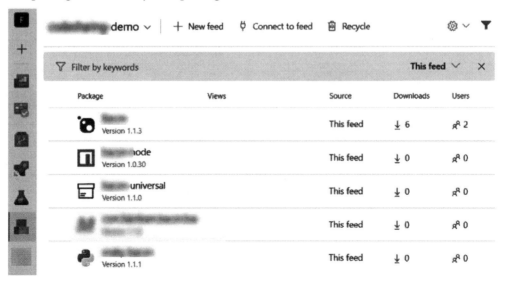

Figure 7.4 – Azure Artifacts packages

Azure Artifacts has the advantage of being in SaaS offering mode, so there is no installation or infrastructure to manage; for more information, the documentation is available here: `https://azure.microsoft.com/en-us/services/devops/artifacts/`.

We finished this overview of package managers with the local NuGet server instance, NPM, Nexus, and Azure Artifacts. Of course, there are many other package manager tools that should be considered according to the company's needs.

After looking at package managers, we will now implement a CI/CD pipeline with a well-known tool called **Jenkins**.

Using Jenkins for CI/CD implementation

Jenkins is one of the oldest CI tools, initially released in 2011. It is open source and developed in Java.

Jenkins has become famous thanks to the large community working on it and its plugins. Indeed, there are more than 1,500 Jenkins plugins that allow you to perform all types of actions within your jobs. And if, despite everything, one of your tasks does not have a plugin, you can create one yourself.

In this section, we will look at the installation and configuration of Jenkins and will create a CI Jenkins job that will be executed during the commit of code that is in a Git repository.

The source code of the demonstration application is a Java project that is open source and available on the GitHub Microsoft repository space here: `https://github.com/microsoft/MyShuttle2`. To be able to use it, you need to fork it into your GitHub account.

Before talking about the Jenkins job, we will see how to install and configure Jenkins.

Installing and configuring Jenkins

Jenkins is a cross-platform tool that can be installed on any type of support, such as **virtual machines** (**VMs**) or even Docker containers. Its installation documentation is available here: `https://jenkins.io/doc/book/installing/`.

For our demo, and to quickly access the configuration of a CI/CD pipeline, we will use Jenkins on an Azure VM. In fact, Azure Marketplace contains a VM with Jenkins and its prerequisites already installed.

These steps show how to create an Azure VM with Jenkins and its basic configuration:

1. To get all the steps to create an Azure VM with Jenkins already installed, read the documentation available here: `https://docs.microsoft.com/en-us/azure/jenkins/install-jenkins-solution-template`.

   The following screenshot shows Jenkins integration on Azure Marketplace:

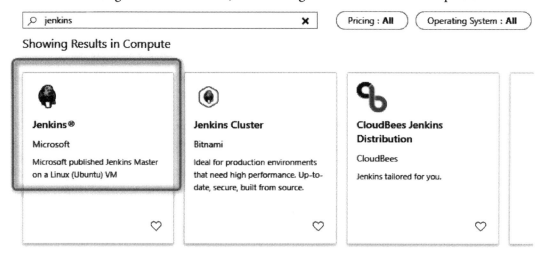

Figure 7.5 – Jenkins on Azure Marketplace

2. Once installed and created, we will access Jenkins in the browser by providing its **Uniform Resource Locator** (**URL**) in the Azure portal in the **DNS name** field, as shown in the following screenshot:

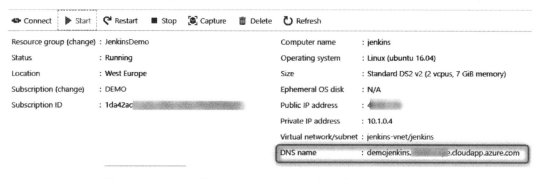

Figure 7.6 – Azure Domain Name System (DNS) name of Jenkins

3. Follow the displayed instructions on the Jenkins home page to enable access to this Jenkins instance via secure **Secure Sockets Layer** (**SSL**) tunneling. For more details about this step, read the documentation at `https://docs.microsoft.com/en-us/azure/jenkins/install-jenkins-solution-template#connect-to-jenkins` and this article: `https://jenkins.io/blog/2017/04/20/secure-jenkins-on-azure/`.

4. Then, follow the configuration instructions on the **Unlock Jenkins** message displayed on the Jenkins screen. Once the configuration is complete, we get Jenkins ready to create a CI job.

In order to use GitHub features in Jenkins, we also installed the **GitHub integration plugin** from the Jenkins plugin management by following this documentation: `https://jenkins.io/doc/book/managing/plugins/`.

The following screenshot shows the installation of the GitHub plugin:

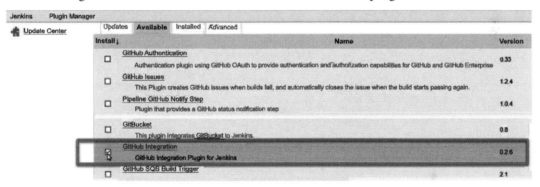

Figure 7.7 – Jenkins GitHub integration

Now that we have installed the GitHub plugin in Jenkins, let's look at how to configure GitHub with a webhook for its integration with Jenkins.

Configuring a GitHub webhook

In order for Jenkins to run a new job, we must first create a webhook in the GitHub repository. This webhook will be used to notify Jenkins as soon as a new push occurs in the repository.

To do this, follow these steps:

1. In the GitHub repository, go to the **Settings | Webhooks** menu.

2. Click on the **Add Webhook** button.

3. In the **Payload URL** field, fill in the URL address of Jenkins followed by / `github-webhook/`, leave the secret input as it is, and choose the **Just the push event** option.

4. Validate the webhook.

The following screenshot shows the configuration of a GitHub webhook for Jenkins:

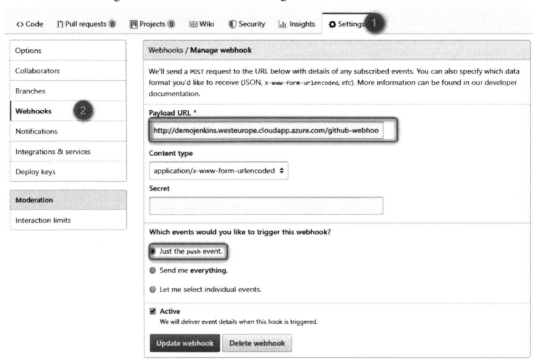

Figure 7.8 – GitHub webhook for Jenkins configuration

5. Finally, we can check on the GitHub interface that the webhook is well configured and that it communicates with Jenkins, as illustrated in the following screenshot:

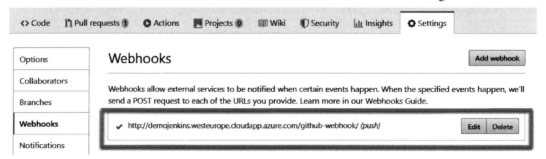

Figure 7.9 – GitHub Webhooks' validation

The configuration of GitHub is done. We will now proceed to create a new CI job in Jenkins.

Configuring a Jenkins CI job

To configure Jenkins, let's follow these steps:

1. First, we will create a new job by clicking on **New Item** or on the **create new jobs** link, as shown in the following screenshot:

Figure 7.10 – Creating a new job in Jenkins

2. On the job configuration form, enter the name of the job—for example, demoCI—and choose the **Freestyle project** template, and then validate that by clicking on **OK**, as shown in the following screenshot:

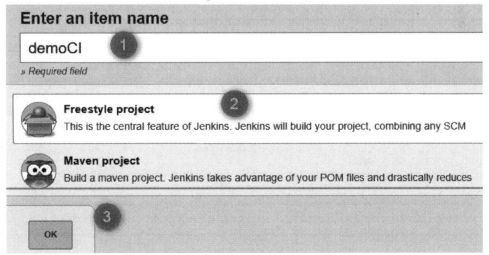

Figure 7.11 – Jenkins job name

3.   Then, we configure the job with the following parameters:

- In the **GitHub project** input, we enter the URL of the GitHub repository, as follows:

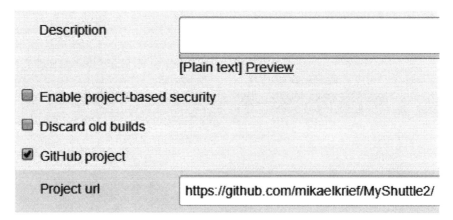

Figure 7.12 – Jenkins job: GitHub

- In the **Source Code Management** section, enter the URL of the GitHub repository and the code branch, like this:

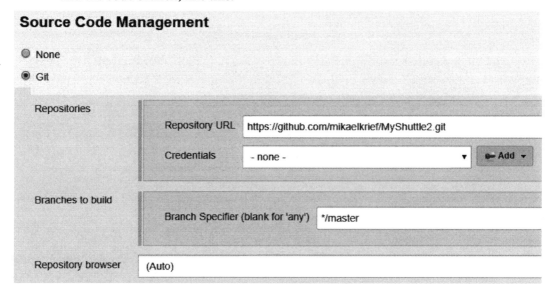

Figure 7.13 – Jenkins job: GitHub configuration

- In the **Build Triggers** section, check the **GitHub hook trigger for GITScm polling** box, like this:

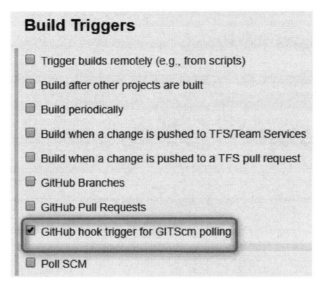

Figure 7.14 – Jenkins job: GitHub hook trigger

- In the **Build** section, in the **Add build step** drop-down list, we'll choose the **Execute shell** step for this lab. You can add as many actions as necessary to your CI (compilation, file copies, and tests). You can see some examples of possible actions in the following screenshot:

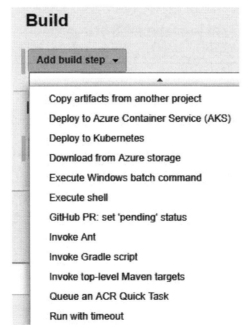

Figure 7.15 – Jenkins job: adding a build step

- Inside the textbox of the shell command, we enter the `printenv` command to be executed during the execution of the job pipeline, as illustrated in the following screenshot:

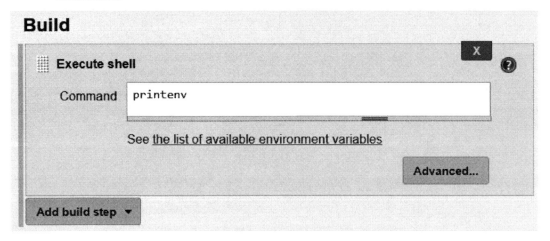

Figure 7.16 – Jenkins job command step sample

4.   Then, we finish the configuration by clicking on **Apply** and then on the **Save** button.

Our Jenkins CI job has now been created and is configured to be triggered during a commit and to perform various actions.

We will now run it manually to test its proper functioning.

Executing a Jenkins job

To test job execution, we will perform these steps:

1.   First, we will modify the code of our GitHub repository—for example, by modifying the `Readme.md` file.

2.   Then, we commit to the master branch directly from the GitHub web interface.

3.   What we see in Jenkins, right after making this commit, is that the `DemoCI` job is queued up and running.

The following screenshot shows the job execution queue:

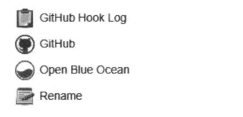

Permalinks

- Last build (#4), 18 sec ago
- Last stable build (#4), 18 sec ago
- Last successful build (#4), 18 sec ago
- Last completed build (#4), 18 sec ago

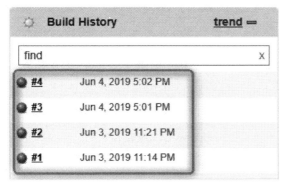

Figure 7.17 – Jenkins job run history

4. By clicking on the job, and then on the link of the **Console Output** menu, we can see the job execution logs, as shown in the following screenshot:

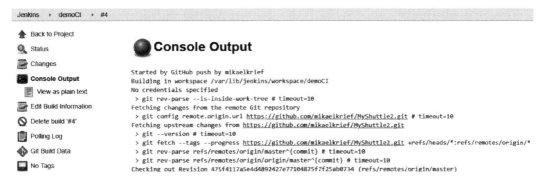

Figure 7.18 – Jenkins job console output

We have just created a CI job in Jenkins that runs during a commit of a Git repository (GitHub, in our example).

In this section, we have looked at the creation of a pipeline in Jenkins. Let's now look at how to create a CI/CD pipeline with another DevOps tool: Azure Pipelines.

Using Azure Pipelines for CI/CD

Azure Pipelines is one of the services offered by Azure DevOps. It was previously known as **Visual Studio Team Services (VSTS)**.

Azure DevOps is a complete DevOps platform provided by Microsoft that is fully accessible via a web browser and requires no installation. It is very useful for the following reasons:

- The DevOps tools manage their code in a **version control system (VCS)**.
- It manages a project in agile mode.
- It deploys applications in a CI/CD pipeline, to centralize packages.
- It performs manual test plans.

Each of these features is combined into services that are summarized in this table:

Service name	Description	Documentation link
Azure Repos	This is an VCS that we looked at in the previous chapter.	`https://azure.microsoft.com/en-us/services/devops/repos/`
Azure Boards	This is a service for project management in agile mode with sprints, backlogs, and boards.	`https://azure.microsoft.com/en-us/services/devops/boards/`
Azure Pipelines	This is a service that allows the management of CI/CD pipelines.	`https://azure.microsoft.com/en-us/services/devops/pipelines/`
Azure Artifacts	This is a private package manager.	`https://azure.microsoft.com/en-us/services/devops/artifacts/`
Azure Test Plans	This allows you to make and manage a manual test plan.	`https://azure.microsoft.com/en-us/services/devops/test-plans/`

Table 7.1 – Azure DevOps services list

Azure DevOps is free for up to five users. Beyond that, there is a license version with per-user costs. For more information on licensing, refer to the product sheet at `https://azure.microsoft.com/en-us/pricing/details/devops/azure-devops-services/`, which also contains a calculator to get a cost estimate for your team.

> **Note**
>
> There is also **Azure DevOps Server**, which is the same product as Azure DevOps, but it installs itself on-premises. To find out the differences between these two products, read the documentation here: `https://docs.microsoft.com/en-us/azure/devops/user-guide/about-azure-devops-services-tfs?view=azure-devops`.

To register with Azure DevOps and create an account, called an organization, we need either a Microsoft live account or a GitHub account, and to then follow these steps:

1. In your browser, go to this URL: `https://azure.microsoft.com/en-us/services/devops/`.

2. Click on the **Sign In** button.

3. On the next page, choose the account to use (either **Live** or **GitHub**).

4. As soon as we register, the first step suggested is to create an organization with a unique name of your choice and the Azure location—for example, `BookLabs` for the name of the organization, and `West Europe` for the location.

5. In this organization, we will now be able to create projects with our CI/CD pipeline, as we learned in *Chapter 6, Managing Your Source Code with Git*.

In this lab, we will show how to set up an **end-to-end** (**E2E**) CI and CD pipeline, starting with the use of Azure Repos to version our code. Then, in Azure Pipelines, we will look at the CI process and end with the automatic deployment of the application in the release.

Versioning of the code with Git in Azure Repos

As we have mentioned, the first prerequisite for setting up a CI process is to have the application code versioned in an SVC, and we will do this in Azure Repos by following these steps:

1. To start our lab, we will create a new project; this operation has already been covered in *Chapter 6, Managing Your Source Code with Git*, in the *Starting with the Git process* section.

2. Then, in Azure Repos, we will import code from another Git repository by using the **Import repository** option of the repository menu, as shown in the following screenshot:

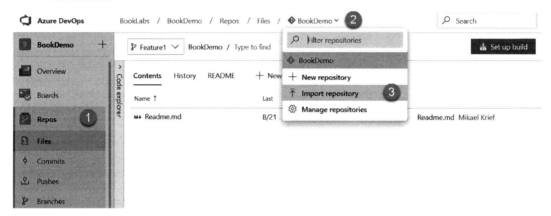

Figure 7.19 – Azure Repos Import repository menu

3. Once the **Import a Git repository** window opens, enter the URL of the Git repository whose sources we want to import. In our lab, we'll import the sources found in the `https://github.com/mikaelkrief/DemoAspNetApp.git` repository, as can be seen in the following screenshot:

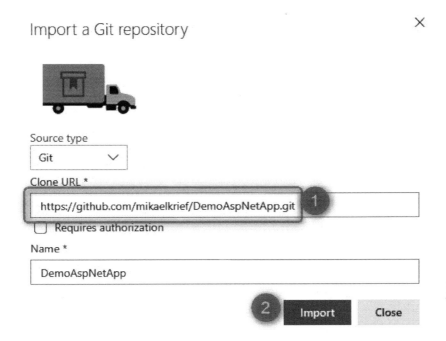

Figure 7.20 – Azure Repos Import repository

4. Click on the **Import** button and then we'll see that the code is imported into our repository. The following screenshot shows the code imported into our Azure Repos repository, which is an ASP.NET code application, and its unit tests:

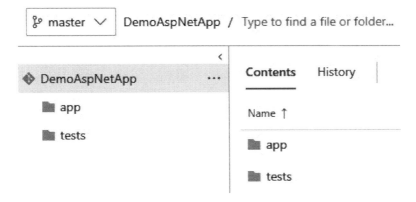

Figure 7.21 – Azure Repos import repository done

Now that we have the code in Azure Repos, we'll set up a CI pipeline that will check and test the code at each user commit.

Creating a CI pipeline

We will create a CI pipeline in Azure Pipelines by following these steps:

1. To create this pipeline, open the **Pipelines | Builds** menu, as shown in the following screenshot. Then, click on the **New pipeline** button:

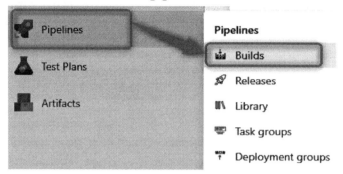

Figure 7.22 – Azure Pipelines: creating a build

2. For the configuration mode, we choose the **Use the classic editor** option, as shown in the following screenshot:

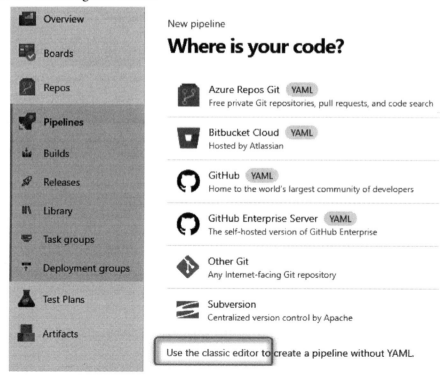

Figure 7.23 – Azure Pipelines classic editor link

In Azure Pipelines, there is the choice of either classic editor mode, which allows us to configure the pipeline via a graphical interface, or YAML pipeline mode, which involves using a **YAML Ain't Markup Language (YAML)** file that describes the configuration of the pipeline.

In this lab, we will use the classic editor mode so that we can visualize the different options and configuration steps.

3. The first configuration step of the pipeline consists of selecting the repository that contains the application's sources.

    Today, Azure Pipelines supports several types of Git systems, such as Azure Repos, GitHub, Bitbucket, and **Subversion (SVN)**. We will therefore select **Azure Repos Git** in the repository that contains the imported sources, as shown in the following screenshot:

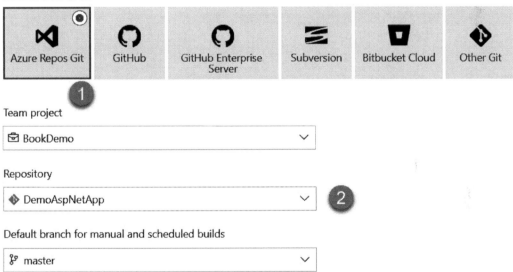

Figure 7.24 – Azure Pipelines: selecting the source repository

4. Azure Pipelines proposes to select a build template that will contain all the preconfigured build steps; there is also the possibility to start from an empty template.

Since our project is an ASP.NET core application, we will choose the **ASP.NET Core** template, as shown in the following screenshot:

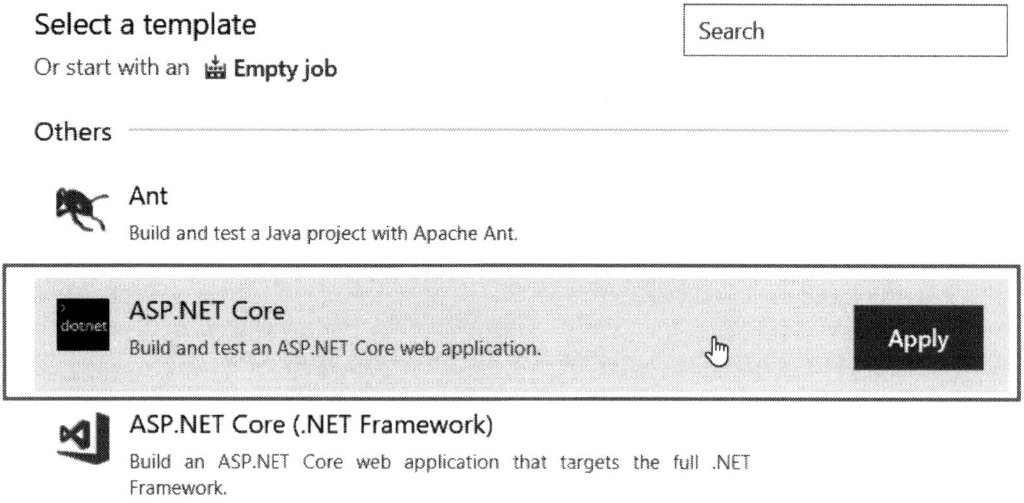

Select a template

Or start with an 👑 **Empty job**

Search

Others ───

🐜 Ant
  Build and test a Java project with Apache Ant.

ASP.NET Core dotnet Build and test an ASP.NET Core web application. 🖑	**Apply**

▷ ASP.NET Core (.NET Framework)
  Build an ASP.NET Core web application that targets the full .NET Framework.

Figure 7.25 – Azure Pipelines: choosing a template

Once the template has been chosen, we reach the configuration page of the build definition.

The configuration of the build definition consists of four main sections, outlined as follows:

- **Variables**
- **Steps**
- **Triggers**
- **Options**

5. We configure the **Variables** section, which allows us to fill in a list of variables in a key form, creating a value that can be used in the steps.

    The following screen shows the **Variables** tab of our build definition:

Figure 7.26 – Azure Pipelines: Variables tab

When we navigate to the **Variables** tab, we see the `BuildConfiguration` and `BuildPlatform` variables, which are already prefilled by the template, and the **+ Add** button, which allows us to add other variables if we wish.

> **Note**
>
> Documentation on variables is available here: https://docs.microsoft.com/en-us/azure/devops/pipelines/process/variables?view=azure-devops&tabs=classic%2Cbatch.

6. We configure the **Tasks** tab, which contains the configuration of all the steps to be performed in the build.

Here is a screenshot of this tab:

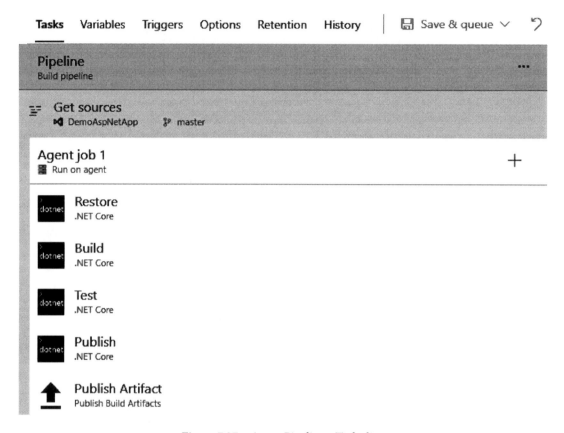

Figure 7.27 – Azure Pipelines: Tasks list

In the preceding screenshot, the first part is **Pipeline**, which allows us to configure the name of the build definition as well as the agent to use.

Indeed, in Azure DevOps, pipelines are executed on agents that are installed on VMs or containers.

Azure DevOps offers free agents from multiple **operating systems (OSes)**, called a hosted agent, but it is also possible to install your own agents, known as **self-hosted** agents.

> **Note**
> To learn more about hosted and self-hosted agents, refer to the following documentation: `https://docs.microsoft.com/en-us/azure/devops/pipelines/agents/agents?view=azure-devops`.

The following screenshot shows the configuration of the **Pipeline** section:

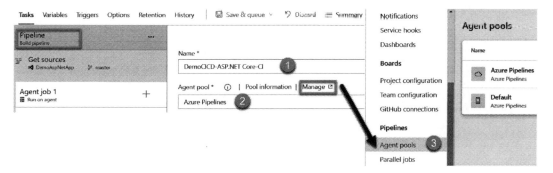

Figure 7.28 – Azure Pipelines: Agent pools configuration

7. Then, we have the **Get sources** phase, which contains the configuration of the sources that we did at the beginning; it is, however, possible to modify it here, as illustrated in the following screenshot:

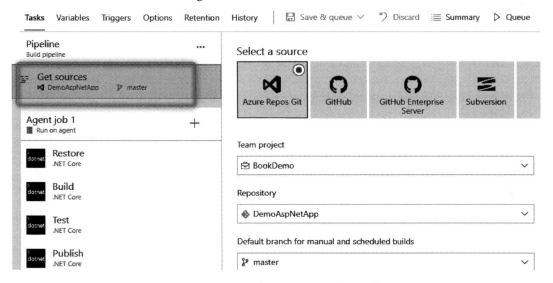

Figure 7.29 – Azure Pipelines: source code configuration

8. We have the **Agent job** part, which contains an ordered list of tasks to be performed in the pipeline. Each of these tasks is configured in the panel on the right.

We can add tasks by clicking on the + button, and then select them from the Azure Pipelines catalog, as follows:

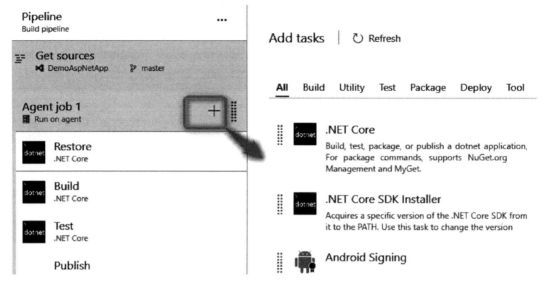

Figure 7.30 – Azure Pipelines: adding a task

By default, Azure Pipelines contains a very rich catalog of tasks; a list of these is available here: `https://docs.microsoft.com/en-us/azure/devops/pipelines/tasks/index?view=azure-devops`. We can also install tasks that can be found in the Azure Marketplace: `https://marketplace.visualstudio.com/search?target=AzureDevOps&category=Azure%20Pipelines&sortBy=Downloads`. If necessary, you can also create tasks for your needs by following the documentation here: `https://docs.microsoft.com/en-us/azure/devops/extend/get-started/node?view=azure-devops`.

Let's define the five tasks in the CI pipeline, as follows:

Step/task	Description
Restore	Restores the packages referenced in the project
Build	Builds the project and generates binaries
Test	Runs unit tests
Publish	Creates a ZIP package that contains the binary files of the project
Publish build artifacts	Defines an artifact that is our ZIP package of the application, which we will publish in Azure DevOps, and which will be used in the deployment release, as seen in the previous section, using a package manager in the CI/CD process

Table 7.2 – Azure Pipelines steps list

9. The last important configuration of our CI pipeline is the configuration of the build trigger in the **Triggers** tab to enable CI, as shown in the following screenshot:

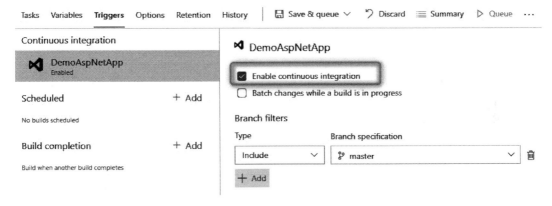

Figure 7.31 – Azure Pipelines: enabling CI

10. The configuration of our CI or build pipeline is complete; we validate and test its execution for the first time by clicking on the **Save & queue** button, as illustrated in the following screenshot:

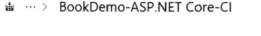

Figure 7.32 – Azure Pipelines: saving and queuing the pipeline

11. At the end of the execution of the build, we have some information that helps us to analyze the status of the pipeline, as follows:

- The following screenshot shows the execution logs. This displays the details of the execution of each task defined in the pipeline:

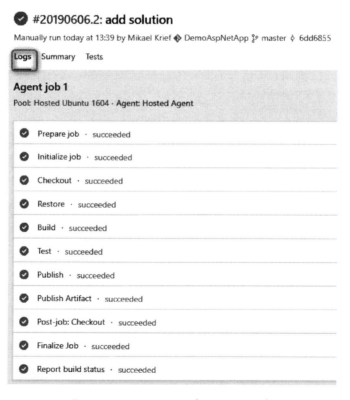

Figure 7.33 – Azure Pipelines run result

- The results of the execution of the unit tests are shown next. The following screenshot displays a report of the executions of unit tests with some important metrics, such as the number of passed/failed tests and the test execution time:

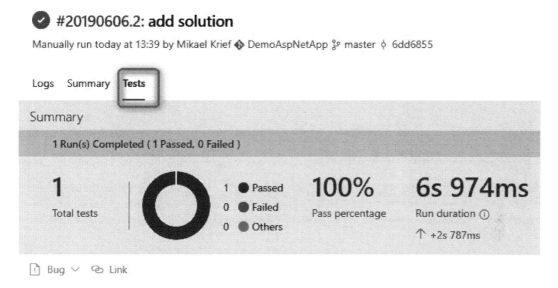

Figure 7.34 – Azure Pipelines: test execution summary

- The following screenshot shows the published artifacts. This provides the possibility to explore or download the published artifacts defined in the **Publish Build Artifact** task of the pipeline.

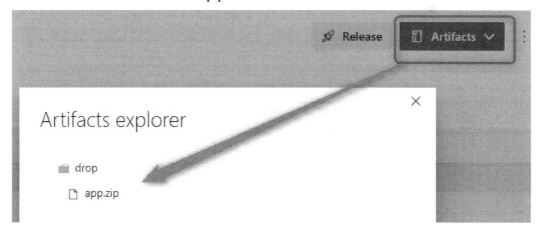

Figure 7.35 – Azure Pipelines: browsing artifacts

Now we know our CI build is configured and operational, we will create and configure a deployment release for the CD pipeline.

Creating a CD pipeline – the release

In Azure Pipelines, the element that allows deployment in the different stages or environments is called the **release**. We will now create a release definition that will deploy our build-generated artifacts to an Azure web app by following these steps:

1. To create a release definition, we go to the **Releases** menu and click on **New pipeline**, as follows:

Figure 7.36 – Azure Pipelines: creating a release definition

2. As for the build, the first step of the configuration is to choose a template already configured. For this lab, we will choose the **Azure App Service deployment** template, as illustrated in the following screenshot:

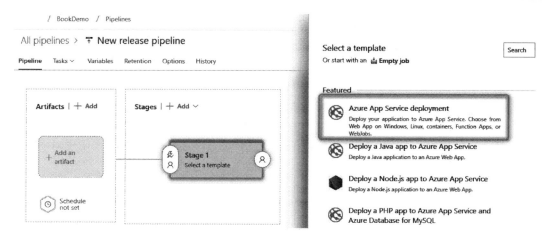

Figure 7.37 – Azure Pipelines: Azure App Service deployment template

3. Then, in the next window, the first stage is named—for example, `CI`—as the CI environment, as illustrated in the following screenshot:

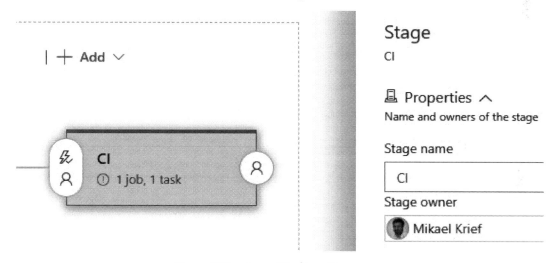

Figure 7.38 – Azure Pipelines: Stage name

4. We configure the entry point of the release in the artifacts part by adding an artifact that is the build definition previously created in the *Creating a CI pipeline* section, as follows:

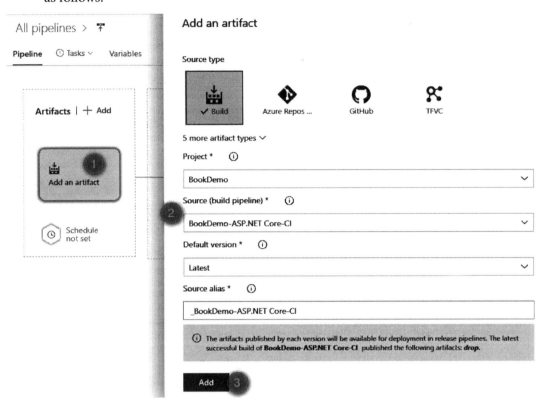

Figure 7.39 – Azure Pipelines: adding a release artifact

5. We configure the automatic release trigger for each successful build execution as follows:

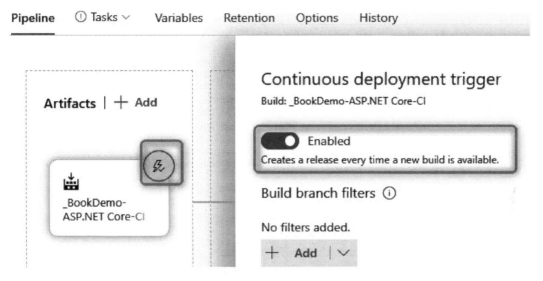

Figure 7.40 – Azure Pipelines: release enabling CD

6. Now, we'll configure the steps that will be executed in the CI stage; by clicking on the stage, we get exactly the same configuration window as the build, with the following information:

    - The agent's choice over the **Run on agent** section
    - The configuration of the steps with their parameters

In our case, we see the deployment task in an Azure web app that was already present in the template. We first fill in the parameters that are located in the **CI** header because they are shared for the CI course, as shown in the following screenshot:

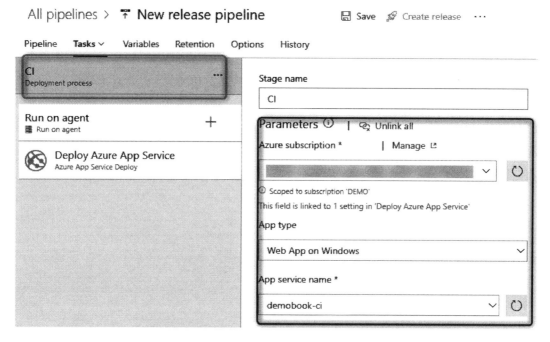

Figure 7.41 – Azure Pipelines: release configuration

We will fill in the following parameters:

- The connection to your Azure subscription

- The name of the Azure web app in which we want to deploy our ZIP package

> **Note**
>
> The web app must already be created before deploying the application in it. If it is not created, you can use the Azure **command-line interface (CLI)** az webapp create command, documented at https://docs.microsoft.com/en-us/cli/azure/webapp?view=azure-cli-latest#az-webapp-create, or the PowerShell New-AzureRmWebApp command, documented at https://docs.microsoft.com/en-us/powershell/module/azurerm.websites/new-azurermwebapp?view=azurermps-6.13.0.

Then, in the parameters of the Azure deployment task, we have nothing to modify.

7. We just have to rename the release with a name that simply describes what it does, and then we save it, as follows:

Figure 7.42 – Azure Pipelines: editing the release name

8. Now, we complete our definition of the release with the deployment of the other environments (or stages), which are, for our example, QA and PROD. To simplify the manipulation, we will clone the CI environment settings in our release and change the name of the **App service name** settings to the name of the web app. The following screenshot shows the clone environment action:

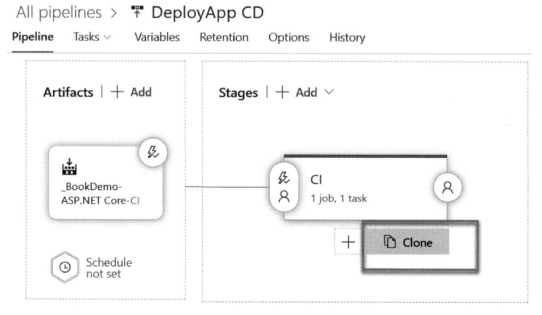

Figure 7.43 – Azure release clone stage

And the following screenshot shows the Azure **App service name** settings with the web app name of the new environment:

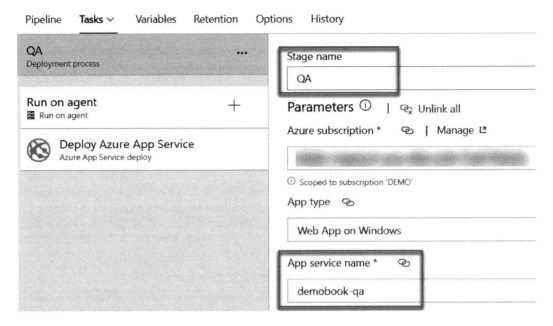

Figure 7.44 – Azure release: editing the app service name

9. We finally get the release definition, as follows:

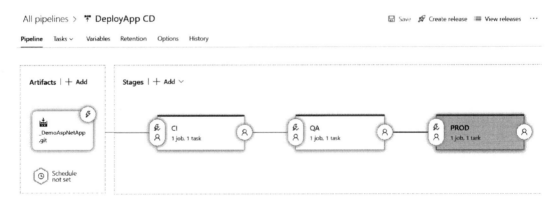

Figure 7.45 – Azure Pipelines: release definition

10. To trigger the deployment of our application, we will create a new release by clicking on the **Create release** button, as shown in the following screenshot:

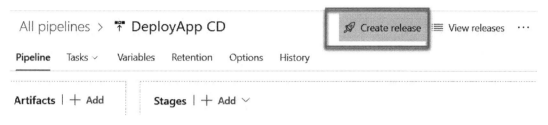

Figure 7.46 – Azure Pipelines: creating a release

11. At the end of its execution, we can see its deployment status, as shown in the following screenshot:

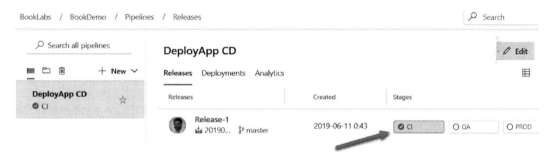

Figure 7.47 – Azure Pipelines: deployment status

In this screenshot, we see that the deployment in the integration environment was successfully completed.

By following the steps in this lab, we have created a CI and CD pipeline in **user interface (UI)** mode (called classical). Now, we will learn how to create a pipeline in code mode with a YAML file.

Creating a full pipeline definition in a YAML file

In the previous sections, we discussed the creation of a CI and CD pipeline in Azure DevOps using the UI, which has some advantages, but one of its inconvenient points is the difficulty to automate the creation of a pipeline for lots of projects.

To solve this problem, Azure DevOps has the possibility to write the entire pipeline definition (CI and CD) inside a YAML file that is saved in the repository.

> **Note**
>
> The objective of this section is to demonstrate an overview of the pipeline YAML of Azure DevOps with only the CI steps. It's not an advanced lab, and if you want to learn more, read the documentation here: `https://docs.microsoft.com/en-us/azure/devops/pipelines/yaml-schema`.

In the following lab, we will learn how to create a basic pipeline definition in a YAML file. Here's how to do this:

1. In Azure Repos, inside the `DemoBook` repository created previously, add a new file named `azure-pipeline.yaml`, with the following content:

```yaml
trigger:
- master
pool:
  vmImage: ubuntu-latest
steps:
- task: DotNetCoreCLI@2
  displayName: "Restore"
  inputs:
    command: restore
    projects: '**/*.csproj'
- task: DotNetCoreCLI@2
  displayName: "build"
  inputs:
    command: 'build'
    projects: '**/*.csproj'
    arguments: '--configuration Release'
- task: DotNetCoreCLI@2
  displayName: "Run tests"
  inputs:
    command: 'test'
    projects: '**/tests/*.csproj'
    arguments: '--configuration Release'
- task: DotNetCoreCLI@2
  displayName: "Code coverage"
  inputs:
```

```
    command: test
    projects: '**/*Tests/*.csproj'
    arguments: '--configuration Release --collect "Code
coverage"'
```

In this file, we have three sections: `trigger`, `pool`, and `steps`. In the `trigger` section, we indicate the branch of the code that triggers the pipeline, so here, any commit on the `master` branch will execute the pipeline.

Then, the `pool` section indicates the agent pool to be used to execute the pipeline. Finally, in the `steps` section, we write all tasks that will be executed during the pipeline. Here, in our lab, we have declared four tasks, as follows:

- The restore of the NuGet packages of the project

- The compilation of the project

- The execution of the tests

- The publication of the code coverage of the executed tests

2. We commit and push this file into the root of the repository, as follows:

Figure 7.48 – Azure Pipelines: YAML pipeline

3. In Azure Pipelines, open the **Pipeline** menu and click on the **Create pipeline** button, as shown in the following screenshot:

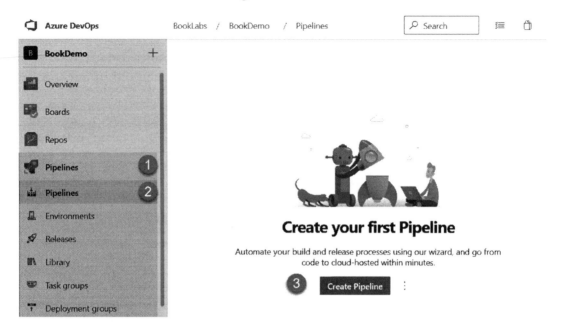

Figure 7.49 – Azure Pipelines: creating a new YAML pipeline

4. Select the source of the code (here, we choose **Azure Repos Git**) and select the repository that contains the YAML file of the pipeline, as illustrated in the following screenshot:

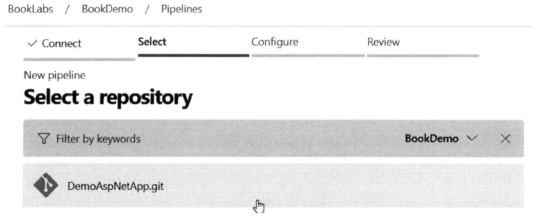

Figure 7.50 – Azure Pipelines: selecting the repository

5. Then, configure the Azure pipeline by choosing the option to use the existing YAML file, as illustrated in the following screenshot:

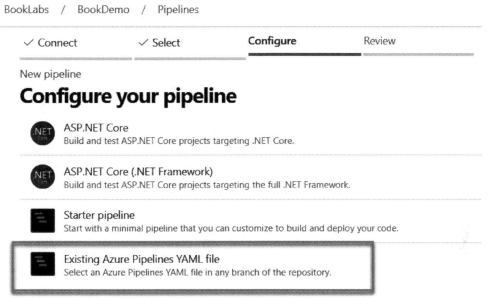

Figure 7.51 – Azure Pipelines: selecting the option to use an existing YAML file

Then, select the path of the pipeline YAML file, as follows:

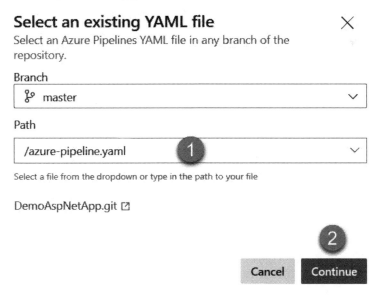

Figure 7.52 – Azure Pipelines: selecting the YAML file

Validate this by clicking on the **Continue** button.

6. The content of the file is displayed on the screen. Finally, to execute the pipeline, click on the **Run** button, as illustrated in the following screenshot:

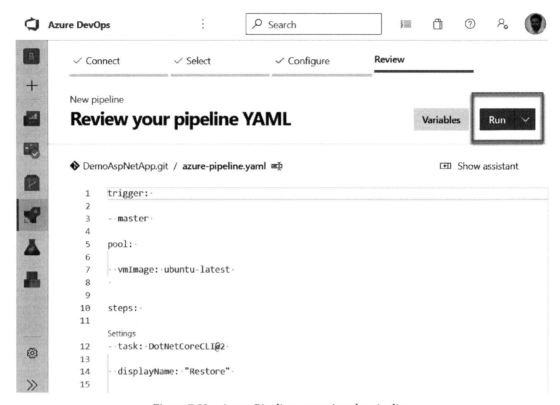

Figure 7.53 – Azure Pipelines: running the pipeline

The pipeline is created and is executed.

7. Finally, we can view the details of the execution of the pipeline, as illustrated in the following screenshot:

Figure 7.54 – Azure Pipelines: job execution

Click on **Job**, as indicated in the preceding screenshot, to display the details of the execution of each task. You should then see a screen like this:

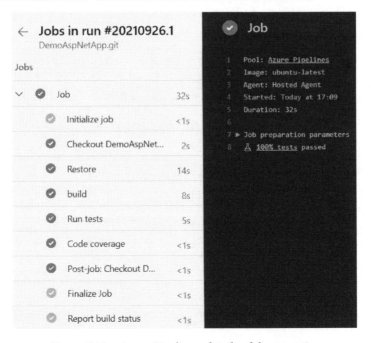

Figure 7.55 – Azure Pipelines: details of the execution

In this section, we learned the basics of how to use YAML files that contain the definition of the pipeline and have many other very interesting features. To learn more, consult the documentation here: `https://docs.microsoft.com/en-us/azure/devops/pipelines/?view=azure-devops`.

Let's now look at creating a CI pipeline using GitLab CI.

Using GitLab CI

In the previous sections of this chapter, we learned how to create CI/CD pipelines with Jenkins and Azure Pipelines.

Now, let's look at a lab using another DevOps tool that is gaining popularity: **GitLab CI**.

GitLab CI is one of the services offered by GitLab (`https://about.gitlab.com/`), which, like Azure DevOps, is a cloud platform with the following attributes:

- A source code manager
- A CI/CD pipeline manager
- A board for project management

The other services it offers are listed here: `https://about.gitlab.com/features/`.

GitLab has a free price model with additional services that are subject to a charge; a price grid is available at `https://about.gitlab.com/pricing/`. The differences between Azure DevOps and GitLab are detailed in this link: `https://about.gitlab.com/devops-tools/azure-devops-vs-gitlab.html`.

In this lab, we'll find out about the following:

1. Authentication at GitLab
2. Creating a new project and versioning its code in GitLab
3. The creation and execution of a CI pipeline in GitLab CI

Authentication at GitLab

Creating a GitLab account is free and can be done either by creating a GitLab account or using external accounts, such as Google, GitHub, Twitter, or Bitbucket.

To create a GitLab account, we need to go to `https://gitlab.com/users/sign_in#register-pane` and choose the type of authentication.

The following screenshot shows the GitLab authentication form:

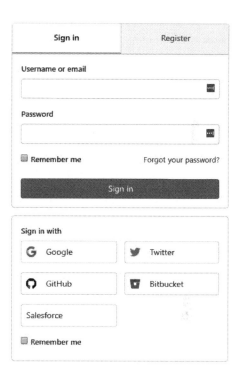

Figure 7.56 – GitLab registration

Once your account has been created and authenticated, you will be taken to the home page of your account, which offers all the functionalities shown in the following screenshot:

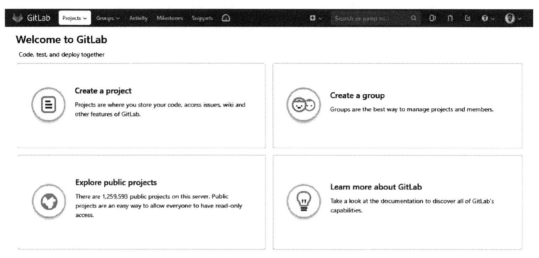

Figure 7.57 – GitLab home page

Now that we are done with authentication, let's go ahead and create a new project.

Creating a new project and managing your source code

To create a new project in GitLab, follow these steps:

1. Click on **Create a project** on the home page, as illustrated in the following screenshot:

Welcome to GitLab

Code, test, and deploy together

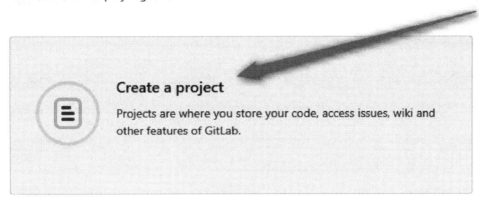

Create a project

Projects are where you store your code, access issues, wiki and other features of GitLab.

Figure 7.58 – GitLab new project

- Then, we can choose from a few options, as follows:

  - To create an empty project (without code), the form asks you to enter the project's name, as illustrated in the following screenshot:

Blank project	Create from template	Import project	CI/CD for external repo

Project name

BookDemo

Project URL

https://gitlab.com/mikakrief/

Project slug

bookdemo

Want to house several dependent projects under the same namespace? Create a group.

Project description (optional)

Description format

Visibility Level ❓

⦿ 🔒 Private
    Project access must be granted explicitly to each user.

○ 🛡 Internal
    The project can be accessed by any logged in user.

○ 🌐 Public
    The project can be accessed without any authentication.

☐ **Initialize repository with a README**
    Allows you to immediately clone this project's repository. Skip this if you plan to push up an existing repository.

[Create project]   [Cancel]

Figure 7.59 – GitLab project configuration

- To create a new project from a built-in template project, proceed as follows:

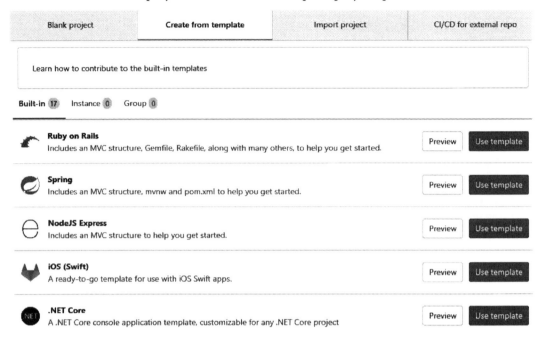

Figure 7.60 – GitLab project template

- To import code from an internal or external repository of another SVC platform, this is as shown in the following screenshot:

Figure 7.61 – GitLab: importing code

- The code to import is located in an external SVC repository, as shown in the following screenshot:

Blank project	Create from template	Import project	CI/CD for external repo

Run CI/CD pipelines for external repositories

Connect your external repositories, and CI/CD pipelines will run for new commits. A GitLab project will be created with only CI/CD features enabled.

If using GitHub, you'll see pipeline statuses on GitHub for your commits and pull requests. More info

Connect repositories from

○ GitHub	git Repo by URL

Figure 7.62 – GitLab: CI/CD for external repositories

In our case, for this lab, we will start with the first option, which is an empty project, and as we saw in the form, we choose a project name such as BookDemo and then validate it by clicking on the **Create a project** button.

2. Once the project is created, we'll have a page that indicates the different Git commands to execute to push its code.

3. To do this, on our local disk, we will create a new gitlab-ci-demo.yml file and then copy the content of our example, which can be found at https://github.com/PacktPublishing/Learning-DevOps-Second-Edition/tree/main/CHAP07, in the gitlab-ci-demo.yml file.

4. Then, we will execute the following commands in a terminal to push the code into the repository, as seen in detail in *Chapter 6, Managing Your Source Code with Git*:

```
git init
git remote add origin <git repo Url>
git add .
git commit -m "Initial commit"
git push -u origin master
```

> **Note**
>
> During execution, an identification window will ask for your GitLab account **identifier** (**ID**) because it is a private project. Once logged in to your account on the GitLab web portal, your username will be available on your account page at https://gitlab.com/profile/account.

Once these commands have been executed, we'll obtain a remote GitLab repository with our lab code.

The following screenshot shows the remote GitLab repository:

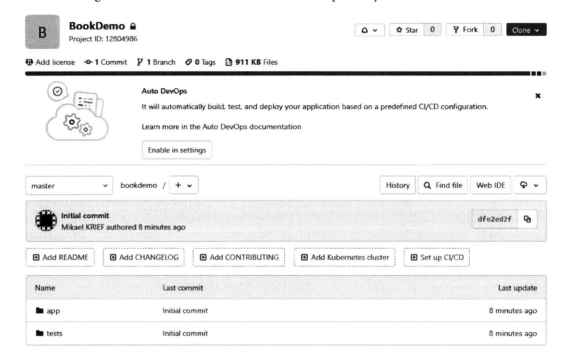

Figure 7.63 – GitLab repository

The code of our application has been deposited in GitLab, and we can now create our CI process with GitLab.

Creating a CI pipeline

In GitLab CI, the creation of a CI pipeline (and CD) is not done via a **graphical UI (GUI)**, but with a YAML file at the root of the project.

This method, which consists of describing the process of a pipeline in a file that is located with the code, can be called **Pipeline as Code (PaC)**, in the same way as **Infrastructure as Code (IaC)**. We'll proceed as follows:

1. To create this pipeline, we will create, at the root of the application code, a `.gitlab-ci.yml` file with the following content:

```
image: microsoft/dotnet:latest
stages:
    - build
    - test
```

```
variables:
    BuildConfiguration: "Release"

build:
    stage: build
    script:
        - "cd app"
        - "dotnet restore"
        - "dotnet build --configuration
$BuildConfiguration"
test:
    stage: test
    script:
        - "cd tests"
        - "dotnet test --configuration
$BuildConfiguration"
```

> **Note**
>
> The code of this file is also available here: https://github.com/
> PacktPublishing/Learning-DevOps-Second-Edition/
> blob/main/CHAP07/gitlab-ci-demo.yml.

We can see at the beginning of this code that we use a microsoft/
dotnet:latest Docker image that will be mounted in a container and in which
the actions of the pipeline will be executed.

Then, we define two stages, one for the build and one for the test execution, as well
as a BuildConfiguration variable that will be used in the scripts.

Finally, we describe each of the stages of the scripts to be executed in their
respective directories. These .NET core scripts are identical to the ones we saw
in the *Using Azure Pipelines for CI/CD* section.

> **Note**
>
> Full documentation on the format and syntax of this .gitlab-ci.yml file
> is available here: https://docs.gitlab.com/ee/ci/yaml/.

2. Then, we will commit and push this file into the remote repository.

3. Just after pushing the code, we can see that the CI process has been triggered.

Our CI pipeline was, therefore, triggered when the code was pushed into the repository, so let's now look at how to see the details of its execution.

Accessing the CI pipeline execution details

To access the execution details of the executed CI pipeline, follow these steps:

1. In the GitLab CI menu, go to **CI / CD | Pipelines**, and you will see a list of pipeline executions, as shown in the following screenshot:

Figure 7.64 – GitLab pipelines

2. To display the details of the pipeline, we click on the desired pipeline execution, as illustrated in the following screenshot:

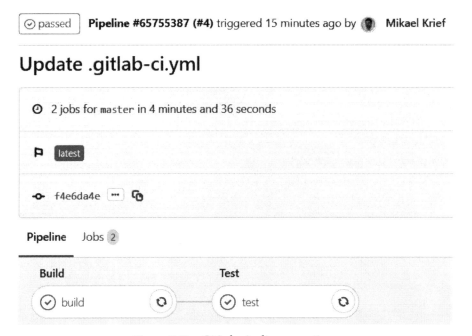

Figure 7.65 – GitLab pipeline execution

3. We can see the execution status, as well as the two stages that you defined in the pipeline YAML file. To view the details of the execution logs for a stage, we click on the stage, as shown in the following screenshot:

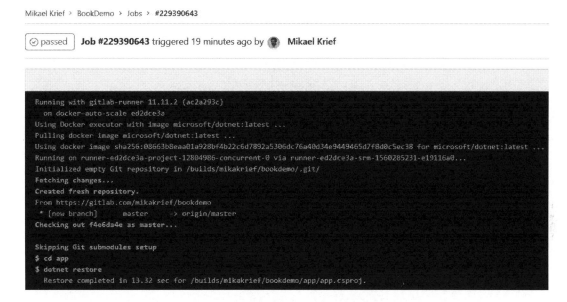

Figure 7.66 – GitLab execution log details

We can see the execution of the scripts written in the pipeline YAML file.

In this section, we have seen the implementation of a CI pipeline in GitLab CI with the initialization of a remote repository and the creation of a YAML file for configuring the pipeline as well as the execution of the pipeline.

Summary

In this chapter, we looked at one of the most important topics in DevOps: the CI/CD process. We started with a presentation of the principles of CI and CD. Then, we focused on package managers, looking at NuGet, npm, Nexus, and Azure Artifacts.

Finally, we saw how to implement and execute an E2E CI/CD pipeline using three different tools: Jenkins, Azure Pipelines, and GitLab CI. For each of them, we looked at the archiving of the application source code, along with the creation of a pipeline and its execution.

After reading this chapter, we should be able to create a pipeline for CI and CD with source code management as the source. In addition, we will be able to choose and use a package manager to centralize and distribute our packages.

In the next chapter, we will learn about the creation of a CI/CD pipeline for an IAC project using Azure DevOps with the objective of executing Packer, Terraform, and Ansible code.

Questions

1. What are the prerequisites for implementing a CI pipeline?
2. When will the CI pipeline be triggered?
3. What is the purpose of a package manager?
4. Which types of packages are stored in a NuGet package manager?
5. Which platform is Azure Artifacts integrated into?
6. Is Jenkins a cloud service?
7. In Azure DevOps, what is the name of the service that allows the management of CI/CD pipelines?
8. What are the three services offered by GitLab?
9. In GitLab CI, which element allows you to build a CI pipeline?

Further reading

If you would like to find out more about CI/CD pipelines, here are some resources you can consult:

- *Hands-On Continuous Integration and Delivery*: https://www.packtpub.com/virtualization-and-cloud/hands-continuous-integration-and-delivery

- *Continuous Integration, Delivery, and Deployment*: https://www.packtpub.com/application-development/continuous-integration-delivery-and-deployment

- *Mastering Jenkins*: https://www.packtpub.com/application-development/mastering-jenkins

- *Azure DevOps Server 2019 Cookbook*: https://www.packtpub.com/networking-and-servers/azure-devops-server-2019-cookbook-second-edition

- *Mastering GitLab 12*: https://www.packtpub.com/cloud-networking/mastering-gitlab-12

8

Deploying Infrastructure as Code with CI/CD Pipelines

In the first part of this book, we learned a lot about **Infrastructure as Code (IaC)**, its advantages, and tools such as Terraform, Packer, and Ansible, and their command lines. Then, in the second part, we discussed Git and dedicated a chapter to the Continuous Integration and Continuous Deployment of applications.

However, we should not neglect to also put CI/CD into practice as IaC, which will allow us to orchestrate and automate the whole process of provisioning the infrastructure.

It is in this second edition of this book that I wanted to add this chapter to reuse all that we have learned in the previous chapters and show how to implement IaC with a CI/CD pipeline, which will be composed of Packer, Terraform, and Ansible.

The pipeline tool that will be used is Azure Pipelines, which we have already covered in detail in *Chapter 7, Continuous Integration and Continuous Delivery*. So we will learn how to write a Azure pipeline in YAML to generate an image with Packer. Then, we will see how to write a YAML pipeline to provision a **Virtual Machine** (**VM**) with Terraform and complete it with the execution of Ansible to install nginx on this VM.

This chapter covers the following topics:

- Running Packer in Azure Pipelines
- Running Terraform and Ansible in Azure Pipelines

Technical requirements

This chapter requires the following:

- An Azure subscription for creating the Packer image and provisioning the VM; you can create a free account here: `https://azure.microsoft.com/en-us/free/search/`.
- An Azure DevOps account for creating the YAML pipelines definition; you can create a free account here: `https://azure.microsoft.com/en-us/pricing/details/devops/azure-devops-services/`.

The source code for this chapter is available at `https://github.com/PacktPublishing/Learning-DevOps-Second-Edition/tree/main/CHAP08`.

Check out the following video to view the Code in Action: `https://bit.ly/3BDT9ne`

Running Packer in Azure Pipelines

To start our IaC pipeline, we will automatically create an Azure VM image using Packer. To perform this operation, we will use Azure Pipelines with a pipeline in YAML format. The goal of this pipeline is to execute a Packer command automatically.

> **Important Note**
>
> For more details on how to create a YAML pipeline in Azure DevOps, read *Chapter 7, Continuous Integration and Continuous Delivery*.

The Packer template that we will use in this section's lab is the code that we learned in *Chapter 4, Optimizing Infrastructure Deployment with Packer*. This source code is available here: `https://github.com/PacktPublishing/Learning-DevOps-Second-Edition/blob/main/CHAP08/packer/.pkr.hcl`.

Before we start using Packer, we need first to create an Azure resource group that will store the created VM image by the pipeline. In our lab, we named this Azure resource group `rg_images`. The following screenshot shows the Azure resource group:

Figure 8.1 – The Azure resource group for the Packer image

Now, we can write the code of the pipeline, which will execute Packer command lines on the Packer template.

To do this, in the same folder as the Packer template, create a new YAML file that will describe the steps of the pipeline, and then write three blocks of code, as follows:

1. The first step is to execute the `packer init` command:

```
- script: packer init $(Build.SourcesDirectory)/CHAP08/
  packer/.pkr.hcl
  displayName:  Packer init
```

2. The second step is to validate the Packer template by running the `packer validate` command:

```
- script: packer validate $(Build.SourcesDirectory)/
  CHAP08/packer/.pkr.hcl
  displayName: Packer validate template
```

3. The last step is to build the image with Packer by running the `packer build` command:

```
- script: packer build $(Build.SourcesDirectory)/CHAP08/
  packer/.pkr.hcl
    displayName: Packer build template
  env:
    PKR_VAR_clientid: $(PKR_VAR_clientid)
    PKR_VAR_clientsecret: $(PKR_VAR_clientsecret)
    PKR_VAR_subscriptionid: $(PKR_VAR_subscriptionid)
    PKR_VAR_tenantid: $(PKR_VAR_tenantid)
```

In this step code, we add to the script the environment variables corresponding to the Azure service principal account. To be used in a Packer template, these environment variables must be in the `PKR_VAR_<variable name>` format.

> **Important Note**
>
> The entire source code of this YAML pipeline file is available here: `https://github.com/PacktPublishing/Learning-DevOps-Second-Edition/blob/main/CHAP08/packer/pipeline.yaml`.

Then, commit and push this file in your Git repository. In this lab, we use GitHub, although you can use other Git repositories such as Azure Repos or Bitbucket.

The last step is to create and run the Azure Pipeline by following these steps:

1. In the Azure Pipelines menu, click on **New pipeline**:

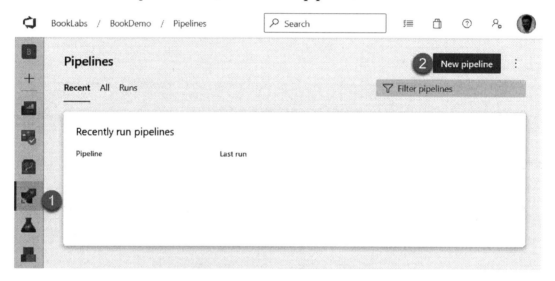

Figure 8.2 – Creating a new pipeline in Azure Pipelines

2. Select the Git repository that contains the Packer templates and the YAML pipeline file, and choose the option to use the existing YAML pipeline file. All the details for this step are explained in the *Creating the full pipeline definition in a YAML file* section of *Chapter 7, Continuous Integration and Continuous Delivery*.

    After creating the pipeline, inside **Edit** mode, add four variables to store the credentials information of the Azure service principal.

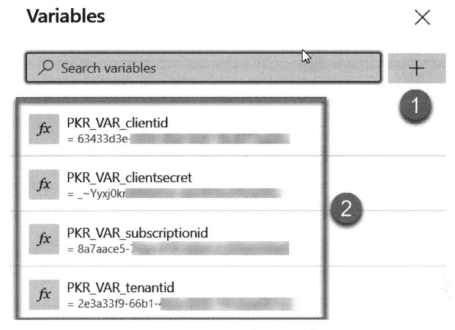

Figure 8.3 – Azure Pipelines variables

These are the variables we used in the YAML pipeline in the latest step script.

3. Then, we can run the pipeline and wait until the end of the execution. In the log panel, we can display all the execution details.

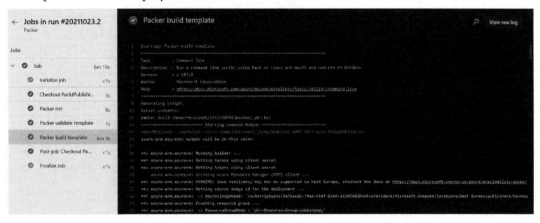

Figure 8.4 – The Azure Pipelines Packer pipeline logs

4. Finally, in the Azure portal, we can see the generated VM image in the Azure resource group.

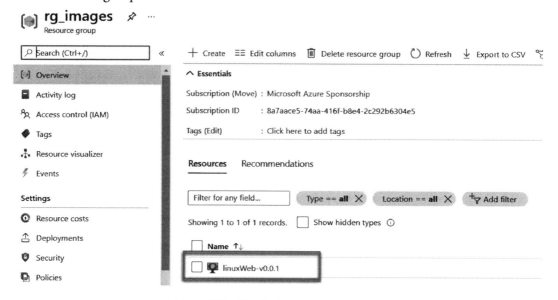

Figure 8.5 – The Packer image on Azure

In this section, we learned how to create Packer images automatically using pipelines in Azure DevOps. In the next section, we will continue with the IaC pipeline to execute Terraform and Ansible commands inside automatic pipelines.

Running Terraform and Ansible in Azure Pipelines

After the creation of the Packer pipeline, we will now create the pipeline for provisioning an Azure VM that uses the image created with Packer and then configures this VM with Ansible. For this demonstration, we will use Ansible to install nginx on this VM.

The Terraform configuration that is used in this code will provision new Azure resource group, a virtual network with a subnet, and a Linux VM with the tag role as the `webserver` value.

This complete Terraform code is available here: `https://github.com/PacktPublishing/Learning-DevOps-Second-Edition/tree/main/CHAP08/terraform`. I will not explain it, since it's the same code that we learned in *Chapter 2, Provisioning Cloud Infrastructure with Terraform*.

The complete Ansible code that we used to install nginx on the Linux machine is available here: `https://github.com/PacktPublishing/Learning-DevOps-Second-Edition/blob/main/CHAP08/ansible/playbookdemo.yml`. We already learned about it in *Chapter 3, Using Ansible for Configuring IaaS Infrastructure*. For the Ansible inventory, we use a **dynamic inventory** that selects VM hosts based on a specific Azure resource group and a tag on a VM.

The configuration code of this dynamic inventory is available here: `https://github.com/PacktPublishing/Learning-DevOps-Second-Edition/blob/main/CHAP08/ansible/inv.azure_rm.yml`.

Now that we have all the Terraform and Ansible code, we can write the YAML code of the Azure Pipelines with the following steps. For this, create a new `azure-pipeline.yaml` file with the following content:

1. The first step is to run Terraform workflow commands with `init`, `plan`, and `apply`:

```
 - script: terraform init --backend-config backend.
tfvars
   displayName:  Terraform init
   workingDirectory: $(Build.SourcesDirectory)/CHAP08/
terraform
   env:
     ARM_CLIENT_ID: $(AZURE_CLIENT_ID)
     ARM_CLIENT_SECRET: $(AZURE_SECRET)
     ARM_SUBSCRIPTION_ID: $(AZURE_SUBSCRIPTION_ID)
     ARM_TENANT_ID: $(AZURE_TENANT)
     ARM_ACCESS_KEY: $(AZURE_ACCESS_KEY)

 - script: terraform plan
   displayName:  Terraform plan
   workingDirectory: $(Build.SourcesDirectory)/CHAP08/
terraform
   env:
     ARM_CLIENT_ID: $(AZURE_CLIENT_ID)
     ARM_CLIENT_SECRET: $(AZURE_SECRET)
     ARM_SUBSCRIPTION_ID: $(AZURE_SUBSCRIPTION_ID)
     ARM_TENANT_ID: $(AZURE_TENANT)
     ARM_ACCESS_KEY: $(AZURE_ACCESS_KEY)
```

```
- script: terraform apply -auto-approve
  displayName:  Terraform apply
  workingDirectory: $(Build.SourcesDirectory)/CHAP08/
terraform
  env:
    ARM_CLIENT_ID: $(AZURE_CLIENT_ID)
    ARM_CLIENT_SECRET: $(AZURE_SECRET)
    ARM_SUBSCRIPTION_ID: $(AZURE_SUBSCRIPTION_ID)
    ARM_TENANT_ID: $(AZURE_TENANT)
    ARM_ACCESS_KEY: $(AZURE_ACCESS_KEY)
```

In these script tasks, we run the following three commands:

- The `terraform init` command using a Terraform state backend configuration.

- The `terraform plan` command for previewing the changes.

> **Important Note**
>
> Optionally, we can add one step here to manually approve the `plan` result before we apply the changes. Here, in this lab, we are confident with the plan changes, and the pipeline can apply the changes directly.

- The `terraform apply` command for applying changes and creating the VM if it does not exist. To this command, we add the `-auto-approve` option to automatically apply changes without asking for confirmation.

For Azure authentication, we use the service principal credentials and the Azure storage access key (for state backend) as environment variables.

2. Then, in this pipeline, we continue with the Ansible execution with the following code:

```
- script: pip install ansible[azure]==2.8.6
  displayName:  Get requirements


- script: ansible-playbook playbookdemo.yml -i inv.
azure_rm.yml
  displayName:  Ansible playbook
  workingDirectory: $(Build.SourcesDirectory)/CHAP08/
ansible
  env:
```

```
AZURE_CLIENT_ID: $(AZURE_CLIENT_ID)
AZURE_SECRET: $(AZURE_SECRET)
AZURE_SUBSCRIPTION_ID: $(AZURE_SUBSCRIPTION_ID)
AZURE_TENANT: $(AZURE_TENANT)
ANSIBLE_HOST_KEY_CHECKING: False
```

In this code, the first script installs the Azure plugins for Ansible that are required for the dynamic inventory.

The second script executes an Ansible playbook and uses the dynamic inventory configured in the `inv.azure_rm.yml` file. We also use the Azure service principal credentials as environment variables.

Then, commit and push this file in your Git repository.

The last step is to create and run the Azure pipeline by following these steps:

1. In the Azure Pipelines menu, click on **New pipeline.**

2. Select the Git repository that contains Packer templates and the YAML pipeline file, and choose the option to use the existing YAML pipeline file.

    All the details for this step are explained in the *Creating the full pipeline definition in a YAML file* section of *Chapter 7, Continuous Integration and Continuous Delivery.*

3. After creating the pipeline, inside **Edit** mode, add five variables to store the credentials information of the Azure service principal and the Azure storage access key for the Terraform state backend.

Figure 8.6 – Azure Pipelines Terraform and Ansible variables

These are the variables we used in the YAML pipeline in all of the script steps.

4. Then, we can run the pipeline and wait until the end of the execution. In the log panel, we can display all the execution details step by step.

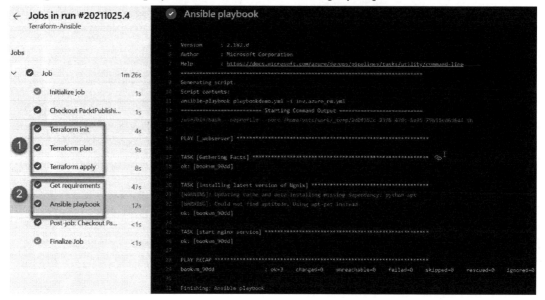

Figure 8.7 – Azure Pipelines Terraform and Ansible log details

We can see on this screen the Terraform command execution and then the Ansible execution.

5. Finally, to verify that the execution is successful, find the public IP on this VM inside the Azure portal.

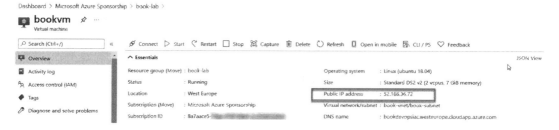

Figure 8.8 – Azure VM public IP

Open a browser and navigate to this public IP:

Welcome to nginx!

If you see this page, the nginx web server is successfully installed and working. Further configuration is required.

For online documentation and support please refer to nginx.org. Commercial support is available at nginx.com.

Thank you for using nginx.

Figure 8.9 – The nginx home page

We can now see the home page of nginx.

In this section, we learned how to write pipeline code to execute Terraform and then Ansible automatically with a YAML pipeline in Azure DevOps, and Terraform and Ansible command lines.

Summary

In this chapter, we implemented a sample pipeline for IaC. In the first section, we learned how to integrate Packer command lines in pipelines. Then, in the second part, we continued the automation of IaC with another pipeline that ran Terraform to provision an Azure VM, and installed nginx on this VM with Ansible.

All the YAML pipeline code used in this chapter was applicable to GitHub and Azure Pipelines, and the process is exactly the same for other CI/CD tools such as Jenkins or GitLab CI.

In the next chapter, we will learn how to build and run a container using Docker.

Questions

1. What is the name of the tool used in this chapter?
2. What is the IaC provisioning order between Terraform, Ansible, and Packer?

Further reading

If you would like to find out more about IaC pipelines, here are some labs:

- DevOps Lab about Terraform on Azure DevOps: `https://azuredevopslabs.com/labs/vstsextend/terraform/`.

- DevOps Lab about Ansible on Azure DevOps: `https://www.azuredevopslabs.com/labs/vstsextend/ansible/`.

Section 3: Containerized Microservices with Docker and Kubernetes

In this part, we present the basic uses of Docker and how to create and run containers from a Dockerfile. Then, we explore the role of Kubernetes and how to deploy more complex applications on Kubernetes.

This section comprises the following chapters:

- *Chapter 9, Containerizing Your Application with Docker*
- *Chapter 10, Managing Containers Effectively with Kubernetes*

9
Containerizing Your Application with Docker

In the last few years, one technology in particular has been making headlines on the net, on social networks, and at events—Docker.

Docker is a containerization tool that became open source in 2013. It allows you to isolate an application from its host system so that the application becomes portable, and the code tested on a developer's workstation can be deployed to production without any concerns about execution runtime dependencies. We'll talk a little about application containerization in this chapter.

A container is a system that embeds an application and its dependencies. Unlike a **virtual machine (VM)**, a container contains only a light **operating system (OS)** and the elements required for the OS, such as system libraries, binaries, and code dependencies.

To learn more about the differences between VMs and containers, and why containers will replace VMs in the future, I suggest you read this blog article: `https://blog.docker.com/2018/08/containers-replacing-virtual-machines/`.

The principal difference between VMs and containers is that each VM that is hosted on a hypervisor contains a complete OS and is therefore completely independent of the guest OS that is on the hypervisor.

Containers, however, don't contain a complete OS—only a few binaries—but they are dependent on the guest OS, and use its resources (**central processing unit (CPU)**, **random-access memory (RAM)**, and network).

In this chapter, we will learn how to install Docker on different platforms, how to create a Docker image, and how to register it in Docker Hub. Then, we'll discuss an example of a **continuous integration/continuous deployment (CI/CD)** pipeline that deploys a Docker image in **Azure Container Instances (ACI)**. After that, we will show how to use Docker to runn tools with **command-line interfaces (CLIs)**.

Finally, we will also learn the basic notions about **Docker Compose** and how to deploy Docker Compose containers in ACI.

This chapter covers the following topics:

- Installing Docker
- Creating a Dockerfile
- Building and running a container on a local machine
- Pushing an image to Docker Hub
- Pushing a Docker image to a private registry (ACR)
- Deploying a container to ACI with a CI/CD pipeline
- Using Docker for running command-line tools
- Getting started with Docker Compose
- Deploying Docker Compose containers in ACI

Technical requirements

This chapter has the following technical requirements:

- An Azure subscription. You can get a free account here: `https://azure.microsoft.com/en-us/free/`.

- For some Azure commands, we will use the Azure CLI. Refer to the documentation here: `https://docs.microsoft.com/en-us/cli/azure/install-azure-cli`.

- In the last part of this chapter, in the *Creating a CI/CD pipeline for the container* section, we will discuss Terraform and the CI/CD pipeline, which were explained in *Chapter 2, Provisioning Cloud Infrastructure with Terraform*, and *Chapter 7, Continuous Integration and Continuous Deployment*.

All of the source code for the scripts included in this chapter is available here: `https://github.com/PacktPublishing/Learning-DevOps-Second-Edition/tree/main/CHAP09`.

Check out the following video to see the code in action:

`https://bit.ly/3t1Jov8`

Installing Docker

Docker's daemon is free and very well suited to developers and small teams—it's what we'll use in this book.

Docker is a cross-platform tool that can be installed on Windows, Linux, or macOS and is also natively present on some cloud providers, such as **Amazon Web Services (AWS)** and Azure.

To operate, Docker needs the following elements:

- **The Docker client**: This allows you to perform various operations on the command line.
- **The Docker daemon**: This is Docker's engine.
- **Docker Registry**: This is a public registry (Docker Hub) or private registry of Docker images.

Before installing Docker, we will first create an account on Docker Hub.

Registering on Docker Hub

Docker Hub is a public space called a **registry**, containing more than 2 million public Docker images that have been deposited by companies, communities, and even individual users.

To register on Docker Hub and list public Docker images, perform the following steps:

1. Go to https://hub.docker.com/, where you will see the following screen:

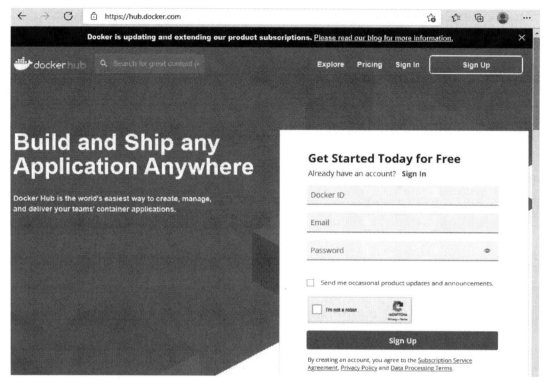

Figure 9.1 – Docker Hub login page

2. Fill in the form with a unique **identifier (ID)**, an email, and a password. Then, click on the **Sign Up** button.

3. Once your account is created, you can then log in to the site, and this account will allow you to upload custom images and download **Docker Desktop**.

4. To view and explore the images available from Docker Hub, go to the **Explore** section, as indicated in the following screenshot:

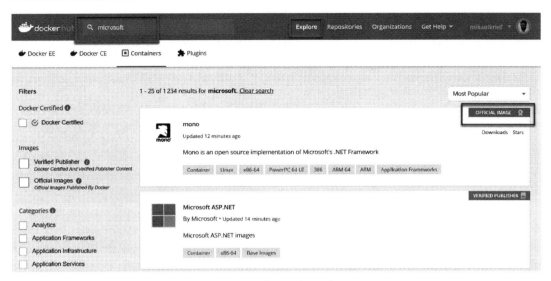

Figure 9.2 – Docker Hub Explore page

A list of Docker images is displayed with a search filter that you can use to search for official images or images from verified publishers, as well as images certified by Docker.

Having created an account on Docker Hub, we will now look at installing Docker on Windows.

Docker installation

We'll now discuss the installation of Docker on Windows in detail.

Before installing Docker Desktop on Windows or macOS, we need to check all license options. For more information about Docker Desktop licensing, read the pricing page (https://www.docker.com/pricing) and the **frequently asked questions (FAQ)** page (https://www.docker.com/pricing/faq).

To install Docker Desktop on a Windows machine, it is necessary to first check the hardware requirements, which are outlined here:

- Windows 10/11 64-bit with at least 4 **gigabytes (GB)** of RAM

- **Windows Subsystem for Linux 2 (WSL 2)** backend or Hyper-V enabled. You can refer to this documentation in the event of any problems: https://docs. docker.com/docker-for-windows/troubleshoot/#virtualization- must-be-enabled.

> **Note**
>
> For more information about WSL, read the documentation here:
>
> `https://docs.microsoft.com/en-us/windows/wsl/`
> `install`
>
> More details about Docker Desktop requirements are specified here:
>
> `https://docs.docker.com/desktop/windows/install/`

To install Docker Desktop, which is the same binary as the Docker installer for Windows and macOS, follow these steps:

1. First, download Docker Desktop by clicking on the **Docker Desktop for Windows** button on the install documentation page at `https://docs.docker.com/desktop/windows/install/`, as indicated in the following screenshot:

Figure 9.3 – Download link for Docker Desktop

2. Once that's downloaded, click on the downloaded **executable (EXE)** file.

3. Then, take the single configuration step, which is a possibility to install required components for the WSL 2 backend, as illustrated in the following screenshot:

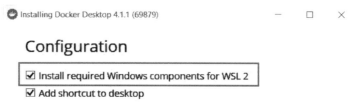

Figure 9.4 – Docker Desktop configuration

In our case, we will check this option to install Windows components using WSL 2 as the backend.

4. Once the installation is complete, we'll get a confirmation message and a button to close the installation, as illustrated in the following screenshot:

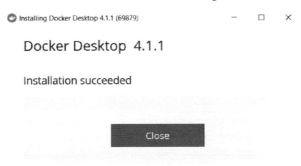

Figure 9.5 – Docker Desktop end installation

5. Finally, to start Docker, launch the Docker Desktop program. An icon will appear in the notification bar indicating that Docker is starting. It will then ask you to log in to Docker Hub via a small window. The startup steps of Docker Desktop are shown in the following screenshot:

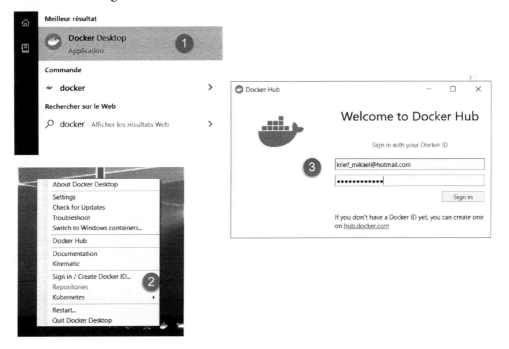

Figure 9.6 – Docker Hub sign-in from Docker Desktop

That's it! We've installed and started Docker on Windows.

To install Docker on another OS, you can read the documentation for each OS at `https://docs.docker.com/get-docker/`. Afterward, you can choose the desired target OS from this page, as shown in the following screenshot:

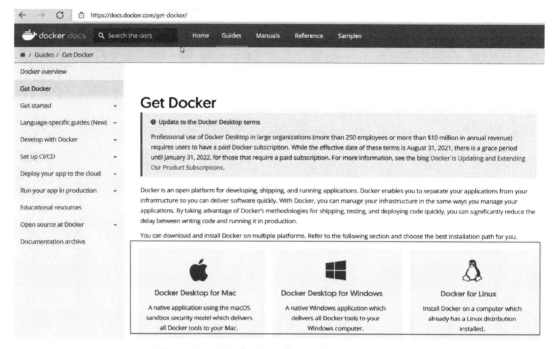

Figure 9.7 – Docker installation documentation

To check your Docker installation, open the Terminal window (it will also work on a Windows PowerShell Terminal) and execute the following command:

```
docker --help
```

You should be able to see something like this:

```
PS C:\Users\mkrief> docker --help
Usage:
  docker [flags]
  docker [command]

Available Commands:
  compose        Docker Compose
  context        Manage contexts
  ecs
  exec           Run a command in a running container
  help           Help about any command
  inspect        Inspect containers
  kill           Kill one or more running containers
  login          Log in to a Docker registry or cloud backend
  logout         Log out from a Docker registry or cloud backend
  logs           Fetch the logs of a container
  prune          prune existing resources in current context
  ps             List containers
  rm             Remove containers
  run            Run a container
  secret         Manages secrets
  serve          Start an api server
  start          Start one or more stopped containers
  stop           Stop one or more running containers
  version        Show the Docker version information
  volume         Manages volumes
```

Figure 9.8 – docker --help command

As you can see in the preceding screenshot, the command displays the different operations available in the Docker client tool.

Before looking at the execution of Docker commands in detail, it is important to have an overview of Docker's concepts.

An overview of Docker's elements

Before executing Docker commands, we will discuss some of Docker's fundamental elements, which are **Dockerfiles**, **containers**, and **volumes**.

First of all, it is important to know that a **Docker image** is a basic element of Docker and consists of a text document called a Dockerfile that contains the binaries and application files we want to containerize.

A **Docker registry** is a centralized storage system for shared Docker images. This registry can be public—as in the case of Docker Hub—or private, such as with **Azure Container Registry** (**ACR**) or JFrog Artifactory.

A container is an instance that is executed from a Docker image. It is possible to have several instances of the same image within a container that the application will run. Finally, a volume is a storage space that is physically located on the host OS (that is, outside the container), and it can be shared across multiple containers if required. This space will allow the storage of persistent elements such as files or databases.

To manipulate these elements, we will use command lines, which will be discussed as we progress through this chapter.

In this section, we discussed Docker Hub and the different steps for creating an account. Then, we looked at the steps for installing Docker Desktop locally, and finally, we finished with an overview of Docker elements.

We will now start working with Docker, and the first operation we will look at is the creation of a Docker image from a Dockerfile.

Creating a Dockerfile

A basic Docker element is a file called a **Dockerfile**, which contains step-by-step instructions for building a Docker image.

To understand how to create a Dockerfile, we'll look at an example that allows us to build a Docker image that contains an Apache web server and a web application.

Let's start by writing a Dockerfile.

Writing a Dockerfile

To write a Dockerfile, we will first create a **HyperText Markup Language** (**HTML**) page that will be our web application. So, we'll create a new `appdocker` directory and an `index.html` page in it, which includes the example code that displays welcome text on a web page, as follows:

```
<html>
  <body>
    <h1>Welcome to my new app</h1>
    This page is test for my demo Dockerfile.<br />
    Enjoy ...
  </body>
</html>
```

Then, in the same directory, we create a Dockerfile (without an extension) with the following content, which we will detail right after:

```
FROM httpd:latest
COPY index.html /usr/local/apache2/htdocs/
```

To create a Dockerfile, start with the FROM statement. The required FROM statement defines the base image, which we will use for our Docker image—any Docker image is built from another Docker image. This base image can be saved either in Docker Hub or in another registry, such as JFrog Artifactory, Nexus Repository, or ACR.

In our code example, we use the Apache httpd image tagged as the latest version, https://hub.docker.com/_/httpd/, and we use the FROM httpd:latest Dockerfile instruction.

Then, we use the COPY instruction to execute the image construction process. Docker copies the local index.html file that we just created into the /usr/local/apache2/htdocs/ directory of the image.

> **Note**
> The source code for this Dockerfile and the HTML page can be found here:
> https://github.com/PacktPublishing/Learning-DevOps-Second-Edition/tree/main/CHAP09/appdocker.

We have just looked at the FROM and COPY instructions of the Dockerfile, but there are other instructions as well that we'll cover in the following section.

Dockerfile instructions overview

We previously mentioned that a Dockerfile file is comprised of instructions, and we also looked at a concrete example with the FROM and COPY instructions. There are other instructions that will allow you to build a Docker image. Here is an overview of the principal instructions that can be used for this purpose:

- FROM: This instruction is used to define the base image for our image, as shown in the example detailed in the preceding *Writing a Dockerfile* section.

- COPY and ADD: These are used to copy one or more local files into an image. The ADD instruction supports an extra two functionalities, to refer to a **Uniform Resource Locator** (**URL**) and to extract compressed files.

> **Note**
>
> For more details about the differences between COPY and ADD, you can read this article: `https://nickjanetakis.com/blog/docker-tip-2-the-difference-between-copy-and-add-in-a-dockerile`.

- RUN and CMD: These instructions take a command as a parameter that will be executed during the construction of the image. The RUN instruction creates a layer so that it can be cached and versioned. The CMD instruction defines a default command to be executed during the call to run the image. The CMD instruction can be overwritten at runtime with an extra parameter provided.

  You can write the following example of the RUN instruction in a Dockerfile to execute the apt-get command:

  ```
  RUN apt-get update
  ```

  With the preceding instruction, we update the apt packages that are already present in the image and create a layer. We can also use the CMD instruction in the following example, which will display a docker message during execution:

  ```
  CMD "echo docker"
  ```

- ENV: This instruction allows you to instantiate environment variables that can be used to build an image. These environment variables will persist throughout the life of the container, as follows:

  ```
  ENV myvar=mykey
  ```

  The preceding command sets a myvar environment variable with the mykey value to the container.

- WORKDIR: This instruction gives the execution directory of the container, as follows:

  ```
  WORKDIR usr/local/apache2
  ```

That was an overview of Dockerfile instructions. There are other instructions that are commonly used, such as EXPOSE, ENTRYPOINT, and VOLUME, which you can find in the official documentation at `https://docs.docker.com/engine/reference/builder/`.

We have just observed that the writing of a Dockerfile is performed with different instructions, such as FROM, COPY, and RUN, which are used to create a Docker image. Now, let's look at how to run Docker in order to build a Docker image from a Dockerfile, and run that image locally to test it.

Building and running a container on a local machine

So far in the chapter, we have discussed Docker elements and have looked at an example of a Dockerfile that is used to containerize a web application. Now, we have all the elements to run Docker.

The execution of Docker is performed by different operations, as outlined here:

- Building a Docker image from a Dockerfile
- Instantiating a new container locally from this image
- Testing our locally containerized application

Let's take a deep dive into each operation.

Building a Docker image

We'll build a Docker image from our previously created Dockerfile that contains the following instructions:

```
FROM httpd:latest
COPY index.html /usr/local/apache2/htdocs/
```

We'll go to a terminal to head into the directory that contains the Dockerfile, and then execute the docker build command with the following syntax:

```
docker build -t demobook:v1 .
```

The -t argument indicates the name of the image and its tag. Here, in our example, we call our image demobook, and the tag we've added is v1.

The . (dot) at the end of the command specifies that we will use the files in the current directory. The following screenshot shows the execution of this command:

Figure 9.9 – docker build command

We can see in this preceding execution the three steps of the Docker image builder, as follows:

1. Docker downloads the defined base image.

2. Docker copies the index.html file in the image.

3. Docker creates and tags the image.

When you execute the docker build command, it downloads the base image indicated in the Dockerfile from Docker Hub, and then Docker executes the various instructions that are mentioned in the Dockerfile.

> **Note**
>
> Note that if during the first execution of the docker build command you get a Get https://registry-1.docker.io/v2/library/httpd/manifests/latest: unauthorized: incorrect username or password error, then execute the docker logout command. Next, restart the docker build command, as indicated in this article: https://medium.com/@blacksourcez/fix-docker-error-unauthorized-incorrect-username-or-password-in-docker-f80c45951b6b.

At the end of the execution, we obtain a locally stored Docker demobook image.

> **Note**
>
> The Docker image is stored in a local folder system depending on your OS. For more information about the location of Docker images, you can read this article: `http://www.scmgalaxy.com/tutorials/location-of-dockers-images-in-all-operating-systems/`.

We can also check if the image is successfully created by executing the following Docker command:

```
docker images
```

Here is the output of the preceding command:

```
PS                   \Learning-DevOps-Second-Edition\CHAP09\appdocker> docker images
REPOSITORY                         TAG                IMAGE ID         CREATED          SIZE
demobook                           v1                 9a3862a66c65     5 minutes ago    143MB
gcr.io/k8s-minikube/kicbase        v0.0.12-snapshot3  25ac91b9c8d7     14 months ago    952MB
```

Figure 9.10 – docker images command

This command displays a list of Docker images on my local machine, and we can see the demobook image we just created. So, the next time the image is built, we will not need to download the httpd image again.

Now that we have created a Docker image of our application, we will instantiate a new container of this image.

Instantiating a new container of an image

To instantiate a new container of our Docker image, we will execute the docker run command in our Terminal, with the following syntax:

```
docker run -d --name demoapp -p 8080:80 demobook:v1
```

The -d parameter indicates that the container will run in the background. In the --name parameter, we specify the name of the container we want. In the -p parameter, we indicate the desired port translation. In our example, this would mean port 80 of the container will be translated to port 8080 on our local machine. And finally, the last parameter of the command is the name of the image and its tag.

The execution of this command is shown in the following screenshot:

```
PS                   \Learning-DevOps-Second-Edition\CHAP09\appdocker> docker run -d --name demoapp -p 8080:80 demobook:v1
6cce2099b174cbe29fcd408d044cd5b2ebbdf50cedfb1a5e2984e346ebee7e1a
```

Figure 9.11 – docker run command

At the end of its execution, this command displays the ID of the container, and the container runs in the background. It is also possible to display a list of containers running on the local machine by executing the following command:

```
docker ps
```

The following screenshot shows the execution with our container:

Figure 9.12 – docker ps command

After the execution of each container, we have its shortcut ID, its associated image, its name, its execution command, and its translation port information displayed.

So, we have built a Docker image and instantiated a new container of that image locally. We will now see how to run a web application that is in the local container.

Testing a container locally

Everything that runs in a container remains inside it—this is the principle of container isolation. However, in the port translation that we did previously, you can test your container on your local machine with the run command.

To do this, open a web browser and enter http://localhost:8080 with 8080, which represents the translation port indicated in the command. You should be able to see the following result:

Figure 9.13 – Docker application launched

We can see the content of our index.html page displayed.

In this section, we looked at the different Docker commands that can be used to build a Docker image. Then, we instantiated a new container from that image, and finally, we tested it locally.

In the next section, we will see how to publish a Docker image in Docker Hub.

Pushing an image to Docker Hub

The goal of creating a Docker image that contains an application is to be able to use it on servers that contain Docker and host the company's applications, just as with a VM.

In order for an image to be downloaded to another computer, it must be saved in a Docker image registry. As already mentioned in this chapter, there are several Docker registries that can be installed on-premises, which is the case for JFrog Artifactory and Nexus Repository.

If you want to create a public image, you can push (or upload) it to Docker Hub, which is Docker's public (and free, depending on your license) registry. We will now see how to upload the image we created in the previous section to Docker Hub. To do this, you need to have an account on Docker Hub, which we created prior to installing Docker Desktop.

To push a Docker image to Docker Hub, perform the following steps:

1. **Sign in to Docker Hub**: Log in to Docker Hub using the following command:

    ```
    docker login -u <your dockerhub login>
    ```

    When executing the command, you will be asked to enter your Docker Hub password and indicate that you are connected to the Docker registry, as shown in the following screenshot:

    ```
    PS            \Learning_DevOps\CHAP07\appdocker> docker login -u mikaelkr
    Password:
    Login Succeeded
    ```

    Figure 9.14 – The docker login command

2. **Retrieve the image ID**: The next step consists of retrieving the ID of the image that has been created. To do so, we will execute the `docker images` command to display a list of images with their ID.

    ```
    PS            \Learning-DevOps-Second-Edition\CHAP09\appdocker> docker images
    REPOSITORY                      TAG                IMAGE ID        CREATED         SIZE
    demobook                        v1                 9a3862a66c65    17 hours ago    143MB
    gcr.io/k8s-minikube/kicbase     v0.0.12-snapshot3  25ac91b9c8d7    14 months ago   952MB
    ```

    Figure 9.15 – Docker images list

3. **Tag the image for Docker Hub**: With the ID of the image we retrieved, we will now tag the image for Docker Hub. To do so, the following command is executed:

    ```
    docker tag <image ID> <dockerhub login>/demobook:v1
    ```

    The following screenshot shows the execution of this command on the created image:

    ```
    PS            \Learning_DevOps\CHAP07\appdocker> docker tag a121d88f6e18 mikaelkrief/demobook:v1
    ```

    Figure 9.16 – docker tag

4. **Push the Docker image to Docker Hub**: After tagging the image, the last step is to push the tagged image to Docker Hub.

For this purpose, we will execute the following command:

```
docker push docker.io/<dockerhub login>/demobook:v1
```

The following screenshot shows the execution of the preceding command:

```
PS              \Learning-DevOps-Second-Edition\CHAP09\appdocker> docker push docker.io/mikaelkrief/demobook:v1
The push refers to repository [docker.io/mikaelkrief/demobook]
f083a28f9cfa: Pushed
4dcdec0b7a0e: Mounted from library/httpd
c86537ee54f9: Mounted from library/httpd
ecd2b49ef243: Mounted from library/httpd
7511c367f47a: Mounted from library/httpd
e8b689711f21: Mounted from library/httpd
v1: digest: sha256:380d9e0b2beb20c495b496c7047bd3d808f048307a5b5c84cc1e1de3fe119e79 size: 1572
```

Figure 9.17 – docker push image

We can see from this execution that the image is uploaded to Docker Hub.

To view the pushed image in Docker Hub, we connect to the Docker Hub web portal at https://hub.docker.com/ and see that the image is present, as shown in the following screenshot:

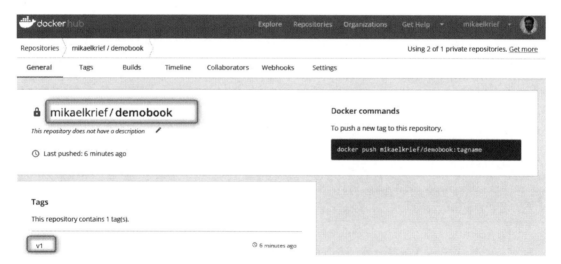

Figure 9.18 – The pushed image in Docker Hub with tag

By default, the image pushed to Docker Hub is in public mode—everybody can view it in the explorer and use it.

We can access this image in Docker Hub in the Docker Hub search engine, as shown in the following screenshot:

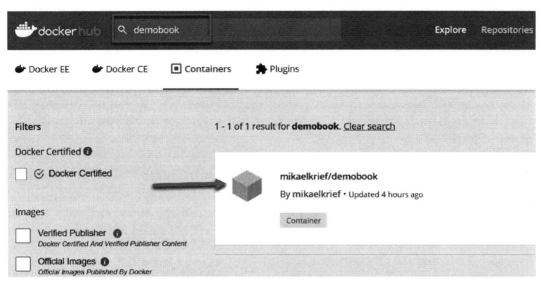

Figure 9.19 – Finding the image in Docker Hub

To make this image private—meaning only you are authenticated to use it—you must go to the **Settings** tab of the image and click on the **Make private** button, as shown in the following screenshot:

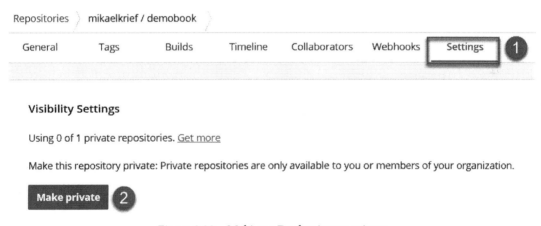

Figure 9.20 – Making a Docker image private

In this section, we looked at the steps and Docker commands for logging in to Docker Hub via the command line, and then we looked at the `tag` and `push` commands for uploading a Docker image to Docker Hub.

In the next section, we will see how to push a Docker image to a private Docker registry using an example ACR instance.

Pushing a Docker image to a private registry (ACR)

In the previous section, we learned how to push a Docker image to Docker Hub, which is a public registry. Now, we will learn how to push a Docker image to a private registry.

There are a lot of on-premises or cloud solutions that enable the Docker private registry. Here is a list of these solutions:

- Docker registry server: `https://docs.docker.com/registry/deploying/`
- Artifactory from JFrog: `https://www.jfrog.com/confluence/display/JFROG/Docker+Registry`
- Amazon **Elastic Container Registry (ECR)**: `https://aws.amazon.com/ecr/`
- **Google Container Registry (GCR)**: `https://cloud.google.com/container-registry`
- ACR: `https://azure.microsoft.com/en-us/services/container-registry/`

In this section, we will study the use of one of these solutions—ACR.

To push a Docker image into ACR, we will proceed with these steps:

1. Before pushing a Docker image, we will create an ACR resource using one of the following:

   - The Azure CLI (`https://docs.microsoft.com/en-us/azure/container-registry/container-registry-get-started-azure-cli`). The `az cli` script that creates a resource group and an ACR resource is shown here:

     ```
     az group create --name RG-ACR --location eastus
     az acr create --resource-group RG-ACR --name acrdemo
     --sku Basic
     ```

   - PowerShell (`https://docs.microsoft.com/en-us/azure/container-registry/container-registry-get-started-powershell`). The PowerShell script that creates a resource group and an ACR resource is shown here:

     ```
     New-AzResourceGroup -Name RG-ACR -Location EastUS
     $registry = New-AzContainerRegistry -ResourceGroupName
     "RG-ARC" -Name "acrdemo" -EnableAdminUser -Sku Basic
     ```

- The Azure portal (`https://docs.microsoft.com/en-us/azure/ container-registry/container-registry-get-started-portal`)

In the next steps, we will use an ACR resource named `demobookacr`.

2. Then, we will connect to our Azure account by running the following `az cli` command:

```
az login
```

3. We connect to the created ACR resource (in *Step 1*) with the following `az acr login` command by passing the `--name` argument as the name of the ACR resource created in *Step 1*, as follows:

```
az acr login --name demobookacr
```

This command will connect to the Docker registry using the `docker login` command in the background.

4. For pushing a Docker image into this ACR resource, we will execute a couple of commands.

The first command is to create a tag to the local image, as illustrated here:

```
docker tag demobook:v1 demobookacr.azurecr.io/demobook:v1
```

The second command is to push the image into the ACR resource, as illustrated here:

```
docker push demobookacr.azurecr.io/demobook:v1
```

These two commands are exactly the same as those we learned for tagging and pushing a Docker image into Docker Hub, with the difference being that the URL of the Docker registry for ACR here is `<acr name>.azurecr.io`.

The following screenshot shows the execution of these commands:

```
PS C:\Users\mkrief> docker tag demobook:v1 demobookacr.azurecr.io/demobook:v1
PS C:\Users\mkrief> docker push demobookacr.azurecr.io/demobook:v1
The push refers to repository [demobookacr.azurecr.io/demobook]
f083a28f9cfa: Pushed
4dcdec0b7a0e: Pushed
c86537ee54f9: Pushed
ecd2b49ef243: Pushed
7511c367f47a: Pushed
e8b689711f21: Pushed
v1: digest: sha256:380d9e0b2beb20c495b496c7047bd3d808f048307a5b5c84cc1e1de3fe119e79 size: 1572
```

Figure 9.21 – Pushing Docker image into ACR

And the following screenshot shows the pushed Docker image in ACR:

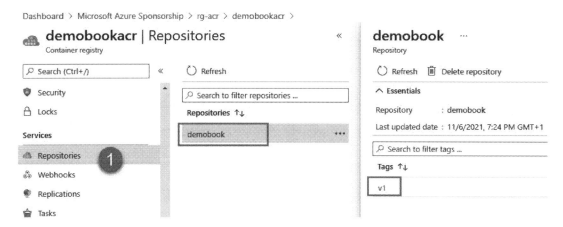

Figure 9.22 – Docker image in ACR

5. Finally, to pull this Docker image, we will use the following command:

```
docker pull demobookacr.azurecr.io/demobook:v1
```

In this section, we learned how to use Docker to push and pull Docker images in a private Docker registry (that is, ACR).

In the next section, we will see how to deploy this image with a CI/CD pipeline in managed cloud container services—ACI and Terraform.

Deploying a container to ACI with a CI/CD pipeline

One of the major reasons Docker has quickly become attractive to developers and operations teams is because the deployment of Docker images and containers has made CI and CD pipelines for enterprise applications easier.

To automate the deployment of our application, we will create a CI/CD pipeline that deploys the Docker image containing our application in ACI.

ACI is a managed service by Azure that allows you to deploy containers very easily, without having to worry about the hardware architecture.

> **Note**
>
> To learn more about ACI, head to the official page at https://azure. microsoft.com/en-us/services/container-instances/.

In addition, we will use Terraform for **infrastructure as code (IaC)**, which we discussed in *Chapter 2, Provisioning Cloud Infrastructure with Terraform*, using the Azure ACI resource and its integration with the Docker image.

We will therefore divide this section into two parts, as follows:

- The Terraform code configuration of the Azure ACI and its integration with our Docker image
- An example of a CI/CD pipeline in Azure Pipelines, which allows you to execute the Terraform code

To start, we will write the Terraform code that allows you to provision an ACI resource in Azure.

Writing the Terraform code for ACI

To provision an ACI resource with Terraform, we navigate to a new `terraform-aci` directory and create a Terraform file, `main.tf`.

In this code, we will provide Terraform code for a resource group and ACI resource using the `azurerm_container_group` Terraform object.

> **Note**
>
> Documentation for the Terraform ACI resource is available here: `https://registry.terraform.io/providers/hashicorp/azurerm/latest/docs/resources/container_group`.

This `main.tf` file contains the following Terraform code, which creates a resource group:

```
resource "azurerm_resource_group" "acidemobook" {
  name = "demoBook"
  location = "westus2"
}
```

In this `main.tf` file, we add `variable` declarations in the Terraform configuration, as follows:

```
variable "imageversion" {
  description ="Tag of the image to deploy"
}
variable "dockerhub-username" {
```

```
   description ="Tag of the image to deploy"
}
```

And we add the Terraform code for the ACI with the `azurerm_container_group` resource block, as follows:

```
resource "azurerm_container_group" "aci-myapp" {
    name = "aci-agent"
    location = "West Europe"
    resource_group_name = azurerm_resource_group.acidemobook.
name
    os_type = "linux"
    container {
        name = "myappdemo"
        image = "docker.io/mikaelkrief/${var.dockerhub-
username}:${var.imageversion}"
        cpu = "0.5" memory = "1.5"
        ports {
        port = 80
        protocol = "TCP"
        }
    }
}
```

In the preceding code snippets, we do the following:

- We declare `imageversion` and `dockerhub-username` variables, which will be instantiated during the CI/CD pipeline and include the username and the tag of the image to be deployed.

- We use the `azurerm_container_group` resource from Terraform to manage the ACI. In its `image` property, we indicate the information of the image to be deployed—meaning, its full name in Docker Hub as well as its tag, which in our example is deported in the `imageversion` variable.

Finally, in order to protect the Terraform state file, we can use the Terraform remote backend by using Azure Blob storage, as we discussed in the *Protecting the state file in the remote backend* section of *Chapter 2, Provisioning Cloud Infrastructure with Terraform*.

> **Note**
>
> The complete source code of this Terraform file is available here: `https://github.com/PacktPublishing/Learning-DevOps-Second-Edition/tree/main/CHAP09/terraform-aci`.

We have the Terraform code that allows us to create an Azure ACI resource that will execute a container of our image. Now, we will create a CI/CD pipeline that will automatically deploy the container of the application.

Creating a CI/CD pipeline for the container

To create a CI/CD pipeline that will build our image and execute the Terraform code, we can use all the tools that we discussed in detail in *Chapter 7, Continuous Integration and Continuous Delivery*.

In this chapter, to visualize the pipeline, we will use **Azure Pipelines**, which is one of the previously detailed tools. It is advisable to carefully read the *Using Azure Pipelines* section of *Chapter 7, Continuous Integration and Continuous Delivery*. For this reason, we will not detail all the stages of the pipeline, but only those relevant to our container subject.

To implement the CI/CD pipeline in Azure Pipelines, we will proceed with these steps:

1. We'll create a new build definition whose **source code** will point to the fork of the GitHub repository (`https://github.com/PacktPublishing/Learning-DevOps-Second-Edition`), and select the root folder of this repository, as shown in the following screenshot:

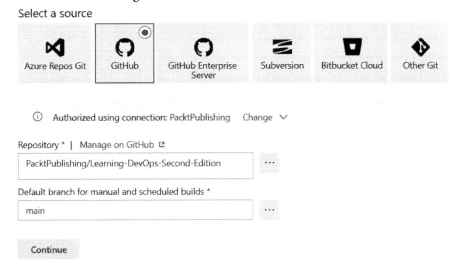

Figure 9.23 – Azure Pipelines with GitHub sources

> **Note**
>
> For more information about forks in GitHub, read *Chapter 16, DevOps for Open Source Projects*.

You are free to use any source control version available in Azure Pipelines.

2. Then, on the **Variables** tab, we will define variables that will be used in the pipeline. The following screenshot shows the information on the **Variables** tab:

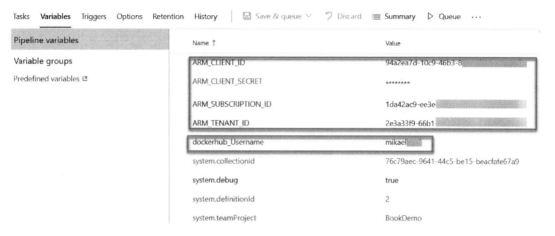

Figure 9.24 – Pipeline variables

We defined four pieces of Terraform connection information for Azure and the username of Docker Hub.

3. Then, on the **Tasks** tab, we must take the following steps:

   A. Run the `docker build` command on the Dockerfile.

   B. Push the image to Docker Hub.

   C. Run the Terraform code to update the ACI resource with the new version of the updated image.

The following screenshot shows the configuration of the tasks:

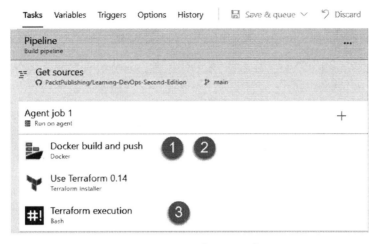

Figure 9.25 – Pipeline steps list

We configure the tasks mentioned in *Step 3* with these steps:

1. The first task, **Docker build and push**, allows you to build the Docker image and push it to Docker Hub. Its configuration is quite simple, as we can see here:

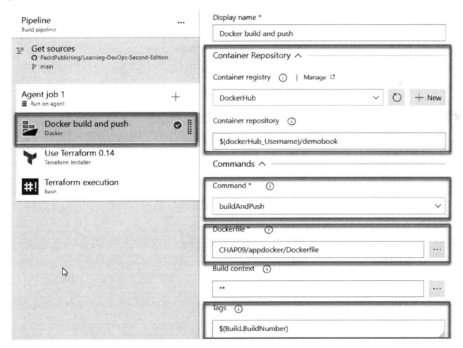

Figure 9.26 – Docker build and push step parameters

These are the required parameters of this task:

- A connection to Docker Hub using Service Connection named DockerHub
- The tag of the image that will be pushed to Docker Hub

2. The second task, **Terraform Installer with the display name Use Terraform 0.14**, allows you to download Terraform on the pipeline agent by specifying the version of Terraform that you want.

> **Note**
> This task is available in the Visual Studio Marketplace at
> `https://marketplace.visualstudio.com/`
> `items?itemName=charleszipp.azure-pipelines-tasks-`
> `terraform&targetId=76c79aec-9641-44c5-be15-`
> `beacfafe67a9.`

The following screenshot shows its configuration, which is very simple:

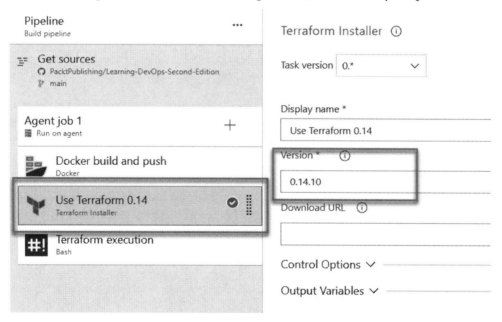

Figure 9.27 – Terraform step parameters

3. The last task, **Bash**, allows you the Terraform execution inside a Bash script, and this screenshot shows its configuration:

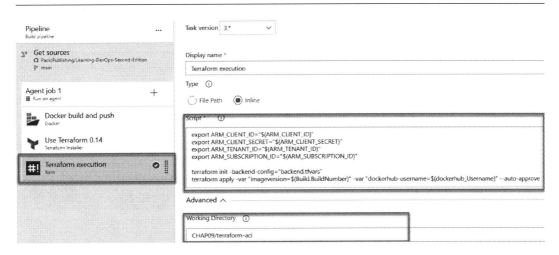

Figure 9.28 – Bash step parameters

The configured script looks like this:

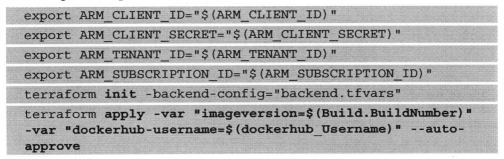

This script performs three actions, which are done in the following order:

A.   Exports the environment variables required for Terraform.

B.   Executes the `terraform init` command.

C.   Executes `terraform apply` to apply the changes, with the two `-var` parameters, which are our Docker Hub username as well as the tag to be applied. These parameters allow the execution of a container with the new image that has just been pushed to Docker Hub.

Then, to configure the build agent to use in the **Agent job** options, we use the Azure Pipelines agent-hosted Ubuntu 16.04, as shown in the following screenshot:

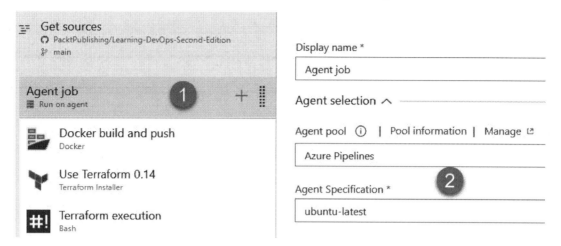

Figure 9.29 – Agent job parameters

Finally, the last configuration is the trigger configuration on the **Triggers** tab, which enables the CI with the trigger of this build at each commit, as shown in the following screenshot:

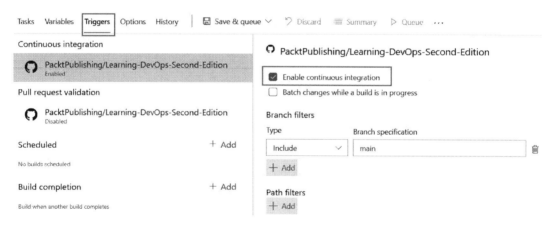

Figure 9.30 – Enabled CI

That completes the configuration of the CI/CD pipeline in Azure Pipelines.

After we trigger this build, we should be able to see a new version of the Docker image at the end of its execution, which corresponds to the number of the build that pushed the Docker image into Docker Hub, as illustrated in the following screenshot:

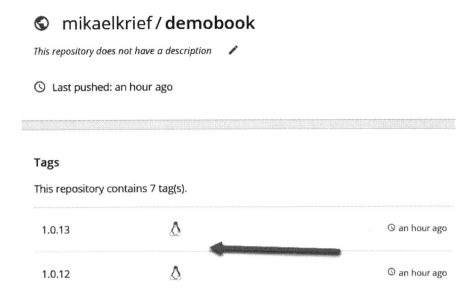

Figure 9.31 – Pushed Docker image in Docker Hub via pipeline

In the Azure portal, we have our `aci-app` ACI resource with our `mydemoapp` container, as you can see in the following screenshot:

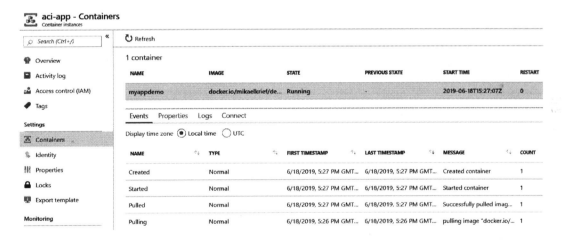

Figure 9.32 – ACI containers

Notice that the container is running well.

Now, to access our application, we need to retrieve the public **fully qualified domain name (FQDN)** URL of the container provided in the Azure portal. The following screenshot shows where you can find this:

Figure 9.33 – FQDN of application container in ACI

We open a web browser with this URL:

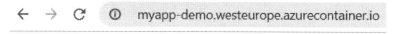

Welcome to my new app

This page is test for my demo Dockerfile.
Enjoy ...

Figure 9.34 – Testing the application

Our web application is displayed correctly.

The next time the application is updated, the CI/CD build is triggered, a new version of the image will be pushed into Docker Hub, and a new container will be loaded with this new version of the image.

In this section, we have looked at writing Terraform code to manage an ACI resource and the creation of a CI/CD pipeline in Azure Pipelines, which allows you to deploy the application's image in Docker Hub and then update the ACI resource with the new version of the image.

In the next section, we will discuss another use case of Docker—that is, for running command-line tools.

Using Docker for running command-line tools

Up to now in this chapter, we have studied use cases of Docker to containerize a web application with Nginx.

Another use case of Docker is to be able to run command-line tools that are in Docker containers.

To illustrate this, we will run a sample of Terraform configuration using the **Terraform** binary, which is not located on a local machine but in a Docker container.

The Terraform configuration that we use in this section is the same as that in the previous section, *Deploying a container to ACI with a CI/CD pipeline*, and the source code is available here: https://github.com/PacktPublishing/Learning-DevOps-Second-Edition/tree/main/CHAP09/terraform-aci.

The goal of this lab is to run this Terraform configuration using the Terraform binary that is in the Docker container. To run this lab, following these steps:

1. First we pull the official Terraform image from the Docker Hub with this command:

    ```
    docker pull hashicorp/terraform
    ```

    The following screenshot shows the execution of this command:

    ```
    PS            \Learning-DevOps-Second-Edition\CHAP09\terraform-aci> docker pull hashicorp/terraform
    Using default tag: latest
    latest: Pulling from hashicorp/terraform
    a0d0a0d46f8b: Pull complete
    2bb95c284368: Pull complete
    e04940e4168e: Pull complete
    Digest: sha256:b54ec7c5c0599bc943373835889ecfae1ef5adcf229854c758a5c94172c30856
    Status: Downloaded newer image for hashicorp/terraform:latest
    docker.io/hashicorp/terraform:latest
    ```

    Figure 9.35 – docker pull command to pull Terraform image

2. Then, inside the folder that contains the Terraform configuration, we will run the Terraform workflow using the following three docker run commands:

    First, we run the terraform init command, as follows:

    ```
    docker run -i -t -v ${PWD}:/usr/tf -w /usr/tf '
    --env ARM_CLIENT_ID="<azure clientId>" '
    --env ARM_CLIENT_SECRET="<azure client secret>" '
    --env ARM_SUBSCRIPTION_ID="<azure subscription>" '
    --env ARM_TENANT_ID="azure tenant id" '
    --env ARM_ACCESS_KEY="azure access key " '
    hashicorp/terraform:latest '
    init -backend-config="backend.tfvars"
    ```

    In this docker run command, we use the following arguments:

    -   -v to create a volume for mounting the current local directory that contains the Terraform code inside the /usr/tf directory on the container

- `-w` to specify the working directory

- `--env` with the environment variable necessary for Terraform to authenticate to Azure

- `Hashicorp/terraform:latest`, which is the name of the image

- `init -backend-config="backend.tfvars"`, which is the argument for the Terraform command to run

Now, we run the `terraform plan` command, as follows:

```
docker run -i -t -v ${PWD}:/usr/tf -w /usr/tf '
--env ARM_CLIENT_ID="<azure clientId>" '
--env ARM_CLIENT_SECRET="<azure client secret>" '
--env ARM_SUBSCRIPTION_ID="<azure subscription>" '
--env ARM_TENANT_ID="azure tenant id" '
--env ARM_ACCESS_KEY="azure access key " '
hashicorp/terraform:latest '
plan -var dockerhub-username="<docker hub username>" -out
plan.tfplan
```

In this preceding command, we use the same argument, with the `plan` command for Terraform.

Finally, we run the `terraform apply` command, as follows:

```
docker run -i -t -v ${PWD}:/usr/tf -w /usr/tf '
--env ARM_CLIENT_ID="<azure clientId>" '
--env ARM_CLIENT_SECRET="<azure client secret>" '
--env ARM_SUBSCRIPTION_ID="<azure subscription>" '
--env ARM_TENANT_ID="azure tenant id" '
--env ARM_ACCESS_KEY="azure access key " '
hashicorp/terraform:latest '
apply plan.tfplan
```

We have just studied a basic example of using a tool (here with Terraform) that runs in a Docker container. This use of Docker has the following advantages:

- It's not necessary to install these tools on its local machine; the installation process is done by the tool editor in the Docker image.

- You can run several versions of the same tool.

In the next section, we will discuss the use of Docker Compose, which allows us to mount several Docker images to the same group of containers.

Getting started with Docker Compose

So far in this chapter, we have studied how to write a Dockerfile, create a Docker image, and run a container of this Docker image.

Today, applications are not working in standalone mode; they need other dependencies such as a service (for example, another application; an **application programming interface (API)**) or a database. This implies that for these applications, the Docker workflow is more consistent. Indeed, when we work with several Docker applications, we have to execute for each of them the `docker build` and `docker run` commands, which requires some effort.

Docker Compose is a more advanced Docker tool that allows us to deploy several Docker containers at the same time in the same deployment cycle. Docker Compose also allows us to manage elements that are common to these Docker containers, such as data volumes and network configuration.

> **Note**
>
> For more details about Docker Compose, read the official documentation here:
>
> `https://docs.docker.com/compose`

In Docker Compose, this configuration—which contains the Docker images, the volumes, and the network that constitutes the artifacts of the same application—is done simply in a configuration file in **YAML Ain't Markup Language (YAML)** format.

In this section, we will learn about the basic mode installation of Docker Compose. Then, we will write a simple Docker Compose configuration file to run an nginx application with a MySQL database in the same context. Finally, we will execute this Docker Compose configuration file and view the result in Docker containers.

Installing Docker Compose

On Windows or macOS, the **Docker Compose** binary is already installed with Docker Desktop.

Follow this documentation to install the Docker Compose binary on Linux: `https://docs.docker.com/compose/install/#install-compose-on-linux-systems`.

We can check if Docker Compose is correctly installed by running the following command:

```
docker-compose version
```

The following screenshot shows the result of this command:

```
PS C:\...........\Learning-DevOps-Second-Edition\CHAP09\docker-compose> docker-compose version
docker-compose version 1.29.2, build 5becea4c
docker-py version: 5.0.0
CPython version: 3.9.0
OpenSSL version: OpenSSL 1.1.1g  21 Apr 2020
```

Figure 9.36 – docker-compose version command

This command displays the version of the installed docker-compose binary.

Now that Docker Compose is installed, we will write the Docker Compose configuration YAML file.

Writing the Docker Compose configuration file

For deploying containers using Docker Compose, we will write a configuration file to run an nginx container coupled with a mysql container.

For this, we will create a new file named docker-compose.yml with the following content that is in two blocks of code.

The first code snippet, in YAML, is for creating an nginx container, as follows:

```yaml
version: '3' #version of the Docker Compose YAML schema
services:
  nginx:
    image: nginx:latest
    container_name: nginx-container
    ports:
    - 8080:80
```

In the preceding code snippet, we start with the services property, which contains a list of services (or Docker applications) to run in Docker. The first service is the nginx service. We configure the nginx docker image to use, the name of the container, and the exposed port, which is 8080, for the local access of the nginx service.

Then, we add the YAML for the MySQL service with the following code:

```
mysql:
    image: mysql:5.7
    container_name: mysql-container
    environment:
     MYSQL_ROOT_PASSWORD: secret
     MYSQL_DATABASE: mydb
     MYSQL_USER: myuser
     MYSQL_PASSWORD: password
```

In the preceding code snippet, we configure the `mysql` service with the Docker image, the name of the container, and the required environment variable for configuring the database access.

> **Note**
>
> The complete source code of this file is available here:
>
> `https://github.com/PacktPublishing/Learning-DevOps-Second-Edition/blob/main/CHAP09/docker-compose/docker-compose.yml`

We have just written the YAML file of the `docker-compose` configuration. Now, we will run Docker Compose to execute the containers described in this configuration.

Executing Docker Compose

For running the Docker containers described in the YAML configuration file, we will run the basic operation of Docker Compose by executing the following command in the folder that contains the `docker-compose.yml` file:

```
docker-compose up -d
```

> **Note**
>
> The `-d` option is added for running the containers in detached mode.
>
> The complete documentation for the `docker-compose` CLI is available here:
>
> `https://docs.docker.com/compose/reference/`

The following screenshot shows the execution of the `docker-compose up -d` command:

```
PS              \Learning-DevOps-Second-Edition\CHAP09\docker-compose> docker-compose up -d
[+] Running 12/12
 - mysql Pulled                                                                              42.7s
   - b380bbd43752 Already exists                                                              0.0s
   - f23cbf2ecc5d Pull complete                                                               0.6s
   - 30cfc6c29c0a Pull complete                                                               2.6s
   - b38609286cbe Pull complete                                                               2.7s
   - 8211d9e66cd6 Pull complete                                                               2.8s
   - 2313f9eeca4a Pull complete                                                               8.7s
   - 7eb487d00da0 Pull complete                                                               8.7s
   - a71aacf913e7 Pull complete                                                               8.8s
   - 393153c555df Pull complete                                                              40.0s
   - 06628e2290d7 Pull complete                                                              40.1s
   - ff2ab8dac9ac Pull complete                                                              40.1s
[+] Running 2/2
 - Container mysql-container   Started                                                        4.0s
 - Container nginx-container   Running                                                        0.0s
```

Figure 9.37 – docker-compose up -d command

At the end of this execution, Docker Compose displays a list of started containers. Here, in our example, these are `nginx` and `mysql`.

To check that the containers are running, we execute the `docker ps` Docker command to display a list of running containers.

The following screenshot shows the execution of the `docker ps` command:

```
PS C:\Users\mkrief> docker ps
CONTAINER ID   IMAGE          COMMAND                CREATED         STATUS         PORTS                      NAMES
2fc77d3debb0   nginx:latest   "/docker-entrypoint..."   3 minutes ago   Up 3 minutes   0.0.0.0:8080->80/tcp       nginx-container
7db499e87466   mysql:5.7      "docker-entrypoint.s..."  3 minutes ago   Up 3 minutes   3306/tcp, 33060/tcp        mysql-container
```

Figure 9.38 – docker ps command

We can see that our two containers are running.

On Windows or macOS, we can also use Docker Desktop, which displays in the containers' list the running containers mounted by Docker Compose inside the `docker-compose` group, as illustrated in the following screenshot:

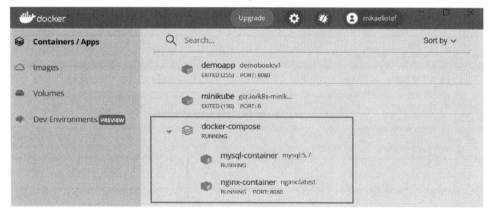

Figure 9.39 – Docker Desktop list of Docker Compose containers

In this section, we learned some basic features for writing Docker Compose configuration files and executing Docker Compose locally to run Docker containers.

In the next section, we will discuss the same execution of these containers remotely on ACI.

Deploying Docker Compose containers in ACI

We discussed ACI in the *Deploying a container to ACI with a CI/CD pipeline* section.

Now, we will learn how to execute containers with Docker Compose configuration in ACI to run a set of containers that are on the same application services.

For this lab, we will use the same Docker Compose configuration we learned in the *Using Docker for running command-line tools* section. The only difference is that the running port on the nginx service is 80 instead of 8080, which we used locally (because my port 80 is already used by another service).

For deploying containers on ACI, we will perform the following steps:

1. Inside our Azure subscription, we will create a new resource group called `rg-acicompose`.

2. Then, in the console terminal, run the following Docker command to log in to Azure:

    ```
    docker login azure
    ```

    The execution of this command opens a window that allows us to authenticate ourselves to our Azure subscription.

3. Create a new Docker context by running the following command:

    ```
    docker context create aci demobookaci
    ```

    By running this command, we choose the Azure subscription and the resource group we created in *Step 1*, as illustrated in the following screenshot:

```
PS              \Learning-DevOps-Second-Edition\CHAP09\docker-compose> docker context create aci demobookaci
? Select a subscription ID Microsoft Azure Sponsorship (8                                    )
? Select a resource group rg-acicompose (westeurope)
Successfully created aci context "demobookaci"
```

Figure 9.40 – Creating Docker context for ACI

4. Check the new Docker context by running the following command:

    ```
    docker context ls
    ```

This command displays a list of Docker contexts and indicates with a * symbol the current context, as illustrated in the following screenshot:

Figure 9.41 – List of Docker contexts

5. Select the newly created `demobookaci` context by running the following command:

```
docker context use demobookaci
```

6. Finally, to deploy the Docker Compose configuration application inside this ACI resource, run the following command:

```
docker compose up
```

The following screenshot shows the result of the execution of this command:

```
PS                 \Learning-DevOps-Second-Edition\CHAP09\docker-compose> docker compose up
[+] Running 3/3
 - Group docker-compose   Created
 - nginx-container        Created
 - mysql-container        Created
```

Figure 9.42 – docker compose up command for deployment to ACI

In our Azure subscription, we can see the created ACI resource with two containers, as indicated in the following screenshot:

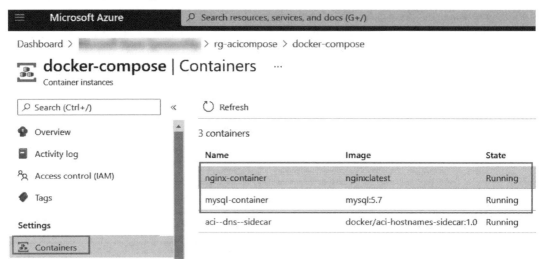

Figure 9.43 – ACI containers created by Docker Compose

Finally, to test and gain access to the deployed application, find the application FQDN in the ACI properties and launch the application in the browser. This is exactly what we learned in the *Deploying a container to ACI with a CI/CD pipeline* section of this chapter.

> **Note**
>
> For another sample of Docker Compose in ACI, read an official tutorial here:
>
> `https://docs.microsoft.com/en-us/azure/container-instances/tutorial-docker-compose`

In this section, we have learned how to deploy multiple containers using Docker Compose in ACI using the `docker-compose` YAML file and some Docker command-line contexts.

Summary

In this chapter, we presented Docker and its essential concepts. We discussed the necessary steps to create a Docker Hub account, and then we installed Docker locally with Docker Desktop.

We created a Dockerfile that details the composition of a Docker image of a web application, and we also looked at the principal instructions that it is composed of— FROM, COPY, and RUN.

We executed the `docker build` and `docker run` commands to build an image from our Dockerfile and execute it locally, and then pushed it to Docker Hub using the `push` command.

In the second part of this chapter, we implemented and executed a CI/CD pipeline in Azure Pipelines to deploy our container in an ACI resource that was provisioned with Terraform. Then, we discussed the use of Docker for running command-line tools such as Terraform.

Finally, we learned to install and use Docker Compose to create multiple application containers and deploy them in ACI.

In the next chapter, we will continue with the subject of containers, and we will look at the use of Kubernetes, which is a tool to manage containers on a large scale. We will use the **Azure Kubernetes Service** (**AKS**) and Azure Pipelines to deploy an application in Kubernetes with a CI/CD pipeline.

Questions

1. What is Docker Hub?

2. What is the basic element that allows you to create a Docker image?

3. In a Dockerfile, what is the instruction that defines a base image to use?

4. Which Docker command allows you to create a Docker image?

5. Which Docker command allows you to instantiate a new container?

6. Which Docker command allows you to publish an image in Docker Hub?

Further reading

If you want to know more about Docker, here are some great books:

- *Docker Cookbook*: `https://www.packtpub.com/virtualization-and-cloud/docker-cookbook-second-edition`

- *Beginning DevOps with Docker*: `https://www.packtpub.com/virtualization-and-cloud/beginning-devops-docker`

10
Managing Containers Effectively with Kubernetes

In the previous chapter, we learned in detail about containers with Docker, about the construction of a Docker image, and about the instantiation of a new container on the local machine. Finally, we set up a **continuous integration/continuous deployment (CI/CD)** pipeline that builds an image, deploys it in Docker Hub, and executes its container in **Azure Container Instances (ACI)**.

All this works well and does not pose too many problems when working with a few containers. But in so-called **microservice applications**—that is, applications that are composed of several services (each of them is a container), we will need to manage and orchestrate these containers.

There are two major container orchestration tools on the market: Docker Swarm and Kubernetes.

For some time now, Kubernetes, also known as **K8S**, has proved to be a true leader in the field of container management and is therefore becoming a *must* for the containerization of applications.

In this chapter, we will learn how to install Kubernetes on a local machine, as well as an example of how to deploy an application in Kubernetes, both in a standard way and with Helm. We will learn in more depth about Helm by creating a chart and publishing it in a private registry on **Azure Container Registry** (**ACR**).

Then, we will talk about **Azure Kubernetes Service** (**AKS**) as an example of a Kubernetes cluster, and finally, we will learn how to monitor applications and metrics in Kubernetes.

This chapter will cover the following topics:

- Installing Kubernetes
- A first example of Kubernetes application deployment
- Using Helm as a package manager
- Publishing a Helm chart in a private registry (ACR)
- Using AKS
- Creating a CI/CD pipeline for Kubernetes with Azure Pipelines
- Monitoring applications and metrics in Kubernetes

Technical requirements

This chapter is a continuation of the previous chapter on Docker, so to understand it properly, it is necessary to have read that chapter and to have installed Docker Desktop (for the Windows **operating system** (**OS**)).

In the CI/CD part of this chapter, you will need to retrieve the source code that was provided in the previous chapter on Docker, which is available at `https://github.com/PacktPublishing/Learning-DevOps-Second-Edition/tree/main/CHAP09/appdocker`.

For the section about Helm charts on ACR, it's necessary to have an Azure subscription (register for free here: `https://azure.microsoft.com/en-us/free/`) and that you have installed the Azure **Command-Line Interface** (**CLI**) binary, available here: `https://docs.microsoft.com/en-us/cli/azure/install-azure-cli`.

The entire source code for this chapter is available at `https://github.com/PacktPublishing/Learning-DevOps-Second-Edition/tree/main/CHAP10`.

Check out the following video to see the Code in Action:

`https://bit.ly/3p7ydjt`

Installing Kubernetes

Before installing Kubernetes, we need to have an overview of its architecture and main components, because Kubernetes is not a simple tool but is a cluster—that is, it consists of a **master** server and other slave servers called **nodes**.

I suggest you explore the architecture of Kubernetes in a simplified way.

Kubernetes architecture overview

Kubernetes is a platform that is made up of several components that assemble together and extend on demand, in order to enable better scalability of applications. The architecture of Kubernetes, which is a client/server type, can be represented simply, as shown in the following diagram:

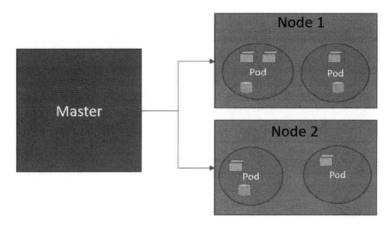

Figure 10.1 – Kubernetes architecture

In the previous diagram, we can see that a cluster is made up of a master component and nodes (also called **worker** nodes), which represent the slave servers.

In each of these nodes, there are **pods**, which are virtual elements that will contain containers and volumes.

Put simply, we can create one pod per application, and it will contain all the containers of the application. For example, one pod can contain a web server container, a database container, and a volume that will contain persistent files for images and database files.

Finally, `kubectl` is the client tool that allows us to interact with a Kubernetes cluster. With this, we have the main requirements that allow us to work with Kubernetes, so let's look at how we can install it on a local machine.

Installing Kubernetes on a local machine

When developing a containerized application that is to be hosted on Kubernetes, it is very important to be able to run the application (with its containers) on your local machine, before deploying it on remote Kubernetes production clusters.

In order to install a Kubernetes cluster locally, there are several solutions, which are detailed next.

The first solution is to use **Docker Desktop** by performing the following steps:

1. If we have already installed Docker Desktop, which we learned about in *Chapter 9, Containerizing Your Application with Docker*, we can activate the **Enable Kubernetes** option in **Settings** on the **Kubernetes** tab, as shown in the following screenshot:

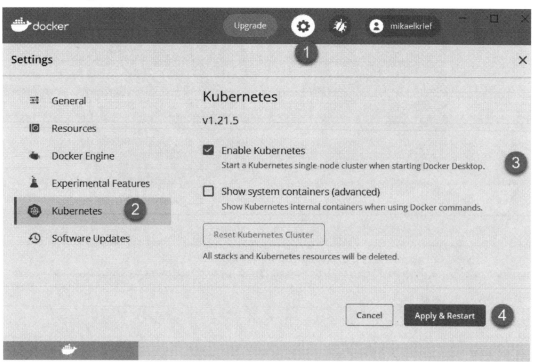

Figure 10.2 – Enabling Kubernetes in Docker Desktop

2. After clicking on the **Apply & Restart** button, Docker Desktop will install a local Kubernetes cluster, and also the `kubectl` client tool, on the local machine.

The second way of installing Kubernetes locally is to install `minikube`, which also installs a simplified Kubernetes cluster locally. Here is the official documentation that you can read: `https://minikube.sigs.k8s.io/docs/start/`.

> **Note**
>
> There are other solutions for installing local Kubernetes, such as `kind` or kubeadm. For more details, read the documentation here: `https://kubernetes.io/docs/tasks/tools/`.

Following the local installation of Kubernetes, we will check its installation by executing the following command in a Terminal:

```
kubectl version --short
```

The following screenshot shows the results for the preceding command:

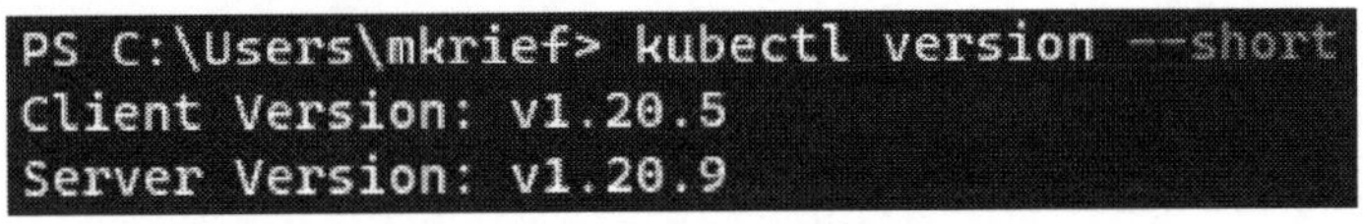

```
PS C:\Users\mkrief> kubectl version --short
Client Version: v1.20.5
Server Version: v1.20.9
```

Figure 10.3 – kubectl getting the binary version

> **Note**
> All of the operations that we carry out on our Kubernetes cluster will be done with `kubectl` commands.

After installing our Kubernetes cluster, we'll need another element, which is the Kubernetes dashboard. This is a web application that allows us to view the status, as well as all the components, of our cluster.

In the next section, we'll discuss how to install and test the Kubernetes dashboard.

Installing the Kubernetes dashboard

In order to install the Kubernetes dashboard, which is a pre-packaged containerized web application that will be deployed in our cluster, we will run the following command in a Terminal:

```
kubectl apply -f https://raw.githubusercontent.com/kubernetes/
dashboard/v2.4.0/aio/deploy/recommended.yaml
```

Its execution is shown in the following screenshot:

```
PS C:\Users\mkrief> kubectl apply -f https://raw.githubusercontent.com/kubernetes/dashboard/v2.4.0/aio/deploy/recommended.yaml
namespace/kubernetes-dashboard created
serviceaccount/kubernetes-dashboard created
service/kubernetes-dashboard created
secret/kubernetes-dashboard-certs created
secret/kubernetes-dashboard-csrf created
secret/kubernetes-dashboard-key-holder created
configmap/kubernetes-dashboard-settings created
role.rbac.authorization.k8s.io/kubernetes-dashboard created
clusterrole.rbac.authorization.k8s.io/kubernetes-dashboard created
rolebinding.rbac.authorization.k8s.io/kubernetes-dashboard created
clusterrolebinding.rbac.authorization.k8s.io/kubernetes-dashboard created
deployment.apps/kubernetes-dashboard created
service/dashboard-metrics-scraper created
deployment.apps/dashboard-metrics-scraper created
```

Figure 10.4 – Kubernetes dashboard installation

From the preceding screenshot, we can see that different artifacts are created, which are outlined as follows: secrets, two web applications, **role-based access control** (**RBAC**) roles, permissions, and services.

> **Note**
>
> Note that the **Uniform Resource Locator** (**URL**) mentioned in the parameters of the command that installs the dashboard may change depending on the versions of the dashboard. To find out the last valid URL to date, consult the official documentation by visiting https://kubernetes.io/docs/tasks/access-application-cluster/web-ui-dashboard/.

Now that we have installed this Kubernetes dashboard, we will connect to it and configure it.

To open the dashboard and connect to it from our local machine, we must first create a proxy between the Kubernetes cluster and our machine by performing the following steps:

1. To create a proxy, we execute the kubectl proxy command in a Terminal. The detail of the execution is shown in the following screenshot:

Figure 10.5 – kubectl proxy command

We can see that the proxy is open on the localhost address (127.0.0.1) on port 8001.

2. Then, in a web browser, open the following URL, http://localhost:8001/api/v1/namespaces/kubernetes-dashboard/services/https:kubernetes-dashboard:/proxy/#/login, which is a local URL (localhost and 8001) that is created by the proxy and that points to the Kubernetes dashboard application we have installed.

The following screenshot shows how to select the Kubernetes configuration file or enter the authentication token:

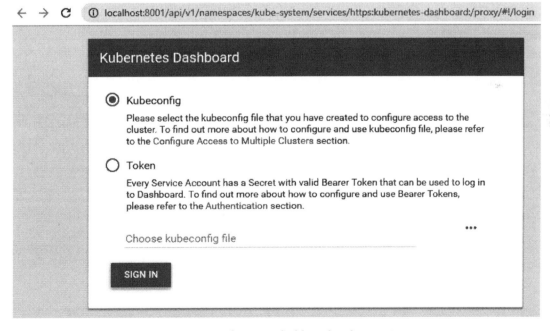

Figure 10.6 – Kubernetes dashboard authentication

3. To create a new user authentication token, we will execute the following script in a PowerShell Terminal:

```
$TOKEN=((kubectl -n kube-system describe secret default |
Select-String "token:") -split " +")[1]
kubectl config set-credentials docker-for-desktop
--token="${TOKEN}"
```

The execution of this script creates a new token inside the local config file.

4. Finally, in the dashboard, we will select the `config` file, which is located in the `C:\Users\<user name>.kube\` folder, as shown in the following screenshot:

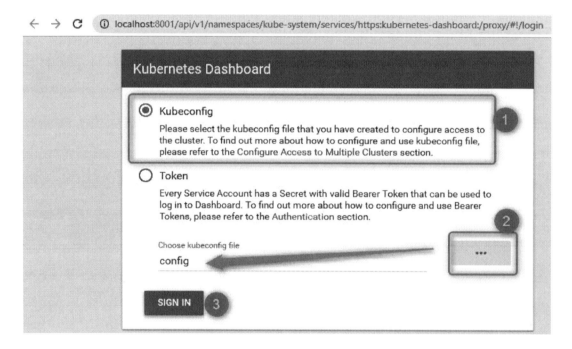

Figure 10.7 – Kubernetes dashboard authentication with the kubeconfig file

> **Note**
>
> For token authentication, read this blog post:
>
> `https://www.replex.io/blog/how-to-install-access-and-add-heapster-metrics-to-the-kubernetes-dashboard`

5. After clicking on the **SIGN IN** button, the dashboard is displayed, as follows:

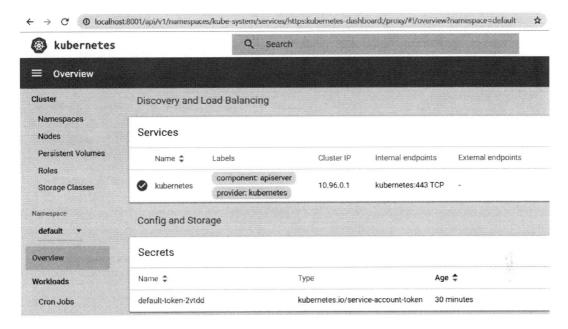

Figure 10.8 – Kubernetes dashboard resources list

We have just seen how to install a Kubernetes cluster on a local machine, and then we installed and configured the Kubernetes web dashboard in this cluster. We will now deploy our first application in the local Kubernetes cluster using **YAML Ain't Markup Language** (**YAML**) specification files and `kubectl` commands.

A first example of Kubernetes application deployment

After installing our Kubernetes cluster, we will deploy an application in it. First of all, it is important to know that when we deploy an application in Kubernetes, we create a new instance of the Docker container in a Kubernetes **pod** object, so we first need to have a Docker image that contains the application.

For our example, we will use the Docker image that contains a web application that we have pushed into Docker Hub in *Chapter 9, Containerizing Your Application with Docker*.

To deploy this instance of the Docker container, we will create a new `k8sdeploy` folder, and inside it, we will create a Kubernetes deployment YAML specification file (`myapp-deployment.yml`) with the following content:

```yaml
---
apiVersion: apps/v1
kind: Deployment
metadata:
    name: webapp
spec:
    selector:
    matchLabels:
        app: webapp
 replicas: 2
template:
    metadata:
    labels:
        app: webapp
    spec:
        containers:
        - name: demobookk8s
            image: mikaelkrief/demobook:latest
        ports:
        - containerPort: 80
```

In this preceding code snippet, we describe our deployment in the following way:

- The `apiVersion` property is the version of `api` that should be used.

- In the `Kind` property, we indicate that the specification type is deployment.

- The `replicas` property indicates the number of pods that Kubernetes will create in the cluster; here, we choose two instances.

In this example, we chose two replicas, which can—at the very least—distribute the traffic load of the application (if there is a high volume of load, we can put in more replicas), while also ensuring the proper functioning of the application. Therefore, if one of the two pods has a problem, the other (which is an identical replica) will ensure the proper functioning of the application.

Then, in the `containers` section, we indicate the image (from Docker Hub) with `name` and `tag`. Finally, the `ports` property indicates the port that the container will use within the cluster.

> **Note**
>
> This source code is also available at `https://github.com/PacktPublishing/Learning-DevOps-Second-Edition/blob/main/CHAP10/k8sdeploy/myapp-deployment.yml`.

To deploy our application, we go to our Terminal and execute one of the essential `kubectl` commands (`kubectl apply`), as follows:

```
kubectl apply -f myapp-deployment.yml
```

The `-f` parameter corresponds to the YAML specification file.

This command applies the deployment that is described in the YAML specification file on the Kubernetes cluster.

Following the execution of this command, we will check the status of this deployment by displaying a list of pods in the cluster. To do this in the Terminal, we execute the `kubectl get pods` command, which returns a list of cluster pods. The following screenshot shows the execution of the deployment and displays the information in the pods, which we use to check the deployment:

```
PS                \Learning-DevOps-Second-Edition\CHAP10\k8sdeploy> kubectl apply -f myapp-deployment.yml
deployment.apps/webapp created                                                                    1
PS                \Learning-DevOps-Second-Edition\CHAP10\k8sdeploy> kubectl get pods
NAME                      READY    STATUS    RESTARTS    AGE
webapp-799697d7d6-gjv7x    1/1      Running   0           100s
webapp-799697d7d6-rd96r    1/1      Running   0           100s                                     2
```

Figure 10.9 – kubectl apply command

What we can see in the preceding screenshot is that the second command displays our two pods, with the name (`webapp`) specified in the YAML file, followed by a **unique identifier** (**UID**), and that they are in a `Running` status.

We can also visualize the status of our cluster on the Kubernetes web dashboard, the `webapp` deployment with the Docker image that has been used, and the two pods that have been created. For more details, we can click on the different links of the elements.

Our application has been successfully deployed in our Kubernetes cluster but, for the moment, it is only accessible inside the cluster, and for it to be usable, we need to expose it outside the cluster.

In order to access the web application outside the cluster, we must add a service type and a `NodePort` category element to our cluster. To add this service type and `NodePort` element, in the same way as for deployment, we will create a second YAML file (`myapp-service.yml`) of the service specification in the same `k8sdeploy` directory, which has the following code:

```
---
apiVersion: v1
kind: Service
metadata:
  name: webapp
  labels:
  app: webapp
spec:
  type: NodePort
  ports:
  - port: 80
    targetPort: 80
    nodePort: 31000
selector:
  app: webapp
```

In the preceding code snippet, we specify the kind, `Service`, as well as the type of service, `NodePort`.

Then, in the `ports` section, we specify the port translation: port `80`, which is exposed internally, and port `31000`, which is exposed externally to the cluster.

> **Note**
>
> The source code of this file is also available at `https://github.com/PacktPublishing/Learning-DevOps-Second-Edition/blob/main/CHAP10/k8sdeploy/myapp-service.yml`.

To create this service on the cluster, we execute the `kubectl apply` command, but this time with our `myapp-service.yaml` file as a parameter, as follows:

```
kubectl apply -f myapp-service.yml
```

The execution of the command creates the service within the cluster, and, to test our application, we open a web browser with the `http://localhost:31000` URL, and our page is displayed as follows:

Welcome to my new app

This page is test for my demo Dockerfile.
Enjoy ...

Figure 10.10 – Demo Kubernetes application

Our application is now deployed on a Kubernetes cluster, and it can be accessed from outside the cluster.

In this section, we have learned that the deployment of an application, as well as the creation of objects in Kubernetes, is achieved using specification files in YAML format and several `kubectl` command lines.

The next step is to use Helm packages to simplify the management of the YAML specification files.

Using Helm as a package manager

As previously discussed, all the actions that we carry out on the Kubernetes cluster are done via the `kubectl` tool and the **YAML specification files**.

In a company that deploys several microservice applications on a Kubernetes cluster, we often notice a large number of these YAML specification files, and this poses a maintenance problem. In order to solve this maintenance problem, we can use **Helm**, which is the package manager for Kubernetes.

> **Note**
>
> For more information on package managers, you can also read the *Using a package manager* section of *Chapter 7, Continuous Integration and Continuous Delivery*.

Helm is, therefore, a repository that will allow the sharing of packages called **charts** that contain ready-to-use Kubernetes specification file templates.

> **Note**
>
> To learn more about Helm and to access its documentation, visit `https://helm.sh/`.

Installing the Helm client

So, we'll see how to install Helm on our local Kubernetes cluster, and later, we'll go through the installation of an application with Helm.

> **Note**
>
> In the first edition of this book, we used a Helm version prior to 3.0, and we learned to install the Helm Tiller plugin. Since version 3.0+, the Tiller plugin doesn't need to be installed, so the Tiller installation guide is deleted in this second edition.

Since version 3, Helm is composed of only one binary: a **client tool** that allows us mainly to install packages of Kubernetes specification files on a target Kubernetes cluster, list the packages of a repository, and indicate the package(s) to be installed.

To install the Helm client, please refer to the installation documentation at `https://helm.sh/docs/using_helm/#installing-the-helm-client`, which details the installation procedure according to the different OSs.

In Windows, for example, we can install it via the **Chocolatey** package manager, with the execution of the following command:

```
choco install kubernetes-helm -y
```

To check its installation, execute the `helm --help` command, as shown in the following screenshot:

```
PS C:\Users\mkrief> helm --help
The Kubernetes package manager

Common actions for Helm:

- helm search:    search for charts
- helm pull:      download a chart to your local directory to view
- helm install:   upload the chart to Kubernetes
- helm list:      list releases of charts
```

Figure 10.11 – helm --help command

The execution of the command tells us that the Helm is properly installed. Now, we will learn how to use a public Helm chart.

Using a public Helm chart from Artifact Hub

The packages contained in a Helm repository are called **charts**. Charts are composed of files that are templates of Kubernetes specification files for an application.

With charts, it's possible to deploy an application in Kubernetes without having to write any YAML specification files. So, to deploy an application, we will use its corresponding chart, and we will pass some configuration variables of this application.

Once Helm is installed, we will install a chart that is in the Helm public repository called **Artifact Hub** and available here: `https://artifacthub.io/`. But first, to display a list of public charts, we run the following command:

```
helm search hub
```

The `hub` parameter is the name of Artifact Hub.

To search for a specific package, we can run the `helm search hub <package name>` command, and if we want to search all `wordpress` packages (for example), we run the following command:

```
helm search hub wordpress
```

Here is an extract from the result, which includes a lot of charts:

```
PS C:\Users\mkrief> helm search hub wordpress
URL                                               CHART VERSION    APP VERSION       DESCRIPTION
https://artifacthub.io/packages/helm/kube-wordp... 0.1.0           1.1               this is my wordpress package
https://artifacthub.io/packages/helm/bitnami/wo... 12.2.3          5.8.2             Web publishing platform for building blogs and ...
https://artifacthub.io/packages/helm/bitnami-ak... 12.2.3          5.8.2             Web publishing platform for building blogs and ...
https://artifacthub.io/packages/helm/groundhog2... 0.4.4           5.8.2-apache      A Helm chart for Wordpress on Kubernetes
https://artifacthub.io/packages/helm/riftbit/wo... 12.1.16         5.8.1             Web publishing platform for building blogs and ...
https://artifacthub.io/packages/helm/homeenterp... 0.1.0           5.8.0-php8.0-apache Blog server
https://artifacthub.io/packages/helm/mcouliba/w... 0.1.0           1.16.0            A Helm chart for Kubernetes
https://artifacthub.io/packages/helm/securecode... 3.4.0           4.0               Insecure & Outdated Wordpress Instance: Never e...
https://artifacthub.io/packages/helm/wordpressm... 1.0.0                             This is the Helm Chart that creates the Wordpre...
https://artifacthub.io/packages/helm/bitpoke/wo... 0.11.1          0.11.1            Bitpoke WordPress Operator Helm Chart
https://artifacthub.io/packages/helm/presslabs/... 0.11.0-alpha.3  0.11.0-alpha.3    Presslabs WordPress Operator Helm Chart
https://artifacthub.io/packages/helm/presslabs/... 0.12.0-rc.2     v0.12.0-rc.2      A Helm chart for deploying a WordPress site on ...
https://artifacthub.io/packages/helm/phntom/bin... 0.0.3           0.0.3             www.binaryvision.co.il static wordpress
https://artifacthub.io/packages/helm/gh-shessel... 1.0.35          5.8.2             Web publishing platform for building blogs and ...
https://artifacthub.io/packages/helm/sonu-wordp... 1.0.0           2                 This is my custom chart to deploy wordpress and...
https://artifacthub.io/packages/helm/uvaise-wor... 0.2.0           1.1.0             Wordpress for Kubernetes
https://artifacthub.io/packages/helm/wordpress/... 0.2.0           1.1.0             Wordpress for Kubernetes
https://artifacthub.io/packages/helm/wordpress-... 1.0.0           2                 This is my custom chart to deploy wordpress and...
https://artifacthub.io/packages/helm/bitpoke/stack 0.11.0-rc.3    0.11.0-rc.3       Your Open-Source, Cloud-Native WordPress Infras...
https://artifacthub.io/packages/helm/securecode... 3.4.0           ▶3.8.20           A Helm chart for the WordPress security scanner...
https://artifacthub.io/packages/helm/viveksahu2... 1.0.0           2                 This is my custom chart to deploy wordpress and...
https://artifacthub.io/packages/helm/presslabs/... 0.11.0-rc.2     v0.11.0-rc.2      Open-Source WordPress Infrastructure on Kubernetes
https://artifacthub.io/packages/helm/presslabs/... 0.12.0-rc.2     v0.12.0-rc.2      Open-Source WordPress Infrastructure on Kubernetes
https://artifacthub.io/packages/helm/six/wordpress 0.2.0          1.1.0             Wordpress for Kubernetes
https://artifacthub.io/packages/helm/jinchi-cha... 0.2.0           1.1.0             Wordpress for Kubernetes
https://artifacthub.io/packages/helm/wordpressm... 0.1.0           1.1
https://artifacthub.io/packages/helm/presslabs/... 0.11.6          0.11.6            Presslabs WordPress Operator Helm Chart
```

Figure 10.12 – Searching for Helm packages

For an easy way to find packages, go to the Artifact Hub site (`https://artifacthub.io/`) and search for the `wordpress` package, as shown in the following screenshot:

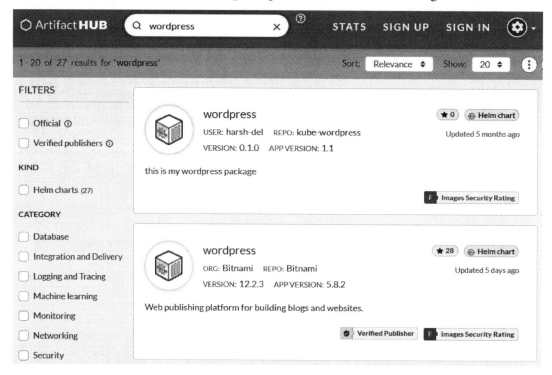

Figure 10.13 – Artifact Hub wordpress search

This page list all `wordpress` packages from all community publishers.

Then, click on the desired package to display details of the package, as illustrated in the following screenshot:

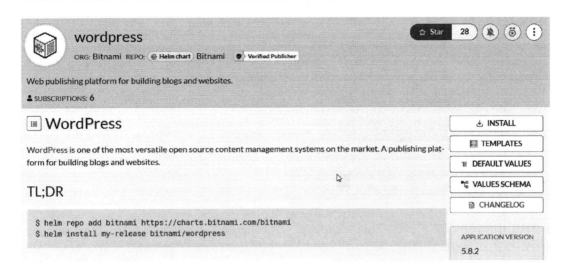

Figure 10.14 – Artifact Hub wordpress details

On this page, we can see the current version of the package and some technical package installation guidelines.

> **Note**
>
> It's also possible to create our private or corporate Helm repository with tools such as Nexus, Artifactory, or even ACR.

Let's now install an application with Helm.

To illustrate the use of Helm, we will deploy a WordPress application in our Kubernetes cluster using a Helm chart.

In order to do this, execute the following commands (mentioned here: `https://artifacthub.io/packages/helm/bitnami/wordpress`):

```
helm repo add bitnami https://charts.bitnami.com/bitnami
helm install wpdemo bitnami/wordpress
```

The first command, `helm repo add`, adds the index of the `bitnami` repository locally. Then, we use the `helm install <release name> <package name>` command to install the desired package on Kubernetes.

The following screenshot shows the execution of these two commands:

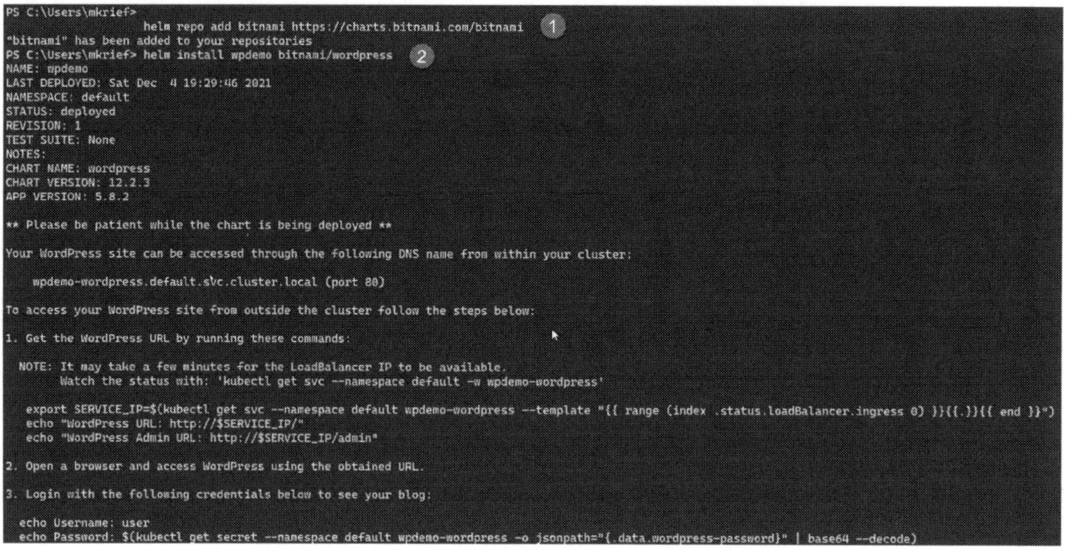

Figure 10.15 – Installing an application with Helm

With the execution of the preceding commands, Helm installs a WordPress instance called wpdemo and all of the Kubernetes components on the local Kubernetes cluster.

We can also display a list of Helm packages that are installed on the cluster by executing the following command:

```
helm ls
```

The following screenshot shows the execution of this command:

Figure 10.16 – Helm list of installed packages

And if we want to remove a package and all of its components (for example, to remove the application installed with this package), we execute the helm delete command, as follows:

```
helm delete wpdemo
```

The following screenshot shows the execution of this command:

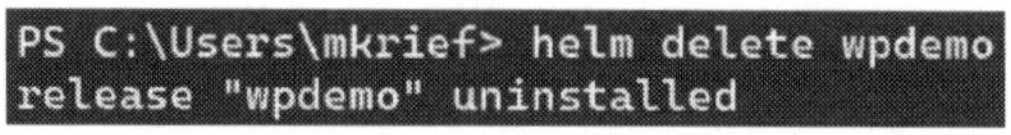

Figure 10.17 – helm delete command

We have discussed the installation of a Helm chart from Artifact Hub to a Kubernetes cluster. In the next section, we will learn how to create a custom Helm chart package.

Creating a custom Helm chart

We have just learned how to use and install a public Helm chart from Artifact Hub, but in companies, we often have some custom applications that require us to create custom Helm charts.

Here are the basic steps to create a custom Helm chart:

1. Inside the folder that will contain the Helm chart file template, run the `helm create <chart name>` command, as follows:

    ```
    helm create demobook
    ```

    The execution of this command will create a directory structure and basic template files for our chart, as shown in the following screenshot:

    Figure 10.18 – Helm chart structure folder

2. Then, customize the chart templates and values by following the technical documentation here: `https://helm.sh/docs/chart_template_guide/`.

3. Finally, we publish the chart in our Kubernetes cluster by running the `helm install <chart name> <chart path root>` command, as follows:

```
helm install demochart ./demobook
```

The following screenshot shows the execution of the preceding command:

```
PS            Learning-DevOps-Second-Edition\CHAP10> helm install demochart ./demobook
NAME: demochart
LAST DEPLOYED: Sun Dec  5 17:16:19 2021
NAMESPACE: default
STATUS: deployed
REVISION: 1
NOTES:
1. Get the application URL by running these commands:
   export POD_NAME=$(kubectl get pods --namespace default -l "app.kubernetes.io/name=demobook,app.kubernetes.io/instance=demochart" -o
jsonpath="{.items[0].metadata.name}")
   export CONTAINER_PORT=$(kubectl get pod --namespace default $POD_NAME -o jsonpath="{.spec.containers[0].ports[0].containerPort}")
   echo "Visit http://127.0.0.1:8080 to use your application"
   kubectl --namespace default port-forward $POD_NAME 8080:$CONTAINER_PORT
```

Figure 10.19 – helm install command

To check the package installation by Helm, run the `kubectl get pods` command to display a list of created pods.

The following screenshot shows a list of created pods:

```
PS            \Learning-DevOps-Second-Edition\CHAP10> kubectl get pods
NAME                                  READY   STATUS    RESTARTS   AGE
demochart-demobook-77458bfd9f-h4mwv   1/1     Running   0          104s
```

Figure 10.20 – kubectl get pods

And run the `helm ls` command to display a list of installed Helm charts, as shown in the following screenshot:

```
PS          \Learning-DevOps-Second-Edition\CHAP10> helm ls
NAME        NAMESPACE   REVISION   UPDATED                             STATUS     CHART            APP VERSION
demochart   default     1          2021-12-05 17:16:19.0370031 +0100 CET  deployed   demobook-0.1.0   1.16.0
```

Figure 10.21 – Helm package list

We can see in the preceding screenshot the `demochart` Helm chart that is installed on the Kubernetes cluster.

In this section, we have seen an overview of the installation and use of Helm, which is the package manager for Kubernetes. Then, we learned about the installation of Helm charts from Artifact Hub. Finally, we learned how to create a custom Helm chart and install this chart on a Kubernetes cluster.

In the next section, we will learn how to publish a custom Helm chart to a private Helm repository—that is, ACR.

Publishing a Helm chart in a private registry (ACR)

In the previous section, we discussed a public Helm repository called Artifact Hub, which is great for public (or community) applications or tools. But for company applications, it's better and recommended to have a private Helm registry.

In the marketplace, there are a lot of private registries such as Nexus or Artifactory, and this documentation explains how to create a private Helm repository: `https://helm.sh/docs/topics/chart_repository/`.

In this section, we will discuss how to use a private Helm repository (that is, ACR, which we have already learned about in *Chapter 9, Containerizing Your Application with Docker*). So, to start our lab, we consider that we have already created an ACR named `demobookacr` on Azure.

> **Note**
>
> If you have not already created an ACR, follow the documentation here:
>
> `https://docs.microsoft.com/en-us/azure/container-registry/container-registry-get-started-azure-cli`

To publish a custom Helm chart in ACR, follow these steps:

1. The first step is to create a package in `tar gz` format of the chart by running the `helm package` command inside the folder where the `chart.yaml` file of the chart is located.

   Run the following command with `"."` as a parameter to indicate that the `chart.yaml` file is in the current folder:

   ```
   helm package .
   ```

   The following screenshot shows the execution of this command:

   ```
   PS          \Learning-DevOps-Second-Edition\CHAP10\demobook> helm package .
   Successfully packaged chart and saved it to:          \Learning-DevOps-Second-Edition\CHAP10\demobook\demobook-0.1.0.tgz
   ```

   Figure 10.22 – Creating a Helm package

   The Helm chart package is created with the name `demobook-0.1.0.tgz`.

2. Then, authenticate to ACR with the following PowerShell script:

   ```
   $env:HELM_EXPERIMENTAL_OCI=1
   $USER_NAME="00000000-0000-0000-0000-000000000000"
   $ACR_NAME="demobookacr"
   ```

```
az login
$PASSWORD=$(az acr login --name $ACR_NAME --expose-token
--output tsv --query accessToken)
helm registry login "$ACR_NAME.azurecr.io" --username
$USER_NAME --password "$PASSWORD"
```

The preceding script performs these operations:

- Sets the HELM_EXPERIMENTAL_OCI environment variable to 1. For more details about environment variables, read this documentation: https://helm.sh/docs/topics/registries/.

- Sets the USER_NAME variable with a 000 fake value.

- Sets the ACR_NAME variable with the name of the ACR.

- Sets the PASSWORD variable dynamically by using the az cli command.

- Uses the Helm registry login to authenticate to the ACR registry.

3. Finally, we push the Helm chart into the ACR registry with the following command:

```
helm push .\demobook-0.1.0.tgz oci://$ACR_NAME.azurecr.
io/helm
```

After the execution of this command, the pushed Helm chart will be in the helm/demobook repository on the ACR.

4. We can check that the Helm chart is correctly pushed to the ACR by running the following command:

```
az acr repository show --name $ACR_NAME --repository
helm/demobook
```

The execution of this command displays the details of the helm/demobook Helm chart.

In the Azure portal, we can see the Helm repository, the Helm chart, and the tag, as shown in the following screenshot:

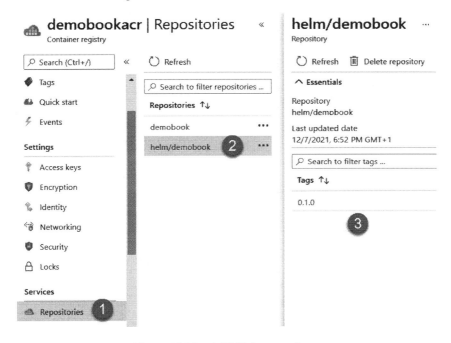

Figure 10.23 – ACR Helm repository

We just learned how to build and push a custom Helm chart into ACR using Helm command lines and `az cli` commands.

Now, in the next section, let's look at an example of a managed Kubernetes service that is hosted in Azure, called AKS.

Using AKS

A production Kubernetes cluster can often be complex to install and configure. This type of installation requires the availability of servers, human resources who have the requisite skills regarding the installation and management of a Kubernetes cluster, and—especially—the implementation of an enhanced security policy to protect the applications.

To overcome these problems, cloud providers offer managed Kubernetes cluster services. This is the case with Amazon with **Elastic Kubernetes Service (EKS)**, Google with **Google Kubernetes Engine (GKE)**, and finally, Azure with AKS. In this section, I propose an overview of AKS, while also highlighting the advantages of a managed Kubernetes cluster.

AKS is, therefore, an Azure service that allows us to create and manage a real Kubernetes cluster as a managed service.

The advantage of this managed Kubernetes cluster is that we don't have to worry about its hardware installation and the management of the master part is done entirely by Azure when the nodes are installed on **virtual machines (VMs)**.

The use of this service is free; what is charged is the cost of the VMs on which the nodes are installed.

> **Note**
>
> To learn more about the benefits offered by AKS, you can read the documentation at `https://docs.microsoft.com/en-us/azure/aks/intro-kubernetes`.

Let's now look at how to create an AKS service.

Creating an AKS service

The creation of an AKS cluster in Azure can be done in three different ways, as outlined here:

- **Manually, via the Azure portal**: The standard way to create an AKS service is to do so via the Azure portal, by creating a Kubernetes service, and then entering its basic Azure properties—that is, the type and number of nodes desired, as shown in the following screenshot:

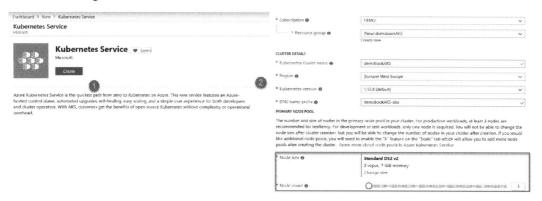

Figure 10.24 – AKS creation via the Azure portal

- **Creation via an az cli script**: You can also use an `az cli` script to automate the creation of the AKS cluster. The script is shown here:

```
#Create the Resource group
az group create --name Rg-AKS --location westeurope
#Create the AKS resource
az aks create --resource-group Rg-AKS --name demoBookAKS
--node-count 2 --generate-ssh-keys --enable-addons
monitoring
```

The `node-count` property indicates the number of nodes, and the `enable-addons` property enables us to monitor the AKS service.

- **Creation with Terraform**: It is also possible to create an AKS service with Terraform. The complete Terraform script is available in the Azure documentation at `https://docs.microsoft.com/en-us/azure/terraform/terraform-create-k8s-cluster-with-tf-and-aks`, and to learn more about using Terraform, you can read *Chapter 2, Provisioning Cloud Infrastructure with Terraform*.

Now that the AKS cluster has been created, we will be able to configure the `kubeconfig` file in order to connect to this AKS cluster.

Configuring the kubeconfig file for AKS

To configure the `kubeconfig` file used by `kubectl` for connecting to the AKS service, we will use the `az cli` tool by executing the following commands in a Terminal:

```
az login
#If you have several Azure subscriptions
az account set --subscription <subscription Id>
az aks get-credentials --resource-group Rg-AKS --name
demoBookAKS
```

This last command takes the resource group as the parameter, and as the name of the created AKS cluster. The role of this command is to automatically create a `.kube\config` file and with this file configure `kubectl` for connection to the AKS cluster, as shown in the following screenshot:

```
C:         1>az aks get-credentials --resource-group Rg-AKS --name demoBookAKS
Merged "demoBookAKS" as current context in                  \.kube\config
```

Figure 10.25 – AKS getting credentials via az cli

To test the connection to AKS, we can execute the following command, `kubectl get nodes`, which displays the number of nodes that are configured when creating an AKS cluster, as shown in the following screenshot:

```
              >kubectl get nodes
NAME                        STATUS    ROLES    AGE    VERSION
aks-nodepool1-41966373-0    Ready     agent    8m     v1.12.8
aks-nodepool1-41966373-1    Ready     agent    8m     v1.12.8
```

Figure 10.26 – kubectl get nodes list

All of the operations that we have seen in the *A first example of Kubernetes application deployment* section of this chapter are identical, whether deploying an application with AKS or with `kubectl`.

After having seen the steps that are taken to create an AKS service in Azure, we will now provide an overview of its advantages.

Advantages of AKS

AKS is a Kubernetes service that is managed in Azure. This has the advantage of being integrated with Azure, as well as some other advantages listed here:

- **Ready to use**: In AKS, the Kubernetes web dashboard is natively installed, and the documentation at `https://docs.microsoft.com/en-us/azure/aks/kubernetes-dashboard` explains how to access it.

- **Integrated monitoring services**: AKS also has all of Azure's integrated monitoring services, including container monitoring, cluster performance management, and log management, as shown in the following screenshot:

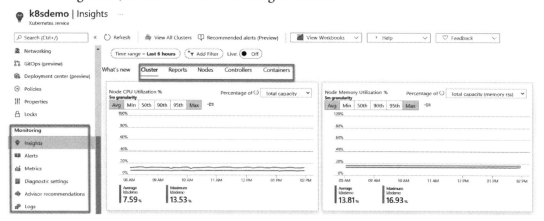

Figure 10.27 – AKS monitoring

- **Very easy to scale**: AKS allows the quick and direct scaling of the number of nodes of a cluster via the portal, or via scripts.

As we can see in the following screenshot, we choose the number of nodes that we want in the Azure portal, and the change is effective immediately:

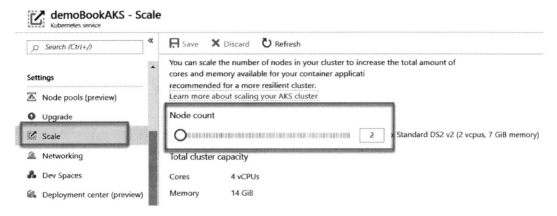

Figure 10.28 – AKS scaling

If we have an Azure subscription and we want to use Kubernetes, it's intuitive and quick to install. AKS has a number of advantages, such as integrated monitoring and scaling in the Azure portal. Using the `kubectl` tool does not require any changes compared to a local Kubernetes instance.

In this section, we have discussed AKS, which is a managed Kubernetes service in Azure. Then, we created an AKS instance and configured the `kubeconfig` file in order to connect to this AKS instance. Finally, we listed its advantages, which are mainly integrated monitoring and fast scalability.

In the next section, we will see some resources for how to deploy an application in Kubernetes by using a CI/CD pipeline with Azure Pipelines.

Creating a CI/CD pipeline for Kubernetes with Azure Pipelines

So far, we have seen how to use `kubectl` to deploy a containerized application in a local Kubernetes cluster or in a remote cluster with AKS.

In the first edition of this book, I explained how to build a complete pipeline in Azure DevOps, from the creation of a new Docker image pushed into Docker Hub to its deployment in an AKS cluster.

Since this first edition, many features have been improved in the different CI/CD tools to deploy in Kubernetes.

That's why in this second edition I won't explain it in detail anymore, but I'll provide you with different resources that are useful for my daily work, as follows:

- The first resource is a great complete video that explains all the details for deploying an application in AKS with Azure DevOps, found at the following link:

  `https://www.youtube.com/watch?v=K4uN16JA7g8`

- On the same subject, there is a great lab on Azure DevOps at the following link:

  `https://www.azuredevopslabs.com/labs/vstsextend/kubernetes/`

- To create an Azure DevOps pipeline in YAML format for deploying to Kubernetes, read the official documentation here:

  `https://docs.microsoft.com/en-us/azure/devops/pipelines/ecosystems/kubernetes/aks-template?view=azure-devops`

- Then, the following documentation also proposes a tutorial for use with Jenkins and Azure DevOps to deploy an application to Kubernetes:

  `https://docs.microsoft.com/en-us/azure/devops/pipelines/release/integrate-jenkins-pipelines-aks?view=azure-devops`

In this section, we have reported some resources for an **end-to-end (E2E)** DevOps CI/CD pipeline in order to deploy an application in a Kubernetes cluster (AKS for our example) with Azure Pipelines.

In the next section, we will learn different ways to monitor applications and metrics on Kubernetes and find out about the tools we can use to do this.

Monitoring applications and metrics in Kubernetes

When we deploy an application in Kubernetes, it's very important—and I consider it a requirement—to have a monitoring strategy for checking and debugging the life cycle of these applications and checking the **central processing unit (CPU)** and **random-access memory (RAM)** metrics.

We will now discuss different ways to debug and monitor your applications in Kubernetes.

Let's start with the basic way, which is the use of the `kubectl` command line.

Using the kubectl command line

To debug applications with the `kubectl` command line, run the commands detailed next:

- To display the state of Kubernetes resources, run the following command:

```
kubectl get pods,svc
```

The output of the preceding command is shown in the following screenshot:

```
PS C:\Users\mkrief> kubectl get pods,svc
NAME                                        READY   STATUS    RESTARTS       AGE
pod/demochart-demobook-77458bfd9f-h4mwv     1/1     Running   2 (3m27s ago)  6d4h
pod/webapp-799697d7d6-gjv7x                 1/1     Running   2 (3m27s ago)  6d7h
pod/webapp-799697d7d6-rd96r                 1/1     Running   2 (3m27s ago)  6d7h

NAME                         TYPE        CLUSTER-IP      EXTERNAL-IP   PORT(S)        AGE
service/demochart-demobook   ClusterIP   10.111.122.236  <none>        80/TCP         6d4h
service/kubernetes           ClusterIP   10.96.0.1       <none>        443/TCP        8d
service/webapp               NodePort    10.110.12.30    <none>        80:31000/TCP   6d6h
```

Figure 10.29 – kubectl getting resources

With this command, we can see if pods are running and find out about services' statuses.

- To display application logs, run the `kubectl logs pod/<pod name>` command, as illustrated in the following screenshot:

```
PS C:\Users\mkrief> kubectl logs pod/webapp-799697d7d6-gjv7x
AH00558: httpd: Could not reliably determine the server's fully qualified domain name, using 10.1.0.35. Set the 'ServerN
ame' directive globally to suppress this message
AH00558: httpd: Could not reliably determine the server's fully qualified domain name, using 10.1.0.35. Set the 'ServerN
ame' directive globally to suppress this message
[Sat Dec 11 20:57:07.523851 2021] [mpm_event:notice] [pid 1:tid 140521422701696] AH00489: Apache/2.4.41 (Unix) configure
d -- resuming normal operations
[Sat Dec 11 20:57:07.532170 2021] [core:notice] [pid 1:tid 140521422701696] AH00094: Command line: 'httpd -D FOREGROUND'
```

Figure 10.30 – kubectl getting pod logs

This command displays the output of the application logs.

For more details on the use of `kubectl` to debug applications, read the documentation here:

`https://kubernetes.io/docs/tasks/debug-application-cluster/ debug-running-pod/`

With the `kubectl` command, we can automate the debugging of applications, but it's necessary to learn all command-line options.

Next, we will discuss debugging applications with some tools.

Using the web dashboard

As already explained in the first section of this chapter, *Installing Kubernetes*, we can use the basic dashboard to display in the web **user interface** (**UI**) details of all resources deployed in Kubernetes.

For cloud-managed Kubernetes services such as AKS for Azure, EKS for **Amazon Web Services** (**AWS**), and GKE for **Google Cloud Platform** (**GCP**), we can use integrated and managed dashboards. For example, for AKS in the Azure portal, we can easily see all logs from the pods. Here's a sample of pod logs in the Azure portal:

Figure 10.31 – AKS live logs

For more details about debugging on AKS, read the documentation here:

```
https://docs.microsoft.com/en-us/azure/architecture/
microservices/logging-monitoring
```

We can also use tier tools such as Octant or Lens.

Using tier tools

There are lots of tools or solutions to monitor and display all resources deployed in a Kubernetes cluster. Among them are two free tools that I often use: Octant and Lens.

Octant

Octant is a VMware community project in a web application launched locally or in a Docker container for visualizing Kubernetes resources and application logs.

The documentation of Octant is available here:

```
https://octant.dev/
```

The source code is available here:

`https://github.com/vmware-tanzu/octant/blob/master/README.md`

Lens

Lens is also a free tool that is installed by the client binary. For me, Lens is the best tool for visualizing and debugging applications. The Lens documentation is available here: `https://k8slens.dev/`.

You can see an overview of the Lens dashboard in the following screenshot:

Figure 10.32 – Lens dashboard

After discussing tools to debug applications, we will see how to display Kubernetes metrics.

Monitoring Kubernetes metrics

All tools just described are great for debugging Kubernetes resources and applications hosted in Kubernetes. But that is not enough—in terms of monitoring, we need to also monitor metrics such as the CPU and RAM used by applications.

With the following basic `kubectl` command line, we can display the CPU and RAM used by nodes and pods:

```
PS C:\Users\mkrief> kubectl top nodes
NAME                            CPU(cores)   CPU%   MEMORY(bytes)   MEMORY%
aks-default-29977126-vmss000000   133m        7%     1875Mi          87%
aks-default-29977126-vmss000001   147m        7%     1986Mi          92%
aks-default-29977126-vmss000002   342m        18%    2017Mi          93%
PS C:\Users\mkrief> kubectl top pods -n vault
NAME                                                            CPU(cores)   MEMORY(bytes)
aks-helloworld-7bfc99f965-m78dl                                 15m          87Mi
consul-consul-connect-injector-webhook-deployment-79b4b98ctt844  4m          38Mi
consul-consul-controller-5bdb877dfd-4rlmw                        2m          22Mi
consul-consul-gjtkq                                              8m          32Mi
consul-consul-kmcl8                                              8m          26Mi
consul-consul-server-0                                          14m          64Mi
consul-consul-tnlds                                             9m           23Mi
consul-consul-webhook-cert-manager-556df5dbfd-k6wfp             3m           20Mi
vault-0                                                         4m           53Mi
vault-1                                                         6m           37Mi
vault-agent-injector-846f9f7bc6-76bjz                          4m           13Mi
web-01enqv6avrgwqgscxzhcsz6rqk-f5984776d-lkzzq                  0m           0Mi
```

Figure 10.33 – kubectl getting metrics

Among the best-known solutions are **Prometheus** and **Grafana**, which monitor the metrics of Kubernetes and provide a lot of dashboard models.

For more details, you can read this article, which explains Kubernetes monitoring with Prometheus and Grafana:

`https://sysdig.com/blog/kubernetes-monitoring-prometheus/`

In this section, we discussed some `kubectl` commands, tools, or solutions such as dashboards, Octant, and Lens to debug applications on Kubernetes.

Summary

In this chapter, we have seen an advanced use of containers with the use of Kubernetes, which is a container manager.

We discussed the different options for installing a small cluster on a local machine using Docker Desktop. Then, using the YAML specification file and the `kubectl` command, we realized the deployment of a Docker image in our Kubernetes cluster in order to run a web application.

We installed and configured Helm, which is the package manager of Kubernetes. Then, we applied it in practice with an example of a chart deployment in Kubernetes.

We also had an overview of AKS, which is a Kubernetes service managed by Azure, looking at its creation and configuration and some resources links that explain how to deploy applications with CI/CD pipelines with Azure DevOps.

Finally, we finished this chapter with a short list of Kubernetes monitoring tools such as the `kubectl` command line, Lens, Prometheus, and Grafana for debugging Kubernetes metrics.

The next chapter begins a new part of this book, which deals with application testing, and we will start with **application programming interface (API)** testing with Postman.

Questions

1. What is the role of Kubernetes?

2. Where is the configuration of the objects that are written in Kubernetes?

3. What is the name of the Kubernetes client tool?

4. Which command allows us to apply a deployment in Kubernetes?

5. What is Helm?

6. What is AKS?

Further reading

If you want to know more about Kubernetes, take a look at the following resources:

*   *The DevOps 2.3 Toolkit*: `https://www.packtpub.com/business/devops-23-toolkit`

*   *Hands-On Kubernetes on Azure*: `https://www.packtpub.com/virtualization-and-cloud/hands-kubernetes-azure`

*   *Hands-On Kubernetes on Azure - Second Edition*: `https://www.packtpub.com/product/hands-on-kubernetes-on-azure-second-edition/9781800209671`

*   *Mastering Kubernetes - Third Edition*: `https://www.packtpub.com/product/mastering-kubernetes-third-edition/9781839211256`

Section 4: Testing Your Application

This part explains some ways of testing APIs with Postman. Then we talk about static code analysis with SonarQube and performance tests involving Postman.

This section comprises the following chapters:

11
Testing APIs with Postman

In the previous chapters, we talked about DevOps culture and **Infrastructure as Code (IaC)** with Terraform, Ansible, and Packer. Then, we saw how to use a source code manager with Git, along with the implementation of a CI/CD pipeline with Jenkins and Azure Pipelines. Finally, we showed the containerization of applications with Docker and their deployment in a Kubernetes cluster.

If you are a developer, you should realize that you use APIs every day, either for client-side use (where you consume the API) or as a provider of the API.

An API, as well as an application, must be testable, that is, it must be possible to test the different methods of this API in order to verify that it responds without error and that the response of the API is equal to the expected result.

In addition, the proper functioning of an API is much more critical to an application because this API is potentially consumed by several client applications, and if it does not work, it will have an impact on all of these applications.

The common API challenges are that we need to script or develop a dedicated application client to test each API individually or a workflow of multiple API execution.

In this chapter, we will learn how to test an API with a specialized tool called **Postman**. We will explore the use of collections and variables, then we will write Postman tests, and finally, we will see how to automate the execution of Postman tests with Newman in a CI/CD pipeline.

This chapter covers the following topics:

- Creating a Postman collection
- Using environments and variables
- Writing Postman tests
- Executing tests locally
- Understanding the Newman concept
- Preparing Postman collections for Newman
- Running the Newman command line
- Integration of Newman in the CI/CD pipeline process

Technical requirements

In this chapter, we will use **Newman**, which is a Node.js package. Therefore, we need to install Node.js and npm on our computer beforehand, which we can download at `https://nodejs.org/en/`.

For the demo APIs that are used in this chapter, we will use an example that is provided on the internet: `https://jsonplaceholder.typicode.com/`.

The GitHub repository, which contains the complete source code used in this chapter, can be found at `https://github.com/PacktPublishing/Learning-DevOps-Second-Edition/tree/main/CHAP11`.

Check out the following video to see the code in action: `https://bit.ly/3s7239U`.

Creating a Postman collection with requests

Postman is a free client tool in a graphical format that can be installed on any type of OS. Its role is to test APIs through requests, which we will organize into collections. It also allows us to dynamize API tests through the use of variables and the implementation of environments. Postman is famous for its ease of use, but also for the advanced features that it offers.

In this section, we will learn how to create and install a Postman account, then we will create a collection that will serve as a folder to organize our requests, and finally, we will create a request that will test a demo API.

Before we use Postman, we will need to create a Postman account by going to `https://www.postman.com/` and clicking on the **Sign Up for Free** button. In the form, click on the **Create Account** link, as shown in the following screenshot:

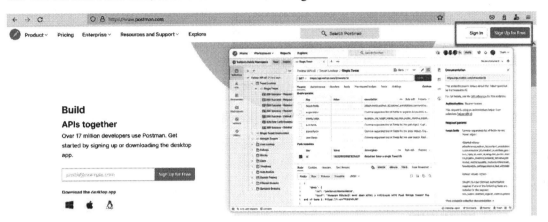

Figure 11.1 – Postman signup

Now, you can either create a Postman account for yourself by filling out the form, or you can create an account using your Google account.

This account will be used to synchronize Postman data between your machine and your Postman account. This way, the data will be accessible on all of your workstations.

After creating a Postman account, we will look at how to download and install it on a local machine.

Installation of Postman

Once the Postman account has been created, those who are using Windows can download Postman from `https://www.getpostman.com/downloads/` and choose the version to install. For those who want to install it on Linux or macOS, just click on the link of your OS. The following screenshot shows the download links according to your OS:

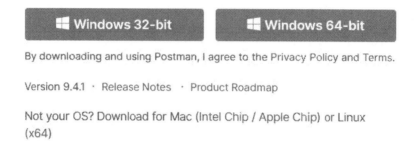

Figure 11.2 – Postman download

Once Postman is downloaded, we need to install it by clicking on the download file for Windows, or for other OSes, follow the installation documentation at `https://learning.getpostman.com/docs/postman/launching_postman/installation_and_updates/`.

We have just seen that the installation of Postman is very simple; the next step is to create a collection in which we will create a request.

> **Note**
> The API that we will test in this chapter is a demo API, which is provided freely on the following site: `https://jsonplaceholder.typicode.com/`.

Creating a collection

In Postman, any request that we test must be added to a directory called `Collection`, which provides storage for requests and allows for better organization.

We will, therefore, create a `DemoBook` collection that will contain the requests to the demo API, and for this, we will perform the following tasks:

1. In Postman, in the left-hand panel, click on the **Collections** | + button.

2. Once the tab opens, we will enter the name `DemoBook`. These steps for creating a new collection are illustrated in the following screenshot:

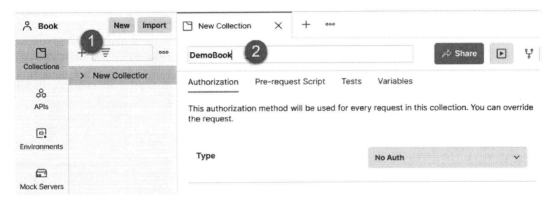

Figure 11.3 – Postman collection creation

So, we have a `Demobook` collection that appears in the left-hand panel of Postman.

This collection is also synchronized with our Postman web account, and we can access it at `https://web.postman.co/me/collections`.

This collection will allow us to organize the requests of our API tests, and it is also possible to modify its properties in order to apply a certain configuration to all the requests that will be included in this collection.

These properties include request authentication, tests to be performed before and after requests, and variables common to all requests in this collection.

To modify the settings and properties of this collection, perform the following actions:

1. Click on the **...** button of the context menu of the collection.

2. Choose the **Edit** option, and the edit form appears, in which we can change all the settings that will apply to the requests in this collection.

3. Switch between all configuration tabs for the edit authorization, scripts, tests, or variables options.

The following screenshot shows the steps that are taken to modify the properties of a collection:

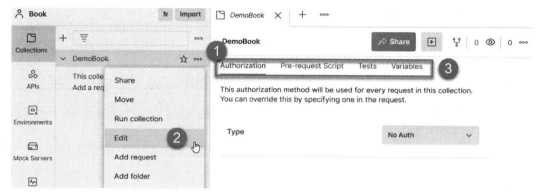

Figure 11.4 – Postman edit collection

So, we have discussed the procedure that is followed in order to create a collection that is the first Postman artifact, and this will allow us to organize our API test requests.

We will now create a request that will call and test the proper functioning of our demo API.

Creating our first request

In Postman, the object that contains the properties of the API to be tested is called a **request**.

This request contains the configuration of the API itself, but it also contains the tests that are to be performed to check that it is functioning properly.

The main parameters of a request are as follows:

- The URL of the API
- Its method: GET/POST/DELETE/PATCH
- Its authentication properties
- Its querystring keys and its body request
- The tests that are to be performed before or after execution of the API

The creation of a request is done in two steps – its creation in the collection, followed by its configuration.

1. **The creation of the request**: To create the request of our API, here are the steps that need to be followed:

    I.   We go to the context menu of the DemoBook collection and click on the **Add Request** option:

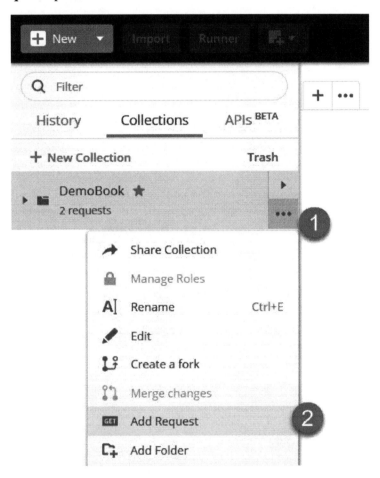

Figure 11.5 – Add Request in Postman

II.   Then, in the new tag, enter the name of the request, `Get all posts`, as shown in the following screenshot:

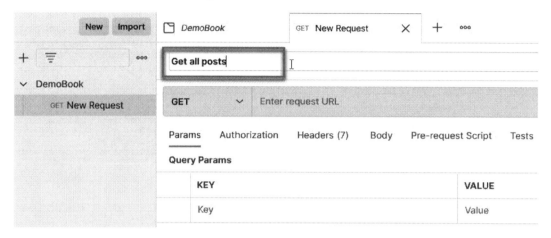

Figure 11.6 – Get all posts in Postman

2.   **The configuration of the request**: After creating the request, we will configure it by entering the URL of the API to be tested, which is `https://jsonplaceholder.typicode.com/posts`, in the **GET** method. After entering the URL, we save the request configuration by clicking on the **Save** button.

The following screenshot shows the parameters of this request with its URL and method:

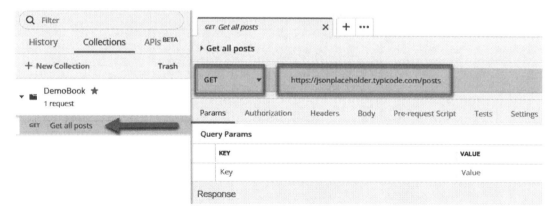

Figure 11.7 – Postman edit request

Finally, to complete the tests, and to add more content to our lab, we will add a second request to our collection, which we will call `Get a single post`. It will test another method of the API, and it will also ensure that we configure it with the `https://jsonplaceholder.typicode.com/posts/<ID of post>` URL.

The following screenshot shows the requests of our collection:

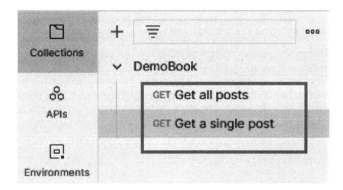

Figure 11.8 – Postman request list

> **Note**
>
> Note that the Postman documentation for collection creation can be found at `https://learning.getpostman.com/docs/postman/collections/creating_collections/`.

In this section, we have learned how to create a collection in Postman, as well as how to create requests and their configurations.

In the next section, we will learn how to dynamize our requests with the use of environments and variables.

Using environments and variables to dynamize requests

When we want to test an API, we need to test it on several environments for better results. For example, we will test it on our local machine and development environment, and then also on the QA environment. To optimize test implementation times and to avoid having a duplicate request in Postman, we will inject variables into this same request to make it testable in all environments.

So, in the following steps, we will improve our requests by creating an environment and two variables; then, we will modify our requests in order to use these variables:

1. In Postman, we will start by creating an **environment** that we call Local, as shown in the following screenshot:

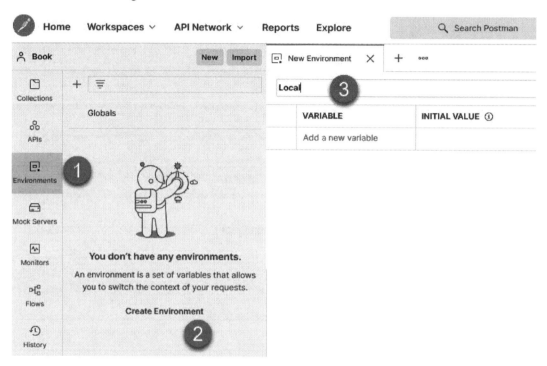

Figure 11.9 – Adding an environment in Postman

2. Then, in this Local environment, we will insert a **variable** named PostID, which will contain the value to pass in the URL of the request. The following screenshot shows the creation of the PostID variable:

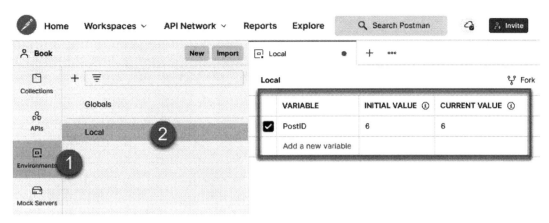

Figure 11.10 – Adding an environment variable in Postman

3. Thus, for the `Local` environment, the value of the `PostID` variable is 6. To have a different value for other environments, it is necessary to create other environments using the same steps that we have just seen, and then add the same variables (with the same name) and their corresponding values. This, for example, shows the variable screen for the `QA` environment:

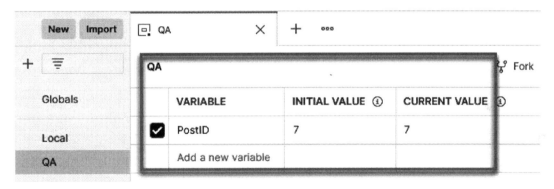

Figure 11.11 – Adding a second environment in Postman

4. Finally, we will modify the request in order to use the variable that we have just declared. In Postman, the usage of a variable is done using the {{variable name }} pattern. So, first, we select the desired environment from the dropdown in the top-right corner. Then, in the request, we will replace the post's ID at the end of the URL with {{PostID}}, as shown in the following screenshot:

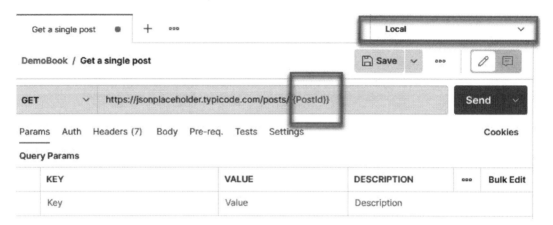

Figure 11.12 – Using a variable environment in Postman

> **Note**
>
> Note that the Postman documentation of environments and variables is available at https://learning.getpostman.com/docs/ postman/environments_and_globals/intro_to_ environments_and_globals/.

In this section, we created a Postman request that will allow us to test an API. Then we made its execution more flexible by creating an environment in Postman that contains variables that are also used in Postman's requests.

In the next section, we will write Postman tests to verify the API result.

Writing Postman tests

Testing an API is not only about checking that its call returns a return code of 200, that is, that the API responds well, but also that its return result corresponds to what is expected, or that its execution time is not too long.

For example, consider an API that returns a response in JSON format with several properties. In the tests of this API, it will be necessary to verify that the result returned is a JSON text that contains the expected properties, and even more so to verify the values of these properties.

In Postman, it is possible to write tests that will ensure that the response of the request corresponds to the expected result in terms of return or execution time using the JavaScript language.

Postman tests are written in the **Tests** tab of the request:

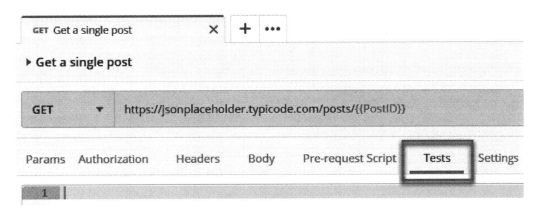

Figure 11.13 – Postman Tests tab

To test our request, we will write several tests, which are as follows:

- That the return code of the request is 200
- That the response time of the request is less than 400 ms
- That the answer is not an empty JSON
- That the return JSON response contains the userId property, which is equal to 1

To perform these tests, we will write the code for the following in the **Tests** tab.

The following code illustrates the return code of the request:

```
pm.test("Status code is 200", function () {
  pm.response.to.have.status(200);
});
```

The following code illustrates a response time of less than 400 ms:

```
pm.test("Response time is less than 400ms", function () {
  pm.expect(pm.response.responseTime).to.be.below(400);
});
```

The following code illustrates that the response in JSON format is not empty:

```
pm.test("Json response is not empty", function (){
  pm.expect(pm.response).to.be.json;
});
```

The following code illustrates that, in the JSON response, the `userId` property is equal to `1`:

```
pm.test("Json response userId eq 1", function (){
  var jsonRes = pm.response.json();
  pm.expect(jsonRes.userId).to.eq(1);
});
```

And so, finally, the **Tests** tab of our request, which tests our API, contains all this code, as shown in the following screenshot:

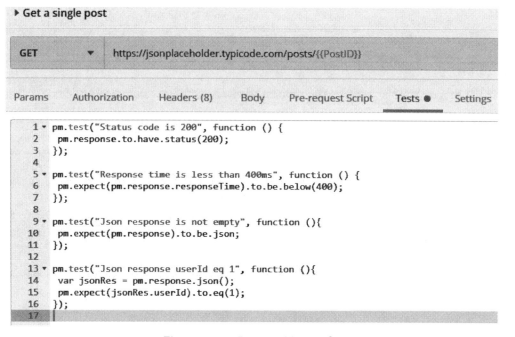

Figure 11.14 – Postman Tests code

We have completed our Postman request with test writing, which will check the proper functioning of the API according to its feedback code, performance, and response content.

> **Note**
>
> For more information about the Postman tests and scripts, you can read the documentation at `https://learning.getpostman.com/docs/postman/scripts/intro_to_scripts`.

In this section, we have just seen how, in Postman, we can write API tests to check the proper functioning of our API. We will now run our Postman request locally in order to test our API.

Executing Postman request tests locally

So far, in Postman, we have created a collection in which two requests contain the parameters and tests of our APIs that are to be tested. To test the proper functioning of the APIs with their parameters and tests, we must now execute our requests that are in Postman. Note that it will only be at the end of this execution that we will know whether our APIs correspond to our expectations.

To execute a Postman request, perform the following actions:

1. You must first choose the desired environment.
2. Click on the **Send** button of the request, as shown in the following screenshot:

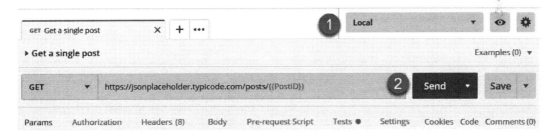

Figure 11.15 – Postman signup

3. In the **Body** tab, we can then view the content of the query response, and if we want to display it in **JSON** format, we can choose the display format. The following screenshot shows the response of the request displayed in JSON format:

Figure 11.16 – Postman body response

4. The **Test Results** tab displays the results of the execution of the tests that we previously wrote, and in our case, the four tests have been executed correctly—they are all green, as shown in the following screenshot:

Figure 11.17 – Postman Test Results

In the preceding screenshot, we can see that the return code of the Postman request is equal to 200, which corresponds to the request's successful execution return code, and its execution time of 23 ms, which is below the threshold (400 ms) that I set for myself as an example.

In the event that one of the tests fails, it will be displayed in red to clearly identify it. An example of a failed test is shown in the following screenshot:

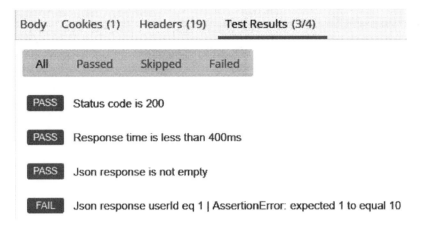

Figure 11.18 – Postman test failed

We have just seen the execution of a Postman request to test an API, but this execution is only for the current request. If we want to execute all Postman requests in a collection, we can use **Postman Collection Runner**.

Postman Collection Runner is a Postman feature that automatically executes all the requests in a collection in the order in which they have been organized.

You can learn more about the Collection documentation by visiting `https://learning.getpostman.com/docs/postman/collection_runs/starting_a_collection_run/`.

The following two screenshots show the **Runner** execution steps, in which we choose the collection to execute, the environment, and the number of iterations. To start its execution, we click on the **Run DemoBook** button:

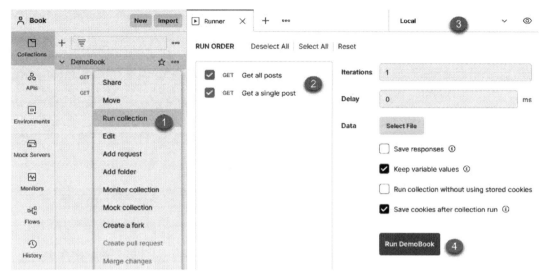

Figure 11.19 – Postman Runner

And so, in the **Runner** tab, we can see the test execution result of all the requests in the collection, as shown in the following screenshot:

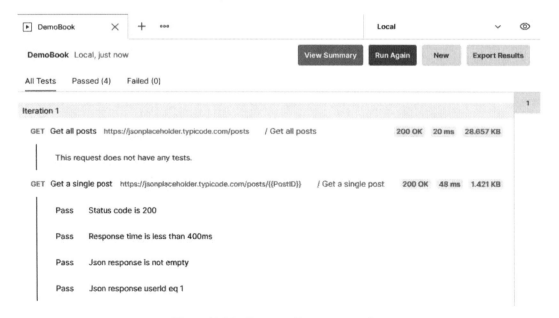

Figure 11.20 – Postman Runner execution

> **Note**
>
> The documentation for Postman Runner can be found at `https://learning.getpostman.com/docs/postman/collection_runs/intro_to_collection_runs`.

In this section, we have learned how to execute Postman requests in order to test an API in a unitary way, before executing all the requests in the collection using Postman Runner. In the following section, we will introduce Newman, which allows us to automate the execution of Postman tests.

Understanding the Newman concept

So far in this chapter, we have talked about using Postman locally to test the APIs that we develop or consume. But what is important in the unit, acceptance, and integration tests is that they are automated so that they can be executed within a CI/CD pipeline.

Postman, as such, is a graphical tool that does not automate itself, but there is another tool called **Newman** that automates tests that are written in Postman.

> **Note**
>
> We can also use another tool called Postman Sandbox to run the Postman API in Node.js or a browser. For more information, read the GitHub repository here: `https://github.com/postmanlabs/postman-sandbox`.

Newman is a free command-line tool that has the great advantage of automating tests that are already written in Postman. It allows us to integrate API test execution in CI/CD scripts or processes.

In addition, it offers the possibility of generating the test results of reports of different formats (HTML, JUnit, and JSON).

Nevertheless, Newman does not allow us to do the following:

- To create or configure Postman requests; as we will see, requests that are executed by Newman will be exported from Postman.
- To execute only one request that is in a collection—it executes all the requests in a collection.

> **Note**
>
> To learn more about Newman, you can visit the product page at `https://www.npmjs.com/package/newman`.

To use Newman, we will need—as stated in the *Technical requirements* section of this chapter—to have Node.js and npm installed, which are available at `https://nodejs.org/en/` (this installer installs both tools).

Then, to install Newman, we must execute this command in the terminal:

```
npm install -g newman
```

The following screenshot shows the execution of the command:

```
PS C:\Users\mkrief> npm install -g newman
C:\Users\mkrief\AppData\Roaming\npm\newman -> C:\Users\mkrief\AppData\Roaming\npm\node_modules\newman\bin\newman.js
+ newman@5.3.0
added 129 packages from 189 contributors in 23.971s
```

Figure 11.21 – Newman installation

This command installs the npm `newman` package and all its dependencies globally, that is, it is accessible on the entire local machine.

Once installed, we can test its installation by running the `newman --help` command, which displays the arguments and options to use, as shown in the following screenshot:

```
                          >newman --help
Usage: newman [options] [command]

Options:
  -v, --version                 output the version number
  -h, --help                    output usage information

Commands:
  run [options] <collection>  URL or path to a Postman Collection.

To get available options for a command:
  newman [command] -h
```

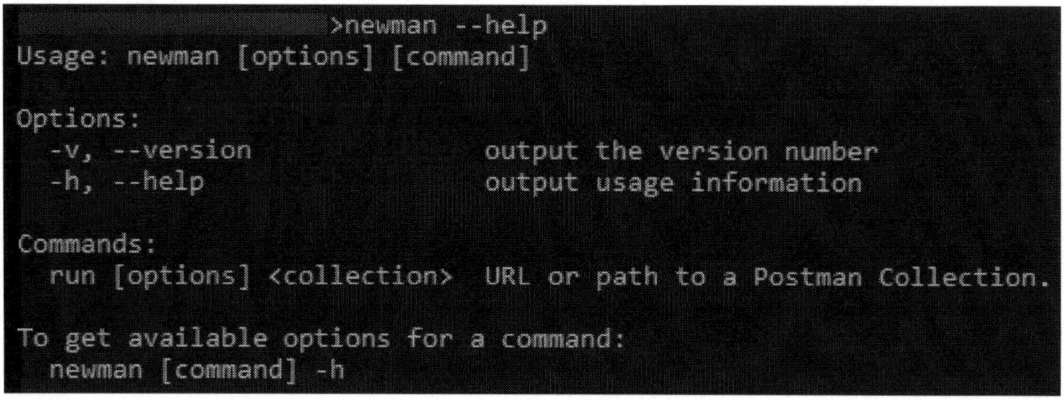

Figure 11.22 – Newman help command

In this section, we introduced Newman by talking about its advantages, and we learned how to install it. In the next section, we will export Postman's collection and environment for use with Newman.

Preparing Postman collections for Newman

As we have just seen, Newman is Postman's client tool, and in order to work, it needs the configuration of the collections, requests, and environments that we have created in Postman.

That's why, before running Newman, we will have to export Postman's collection and environments, and this export will serve as Newman's arguments. So, let's start exporting the DemoBook collection that we created in Postman.

Exporting the collection

The exporting of a Postman collection consists of obtaining a JSON file that contains all the settings of this collection and the requests that are inside it.

It is from this JSON file that Newman will be able to run the same API tests as when we ran them from Postman.

To do this export, perform the following tasks:

1. Go to the context menu of the collection that we want to export.
2. Choose the **Export** action.
3. Then, in the window that opens, uncheck the **Collection v2.1 (recommended)** checkbox.
4. Finally, validate by clicking on the **Export** button.

These steps are shown in the following screenshot:

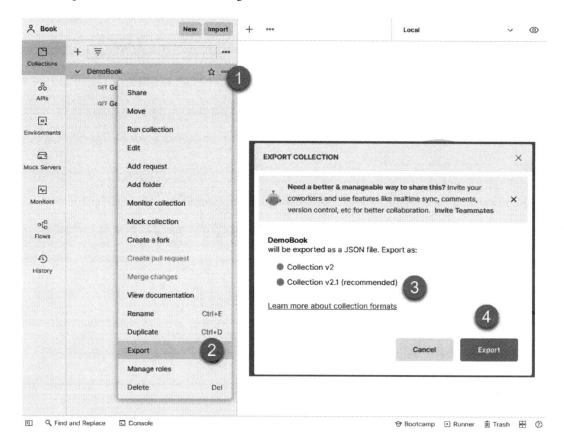

Figure 11.23 – Postman export collection

Clicking on the **Export** button exports the collection to a JSON format file, DemoBook. postman_collection.json, which we save in a folder that we create, which is dedicated to Newman.

After exporting the collection, we also need to export the environment and variable information because the requests in our collection depend on it.

Exporting the environments

We could stop there for Newman's configuration, but the problem is that our Postman requests use variables that are configured in environments.

It is for this reason, therefore, that we will also have to export the information from each environment in JSON format so that we can also pass it on as an argument to Newman.

To export the environments and their variables, perform the following tasks:

1. Open **ENVIRONMENTS** from the left panel in Postman.
2. Then, click on the **Export** environment button.

These steps are shown in the following screenshot:

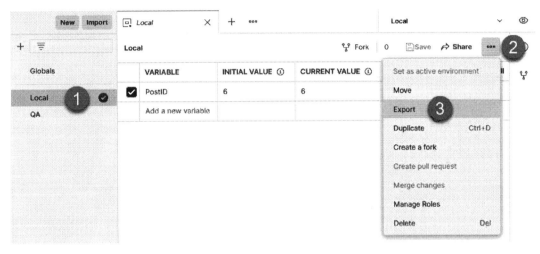

Figure 11.24 – Postman Export environment

So, for each environment, we will export their configurations in a JSON file, which we save in the same folder where we exported the collection.

Finally, we have a folder on our machine that contains three Postman JSON files:

- One JSON file for the collection
- One JSON file for the Local environment
- One JSON file for the QA environment

The following screenshot shows the contents of the local folder that contains Postman's exports:

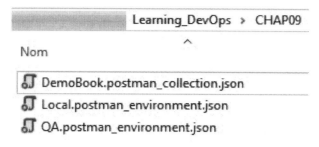

Figure 11.25 – Postman export file folder

We have just covered the export of all the configurations of our Postman requests, including the collection and the environments, and we will now look at the execution of the Newman command line.

Running the Newman command line

After exporting the Postman configuration that we saw earlier, we will run the Newman utility on our local machine.

To execute Newman, go to the Terminal, then to the folder where the JSON configuration files are located, and execute the following command:

```
newman run DemoBook.postman_collection.json -e Local.postman_
environment.json
```

The newman run command takes the JSON file of the collection that we exported as an argument and a parameter, -e, which is the JSON file of the exported environment.

> **Note**
> For more details about all the arguments of this command, read the documentation at https://www.npmjs.com/package/newman#newman-options.

Newman will execute the Postman requests from the collection we exported. It will also use the variables of the exported environment and will also perform the tests we wrote in the request.

The result of its execution, which is quite detailed, is shown in the following screenshot:

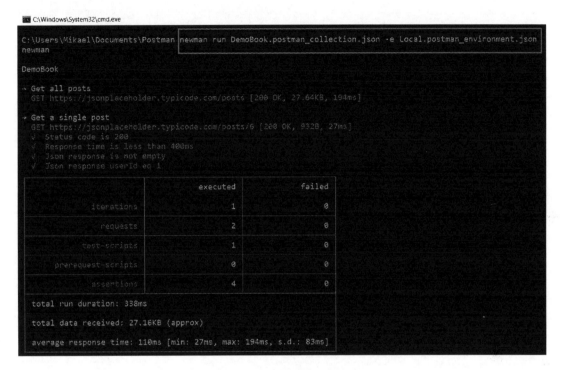

Figure 11.26 – Newman execution

And here is another screenshot that shows the result of its execution in case there is an error in the test:

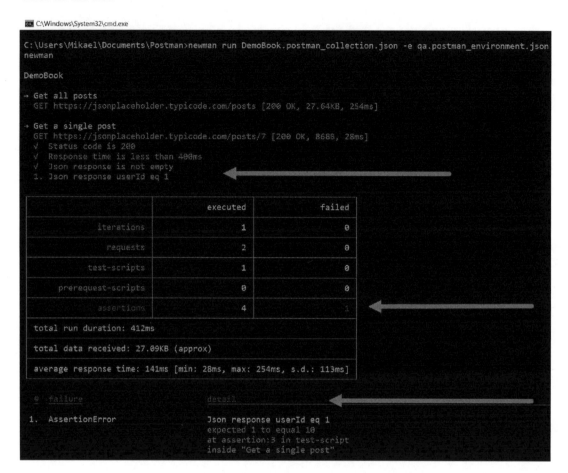

Figure 11.27 – Newman failed tests

We can see the details of the test that shows an error and what is expected in the request. In this section, we have learned how to run Newman on a local machine, and we will now learn how Newman is integrated in a CI/CD pipeline.

Integration of Newman in the CI/CD pipeline process

Newman is a tool that automates the execution of Postman requests from the command line, which will quickly allow us to integrate it into a CI/CD pipeline.

To simplify its integration in a pipeline, we go to the first step in the directory that contains the JSON files that were exported from Postman and create an npm configuration file—`package.json`.

This will have the following content:

```
{
  "name": "postman",
  "version": "1.0.0",
  "description": "postmanrestapi",
  "scripts": {
      "testapilocal": "newman run
DemoBook.postman_collection.json -e
Local.postman_environment.json -r junit,cli –reporter
junit-export result-tests-local.xml",
      "testapiQA": "newman run
DemoBook.postman_collection.json -e
QA.postman_environment.json -r junit,cli --reporter-junit
export result-tests-qa.xml"
  },
  "devDependencies": {
      "newman": "^5.3.0"
  }
}
```

In the `scripts` section, we put the two scripts that will be executed with the command lines that we saw in the previous section and we add to them the `-r` argument, which allows the output of the command with reporting in JUnit format, while, in the `DevDependencies` section, we indicate that we need the Newman package.

That's it; we have all the files that are necessary for integrating Newman's execution into a CI/CD pipeline.

To show Newman's integration into a CI/CD pipeline, we will use **Azure Pipelines**—an Azure DevOps service that we saw in *Chapter 7, Continuous Integration and Continuous Delivery*, and *Chapter 9, Containerizing Your Application with Docker*, and which has the advantage of having a graphic representation of the pipeline.

As a prerequisite for the pipeline, the directory that contains the JSON files of the Postman export, as well as the `package.json` file, must be committed in a source control version. In our case, we will use the GitHub repository, which contains the complete source code of this chapter: `https://github.com/PacktPublishing/Learning-DevOps-Second-Edition/tree/main/CHAP11`.

Build and release configuration

In Azure Pipelines, we will create a build and release configuration by following these actions:

1. We create a new **build definition** that copies the files that are needed to run Newman into the build artifacts, as shown in the following screenshot:

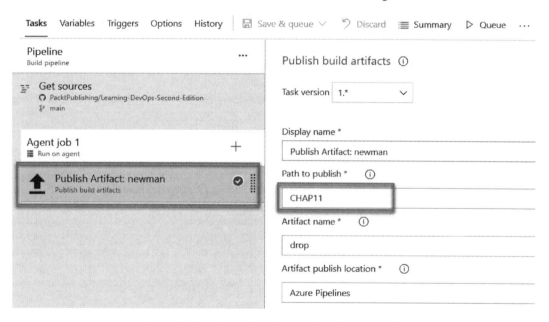

Figure 11.28 – Azure Pipelines publish Newman files

We also enable the continuous integration option in the **Triggers** tab. Then, to run this build, we save and queue this build definition.

2. Then, we create a new **release definition**, which will be in charge of running Newman for each environment. This release will get the artifacts of the build, and will be composed of two stages, DEV and QA, as shown in the following screenshot:

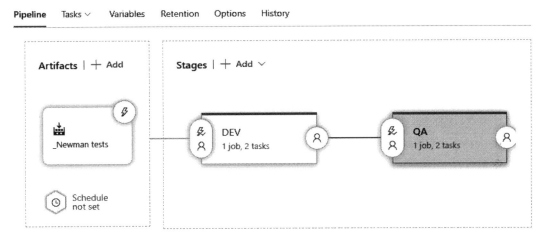

Figure 11.29 – Azure Pipelines Newman execution release

For each of these stages, we configure three tasks that go as follows, based on the package.json file:

1. Install Newman.
2. Run Newman.
3. Publish the test results in Azure Pipelines.

The following screenshot shows the configuration of the tasks for each stage:

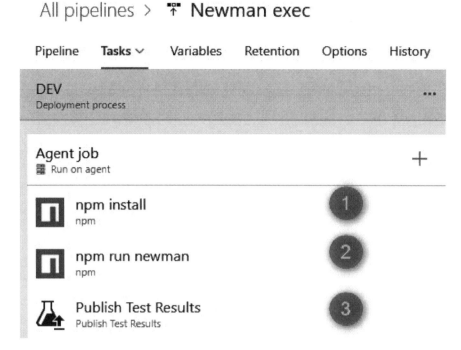

Figure 11.30 – Azure Pipelines Newman release steps

Let's look at the details of the parameters of these tasks in order.

npm install

The parameters of the **npm install** task are as follows:

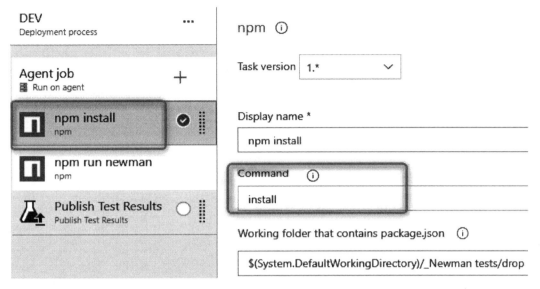

Figure 11.31 – Azure Pipelines npm install

Here, the command that is to be executed in the directory containing the artifact files is npm install.

npm run newman

The parameters of the **npm run newman** task are as follows:

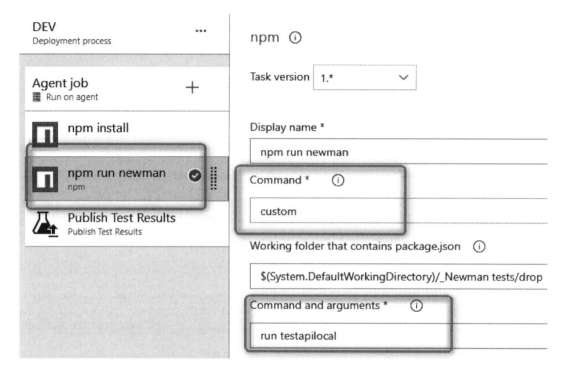

Figure 11.32 – Azure Pipelines run newman

Here, the custom command that is to be executed is npm run testapilocal in the directory that contains the artifact files, with the testapilocal command being defined in the package.json file in the script section (as seen previously), and which executes Newman's command line.

Publish Test Results

The parameters of the **Publish Test Results** task, which allows us to publish the results of the tests that are performed by Newman in Azure Pipelines, are as follows:

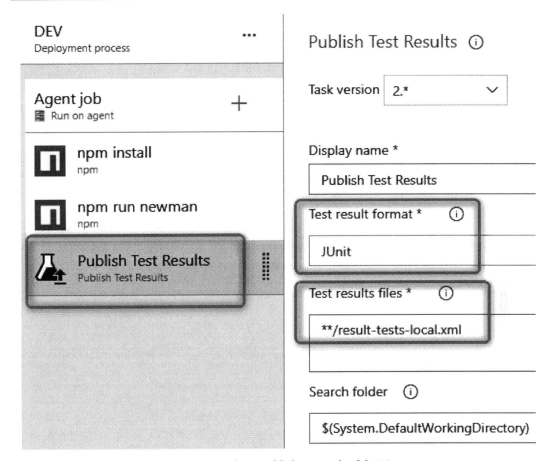

Figure 11.33 – Azure Pipelines publishing result of the Newman tests

In the parameters of this task, we indicate the JUnit XML reporting files that are generated by Newman, and in the **Control Options** field of this task, we select an option to execute the task, even if the **npm run newman** task fails.

The following screenshot shows the parameters of **Control Options** to run this task: **Even if a previous task has failed, unless the deployment was canceled**:

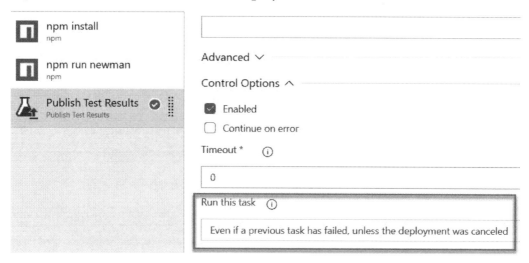

Figure 11.34 – Azure Pipelines publishing result of the Newman tests option

The configuration of the pipeline is complete—we will now proceed to its execution.

The pipeline execution

Once the configuration of the release is finished, we can execute this release, and at the end, we can see the reporting of the Newman tests in the **Tests** tab.

The following screenshot shows the reporting of the Newman tests in Azure Pipelines:

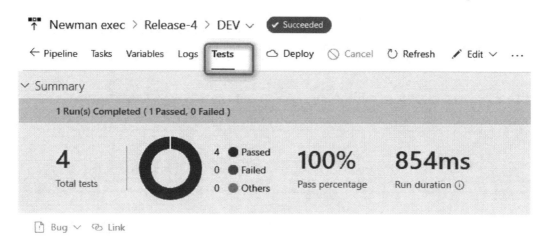

Figure 11.35 – Azure Pipelines view result of the Newman tests

All Postman tests were completed successfully.

Here is a screenshot that shows the reporting of the tests in case one of the tests fails:

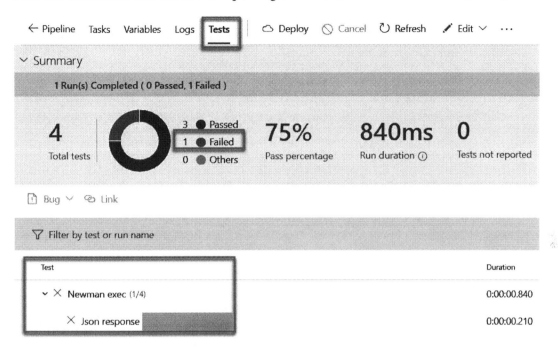

Figure 11.36 – Azure Pipelines view result of the Newman failed tests

So, we integrated Newman's execution successfully, and thus we were able to automate the requests of our API, which we had configured in Postman, in a CI/CD pipeline.

Regarding the integration of Newman executions in **Jenkins**, read the documentation at `https://learning.getpostman.com/docs/postman/collection_runs/integration_with_jenkins`, and for integration with **Travis CI**, the documentation can be found at `https://learning.getpostman.com/docs/postman/collection_runs/integration_with_travis`.

In this section, we learned how to create and configure a CI/CD pipeline in Azure Pipelines, which performs Postman tests that have been exported for Newman.

Summary

In this chapter, we introduced Postman, which is an excellent tool for testing APIs. We created a Postman account and installed it locally.

Then, we created collections and environments, in which we created requests that contain the settings of our APIs that are to be tested.

We also talked about automating these tests using the Newman command-line tool, with the exporting of Postman collections and environments.

Finally, in the last part of this chapter, we created and executed a CI/CD pipeline in Azure DevOps that automates the execution of API tests in a DevOps process.

In the next chapter, we will stay on the subject of testing, and we will look at the analysis of static code with a well-known tool called **SonarQube**.

Questions

1. What is the goal of Postman?
2. What is the first element that needs to be created in Postman?
3. What is the name of the element that contains the configuration of the API that is to be tested?
4. Which tool in Postman allows us to execute all the requests of a collection?
5. Which tool allows us to integrate Postman API tests in a CI/CD pipeline?

Further reading

If you want to know more about Postman, here are some additional resources:

*   Postman Learning Center: `https://learning.getpostman.com/`
*   Videos and tutorials about Postman: `https://www.getpostman.com/resources/videos-tutorials/`

12
Static Code Analysis with SonarQube

In the previous chapter, we looked at how to test the functionality of an **application programming interface (API)** with Postman, a free tool for testing APIs, and the integration and automation of these tests in a **continuous integration/continuous deployment (CI/CD)** pipeline using Newman.

Testing the functionality of an API or application is a good practice when we wish to improve the quality of applications. In a company, the quality of an application must be considered by all its members because an application that brings business value to users increases the company's profits.

However, we often neglect to test the quality of an application's code because we think that what matters is how the application works and not how it is coded. This way of thinking is a big mistake because poorly written code can contain security vulnerabilities and can also cause performance problems. Moreover, the quality of the code has an impact on its maintenance and scalability because code that is too complex or poorly written is difficult to maintain and, therefore, will cost more for the company to fix.

In this chapter, we will focus on static code analysis with a well-known tool called **SonarQube**. We will provide a brief overview of it and go over how to install it. Then, we will use SonarLint to analyze the code locally. Finally, we will integrate SonarQube into a CI/CD pipeline on Azure Pipelines.

In this chapter, we will cover the following topics:

- Exploring SonarQube
- Installing SonarQube
- Real-time analysis with SonarLint
- Executing SonarQube in a CI process

Technical requirements

To use SonarQube and SonarLint, we have to install the **Java Runtime Environment** (**JRE**), which can be found at `https://www.oracle.com/technetwork/java/javase/downloads/jre8-downloads-2133155.html` (an Oracle account is required), on the server where we have SonarQube and on the local development environment where we have SonarLint.

To integrate SonarQube into an Azure DevOps pipeline, we must install the following extension on our Azure DevOps organization: `https://marketplace.visualstudio.com/items?itemName=SonarSource.sonarqube`.

The complete code source for this chapter is available at `https://github.com/PacktPublishing/Learning-DevOps-Second-Edition/tree/main/CHAP12`.

Check out the following video to see the code in action: `https://bit.ly/3s96XTR`.

Exploring SonarQube

SonarQube is an open source tool from SonarSource (`https://www.sonarsource.com/`) that's written in Java. It allows us to perform static code analysis to verify the quality and security of an application's code.

SonarQube is designed for developer teams and provides them with a dashboard and reports that are customizable so that they can present the quality of the code in their applications.

It allows for the analysis of static code in a multitude of languages (over 25), such as **PHP: Hypertext Preprocessor (PHP)**, Java, .NET, JavaScript, Python, and so on. A complete list can be found at `https://www.sonarqube.org/features/multi-languages/`.

In addition, apart from code analysis with security issues, code smell, and code duplication, SonarQube also provides code coverage for unit tests. For more details about these issue concepts, read the documentation here: `https://docs.sonarqube.org/latest/user-guide/concepts/`.

Finally, SonarQube integrates very well into CI/CD pipelines so that it can automate the code analysis during developer code commits. This reduces the risk of deploying an application that has security vulnerabilities or code complexity that is too high.

On the other hand, it is important to note that they have a multitude of plugins that can be paid for. A list of plugins is available here: `https://www.sonarplugins.com/`.

Now that we've provided an overview of SonarQube, we will look at its architecture and components. Finally, we will look at the different ways of installing it.

Installing SonarQube

SonarQube is an on-premises solution—in other words, it must be installed on servers or **virtual machines (VMs)**. In addition, SonarQube consists of several components that will analyze the source code of applications, retrieve and store the data from this analysis, and provide reports on the quality and security of the code.

Before we install SonarQube, it is essential that we look at its architecture and components.

Overview of the SonarQube architecture

SonarQube is a client/server tool, which means that its architecture is composed of artifacts on the server side and also on the client side.

A simplified SonarQube architecture is shown in the following diagram:

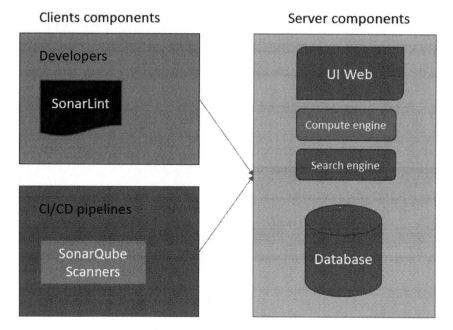

Figure 12.1 – SonarQube architecture with Client and Server components

Let's look at the components that are shown in the preceding diagram. The components that make up SonarQube on the server side are listed here:

- A SQL Server, MySQL, Oracle, or PostgreSQL database that contains all the analysis data.

- A web application that displays dashboards.

- The compute engine, which is in charge of retrieving the analysis and processes and putting them in the database.

- A search engine built with Elasticsearch.

The client-side components are listed here:

- The scanner, which scans the source code of the applications and sends the data to the compute engine.

- The scanner is usually installed on build agents that are used to execute CI/CD pipelines.

- SonarLint is a tool that's installed on developers' workstations for real-time analysis. We will look at it in detail later in this chapter.

For more details on this architecture, we can consult the SonarQube architecture and integration documentation, which can be found at `https://docs.sonarqube.org/latest/user-guide/concepts/`.

Now that we have looked at its architecture and components, we will learn how to install it.

SonarQube installation

SonarQube can be installed in different ways—either manually or by installing a Docker container from the Sonar image. Alternatively, if we have an Azure subscription, we can use a SonarQube VM from the Marketplace. Let's take a closer look at each of these options.

Manual installation of SonarQube

If we want to install the SonarQube server manually, we must take the prerequisites into account. These prerequisites are that Java must already be installed on the server and that we need to check the hardware configuration shown at `https://docs.sonarqube.org/latest/requirements/requirements/`.

Then, we must manually install the server components in order, like so:

1. Install the database. This can be either MSSQL, Oracle, PostgreSQL, or MySQL.

2. Then, for the web application, download the Community Edition of SonarQube from `https://www.sonarqube.org/downloads/` and unzip the downloaded ZIP file.

3. In the `$SONARQUBE-HOME/conf/sonar.properties` file, configure access to the database we installed in *Step 1* and the storage path of Elasticsearch, as detailed in the following documentation: `https://docs.sonarqube.org/latest/setup/install-server/`.

4. Start the web server.

To find out about all the details regarding this installation according to the chosen database and our **operating system (OS)**, we can consult the following documentation: `https://docs.sonarqube.org/latest/setup/install-server/`.

Installation via Docker

If we want to install SonarQube Community edition for tests or demonstration purposes, we can install it via the official Docker image that is available from Docker Hub at `https://hub.docker.com/_/sonarqube/`.

Be careful as this image uses a small integrated database that is not made for production.

Installation in Azure

If we have an Azure subscription, we can quickly access the entire SonarQube server using the SonarQube VM from the Azure Marketplace. Follow these steps to create a SonarQube VM in Azure:

1. In the Azure Marketplace, search and select the **SonarQube** image. The following screenshot shows the SonarQube page of the Marketplace:

Figure 12.2 – Azure SonarQube in the Marketplace

2. Click on the **Create** button to get started.

3. In the VM form, on the **Basics** tab, select the **Resource group** type and provide the **Virtual machine name** information, as shown in the following screenshot:

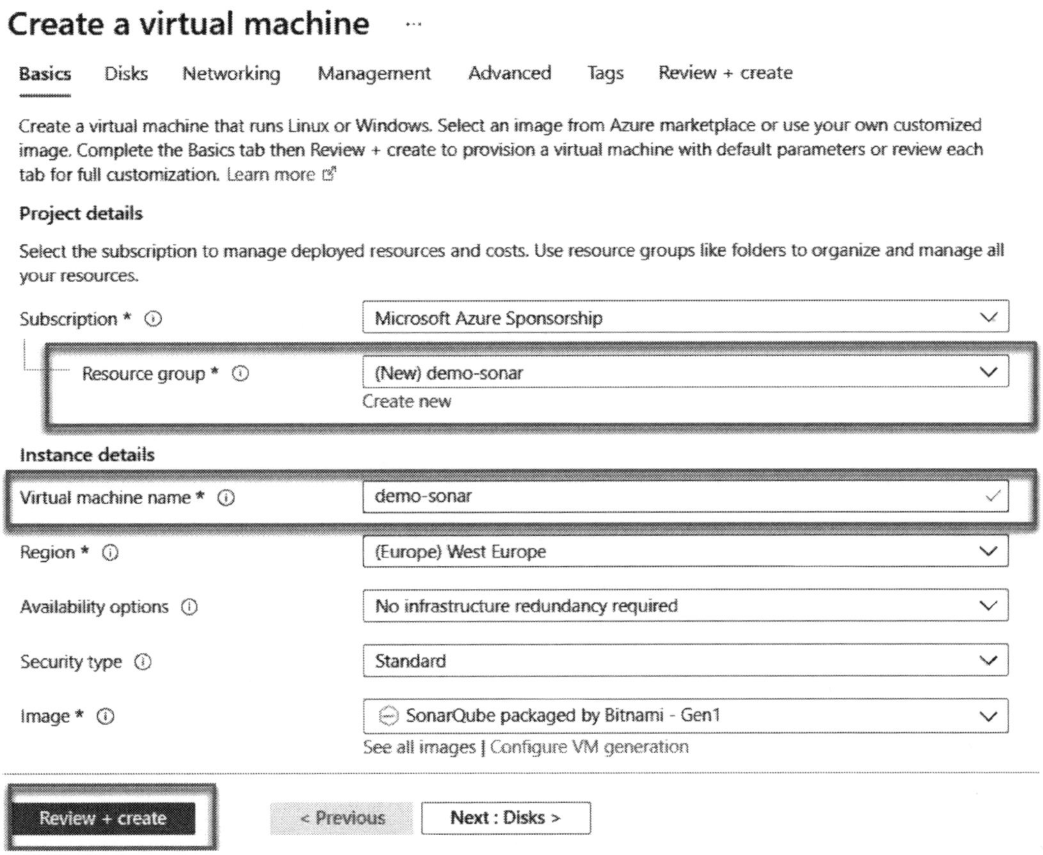

Create a virtual machine ⋯

Basics Disks Networking Management Advanced Tags Review + create

Create a virtual machine that runs Linux or Windows. Select an image from Azure marketplace or use your own customized image. Complete the Basics tab then Review + create to provision a virtual machine with default parameters or review each tab for full customization. Learn more ☐

Project details

Select the subscription to manage deployed resources and costs. Use resource groups like folders to organize and manage all your resources.

Subscription * ⓘ	Microsoft Azure Sponsorship	⌄
Resource group * ⓘ	(New) demo-sonar	⌄
	Create new	

Instance details

Virtual machine name * ⓘ	demo-sonar	✓
Region * ⓘ	(Europe) West Europe	⌄
Availability options ⓘ	No infrastructure redundancy required	⌄
Security type ⓘ	Standard	⌄
Image * ⓘ	⊝ SonarQube packaged by Bitnami - Gen1	⌄
	See all images | Configure VM generation	

[Review + create]   < Previous   Next : Disks >

Figure 12.3 – SonarQube Azure creation

We can also change some optional VM options in the **Disks** and **Networking** tabs. Then, we validate these changes by clicking on the **Review + create** button.

At the end of the resource creation, we can view the status of the deployment in the Azure portal, which in this case is successful:

✅ Your deployment is complete

⊖ Deployment name: CreateVm-bitnami.sonarqube-6-4-2019072815...   Start time: 7/28/2019, 3:40:26 PM
Subscription: Microsoft Azure Sponsorship   Correlation ID: 6bfacfb4-78eb-4e07-8f79-8
Resource group: demo-sonar

∧ **Deployment details** (Download)

RESOURCE	TYPE	STATUS	OPERATION DETAILS
✅ demo-sonar	Microsoft.Compute/virt...	OK	Operation details
✅ demo-sonar592	Microsoft.Network/netw...	Created	Operation details
✅ demosonardiag	Microsoft.Storage/stora...	OK	Operation details
✅ demo-sonar-vnet	Microsoft.Network/virtu...	OK	Operation details
✅ demo-sonar-nsg	Microsoft.Network/netw...	OK	Operation details
✅ demo-sonar-ip	Microsoft.Network/publ...	OK	Operation details

Figure 12.4 – SonarQube Azure deployment

4. To access the installed SonarQube server, view the details of the VM and get the **Public IP address** value, as shown in the following screenshot:

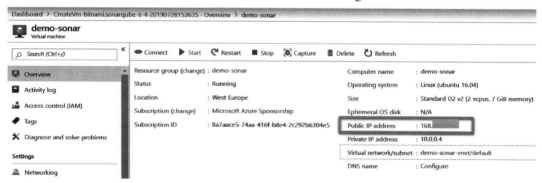

Figure 12.5 – SonarQube Azure Internet Protocol (IP) address

Open a web browser with this IP address as a **Uniform Resource Locator** (URL). The SonarQube authentication page will be displayed, as illustrated in the following screenshot:

Figure 12.6 – SonarQube login screen

The default login is `admin` and is accessible via the VM boot diagnostics information, as indicated in the documentation (`https://docs.bitnami.com/azure/faq/get-started/find-credentials/`). The following screenshot shows how to perform password recovery via the **Boot diagnostics** option:

Figure 12.7 – SonarQube Azure password recovery

Once authenticated, we can access the SonarQube dashboard, which looks like this:

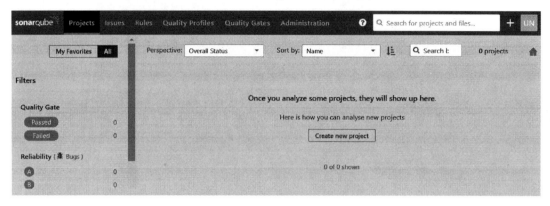

Figure 12.8 – SonarQube home page

We have learned the steps to install SonarQube inside a VM, so now, we will learn to install SonarQube on Kubernetes.

Installing SonarQube on Kubernetes

For installing SonarQube on a Kubernetes cluster, we will use the `helm-chart` package provided here: `https://github.com/SonarSource/helm-chart-sonarqube/tree/master/charts/sonarqube`.

Before installing SonarQube on Kubernetes, it's important to read about the requirements here: `https://docs.sonarqube.org/latest/setup/sonarqube-on-kubernetes/`.

For installing SonarQube on Kubernetes, run the following script:

```
helm repo add sonarqube https://SonarSource.github.io/helm-chart-sonarqube
helm repo update
kubectl create namespace sonarqube
helm upgrade --install -n sonarqube sonarqube/sonarqube
```

The first line of this script adds the SonarQube Helm registry locally.

The second line updates the index of this registry.

Then, the script creates the `sonarqube` namespace.

Finally, the last line installs the `sonarqube` Helm chart.

At the end of the execution of this script, the Helm chart execution displays the script to use the installed SonarQube instance on the console, as shown in the following screenshot:

```
PS C:\Users\mkrief> helm upgrade --install -n sonarqube sonarqube sonarqube/sonarqube
Release "sonarqube" does not exist. Installing it now.
NAME: sonarqube
LAST DEPLOYED: Sun Dec 19 15:05:26 2021
NAMESPACE: sonarqube
STATUS: deployed
REVISION: 1
NOTES:
1. Get the application URL by running these commands:
   export POD_NAME=$(kubectl get pods --namespace sonarqube -l "app=sonarqube,release=sonarqube" -o jsonpath="{.items[0].metadata.name}")
   echo "Visit http://127.0.0.1:8080 to use your application"
   kubectl port-forward $POD_NAME 8080:9000 -n sonarqube
```

Figure 12.9 – SonarQube installation on Kubernetes with Helm

> **Note**
>
> Before executing this script, check that all pods are running by executing the following command:
>
> ```
> kubectl get pods -n sonarqube
> ```

In this section, we have looked at the architecture of SonarQube, along with details about the client and server components. Then, we looked at the different installation methods that are available and the configuration of SonarQube. In the next section, we will look at how developers can perform real-time code analysis using SonarLint before they commit their code.

Real-time analysis with SonarLint

Developers who use SonarQube in a CI context often face the problem of having to wait too long before they get the results of the SonarQube analysis. They must commit their code and wait for the end of the CI pipeline before they get the results of the code analysis.

To address this problem and, therefore, improve the daily lives of developers, SonarSource—the editor of SonarQube—provides another tool, **SonarLint**, which allows real-time code analysis.

SonarLint is a free and open source tool (`https://www.sonarlint.org/`) that downloads differently depending on your development tool and development language. SonarLint is available for Eclipse, IntelliJ IDEA, Visual Studio, and **Visual Studio Code (VS Code) integrated development environments (IDEs)**.

In this book, we will look at an example of using SonarLint on an application written in TypeScript using the VS Code IDE. The prerequisite to using SonarLint is having the JRE installed on the local development computer. It can be downloaded from `https://www.oracle.com/technetwork/java/javase/downloads/jre8-downloads-2133155.html`.

To learn more about the concrete use of SonarLint, follow these steps:

1. In VS Code, install the SonarLint extension by going to the following page on the Azure Marketplace:

Figure 12.10 – SonarLint VS Code extension

2. Then, in VS Code, in the **User** settings, configure the extension with the installation path of the JRE, shown as follows:

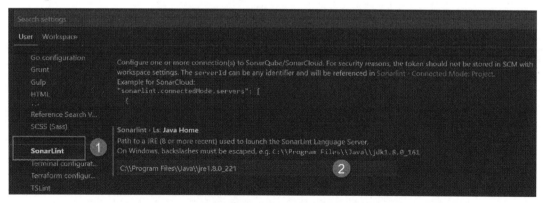

Figure 12.11 – SonarLint VS Code extension configuration

3. In our project, create a `tsApp` folder. Inside that folder, create an `app.ts` file that contains the code of our application. The source code is available here: `https://github.com/PacktPublishing/Learning-DevOps-Second-Edition/blob/main/CHAP12/tsApp/app.ts`.

4. Note that in this SonarLint sample code, it states that the code is not correct, as shown in the following screenshot:

```
1  var x=4
2  if (x && x)
3
4  }      var x: number

          Correct one of the identical sub-expressions on both sides of operator "&&"
          (typescript:S1764) sonarlint(typescript:S1764)

          Quick Fix...  Peek Problem
```

Figure 12.12 – SonarLint sample check code

SonarLint allows us to learn more about this error by displaying detailed information regarding the error and how to fix it, as shown in the following screenshot:

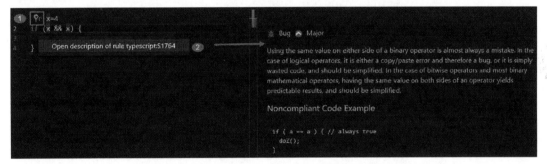

Figure 12.13 – SonarLint sample check code error details

Thus, SonarLint and its integration with various IDEs allow us to detect static code errors in real time as soon as possible—that is, while the developer writes their code and before they commit it in the source control version.

In this section, we learned how to install SonarLint in VS Code and how to use it to perform real-time code analysis.

In the next section, we will discuss how to integrate SonarQube analysis into a CI process in Azure Pipelines.

Executing SonarQube in a CI process

So far in this chapter, we have looked at how to install SonarQube and how developers use SonarLint on their local machines.

Now, we will look at how to perform code analysis during CI to ensure that each time a code commit is made, we can check the application code that's provided by all team members.

In order to integrate SonarQube into a CI process, we will need to perform the following actions:

1. Configure SonarQube by creating a new project.
2. Create and configure a CI build in Azure Pipelines.

Let's start by examining the creation of a new project in SonarQube.

Configuring SonarQube

SonarQube's configuration consists of creating a new project and retrieving an identification token. To create a new project, follow these steps:

1. Click on the **Create new project** link on the dashboard.
2. Then, enter a unique demobook key and a name for this project as demo-book in the form.
3. To validate this, click on the **Set Up** button to create the project. The steps are shown in the following screenshot:

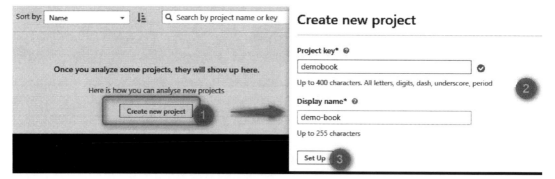

Figure 12.14 – SonarQube project creation

As soon as the project is created, the SonarQube assistant proposes that we create a token (unique key) that will be used for analysis.

To generate and create this token, follow these steps:

1. In the input, type a desired token name.
2. Then, validate it by clicking on the **Generate** button.
3. The unique key is then displayed on the screen. This key is our token, and we must keep it safe. The following screenshot shows the steps for generating the token:

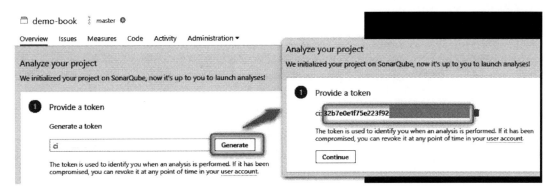

Figure 12.15 – SonarQube token generation

The configuration of SonarQube with our new project is complete. Now, we will configure our CI pipeline to perform the SonarQube analysis.

Creating a CI pipeline for SonarQube in Azure Pipelines

To illustrate the integration of a SonarQube analysis into a CI pipeline, we will use Azure Pipelines, which we looked at in detail in *Chapter 7, Continuous Integration and Continuous Delivery*.

The application that we'll use as an example in this section has been developed in Node.js, which is a simple calculator that contains some methods, including unit test methods.

> **Note**
>
> Note that the purpose of this section is not to discuss the application code, but rather the pipeline. You can access the application source code at `https://github.com/PacktPublishing/Learning-DevOps-Second-Edition/tree/main/CHAP12/AppDemo`.

To use SonarQube in Azure Pipelines, we must install the **SonarQube extension** in our Azure DevOps organization from the Visual Studio Marketplace, which is located at `https://marketplace.visualstudio.com/items?itemName=SonarSource.sonarqube`, as described in the *Technical requirements* section of this chapter.

The following screenshot shows the header and button to install the extension from the Visual Studio Marketplace:

Figure 12.16 – SonarQube Azure DevOps extension

Once the extension has been installed, we can configure our CI build.

In Azure Pipelines, we will create a new build definition with the following configuration:

1. In the **Get Sources** tab, select the repository and the branch that contains the source code of the application, as shown in the following screenshot:

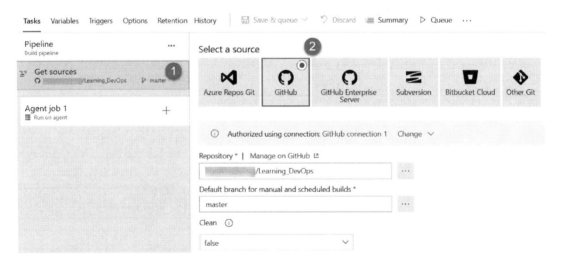

Figure 12.17 – Azure DevOps selected repository

2. Then, in the **Tasks** tab, configure the schedule of the tasks, shown as follows:

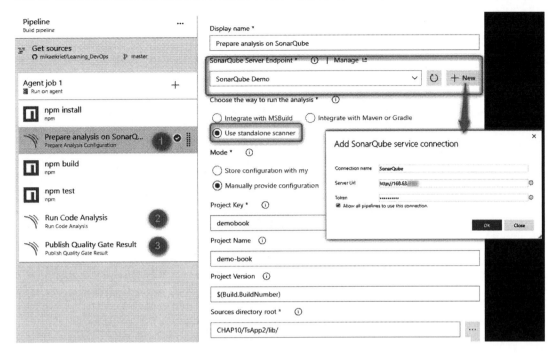

Figure 12.18 – Azure Pipelines SonarQube: preparing analysis

Here are the details of the configuration of these tasks:

1. The **Prepare analysis on SonarQube** task includes configuring SonarQube with the following:

    - An endpoint service, which is the connection to SonarQube with its URL and token that we generated previously in the SonarQube configuration

    - The key and name of the SonarQube project

    - The version number of the analysis

2. Then, we build and execute the unit tests of the application with npm build and npm test.

3. The **Run Code Analysis** task retrieves the test results, analyzes the TypeScript code of our application, and sends the data from the analysis to the SonarQube server.

Then, we save, start executing the CI build, and wait for it to finish.

The SonarQube dashboard has been updated with the code analysis, as shown in the following screenshot:

Figure 12.19 – SonarQube dashboard analysis

Here, we can see the measurements of bug numbers, code maintainability, and also code coverage. By clicking on each of these pieces of data, we can access details of the element.

In this section, we have looked at how to integrate SonarQube analysis into a CI pipeline that will provide a dashboard, along with the results and reports of the code analysis of each code commit.

Summary

In this chapter, we looked at how to analyze the static code of an application using SonarQube. This analysis can detect and prevent code syntax problems and vulnerabilities in the code, and can also indicate the code coverage provided by unit tests.

Then, we discussed in detail the use of SonarLint, which allows developers to check their code in real time as they write their code.

Finally, we looked at the configuration of SonarQube and its integration into a CI process to ensure continuous analysis that will be triggered at each code commit of a team member.

In the next chapter, we will look at some security practices by performing security tests with the **Zed Attack Proxy** (**ZAP**) tool, executing performance tests with Postman, and launching load tests with Azure DevOps.

Questions

1. Which language is SonarQube developed in?
2. What are the requirements for installing SonarQube?
3. What is the role of SonarQube?
4. What is the name of the tool that allows real-time analysis by developers?

Further reading

If you want to find out more about SonarQube, here is a resource to help you with this:

- SonarQube documentation: `https://docs.sonarqube.org/latest/`

13
Security and Performance Tests

In *Chapter 11, Testing APIs with Postman*, and *Chapter 12, Static Code Analysis with SonarQube*, we talked about test automation with API tests with Postman and static code analysis with SonarQube, respectively.

In this chapter, we will discuss how to carry out security and penetration tests on a web application using the ZAP tool based on the OWASP recommendations. Then, we will add to our Postman skills so that we can perform performance tests on APIs.

We will be covering the following topics:

- Applying web security and penetration testing with ZAP
- Running performance tests with Postman

Technical requirements

To use ZAP, we need to install the **Java Runtime Environment** (**JRE**), which is available at `https://www.oracle.com/technetwork/java/javase/downloads/jre8-downloads-2133155.html` (an Oracle account is required).

In this chapter, we'll talk about Postman, which we discussed in *Chapter 11, Testing APIs with Postman*.

Check out the following video to see the Code in Action: `https://bit.ly/3HbOgD0`.

Applying web security and penetration testing with ZAP

Today, application security must be at the heart of companies' concerns. As soon as a web application (or website) is publicly exposed on the internet, it is a candidate for an attack by malicious people. In addition, it is important to note that application security is even more important if it is used to store sensitive data such as bank accounts or your personal information.

To address this problem, there's **Open Web Application Security Project** (**OWASP**) (`https://www.owasp.org/index.php/Main_Page`), a worldwide organization that studies application security issues. The goal of this organization is to publicly highlight the security problems and vulnerabilities that can be encountered in an application system. In addition to this valuable security information, OWASP provides recommendations, solutions, and tools for testing and protecting applications.

One of the important and useful projects and documents that's provided by OWASP is the top 10 application security issues. This document is available at `https://owasp.org/www-project-top-ten/`. The document is very detailed and provides an explanation, examples, and a solution for each security issue. In this document, we can see that the top security vulnerability that applications are most vulnerable to is injection vulnerability, such as SQL injection, which consists of injecting code or requests into an application to collect, delete, or corrupt data from the application.

At the time of writing, the top 10 OWASP mitigation techniques are as follows:

1. Ongoing risk assessment
2. Use automated as well as manual means for assessments
3. Choose a strong **Web Application Firewall** (**WAF**)

4. Ensure that the web development framework and coding practices have inbuilt security

5. Enforce **multi-factor authentication (MFA)**

6. Encrypt all data

7. Apply all software updates instantly

8. Ensure that the web application is sanitized

9. Have formal awareness initiatives

10. Adhere to OWASP compliance standards

For more details about these mitigation techniques, read the following article: `https://www.indusface.com/blog/owasp-top-10-mitigation-techniques/`.

We also have another known security flaw in this document, which is **cross-site scripting (XSS)**. This consists of executing HTML or malicious JavaScript code on a user's web browser.

The challenge for companies is to be able to automate the security tests of their applications to protect them and take steps as quickly as possible when a flaw is discovered.

There are many security and penetration testing tools available. A very complete list is available at `https://www.owasp.org/index.php/Appendix_A:_Testing_Tools`. Among them, we learned about SonarQube in the previous chapter, which allows you to analyze code to detect security vulnerabilities.

Another tool in this list that is very interesting is **Zed Attack Proxy (ZAP)** (`https://www.owasp.org/index.php/OWASP_Zed_Attack_Proxy_Project`), which was developed by the OWASP community.

Let's learn how to use ZAP to perform security tests on our applications.

Using ZAP for security testing

ZAP is a free and open source graphical tool that allows you to scan websites and perform a multitude of security and penetration tests.

Unlike SonarQube, which also performs security analysis in the application's source code but does not execute it, ZAP runs the application and performs security tests.

When running, ZAP will act as a proxy between the user and the application by scanning all the URLs of the application, then performing a series of penetration tests on these different URLs. It is currently one of the most widely used tools in application testing because, in addition to being free, it provides many very interesting features, such as the ability to configure Ajax penetration tests, as well as also advanced test configurations. In addition, it integrates very well with many CI/CD pipeline platforms. Finally, it is possible to control it using REST APIs. The respective documentation is available at `https://www.zaproxy.org/docs/api/`.

What I propose to do is make a small lab using ZAP on a public demonstration website that has security holes. As we mentioned in the *Technical requirements* section, one prerequisite of using ZAP is to have Java installed on the machine that will perform the tests. It can be a local machine or a build agent.

We can download ZAP at `https://www.zaproxy.org/download/`; download the package that corresponds to your OS.

Then, install ZAP by following the software installation procedures of your OS. Once the installation is complete, we can open ZAP and access its interface.

The following screenshot shows the default ZAP interface:

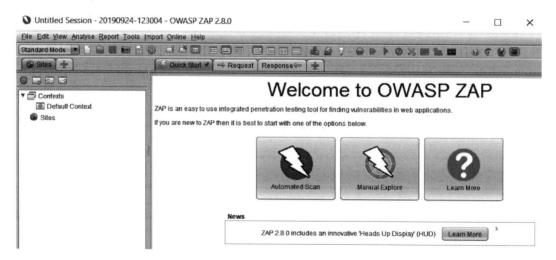

Figure 13.1 – OWASP ZAP tool

We will perform our first piece of security analysis with ZAP by following these steps:

1. In the right-hand panel, click on the **Automated Scan** button, which will open a form where we can enter the URL to be scanned.

2. In the **URL to attack** field, enter the URL of the website to analyze. In our example, we will enter the URL of a demo site: `http://demo.guru99.com/Security/SEC_V1/`.

3. Then, to start the analysis, click on the **Attack** button.

The following screenshot shows the preceding steps visually:

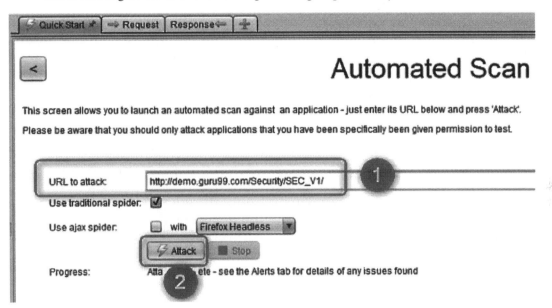

Figure 13.2 – OWASP ZAP – Automated Scan

We must wait for the security test analysis of this website to be completed.

4. As soon as the analysis is completed, we can see what security problems were encountered in the panel at the bottom left.

5. Finally, clicking on one of the alerts displays the details of the problem and helps us solve it.

The following screenshot shows the analysis results that we have just mentioned:

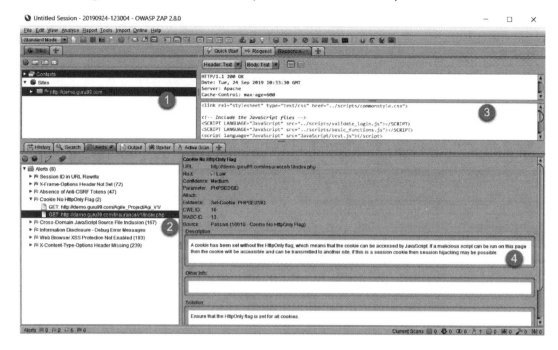

Figure 13.3 – OWASP ZAP scan result

With that, we've learned how to use ZAP, a graphical tool that's used to analyze the security vulnerabilities of a website very quickly.

Now, let's look at the different ways to automate the execution of ZAP.

Ways to automate the execution of ZAP

We can also automate this ZAP analysis by installing it on an agent server of our CI/CD pipeline and using the `zap-cli` tool, which is available at `https://github.com/Grunny/zap-cli`. This is used in the command line and calls the ZAP APIs.

The following screenshot shows using `zap-cli` on the command line to analyze our demo website:

Figure 13.4 – zap-cli scan command line

In the preceding execution, two commands are used:

- The first, `zap-cli active-scan`, analyzes the website that was passed as a command parameter.

- The second, `zap-cli report`, generates a report of the scan result in HTML format.

> **Note**
>
> In the preceding commands, we used the `--api-key` parameter. To retrieve your API key value, go to the **Tools | Options | API** menu in your ZAP tool instance.

If we use Azure DevOps as a CI/CD pipeline platform, we can use the OWASP Zed Attack Proxy Scan task of Visual Studio Marketplace, which is available at `https://marketplace.visualstudio.com/items?itemName=kasunkodagoda.owasp-zap-scan`. If we have an Azure subscription, Azure Pipelines can also run ZAP in a Docker container, hosted in an Azure Container instance, as explained and detailed at `https://devblogs.microsoft.com/premier-developer/azure-devops-pipelines-leveraging-owasp-zap-in-the-release-pipeline/`.

If we're using Jenkins as a build factory, then look at the following article, which explains how to integrate and use the ZAP plugin when you're running a job: `https://www.breachlock.com/integrating-owasp-zap-in-devsecops-pipeline/`.

We've just learned how to perform security tests on our web applications with ZAP, which is developed by the OWASP community. We looked at its basic use via its graphical interface and performed security tests on a demonstration application. Then, we saw that it is also possible to automate its execution with `zap-cli` so that we can integrate it into a DevOps CI/CD pipeline.

Now, let's learn how to do performance tests with Postman.

Running performance tests with Postman

Among the tests that need to be done to guarantee the quality of our applications and ensure they are functional, including code analysis and security tests, there are also performance tests. The purpose of performance testing isn't to detect bugs in applications; it's to ensure that the application (or API) responds within an acceptable time frame to provide a good user experience.

The performance of an application is determined by metrics such as the following:

- Its response times
- What resources it uses (CPU, RAM, and network)
- The error rates
- The number of requests per second

Performance tests are divided into several types of tests, such as load tests, stress tests, and scalability tests.

Many tools are available to perform performance tests. The following article lists the 15 best ones: `https://www.softwaretestinghelp.com/performance-testing-tools-load-testing-tools/`. Among the tools we've already seen in this book, Postman is not a dedicated tool for performance testing, especially since it focuses mainly on APIs and not on monolithic web applications. However, Postman can provide a good indication of the performance of our API.

We discussed its usage in detail for API testing in *Chapter 11, Testing APIs with Postman*. When you're executing a request that tests an API in a unitary way, Postman provides the execution time of that API, as shown in the following screenshot:

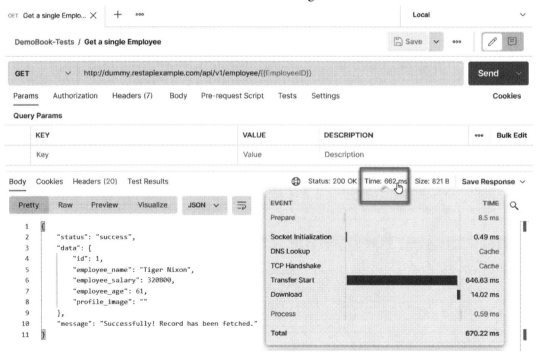

Figure 13.5 – Postman performance test

In addition, in Postman's **Collection Runner**, it is possible to execute all the requests of a collection and indicate the number of iterations; that is, the number of times the runner will execute the loop tests. This simulates several connections that call the API, and it is also where the execution time that's rendered by Postman becomes very interesting.

The following screenshot shows the configuration of Postman's **Runner** with several iterations in the input parameters:

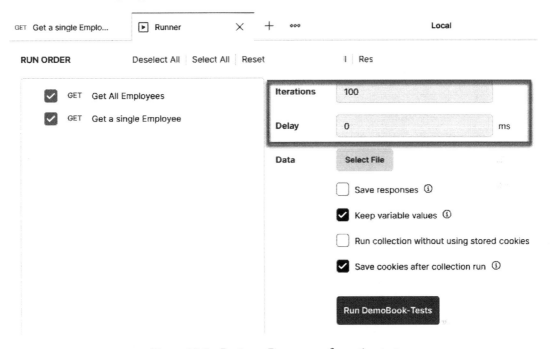

Figure 13.6 – Postman Runner configuration test

The following screenshot shows the results of the runner:

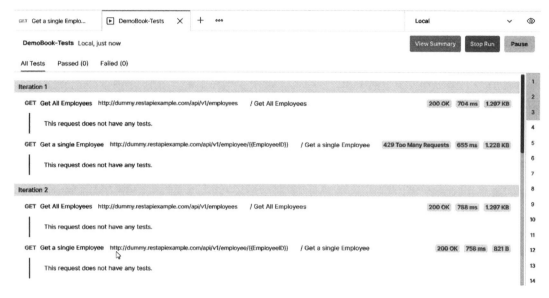

Figure 13.7 – Postman Runner test results

Here, we can see that the runner displays the execution time of each request, which means we can identify overload problems on an API.

Now that we've learned how to perform performance tests with Postman, let's summarize this chapter.

Summary

In this chapter, we looked at how to use ZAP, a tool that's developed by the OWASP community to automate the execution of web application security tests. We also saw how Postman can provide information on API performance.

In the next chapter, we will continue to talk about security and DevSecOps by learning how to automate infrastructure testing with Inspec, how to protect secrets with Hashicorp's Vault, and using Secure DevOps Kit for Azure to check the security compliance of Azure infrastructures.

Questions

Answer the following questions to test your knowledge of this chapter:

1. Is ZAP a tool that analyzes the source code of an application?

2. In Postman, what is the metric that allows us to have performance information?

Further reading

To learn more about what was covered in this chapter, take a look at the following resources:

- *Learn Penetration Testing*: `https://www.packtpub.com/networking-and-servers/learn-penetration-testing`

- Pluralsight videos about OWASP and ZAP: `https://www.pluralsight.com/search?q=owasp`

Section 5: Taking DevOps Further/More on DevOps

This part explains advanced topics relating to DevOps processes with security integration in DevOps (DevSecOps), some techniques concerning Blue-Green deployment, and how to apply DevOps in an open source project.

This section comprises the following chapters:

- *Chapter 14, Security in the DevOps Process with DevSecOps*
- *Chapter 15, Reducing Deployment Downtime*
- *Chapter 16, DevOps for Open Source Projects*
- *Chapter 17, DevOps Best Practices*

14
Security in the DevOps Process with DevSecOps

So far in this book, we have discussed in detail the **development-operations (DevOps)** culture as well as the DevOps tools that will facilitate communication and collaboration between developers and operations people (**information technology-operations, or ITOps**).

However, in this union, we have noticed that a very important aspect is often missing, which is security. Indeed, **continuous integration/continuous deployment (CI/CD)** pipelines and **infrastructure as code (IaC)** allow faster deployment of infrastructure and applications, but the problem is that to deploy faster, we do not include security teams, which causes the following:

- Security teams block or slow down deployments and therefore lead to longer deployment cycles.
- Security problems are detected very late in the infrastructure and in applications.

This is why, for some time now, security has been included in the DevOps culture by becoming a **development-security-operations (DevSecOps)** culture more broadly. There is nothing outside the ambit of security. Since we are developing at rapid speeds, it makes ample sense to make security part of the process rather than outside it.

The DevSecOps culture or approach is, therefore, the union of developers and operations with the integration of security as early as possible in the implementation and design of projects. The DevSecOps approach is also the automation of compliance and security verification processes in CI/CD pipelines, to guarantee constant security and not slow down application deployment cycles.

Today, the DevOps culture must absolutely integrate security teams but also all security processes, whether on tools, infrastructure, or applications. This is to provide not only better quality but also more secure applications.

In this chapter, we'll focus on the DevSecOps approach. First, we'll see how to test the compliance of an Azure infrastructure using InSpec from Chef. Then, we'll learn how to protect all infrastructure and application secrets with Vault from HashiCorp.

This chapter will cover the following topics:

- Testing Azure infrastructure compliance with Chef InSpec
- Keeping sensitive data safe with HashiCorp Vault

Technical requirements

In this chapter, we'll see the use of InSpec, which requires **Ruby** version 2.4 or later to be installed on the local machine. To install Ruby according to your specific **operating system (OS)**, read this documentation: `https://www.ruby-lang.org/en/documentation/installation/`.

In the *Keeping sensitive data safe with HashiCorp Vault* section, we'll discuss the integration between Vault and Terraform without looking into the details of Terraform, so I suggest you first read *Chapter 2, Provisioning Cloud Infrastructure with Terraform*.

The complete source code for this chapter is available here:

`https://github.com/PacktPublishing/Learning-DevOps-Second-Edition/tree/main/CHAP14`

Check out the following video to see the Code in Action:

`https://bit.ly/3In9kb2`

Testing Azure infrastructure compliance with Chef InSpec

One of the important practices of DevOps culture is IaC, detailed in *Chapter 1, The DevOps Culture and Infrastructure as Code Practices*, which consists of coding the configuration of an infrastructure and then being automatically deployed via CI/CD pipelines. IaC allows cloud infrastructure to be deployed and provisioned very quickly, but the question that often arises is: *Does the automatically provisioned infrastructure meet functional compliance and security requirements?*

To answer this question, we'll have to write and automate infrastructure tests that will verify the following:

- The infrastructure deployed corresponds well to the application and enterprise architecture specifications.

- The company's security policies are properly applied to the infrastructure.

These tests can be written in any scripting language that can interact with our cloud provider, and if we have an Azure subscription, we can use—for example—the Azure **command-line interface (CLI)** or Azure PowerShell commands to code the tests of our Azure resources. Also, if we use PowerShell, we can use **Pester** (`https://pester.dev/docs/quick-start/#what-is-pester`), which is a library that allows us to perform PowerShell tests and, combined with Azure PowerShell, allows us to perform infrastructure compliance tests.

> **Note**
>
> To get an example of how to use Pester to test an Azure infrastructure, I suggest you read this article: `https://dzone.com/articles/azure-security-audits-with-pester`. Also, have a look at this blog post: `https://dev.to/omiossec/unit-testing-in-powershell-introduction-to-pester-1de7`.

The problem with these scripting tools is that they require a lot of code to be written. Also, these tools are dedicated to a specified cloud provider, and they require learning a new scripting language.

One of the IaC tools is **InSpec** (`https://www.inspec.io/`), which performs infrastructure compliance tests.

In this section, we'll see in detail the use of InSpec to test the compliance of Azure infrastructure and, to start with its implementation, I will provide you with an overview of InSpec.

Overview of InSpec

InSpec is an open source tool written in Ruby that runs on the command line and is produced by one of the leading DevOps tools, **Chef**, whose website is `https://www.chef.io/`. It allows users writing declarative-style code to test the compliance of a system or infrastructure.

To use InSpec, it's not necessary to learn a new scripting language; we should already have enough knowledge to write the desired state of the infrastructure resources or the system we want to test.

With InSpec, we can test the compliance of remote machines and data and, since the latest version, it is also possible to test a cloud infrastructure such as Azure, **Amazon Web Services** (**AWS**), and **Google Cloud Platform** (**GCP**).

After this little overview of InSpec, let's look at how to download and install it.

Installing InSpec

We have seen in the *Technical requirements* section that InSpec needs to have **Ruby** (>2.4) installed on our machine.

InSpec can be installed either manually or via a script, as outlined here:

- **Manually**: This can be done by downloading the package corresponding to our OS from `https://www.chef.io/downloads/tools/inspec`.

- **With a script**: We can install InSpec by executing the commands detailed next in a terminal.

On Windows, we can download and install InSpec using the Chocolatey package at `https://community.chocolatey.org/packages/inspec` with the following command:

```
choco install inspec -y
```

On Linux, use the following script:

```
curl https://omnitruck.chef.io/install.sh | sudo bash -s -- -P
inspec
```

The following screenshot shows the installation of InSpec via the **Chocolatey package**:

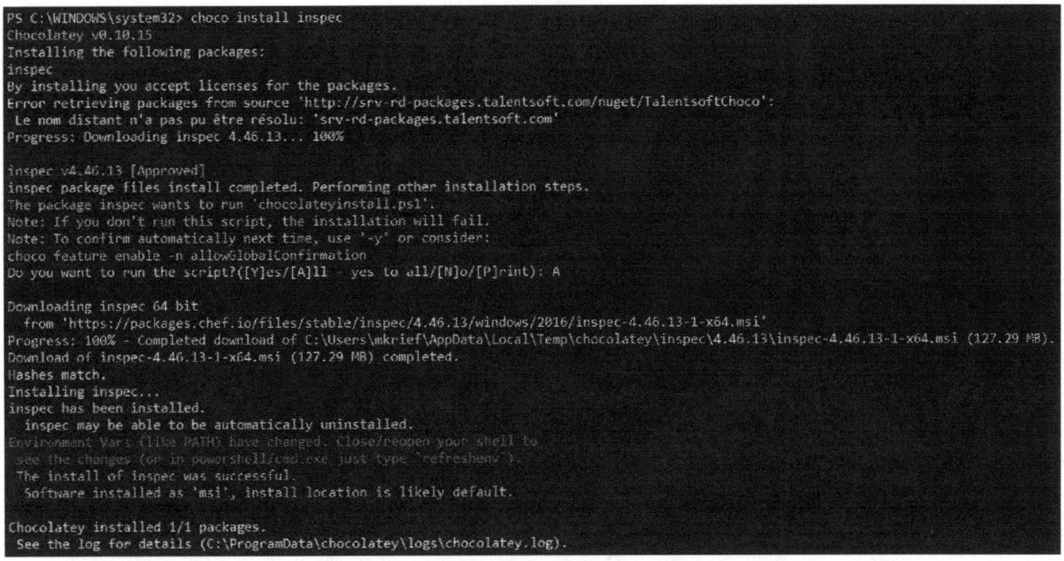

Figure 14.1 – InSpec installation on Windows

> **Note**
>
> For more information on the installation of InSpec for all OSes, refer to this documentation: `https://docs.chef.io/inspec/install/`.

To verify that InSpec has been correctly installed and is working, we run the `inspec --version` command to display its version, and the `inspec` command to display the list of available commands.

The following screenshot shows the execution of these commands:

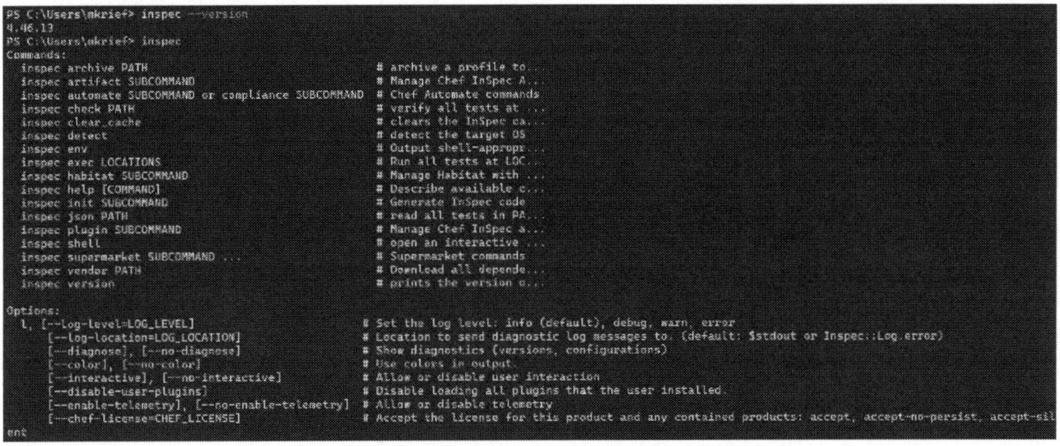

Figure 14.2 – Checking the InSpec version and displaying InSpec options

Also, as with many of the tools already detailed in this book, InSpec has been integrated into the **Azure Cloud Shell** tool suite, as shown in the following screenshot:

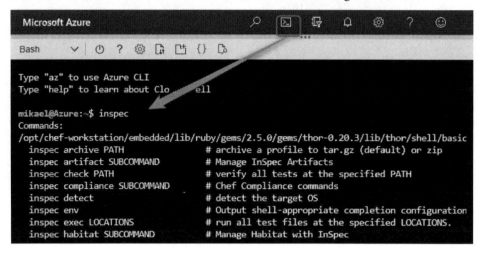

Figure 14.3 – InSpec in Azure Cloud Shell

We have just seen the different ways to install InSpec, and we'll now see the configuration of Azure for InSpec.

Configuring Azure for InSpec

Before writing test cases to test the compliance of our Azure infrastructure, we need to create an Azure service principal that has read permission on the Azure resources that will be tested.

To create this Azure service principal, we'll use the same procedure that we already detailed in the *Configuring Terraform for Azure* section of *Chapter 2, Provisioning Cloud Infrastructure with Terraform.*

Using the **Azure CLI** tool, we execute the following az cli command:

```
az ad sp create-for-rbac -name="<SP name> -role="Reader"
-scopes="/subscriptions/<subscription Id>"
```

This preceding command requires the following parameters:

- --name is the name of the Azure service principal to be created.

- --scopes is the **identifier (ID)** of the subscription (or other scopes) in which the Azure resources will be present.

- --role is the role name that the service principal will have on the specified resource scope.

The execution of this preceding command returns the following three pieces of authentication information relating to the created service principal:

- The client ID

- The client secret

- The tenant ID

> **Note**
>
> For more details on service principals, see the following documentation:
>
> https://docs.microsoft.com/en-us/cli/azure/create-
> an-azure-service-principal-azure-cli?view=azure-
> cli-latest

We'll see how to use this authentication information when running InSpec, but before it is executed, we need enough knowledge to write InSpec tests. Let's see how to do this.

Writing InSpec tests

After installing InSpec and configuring authentication for Azure, we can start using InSpec. To show an example of InSpec tests, we'll write tests that will check that the Azure infrastructure we provisioned with Terraform in *Chapter 2, Provisioning Cloud Infrastructure with Terraform*, is compliant with the specifications of our Azure infrastructure, which must be composed of the following:

- One resource group named bookRg

- One **virtual network (VNet)** with one subnet inside it named book-subnet

- One **virtual machine (VM)** named bookvm

As a first step in writing our InSpec tests, we'll create an InSpec profile file.

Creating an InSpec profile file

To create an InSpec profile file, we'll generate the test directory structure, then modify the InSpec profile file that was generated.

To perform this manipulation, we create a test folder structure and an InSpec profile that defines some metadata and the InSpec configuration. To create a structure and an InSpec profile file, on your machine, go to the directory of your choice and execute the following command:

```
inspec init profile azuretests
```

This command initializes a new profile by creating a new folder, `azuretests`, that contains all of the artifacts needed for InSpec tests, with the following:

- Controls (tests)
- Libraries
- A profile file, `inspec.yml`, with some default metadata

Then, we modify this `inspec.yml` profile file with some personal metadata and add the **Uniform Resource Locator** (**URL**) link from the InSpec-Azure resource pack to the sample code, as follows:

```
name: azuretests
title: InSpec Profile
maintainer: Your name
copyright: Your name
copyright_email: you@example.com
license: All Rights Reserved
summary: An InSpec Compliance Profile
version: 0.1.0
inspec_version: '>= 4.6.9'
depends:
  - name: inspec-azure
    url: https://github.com/inspec/inspec-azure.git
```

In this code, we have entered some personal information, such as our name, and information about the license type of this code. Then, finally, in the last part of this file, we indicated a dependency with the URL of the InSpec-Azure resource library pack.

In fact, since version 2.2.7 of InSpec, we can use a set of InSpec libraries that use the Azure API and hence allow us to access all Azure resources. From there, the InSpec team creates an Azure resource pack that contains a lot of libraries to test a wide range of Azure resources such as Azure users, Azure Monitor, Azure networking (VNet and subnets), Azure SQL Server, **Azure Virtual Machines (Azure VMs)**, and many other Azure resources.

> **Note**
>
> For a complete list of available Azure resources, refer to the InSpec documentation for the InSpec Azure resource pack:
>
> `https://www.inspec.io/docs/reference/`
> `resources/#azure-resources`

After generating our directories that contain the tests and profile file updates, we'll write our infrastructure compliance tests.

Writing compliance InSpec tests

To answer our example specification, we'll write tests that will verify our provisioned infrastructure contains a resource group, VM, and subnet.

All of the tests we'll be drafting are located in the `controls` folder and are written in a Ruby file (`.rb`) with very simple code that's human-readable.

To begin, we'll write a test that checks the existence of the resource group, and for this, we'll delete the `example.rb` example file in the `controls` folder, which is an example of the tests provided in the test templates, and create a new file named `resourcegroup.rb` that contains the following code content:

```
control 'rg' do
  describe azure_resource_groups do  #call the azurerm_resource_
groups of Azure Resource Pack
      its('names') { should include 'bookRg' } #test assert
  end
end
```

In this declarative code, the desired state of the resources is described and the following actions have been taken:

1. Create a control (or test) called `test_rg`.

2. In this control, we'll create a method of the `describe` type, in which we use the `azure_resource_groups` library of the Azure resource packs, which allows us to test the existence of a resource group.

3. In this `describe` method, we write a test assertions that checks whether there is a `bookRg` resource group in the Azure subscription.

Then, we'll continue to write our tests for the VM and subnet. To do this, we manually create a `subnet.rb` file in the `controls` directory that contains the following code:

```ruby
control "subnet" do
  describe azure_subnet(resource_group: 'bookRg', vnet: 'book-vnet', name: 'book-subnet') do
      it { should exist }
      its('address_prefix') { should eq '10.0.10.0/24' }
  end
end
```

In this code, we use the `azurerm_subnet` library, which allows us to test the existence of a subnet in a VNet. In this test, we check that the `book-subnet` subnet exists in the `book-vnet` VNet and that it has the IP range `10.0.10.0/24`.

Finally, here, we finish with writing the tests that allow us to check our VM with the following code in the `vm.rb` file:

```ruby
control 'vm' do
  describe azure_virtual_machine(resource_group: 'bookRg', name: 'bookvm')
  do
  it { should exist }
  its('properties.location') { should eq 'westeurope'}
  its('properties.hardwareProfile.vmSize') { should eq 'Standard_DS1_v2'}
  its('properties.storageProfile.osDisk.osType') { should eq 'Linux' }
}
```

```
    end
    end
```

In this code, we use the `azurerm_virtual_machine` library and test that the VM named `demovm` exists in the `bookRg` resource group. We also check some of its properties, such as region, OS type, and the size of the VM.

We have finished writing the InSpec tests that will be used to check the compliance of our Azure infrastructure, and we'll now see the execution of InSpec with these tests that we have just written.

Executing InSpec

To execute InSpec, we'll perform the following steps:

1. We'll configure the InSpec authentication to Azure; for this, we'll create environment variables with the values of the Azure service principal information that we created previously in the *Configuring Azure for InSpec* section. The four environment variables and their values are listed here:

   - `AZURE_CLIENT_ID` with the client ID of the service principal
   - `AZURE_CLIENT_SECRET` with the secret client of the service principal
   - `AZURE_TENANT_ID` with the tenant ID
   - `AZURE_SUBSCRIPTION_ID` with the ID of the subscription that contains the resources and whose service principal has reader permissions

   Here is an example of how to create these variables in a Linux OS:

   ```
   export AZURE_SUBSCRIPTION_ID="<Subscription ID"
   export AZURE_CLIENT_ID="<Client Id>"
   export AZURE_CLIENT_SECRET="<Secret Client>"
   export AZURE_TENANT_ID="<Tenant Id>"
   ```

2. Then, in a Terminal, we'll place ourselves in the directory containing the profile file, `inspec.yml`, and run the `inspec vendor .` command to download all dependencies and generate a lock file in the `vendor` directory.

3. Then, execute the following `inspec` command to check that the syntax of the tests is correct:

   ```
   inspec check .
   ```

The argument to be provided to this command is the path to the directory that contains the `inspec.yml` file. Here, in this command, we use `.` (dot) in the argument to indicate that the `inspec.yml` file is in the current directory, and the following screenshot shows the result of the execution of this command:

```
PS                      \Learning-DevOps-Second-Edition\CHAP14\azuretests> inspec check
Location :    .
Profile  :    azuretests
Controls :    3
Timestamp :   2021-12-26T16:21:45+01:00
Valid :       true

No errors or warnings
```

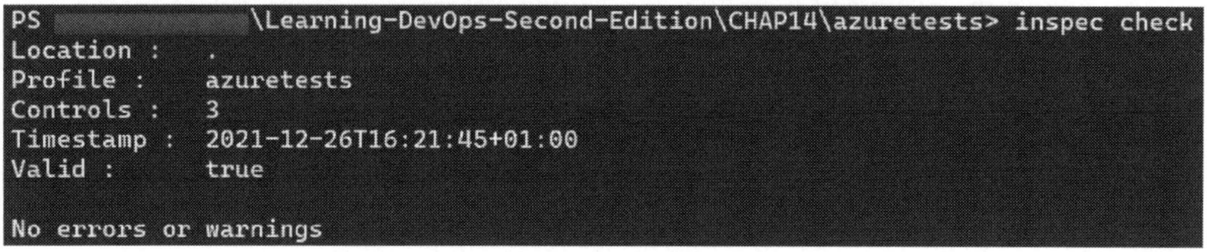

Figure 14.4 – InSpec check profile

4. Finally, we execute InSpec to execute the tests with the `inspec exec` command, as follows:

```
inspec exec . -t azure://
```

This command takes as an argument the path of the directory that contains the `inspec.yml` file (here, it is the dot). We also add the `-t` option, which takes the value of the tests to the target—that is, `azure`.

The following screenshot shows the result of the execution of this command:

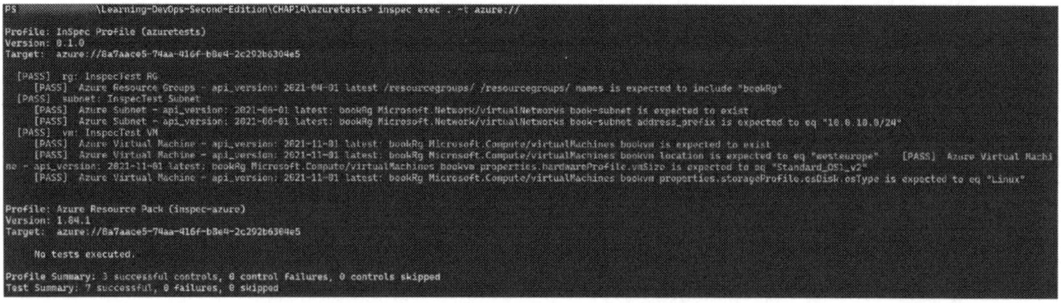

Figure 14.5 – InSpec exec tests

We can see from this result that all of the tests are green and therefore successful, so the compliance of the infrastructure is very successful.

We have just explained in this section how to write InSpec tests and run them to verify the compliance of our Azure infrastructure.

InSpec is a very powerful tool; it also allows you to test the configuration of a VM. That's why I invite you to view the following documentation: `https://www.inspec.io/docs/`.

We have just seen here the installation of InSpec, then the writing of InSpec tests, and finally how to use it with its command line to test the compliance of Azure infrastructure. In the next section, we'll look at another aspect of security with the protection of sensitive data using the secrets manager, Vault, from HashiCorp.

Keeping sensitive data safe with HashiCorp Vault

Today, when we talk about security in information systems, the most expected topic is the protection of sensitive data between different components of the system. This sensitive data that needs to be protected includes server access passwords, database connections, **application programming interface (API)** authentication tokens, and application user accounts. Indeed, many security attacks occur because this type of data is decrypted in the source code of applications or in poorly protected files that are exposed to local workstations. Many known tools can be used to secure this sensitive data, such as these:

- KeyPass (`https://keepass.info/`)
- LastPass (`https://www.lastpass.com/`)
- Ansible Vault, the use of which we discussed *Chapter 3, Using Ansible for Configuring IaaS Infrastructure*
- Vault from HashiCorp

Also, cloud providers offer their own secrets protection services such as the following:

- Azure Key Vault: `https://azure.microsoft.com/en-us/services/key-vault/`
- **Key Management Service (KMS)** for Google Cloud Platform: `https://cloud.google.com/kms/`
- AWS Secrets Manager for AWS: `https://aws.amazon.com/secrets-manager/?nc1=h_ls`

Out of all of the tools we have mentioned, we'll look at the use of **Vault** from HashiCorp, which is free and open source and can be installed on any type of OS as well as on Kubernetes.

These are the main features and benefits of Vault:

- It allows the storage of static secrets as well as dynamic secrets.
- It also has a system for rotating and revoking secrets.

- It allows data to be encrypted and decrypted without having to store it.

- It also has a web interface that allows the management of secrets.

- It integrates with a multitude of authentication systems.

- All secrets are stored in a single centralized tool.

- It allows you to be independent of your architecture by being accessible with all major cloud providers, Kubernetes, or even on internal data centers (on-premises).

> **Note**
>
> For more information on Vault features, see the product page at `https://www.vaultproject.io/docs/what-is-vault/index.html`.

With all of these very interesting features, Vault is therefore a tool that I recommend for any company that wants to protect its sensitive information and integrate its secure accessibility into a CI/CD pipeline. Indeed, in addition to being very efficient for data protection, Vault integrates very well in CI/CD pipelines. These pipelines will be able to use this protected data when provisioning infrastructure and deploying applications.

After an overview of Vault, we'll proceed with the installation of Vault on a local machine and use it for encrypting and decrypting data. We'll also give an overview of the Vault **user interface** (**UI**), and finally, we'll expose the process of how to retrieve data from Vault in Terraform.

Installing Vault locally

If you decide to use Vault, it is important to know that it is a tool that is responsible for the security of your sensitive infrastructure and application data. In practice, Vault is not just a tool, and before installing it in production, you need to understand its concepts and its different architectural topologies.

> **Note**
>
> To learn more about Vault architecture topologies, please refer to the documentation at `https://learn.hashicorp.com/vault/operations/ops-reference-architecture`.

The purpose of this chapter is therefore not to go into the details of the concepts and architecture of Vault but to explain the installation and use of Vault in development mode. In other words, we'll install Vault on a local workstation to have a small instance that's used for testing and development.

We have already detailed the use of HashiCorp tools in this book with Terraform and Packer, and similarly, Vault can be installed either manually or via a script, as follows:

- To **install Vault manually**, the procedure is exactly the same as that of installing Terraform and Packer, so you need to do the following:

  A. Navigate to the download page: `https://www.vaultproject.io/downloads.html`.

  B. Download the package related to your OS in the folder of your choice.

  C. Unzip the package and update the `PATH` environment variable with its path to this folder.

- To **install Vault automatically**, we'll use a script, the code of which depends on our OS.

For **Linux**, in a Terminal, run the following script (from `https://www.vaultproject.io/downloads`):

```
curl -fsSL https://apt.releases.hashicorp.com/gpg | sudo
apt-key add -sudo apt-add-repository "deb [arch=amd64] https://
apt.releases.hashicorp.com $(lsb_release -cs) main"sudo apt-get
update && sudo apt-get install vault
```

This script performs the following actions:

1. It registers to the HashiCorp package registry.
2. Installs the Vault package.

For **Windows**, to install Vault via a script, we'll use **Chocolatey**, which is the Windows software package manager (`https://chocolatey.org/`), by executing the following command in a Terminal:

```
choco install vault -y
```

This command downloads and installs Vault from Chocolatey.

Apart from these scripts that allow Vault to be installed on a local workstation, HashiCorp also provides Terraform code that allows you to create a complete Vault infrastructure on different cloud providers.

> **Note**
> This Terraform code is available for Azure at `https://github.com/hashicorp/terraform-azurerm-vault`; for AWS, it is available at `https://github.com/hashicorp/terraform-aws-vault`; and for GCP, it is available at `https://github.com/hashicorp/terraform-google-vault`.

For **Kubernetes**, we can use a Helm chart to install Vault inside a Kubernetes instance using the following script:

```
helm repo add hashicorp https://helm.releases.hashicorp.com
kubectl create namespace vault
helm install vault hashicorp/vault --namespace vault
```

In the preceding script, we perform the following actions:

1. Add the Hashicorp Helm repository locally.

2. Create a `vault` namespace.

3. Install Vault in the `vault` namespace using the Helm chart.

For more details about Vault installation on Kubernetes, read the tutorial here:

`https://learn.hashicorp.com/tutorials/vault/kubernetes-raft-deployment-guide?in=vault/kubernetes`

After installing Vault, we'll test its installation by running the following command in the Terminal:

```
vault --version
```

This command displays the installed version of Vault. We can also execute the `vault --help` command to display a list of available commands.

We have just seen the different ways to install Vault on a local machine or on Kubernetes; the next step is to start the Vault server.

Starting the Vault server

Vault is a client/server tool that consists of a client component that's used by developers for applications and a server component that is responsible for protecting data in remote backends.

> **Note**
>
> Vault supports a very large number of backends, a list of which is available here:
>
> `https://www.vaultproject.io/docs/configuration/storage/index.html`

After installing Vault locally, we only have access to the client part, and to be able to use Vault, we'll start the server component.

To start the Vault server component in development mode, we'll execute this command in a second Terminal:

```
vault server -dev
```

This command starts and configures the Vault server with a minimal configuration that contains an authentication token and a default backend called **in-memory**, which stores all secrets data in the memory of the server, as shown in the following screenshot:

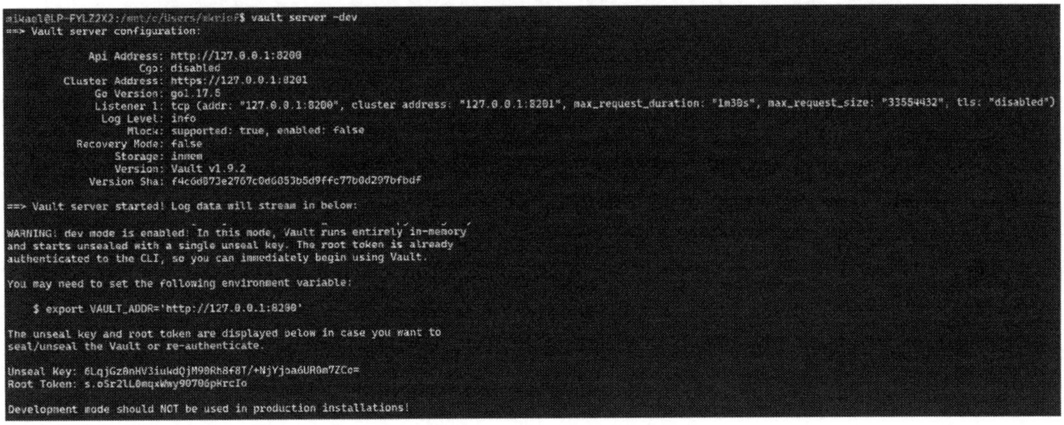

Figure 14.6 – Vault start -dev mode

> **Important Consideration**
>
> This Terminal must remain open to keep the Vault server running.

Also, since we are in development mode and the backend storage is just in memory, as soon as the Vault server stops, all of the secret data is deleted from the memory.

Then, as indicated during this execution, we'll export the VAULT_ADDR environment variable with this command in another Terminal:

```
export VAULT_ADDR='http://127.0.0.1:8200'
```

Finally, to check the execution status of the Vault server, we execute the following command:

```
vault status
```

Here is the command output, which displays the properties of the Vault server:

```
root@mkrief:/home/mikaelkrief# vault status
Key                Value
---                -----
Seal Type          shamir
Initialized        true
Sealed             false
Total Shares       1
Threshold          1
Version            1.2.1
Cluster Name       vault-cluster-9e7d6ef4
Cluster ID         82bfd424-73ce-9c3d-1dd1-dae6d88bb604
HA Enabled         false
```

Figure 14.7 – Vault status

> **Note**
>
> To learn more about the Vault server started in development mode, read the documentation at https://www.vaultproject.io/docs/concepts/dev-server.html.

Now that Vault is installed and the server is started, we'll see how to write data to Vault to protect it, and read that data so that it can be used from a third-party application.

Writing secrets to Vault

When you want to protect sensitive data that will be used by an application or infrastructure resources, the first step is to store this data in the secrets data manager that has been chosen by the company. We'll see in practice the steps for writing data to Vault.

To protect data in Vault, we go to a Terminal and execute the following command:

```
vault kv put secret/vmadmin vmpassword=admin123*
```

The following screenshot shows its execution:

```
root@mkrief:/home/mikaelkrief# vault kv put secret/vmadmin vmpassword=admin123*
Key              Value
...              .....
created_time     2019-08-13T13:56:14.5200652Z
deletion_time    n/a
destroyed        false
version          1
```

Figure 14.8 – Vault put secret with vault kv put command line

The command, with the put operation, creates new secret data in memory with the title vmadmin of the key-value type, which in this example is the admin account of a VM, in the secret/ path.

In Vault, all protected data is stored in a path that corresponds to an organizational location in Vault. The default path for Vault is secret/, and it is possible to create custom paths that will allow better management of secret rights and better organization by domain, topic, or application.

In terms of secrets stored in Vault, one of their advantages is that it is possible to store multiple data in the same secret; for example, we'll update the secret data that we have created with another secret, which is the login admin of the VM.

For this, we'll execute the following command that adds another key-value secret in the same Vault data:

```
vault kv put secret/vmadmin vmpassword=admin123*
vmadmin=bookadmin
```

As we can see in this execution, we used exactly the same command with the same secret, and we added new key-value data—that is, vmadmin.

> **Note**
>
> For more information on this kv put command, read the documentation at https://www.vaultproject.io/docs/commands/kv/put.html.

We learned how to use commands to create a secret in Vault and the various uses of secrets, and we'll now have a look at the command to read this secret in order to use it inside an application or in infrastructure resources.

Reading secrets in Vault

Once we have created secrets in Vault, we'll have to read them to use them in our applications or infrastructure scripts.

To read a key that is stored in Vault, we go to a Terminal to execute this command:

```
vault kv get secret/vmadmin
```

In this command, we use the `kv` operation with the `get` operator, and we indicate in the parameter the complete path of the key to get the protected value within our example, `secret/vmadmin`.

The following screenshot shows the command execution, as well as its output:

Figure 14.9 – Vault get secret with vault kv get command line

What we notice in the output of this command is the following:

- The version number of the secret here is 2 because we executed the `kv put` command twice, so the version number was incremented at each execution.

- There are two key-value data items that we protected in the secret in the previous *Writing secrets to Vault* section.

If you want to access the data stored in this secret but from an earlier version, you can execute the same command by optionally specifying the desired version number, as in this example:

```
vault kv get -version=1 secret/vmadmin
```

The following screenshot shows its execution:

```
root@mkrief:/home/mikaelkrief# vault kv get -version=1 secret/vmadmin
====== Metadata ======
Key                Value
---                -----
created_time       2019-08-13T13:56:14.5200652Z
deletion_time      n/a
destroyed          false
version            1

====== Data ======
Key                Value
---                -----
vmpassword         admin123*
root@mkrief:/home/mikaelkrief#
```

Figure 14.10 – Vault get secret by its version

We can see in this output, in the Data section, version 1 of the key-value data we had during the first execution of the kv put command.

> **Note**
>
> For more information on the kv get command, read the documentation at https://www.vaultproject.io/docs/commands/kv/get.html.

We have just seen the use of the kv get Vault command to retrieve all or specific versions of the values of a secret; we'll now briefly see how to use the Vault UI web interface for better management of secrets.

Using the Vault UI web interface

One of the interesting features of Vault is that, apart from the client-side tool that allows you to perform all operations on the Vault server, Vault has a UI web interface that allows you to manage secrets, but more visually and graphically.

To open and use the Vault web interface to visualize the secrets that we have created with the client tool, we must follow these steps:

1. In a browser, enter the URL provided when starting the server—that is, http://127.0.0.1:8200/ui, which is the default local Vault URL.

2. In the authentication form, enter the token that was provided in the Terminal in the root token information, as shown in the following screenshot:

```
root@mkrief:/home/mikaelkrief# vault server -dev
==> Vault server configuration:

            Api Address: http://127.0.0.1:8200
                    Cgo: disabled
        Cluster Address: https://127.0.0.1:8201
             Listener 1: tcp (addr: "127.0.0.1:8200", cluster address: "127.0.0.1:8
              Log Level: info
                  Mlock: supported: true, enabled: false

    $ export VAULT_ADDR='http://127.0.0.1:8200'                         o

The unseal key and root token are displayed below in case you want to
seal/unseal the Vault or re-authenticate.

Unseal Key: fh7vj+J8lHHXr+AtTva4DU2Ru4kcPtqQuM9jKBoO1BA=
   Root Token: s.6MGUVmH1bnhD36aWf0Fb9oR4

Development mode should NOT be used in production installations!
```

Figure 14.11 – Vault getting the root token

3. Click on the **Sign In** button to authenticate, as illustrated here:

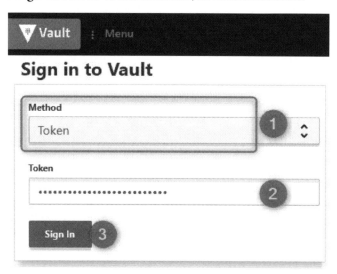

Figure 14.12 – Vault UI sign-in

4. The home of the interface displays a list of secret paths, called **Secrets Engines**, containing secrets that have been stored, as illustrated in the following screenshot:

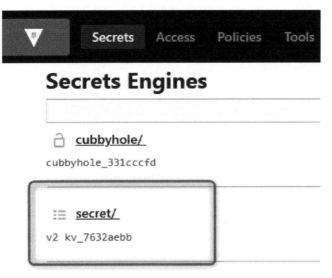

Figure 14.13 – Vault UI Secrets Engines

5. By clicking on each secret engine, you can see a list of secrets that have been saved. The following screenshot shows the secret engine page, which displays the secret we created on the command line in the previous section:

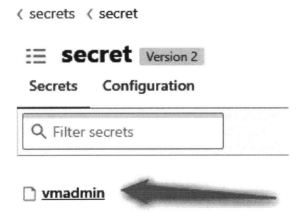

Figure 14.14 – Vault UI secret

6. By clicking on a specific secret, you can access a list of data that we have protected, with the possibility of viewing the values of each key in cleartext. We can also display the history of the content of a secret by selecting the desired version in the **History** drop-down menu, as illustrated in the following screenshot:

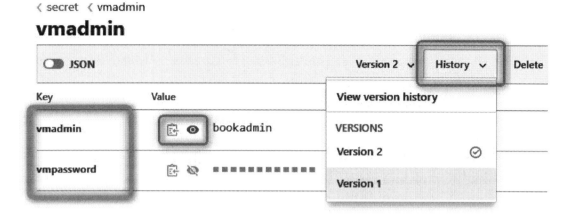

Figure 14.15 – Vault UI: reading secrets' details

The Vault web interface also allows you to perform all management operations on secrets and other Vault components.

> **Note**
> If you want to know more about this web interface, read this article:
> `https://www.hashicorp.com/resources/vault-oss-ui-introduction`

We have seen that the Vault web interface is a very good alternative to the client tool that allows you to view and manage Vault elements. After this overview of Vault and its operations, I propose a small Vault use case that shows you how to get secrets in Terraform code.

Getting Vault secrets in Terraform

As we have already seen in *Chapter 2, Provisioning Cloud Infrastructure with Terraform*, it is very important to protect the infrastructure configuration information that we write in Terraform code. One way to protect this sensitive data is to store it in a secrets manager such as Vault and recover it directly with Terraform dynamically.

Here is an example of Terraform code that allows you to retrieve the password of a VM that you want to provision from Vault. This Terraform code example is composed of three blocks, which are detailed as follows:

1. First, we use the Vault provider for configuring the Vault URL by executing the following code:

    ```
    provider "vault" {
        address = "http://127.0.0.1:8200" #Local Vault Url
    }
    ```

    The Vault provider is configured with the Vault server configuration and its authentication.

    In our case, we configure the Vault server URL in the Terraform code, and for the authentication of a token, we'll use an environment variable when running Terraform after an explanation of the code.

    > **Note**
    >
    > For more details on the Terraform Vault provider and its configuration, see the following documentation:
    >
    > https://www.terraform.io/docs/providers/vault/index.html

2. Then, we add the Terraform data block, `vault_generic_secret`, which is used for retrieving a secret from a Vault server. The code is illustrated in the following snippet:

    ```
    data "vault_generic_secret" "vmadmin_account" {
        path = "secret/vmadmin"
    }
    ```

    This data block allows us to retrieve (in read-only mode) the content of a secret stored in Vault. Here, we ask Terraform to retrieve the secret that is in the `secret/vmadmin` Vault path that we created earlier in this section.

    > **Note**
    >
    > For more details on `vault_generic_secret` data and its configuration, see the following documentation:
    >
    > https://www.terraform.io/docs/providers/vault/d/generic_secret.html

3. Finally, we add an `output` block to use the decrypted value of the secret, as follows:

```
output "vmpassword" {
value = "${data.vault_generic_secret.vmadmin_account.
data["vmpassword"]}"
  sensitive = true

}
```

This block provides an example of the exploitation of the secret.

The `data.vault_generic_secret.vmadmin_account.data["vmpassword"]` expression is used to get the secret returned by the previously used data block. In the `data` array, we add the name of only those keys for which we need the encrypted values to be recovered. Also, this output is considered *sensitive* so that Terraform does not display its value in plaintext when it is executed.

> **Note**
>
> The complete Terraform source code is also available here:
> `https://github.com/PacktPublishing/Learning-`
> `DevOps-Second-Edition/blob/main/CHAP14/vault/`
> `terraform_usevault/main.tf`

We have finished writing the Terraform code; we'll now quickly execute it to see the recovery of the secret.

> **Note**
>
> For the execution of the code, which we have already detailed in *Chapter 2, Provisioning Cloud Infrastructure with Terraform*, we'll only quote the commands without further detailing them in this section.

To execute Terraform, we go in a Terminal to the folder that contains the Terraform code, and then we proceed in this order:

1. Export the VAULT_TOKEN environment variable with the value of the Vault token. In our development mode case, this token is provided at the start of the Vault server.

   The following command shows the export of this environment variable on a Linux OS:

```
export VAULT_TOKEN=xxxxxxxxxxxx
```

2. Then, we'll execute Terraform with these commands:

```
terraform init
terraform plan
terraform apply
```

Here is a quick summary of the details of these commands:

- The `terraform init` command initializes the context and downloads all necessary providers.

- The `terraform plan` command displays a preview of all changes that will be applied by Terraform.

- The `terraform apply` command applies all changes on the infrastructure and displays the output values.

> **Note**
>
> To learn all the details of the main Terraform commands and the Terraform life cycle, read *Chapter 2* of this book, *Provisioning Cloud Infrastructure with Terraform*.

The following screenshot shows the execution of the `apply` command:

```
PS                Learning-DevOps-Second-Edition\CHAP14\vault\terraform_usevault> terraform apply

An execution plan has been generated and is shown below.
Resource actions are indicated with the following symbols:

Terraform will perform the following actions:

Plan: 0 to add, 0 to change, 0 to destroy.

Changes to Outputs:
  + vmpassword = (sensitive value)

Do you want to perform these actions?
  Terraform will perform the actions described above.
  Only 'yes' will be accepted to approve.

  Enter a value: yes


Apply complete! Resources: 0 added, 0 changed, 0 destroyed.

Outputs:

vmpassword = <sensitive>
```

Figure 14.16 – Terraform sensitive output

We can see that the value in the Terraform output named `vmpassword` is not displayed in clear text in the Terminal.

3. Finally, we display the Terraform output value in **JavaScript Object Notation (JSON)** format with the `terraform output` command and the `-json` option, as follows:

```
PS                    Learning-DevOps-Second-Edition\CHAP14\vault\terraform_usevault> terraform output -json
{
  "vmpassword": {
    "sensitive": true,
    "type": "string",
    "value": "admin123*"
  }
}
```

Figure 14.17 – Terraform output command in JSON format

We see that Terraform has displayed the value of the key that was in the secret, which we had inserted in Vault. This value can now be used for any sensitive data that should not be stored in Terraform code, such as VM passwords.

> **However, Be Careful**
>
> We have protected our Terraform code by outsourcing all sensitive data to a secrets manager, but it should not be forgotten that Terraform stores all information—including data and output information—in the Terraform state file. It is therefore very important to protect it by storing the Terraform state file in a protected remote backend, as we saw in the *Protecting the state file in a remote backend* section of *Chapter 2, Provisioning Cloud Infrastructure with Terraform*.

In this section, we have studied the use of HashiCorp's Vault, which is a secret data manager. We have seen how the installation on different OSes can be done manually and automatically. We used its command lines to protect and read data that we have protected inside. Then, we discussed how to manage secrets in Vault using its web interface. Finally, we wrote and executed Terraform code that uses the Vault provider and allows us to retrieve secrets that we stored in a Vault server.

Summary

This chapter is dedicated to integrating security into DevOps practices. We presented three tools to verify and secure your data and cloud infrastructure. We discussed how to check the compliance of an Azure infrastructure using **InSpec** from Chef.

To do this and check infrastructure compliance, we installed InSpec and then detailed the writing of InSpec tests. We used its command lines to verify the compliance of Azure infrastructure.

In the last section, we saw how to protect sensitive data with **Vault** from HashiCorp. In this section, we looked at data encryption and decryption in Vault and wrote Terraform code that will dynamically retrieve the secrets stored in Vault.

In the next chapter, we'll present the concept of **blue-green deployment** with its patterns for reducing deployment downtime. Then, we'll learn how to implement it in an application as well as in the deployment of Azure infrastructure.

Questions

1. What is the role of InSpec?
2. What is the name of the package manager that allows you to download InSpec via the command line?
3. Which InSpec command allows you to execute InSpec tests?
4. Who is the publisher of Vault?
5. Which command starts Vault in development mode?
6. When Vault is installed locally, can it be used for production?
7. In local mode, where is Vault's encrypted data stored?

Further reading

If you want to know more about DevSecOps with InSpec, Vault, and **Secure DevOps Kit for Azure (AzSK)**, here are some resources:

*   InSpec documentation: `https://www.inspec.io/`
*   HashiCorp Vault documentation: `https://www.vaultproject.io/docs/`
*   Learn about HashiCorp Vault: `https://learn.hashicorp.com/vault`

15
Reducing Deployment Downtime

So far in this book, we have discussed **DevOps** practices such as **Infrastructure as Code (IaC)**, **continuous integration/continuous deployment (CI/CD)** pipelines, and the automation of different types of tests.

In *Chapter 1, The DevOps Culture and Infrastructure as Code Practices*, we saw that these DevOps practices will improve the quality of applications and thus improve the financial gain of a company. We will now go deeper into DevOps practices by looking at how to ensure the continuous availability of your applications even during your deployments, and how to deliver new versions of these applications more frequently in production.

Often, what we see is that deployments require your applications to be interrupted by—for example—infrastructure changes or service shutdowns. Moreover, what we also see is that companies are still reluctant to deliver more frequently in production. They are not equipped to test the application in the production environment, or they are waiting for other dependencies.

In this chapter, we will look at several practices that will help you improve application delivery processes. We'll start with a way to reduce the downtime of your infrastructure and applications during Terraform deployments. Then, we will discuss the concept and patterns of blue-green deployment and how to configure it with some Azure resources. Finally, we will present the details of implementing a feature flag in your application, which will allow you to modify the operation of an application without having to redeploy it in production.

You will also learn how to configure Terraform code to reduce application downtime. You'll be able to configure Azure resources with blue-green deployment and implement feature flags in your applications with either an open source component or the LaunchDarkly platform.

In this chapter, we will cover the following topics:

- Reducing deployment downtime with Terraform
- Understanding blue-green deployment concepts and patterns
- Applying blue-green deployments on Azure
- Introducing feature flags
- Using an open source framework for feature flags
- Using the LaunchDarkly solution

Technical requirements

In order to understand the Terraform concepts that will be presented in this chapter, you need to have read *Chapter 2, Provisioning Cloud Infrastructure with Terraform*.

We will look at an example of how to implement blue-green deployment in Azure. If you don't have an Azure subscription, you can create a free Azure account here: `https://azure.microsoft.com/en-gb/free/`.

Then, we will look at an example of how to use feature flags in an ASP.NET Core application. To use our example, you will need to install the .NET Core **software development kit (SDK)**, which can be downloaded from `https://dotnet.microsoft.com/download`.

For code editing, we used the free **Visual Studio Code (VS Code)** editor, which is available for download here: `https://code.visualstudio.com/`.

The complete source code for this chapter can be found at `https://github.com/PacktPublishing/Learning-DevOps-Second-Edition/tree/main/CHAP15`.

Check out the following video to see the Code in Action:

`https://bit.ly/3hcvrVH`

Reducing deployment downtime with Terraform

In *Chapter 2, Provisioning Cloud Infrastructure with Terraform*, we detailed the use of Terraform by looking at its commands and life cycle and put it into practice with an implementation in Azure.

One of the problems with Terraform is that, depending on the infrastructure changes that need to be implemented, Terraform may automatically destroy and rebuild certain resources.

To fully understand this behavior, let's look at the output of this following Terraform execution, which provisioned an Azure Web App in Azure and has been modified with a name change:

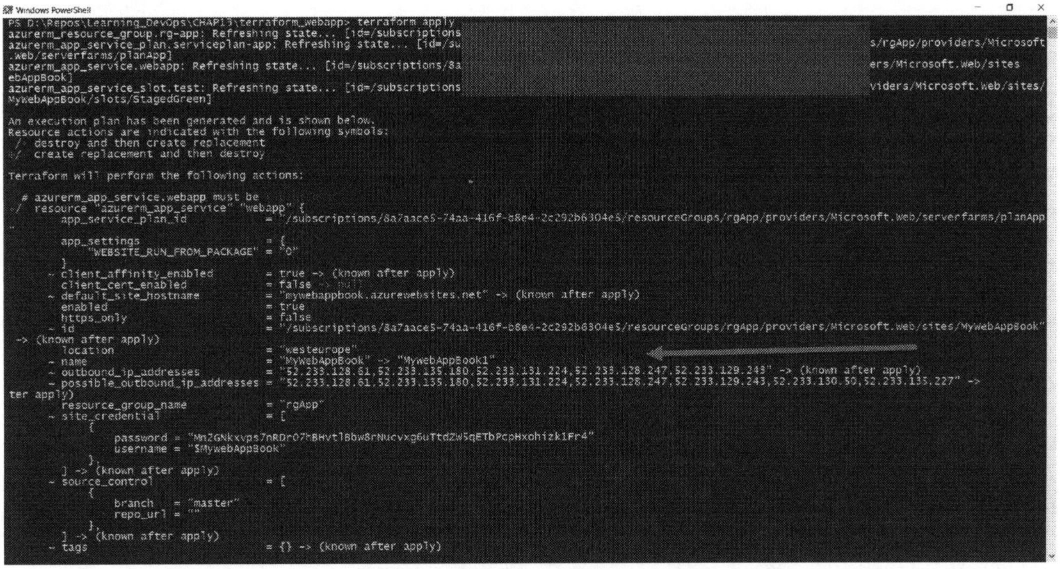

Figure 15.1 – Terraform downtime

Here, we can see that Terraform will destroy the web app and then rebuild it with the new name. Although destruction and reconstruction are done automatically, while Terraform is destroying and rebuilding the web app, the application will be inaccessible to users.

To solve this problem of downtime, we can add the Terraform `create_before_ destroy` option, as follows:

```
resource "azurerm_app_service" "webapp" {
    name = "MyWebAppBook1" #new name
    location = "West Europe"
    resource_group_name = "${azurerm_resource_group.rg-app.
name}"
    app_service_plan_id = "${azurerm_app_service_plan.
serviceplan-app.id}"
    app_settings = {
        WEBSITE_RUN_FROM_PACKAGE = var.package_zip_url"
    }
    lifecycle { create_before_destroy = true}
}
```

By adding this option, Terraform will do the following:

1. First, Terraform creates a new web app with a new name.
2. During the provisioning of the new web app, it uses the **Uniform Resource Locator** (**URL**) for the application package in ZIP format that's provided in the `app_settings` property. Use `WEBSITE_RUN_FROM_PACKAGE` to launch the application.
3. Then, Terraform will destroy the old web app.

Using the `Terraform create_before_destroy` option will ensure the viability of our applications during deployments.

However, be careful, as this option will only be useful if the new resource that's being created allows us to have the application running very quickly at the same time as it's provisioning so that a service interruption doesn't occur.

In our example of a web app, this worked when we used the `WEBSITE_RUN_ FROM_PACKAGE` property of the web app. For a **virtual machine** (**VM**), we can use a VM image created by **Packer**. As we saw in *Chapter 4, Optimizing Infrastructure Deployment with Packer*, Packer contains information regarding the VM applications that have already been updated inside the VM image.

> **Note**
>
> For more information on the `create_before_destroy` option,
> please view the following Terraform documentation: `https://www.`
> `terraform.io/language/meta-arguments/lifecycle`.

We have just seen that, with Terraform and IaC, it is possible to reduce downtime during deployments in the case of resource changes.

We will now look at the concepts and patterns of a practice called **blue-green deployment**, which allows us to deploy and test an application in production with great confidence.

Understanding blue-green deployment concepts and patterns

Blue-green deployment is a practice that allows us to deploy a new version of an application in production without impacting the current version of the application. In this approach, the production architecture must be composed of **two identical environments**; one environment is known as the **blue** environment while the other is known as the **green** environment.

The element that allows routing from one environment to another is a router—that is, a load balancer.

The following diagram shows a simplified schematic of a blue-green architecture:

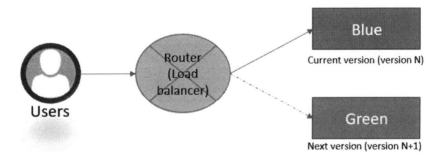

Figure 15.2 – Blue-green architecture

As we can see, there are two identical environments—the environment called **blue**, which is the current version of the application, and the environment called **green**, which is the new version or the next version of the application. We can also see a router, which redirects users' requests either to the blue environment or the green environment.

Now that we've introduced the principle of blue-green deployment, we will look at how to implement it in practice during deployment.

Using blue-green deployment to improve the production environment

The basic usage pattern of blue-green deployment goes like this: when we're deploying new versions of the application, the application is deployed in the blue environment (version N) and the router is configured in this environment.

When deploying the next version (version $N+1$), the application will be deployed in the green environment, and the router is configured in this environment.

The blue environment becomes unused and idle until the deployment of version $N+2$. It also will be used in the case of rapid rollback to version N.

This practice of blue-green deployment can also be declined on several patterns—that is, the canary release and dark launch patterns. Let's discuss the implementation of each of these patterns in detail. We will start with the canary release pattern.

Understanding the canary release pattern

The canary release technique is very similar to blue-green deployment. The new version of the application is deployed in the green environment, but only for a small, restricted group of users who will test the application in real production conditions.

This practice is done by configuring the router (or load balancer) to be redirected to both environments. On this router, we apply redirection restrictions of a user group so that it can only be redirected to the green environment, which contains the new version.

Here is a sample diagram of the canary release pattern:

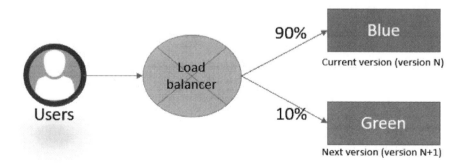

Figure 15.3 – Blue-green canary release

In the preceding diagram, the router redirects 90% of users to the blue environment and 10% of users to the green environment, which contains the new version of the application.

Then, once the tests have been performed by this user group, the router can be fully configured in the green environment, thus leaving the blue environment free for testing the next version (*N+2*).

As shown in the following diagram, the router is configured to redirect all users to the green environment:

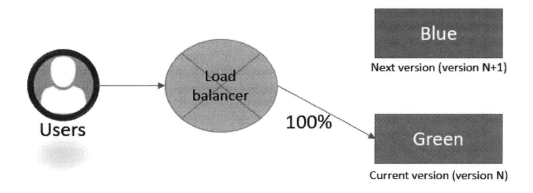

Figure 15.4 – Blue-green architecture with router

This deployment technique thus makes it possible to deploy and test the application in the real production environment without having to impact all users.

We will look at a practical implementation of this blue-green deployment pattern in Azure later in this chapter, in the *Applying blue-green deployments on Azure* section. But before that, let's look at another blue-green deployment pattern— the dark launch pattern.

Exploring the dark launch pattern

The dark launch pattern is another practice related to blue-green deployment that consists of deploying new features in hidden or disabled mode (so that they're inaccessible) into the production environment. Then, when we want to have access to these features in the deployed application, we can activate them as we go along without having to redeploy the application.

Unlike the canary release pattern, the dark launch pattern is not a blue-green deployment that depends on the infrastructure but is implemented in the application code. To set up the dark launch pattern, it is necessary to encapsulate the code of each feature of the application in elements called **feature flags** (or **feature toggles**), which will be used to enable or disable these features remotely.

We will look at the implementation and use of feature flags with an open source framework and a cloud platform in the last few sections of this chapter.

In this section, we have presented the practice of blue-green deployment, along with its concepts and patterns, such as the canary release and dark launch patterns. We have discussed that this practice requires changes to be made in the production infrastructure since it's composed of two instances of the infrastructure—one blue and one green—as well as a router that redirects users' requests.

Now that we've talked about blue-green deployment patterns, we will look at how to implement one in practice in an Azure cloud infrastructure.

Applying blue-green deployments on Azure

Now that we've looked at blue-green deployment, we'll look at how to apply it to an Azure infrastructure using two types of components—App Service slots and Azure Traffic Manager.

Let's start by looking at the most basic component—App Service slots.

Using App Service with slots

If we have an Azure subscription and want to use blue-green deployment without investing a lot of effort, we can use App Service slots (Azure Web Apps or Azure Functions).

In Azure App Services such as a Web App, we can create a second instance of our Web App by creating a slot for it (up to 20 slots, depending on the App Service plan). This slot is a secondary web app but is attached to our main web app.

In other words, the main web app represents the blue environment, and the slot represents the green environment.

To use this web app and its slot as a blue-green architecture, we will perform the following configuration steps:

1. Once the web app slot has been created, the new version of the application will be deployed in this slot and we can assign a percentage of traffic, as shown in the following screenshot:

Figure 15.5 – Azure deployment slots

Here, we've assigned 10% of traffic to the web app slot, which includes changes to the new version of the application.

2. As soon as the new version of the application has been tested on the slot, we can swap the slot to the main web app (the blue environment), as shown in the following screenshot:

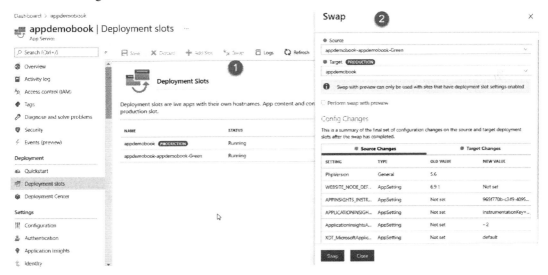

Figure 15.6 – Azure swap slots

With this swap, the web app takes the content of its slot, and vice versa.

The web app now contains the new version (*N+1*) of the application, and the slot contains the older version (*N*). In case there is an urgent problem, we can recover the previous version of the application by redoing a swap.

> **Note**
>
> To learn more about configuring and using Web App slots, you can read the following documentation: `https://docs.microsoft.com/en-us/ azure/app-service/deploy-staging-slots`.

This is exactly what we saw in the canary release pattern, which allows us to distribute production traffic for a group of users as well as route the application to the environment that has the *N+1* version of the application.

Now that we've discussed the use of slots, we'll take a look at the Azure Traffic Manager component, which also allows us to implement blue-green deployment.

Using Azure Traffic Manager

In Azure, there is a component called **Azure Traffic Manager** that allows us to manage traffic between several resource endpoints, such as two web apps.

To do this, we need to have two web apps: one for the blue environment and another for the green environment.

Then, in our Azure subscription, we have to create a Azure Traffic Manager that we'll configure with the following steps:

1. In the Traffic Manager, we will first configure a profile that determines the traffic routing method. In our case, we will configure a **Weighted** profile—that is, configure it according to a weight that we will assign in our web app. The following screenshot shows the configuration of the profile by weight:

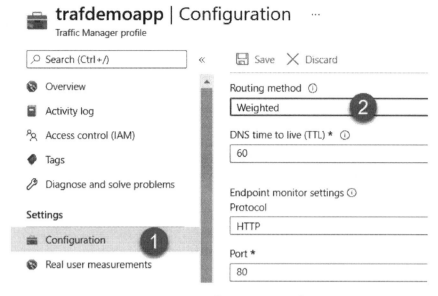

Figure 15.7 – Azure Traffic Manager configuration

> **Note**
>
> To find out about the other profile configuration options and how they
> work, you can read the following documentation: `https://docs.`
> `microsoft.com/en-us/azure/traffic-manager/traffic-`
> `manager-routing-methods`.

2. Then, we will record the endpoints that make up our two web apps. For each of
    them, we'll configure a preponderance weight, as shown in the following screenshot:

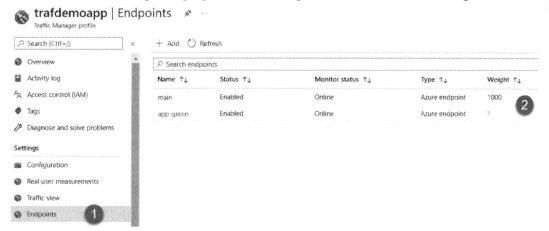

Figure 15.8 – Azure Traffic Manager endpoints

Thus, the main endpoint (that is, the blue environment) has the maximum weight, which is equivalent to 100% traffic.

> **Note**
>
> If you would like to know more about configuring Traffic Manager, you can follow this tutorial: https://docs.microsoft.com/en-us/ azure/traffic-manager/tutorial-traffic-manager- weighted-endpoint-routing.

As for the App Service slots, with Traffic Manager, we can adjust this weight according to the traffic we want on each endpoint and then apply blue-green deployment.

We have just discussed the implementation of blue-green deployment and, more specifically, with the canary release pattern in an Azure infrastructure using a couple of solutions, as summarized here:

- For the first solution, we used a slot that was under a web app and we configured their user-traffic percentage.
- For the second solution, we used and configured an Azure Traffic Manager resource that acts as a router between two web apps.

Now, let's look at the dark launch pattern in detail, starting with an introduction to feature flags and their implementation.

Introducing feature flags

Feature flags (also called feature toggles) allow us to dynamically enable or disable a feature of an application without having to redeploy it.

Unlike blue-green deployment with the canary release pattern, which is an architectural concept, feature flags are implemented in the application's code. Their implementation is done with a simple encapsulation using conditional if rules, as shown in the following code example:

```
if(activateFeature("addTaxToOrder")==True) {
    ordervalue = ordervalue + tax
}else{
    ordervalue = ordervalue
}
```

In this example code, the `activateFeature` function allows us to find out whether the application should add the tax to order according to the `addTaxToOrder` parameter, which is specified outside the application (such as in a database or configuration file).

Features encapsulated in feature flags may be necessary either for the running of the application or for an internal purpose such as log activation or monitoring.

The activation and deactivation of features can be controlled either by an administrator or directly by users via a graphical interface.

The lifetime of a feature flag can be either of the following:

- **Temporary**: To test a feature. Once validated by users, the feature flag will be deleted.
- **Definitive**: To leave a feature flagged for a long time.

Thus, using feature flags, a new version of an application can be deployed to the production stage faster. This is done by disabling the new features of the release. Then, we will reactivate these new features for a specific group of users such as testers, who will test these features directly in production.

Moreover, if we notice that one of the application's functionalities is not working properly, it is possible for the feature flags to disable it very quickly, without us having to redeploy the rest of the application.

Feature flags also allow A/B testing—that is, testing the behavior of new features by certain users and collecting their feedback.

There are several technical solutions when it comes to implementing feature flags in an application, as outlined here:

- You develop and maintain your custom feature flags system, which has been adapted to your business needs. This solution will be suitable for your needs but requires a lot of development time, as well as the necessary considerations of architecture specifications such as the use of a database, data security, and data caching.

- You use an open source tool that you must install in your project. This solution allows us to save on development time but requires a choice of tools, especially in the case of open source tools. Moreover, among these tools, few offer portal or dashboard administration that allows for the management of feature flags remotely. There is a multitude of open source frameworks and tools for feature flags. Please go to `http://featureflags.io/resources/` to find them. Please refer to the following as well:

  - RimDev.FeatureFlags (`https://github.com/ritterim/RimDev.FeatureFlags`)

  - Flagr (`https://github.com/checkr/flagr`)

  - Unleash (`https://github.com/Unleash/unleash`)

  - Togglz (`https://github.com/togglz/togglz`)

  - Flip (`https://github.com/pda/flip`).

- You can use a cloud solution (a **platform as a service**, or **PaaS**) that requires no installation and has a back office for managing feature flags, but most of them require a financial investment for large-scale use in an enterprise. Among these solutions, we can mention the following:

  - LaunchDarkly (`https://launchdarkly.com/`)

  - Rollout (`https://app.rollout.io/signup`)

  - Featureflag.tech (`https://featureflag.tech/`)

  - Featureflow (`https://www.featureflow.io/`).

In this section, we have talked about how the use of feature flags is a development practice that allows you to test an application directly in the production stage.

We also mentioned the different feature flag usage solutions and illustrated their implementation. Let's discuss one of its implementations with an open source tool known as `RimDev.FeatureFlags`.

Using an open source framework for feature flags

As we've seen, there are a large number of open source tools or frameworks that allow us to use feature flags in our applications.

In this section, we will look at an example of implementing feature flags within a .NET (Core) application using a simple framework called `RimDev.FeatureFlags`.

`RimDev.FeatureFlags` is a framework written in .NET that's free and open source (`https://github.com/ritterim/RimDev.FeatureFlags`) and is packaged and distributed via a NuGet package. It can be found here: `https://www.nuget.org/packages/RimDev.AspNetCore.FeatureFlags`.

To store the feature flag data, `RimDev.FeatureFlags` uses a database that must be created beforehand. The advantage of `RimDev.FeatureFlags` is that once implemented in our application, it provides a web **user interface** (**UI**) that allows us to enable or disable feature flags.

As a prerequisite for this example, we need to have an ASP.NET Core MVC application already initialized. We will use a SQL Server database that has been created to store feature flag data.

To initialize `RimDev.FeatureFlags` in this application, we will perform the following steps:

1. The first step consists of referencing the NuGet `RimDev.FeatureFlags` package in our application and modifying (with any text editor) the `.csproj` file of the application, which is located at the root of the application's files and contains some application parameters, by adding a `PackageReference` element, as follows:

    ```
    <ItemGroup>
        ...
        <PackageReference Include="RimDev.AspNetCore.
    FeatureFlags" Version="2.1.3" />
    </ItemGroup>
    ```

    Alternatively, we can execute the following command in a terminal command line to reference a NuGet package in the existing project:

    ```
    dotnet add package RimDev.AspNetCore.FeatureFlags
    ```

2. Then, we'll go to the `appsettings.json` configuration file to configure the connection string to the database we created beforehand with the following code:

    ```
    "connectionStrings": {
    "localDb": "Data Source=<your database
    server>;Database=FeatureFlags.AspNetCore;User ID=<your
    user>;Password=<password data>
    }
    ```

3. In the `startup.cs` file, which is located at the root of the application's files, we'll add the configuration to `RimDev.FeatureFlags` with this block of code:

```
private readonly FeatureFlagOptions options;
public Startup(IConfiguration configuration)
{
    Configuration = configuration;
    options = new FeatureFlagOptions()
.UseCachedSqlFeatureProvider(Configuration.
GetConnectionString("localDb"));
}
```

In the preceding code snippet, we initialized the options of `RimDev.FeatureFlags` by using the database connection. We can configure service loading with the following code:

```
public void ConfigureServices(IServiceCollection
services)
{
    ...
    services.AddFeatureFlags(options);
}
public void Configure(IApplicationBuilder app,
IHostingEnvironment env)
{
    ...
    app.UseFeatureFlags(options);
    app.UseFeatureFlagsUI(options);
}
```

As soon as the application starts, `RimDev` will load the feature flag data into the application context. With this, we've configured `RimDev.FeatureFlags` in our project.

Now, we will create feature flags and use them in the application. For this example, we will create a feature flag called ShowBoxHome that may or may not display the image in the middle of our application's home page. Let's look at how to create and manipulate these feature flags in our project, as follows:

1. First, we will create feature flags by creating a new class that contains the following code:

```
using RimDev.AspNetCore.FeatureFlags;
    namespace appFeatureFlags.Models{
        public class ShowBoxHome : Feature {
            public override string Description { get;
} = "Show the home center box.";
        }
    }
```

This class contains the ShowBowHome feature flag. An override description is given to this feature flag.

2. Then, in our controller, we call the ShowBoxHome class with the following code:

```
public class HomeController : Controller {
        private readonly ShowBoxHome showboxHome;
        public HomeController (ShowBoxHome showboxHome){
            this.showboxHome = showboxHome;
        }
        public IActionResult Index() {
            return View(new HomeModel{ShowboxHome = this.
showboxHome.Value});
        }
        ...
}
```

The controller receives the values of the feature flags stored in the database, which were loaded when the application was started.

3. We'll also create a `HomeModel` class that will list all the feature flags needed for the home page, as follows:

```
public class HomeModel
{
    public bool ShowBoxHome { get; set; }
}
```

4. Finally, in `Views/Home/index.chtml`, we'll use this model to display the image in the center of the home page, depending on the value of the feature flag, with the following code:

```
@if(Model.ShowBoxHome){
    <div><img src="img/test.png"></div>
}
```

Once the development process has come to an end, deploy and run our application. By default, there is no image in the middle of the home page, as shown in the following screenshot:

Figure 15.9 – Feature flag demonstration home application

To display the image, we need to activate the feature dynamically, like so:

1. Go to the back office at `http://<yoursite>/_features`. We'll see a switch called `ShowHomeBow`.

2. We activate the flags by switching on the toggle, as shown in the following screenshot:

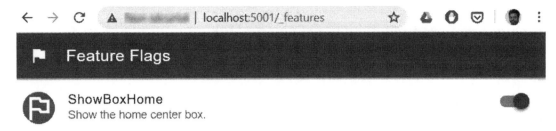

Figure 15.10 – Feature flag demonstration feature toggle

Reload the home page of our application. Here, we can see that the image is displayed in the center of the page:

Figure 15.11 – Feature flag demonstration application

By using the `RimDev.FeatureFlags` framework and feature flags, we were able to enable or disable a feature of our application without having to redeploy it.

> **Note**
> The complete source code for this application can be found at `https://github.com/PacktPublishing/Learning-DevOps-Second-Edition/tree/main/CHAP15/appFF`.

We have just seen how to use an open source tool to implement basic feature flags in a .NET Core application. We noticed that, with the use of an open source tool, we can create a database in our infrastructure. This use of feature flags is quite basic, and moreover, access to the UI for managing feature flags is not secure.

Finally, as with any open source tool, it is important to check whether it is maintained and updated regularly by its editor or community. However, the use of open source tools for feature flags remains appealing and inexpensive for small business projects.

Now, let's look at another tool solution for feature flags, which is to use a PaaS solution in the cloud. One example of such a solution is LaunchDarkly.

Using the LaunchDarkly solution

In the previous section, we discussed using open source tools for feature flags, which can be a good solution but requires some infrastructure components and is dependent on a development language (in our example, it was .NET Core).

For better use and management of feature flags, we can use a cloud solution that does not require the implementation of an architecture and provides a lot of features around feature flags.

Among these cloud solutions (**software as a service**, or **SaaS**), there is **LaunchDarkly** (`https://launchdarkly.com/`), which is a SaaS platform that is composed of a feature flag management back office and SDKs that allow us to manipulate the feature flags in our applications.

The LaunchDarkly SDKs are available for many development languages, such as .NET, JavaScript, Go, and Java. A complete list of SDKs is available here: `https://docs.launchdarkly.com/sdk`.

In addition to the classic version of feature flag management with `RimDev.FeatureFlags`, LaunchDarkly allows feature flags to be managed by a user and also provides A/B testing features that are linked to feature flags. A/B testing can measure the use of the application's features through feature flags.

However, LaunchDarkly is a paid solution (`https://launchdarkly.com/pricing/`). Fortunately, it provides a 30-day trial so that we can test it out. Please take a look at how to use LaunchDarkly so that you can implement feature flags in a .NET application.

For that, we will start by creating some feature flags, as follows:

1. First, log in to your LaunchDarkly account by clicking on the **Sign In** button that is located in the top menu of the LaunchDarkly site. Alternatively, you can go to `https://app.launchdarkly.com/`.

2. Once we're connected to our account, in the **Account settings** section, we can create a new project called `DemoBook`, as illustrated in the following screenshot:

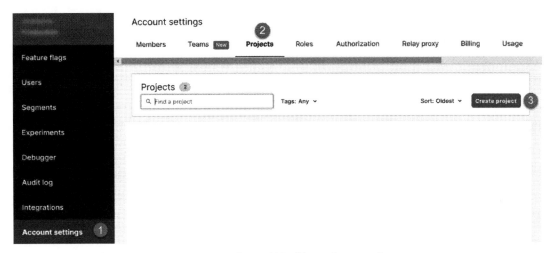

Figure 15.12 – LaunchDarkly project creation

By default, two environments are created in the project. We'll be able to create our own environments and then test the feature flags in different environments. In addition, each of these environments has a unique SDK key that will serve as authentication for the SD3.

1. Then, in the environment called **Test**, we'll navigate to the **Feature flags** menu and click on the **Create flag** button, then we'll create a feature flag called ShowBoxHome, as shown in the following screenshot:

Figure 15.13 – LaunchDarkly feature flag creation

Once created, we can activate it by clicking on the **On/Off** toggle switch.

Now that we have configured and created a feature flag in the LaunchDarkly portal, we will see how we can use the SDK in the application code.

> **Note**
>
> In LaunchDarkly, the variations that are made to feature flags are done by users connected to the application. This means that the application must provide an authentication system.

To use the SDK and launch the application, follow these steps:

1. The first step is to choose an SDK that corresponds to the application development language. We can do this by going to `https://docs.launchdarkly.com/docs/getting-started-with-launchdarkly-sdks#section-supported-sdks`. In our case, we have a .NET application, so we will follow this procedure: `https://docs.launchdarkly.com/docs/dotnet-sdk-reference`.

2. Now, let's integrate the reference to the NuGet `LaunchDarkly.ServerSdk` package (`https://www.nuget.org/packages/LaunchDarkly.ServerSdk/`) in the `.csproj` file of our application by adding it to the reference packages, like so:

```
<ItemGroup>
  <PackageReference Include="LaunchDarkly.ServerSdk"
  Version="6.3.1" />
  . . .
</ItemGroup>
```

3. In the .NET code, we do this in the controller. To do this, we need to import the SDK with the `using` command, as follows:

```
using LaunchDarkly.Client;
```

4. Still in the controller code, we add the connection to LaunchDarkly, as invoked by `FeatureFlag`. The code is illustrated in the following snippet:

```
public IActionResult Index() {
  LdClient ldClient = new LdClient("sdk-eb0443dc-xxxx-xxx-xx-xxx");
  User user = LaunchDarkly.Client.User.WithKey(User.Identity.Name);
  bool showBoxHome = ldClient.BoolVariation("show-box-home", user, false);
  return View(new HomeModel{ShowBoxHome = showBoxHome});
}
```

For the connection to LaunchDarkly, we need to use the SDK key that was provided when the project was created. Then, in the preceding code, we connect the user who is connected to the application to the feature flag that we created previously in the portal.

5. Finally, in the Home/Index.chtml view, we add the following code to add a condition that will display the image, depending on the value of the feature flag:

```
<div class="text-center">
    @if(Model.ShowBoxHome){
        <div><img src="img/test.png"></div>
    }
<div>
```

6. Finally, we deploy and execute the application. As illustrated in the following screenshot, the home page shows the central image because the feature flags are set to true by default:

appdemoLD   Home   Privacy   Hello mikael@test.fr!   Logout

Welcome

Learn about building Web apps with ASP.NET Core.

Figure 15.14 – LaunchDarkly feature flag demonstration application

7.   Then, we go to the LaunchDarkly portal and modify the configuration of this feature flag for the current user with a `false` value. On the **Users** management page, we select the user, as illustrated in the following screenshot:

Figure 15.15 – LaunchDarkly user

Then, we update the value of the feature flag to `false`, as illustrated in the following screenshot:

Figure 15.16 – LaunchDarkly feature flag user settings

8.   By reloading the page, we can see that the central image is no longer displayed, as illustrated here:

appdemoLD   Home   Privacy   Hello mikael@test.fr!   Logout

Welcome

Learn about building Web apps with ASP.NET Core.

Figure 15.17 – Feature flag demo application with LaunchDarkly

This is an example of how to use LaunchDarkly, which has many other interesting features, such as a user management system, feature usage with A/B testing, integration with CI/CD platforms, and reporting.

> **Note**
>
> The complete code source for this application can be found at `https://github.com/PacktPublishing/Learning-DevOps-Second-Edition/tree/main/CHAP15/appdemoLD`.

What we have discussed in this section is an overview of LaunchDarkly, which is a feature flag cloud platform. We studied its implementation in a web application with the creation of feature flags in the LaunchDarkly portal.

Then, we manipulated this feature flag in the application code via the SDK provided by LaunchDarkly. Finally, in the LaunchDarkly portal, we enabled/disabled a feature for a user who wants to test a new feature of the application without having to redeploy it.

Summary

In this chapter, we focused on improving production deployments. We started by using Terraform to reduce downtime during provisioning and resource destruction.

Then, we focused on the practice of blue-green deployment and its patterns, such as canary release and dark launch. We looked at the implementation of a blue-green deployment architecture in Azure using App Service and the Azure Traffic Manager component.

Finally, we detailed the implementation of feature flags in a .NET application using two types of tools—`RimDev.FeatureFlags`, which is an open source tool that offers a basic feature flag system, and LaunchDarkly, which is a cloud-based solution. It's not free of charge but provides complete and advanced feature flag management.

The next chapter is dedicated to GitHub. Here, we will look at the best practices for contributing to open source projects.

Questions

1. In Terraform, which option can we use to reduce downtime?

2. What is a blue-green deployment infrastructure composed of?

3. What are the two blue-green deployment patterns that we looked at in this chapter?

4. In Azure, what are the components that allow us to apply a blue-green deployment practice?

5. What is the role of feature flags?

6. What is the `RimDev.FeatureFlags` tool?

7. Which feature flag tool discussed in this chapter is a SaaS solution?

Further reading

If you want to find out more about zero-downtime and blue-green deployment practices, take a look at the following resources:

- *Zero Downtime Updates with HashiCorp Terraform*: `https://www.hashicorp.com/blog/zero-downtime-updates-with-terraform`

- *BlueGreenDeployment* by *Martin Fowler*: `https://martinfowler.com/bliki/BlueGreenDeployment.html`

- *Feature Toggles (aka Feature Flags)* by *Martin Fowler*: `https://martinfowler.com/articles/feature-toggles.html`

- *Blue-Green Deployment on Azure with Zero Downtime* (article): `http://work.haufegroup.io/Blue-Green-Deployment-on-Azure/`

- Feature flag guide: `http://featureflags.io/`

- LaunchDarkly feature flag use cases: `https://launchdarkly.com/use-cases/`

16
DevOps for Open Source Projects

Until a few years ago, the open source practice, which consists of delivering the source code of a product to the public, was essentially only used by the Linux community. Since then, many changes have taken place regarding open source with the arrival of GitHub. Microsoft has since made a lot of its products open source and is also one of the largest contributors to GitHub.

Today, open source is a must in the development and enterprise world, regardless of whether we wish to use a project or even contribute to it.

However, open source applications are not always free. There are sometimes licensing fees for plugins, support, or enterprise features. Also, in terms of support, using open source software can sometimes present difficulties and pitfalls when it comes to product support.

Throughout this book, we have seen many instances where open source tools such as Terraform, Ansible, Packer, Vagrant, Jenkins, and SonarQube have been used. However, one of the great advantages of open source is not only the use of products but also the fact that we can contribute to them.

To contribute to an open source project, we need to participate in its evolution by discussing issues with its use or by making suggestions regarding improving it. In addition, if you are a developer, you can also modify its source code to make it evolve.

Finally, as a developer or a member of an operational team, we can share our project in open source and make it available to the community.

In this chapter, we'll discuss open source contributions and why it's important to apply DevOps practices to all open source projects.

All of these practices, such as the use of Git, a CI/CD pipeline, and security analysis, have already been discussed throughout this book. However, in this chapter, we'll focus more on how to apply them in the context of our open source project.

We will start by learning how to share the code of a project in GitHub and how to initialize a contribution to another project. We will also discuss how to manage pull requests, which is one of the most important features of the contribution. In addition, we will look at how to indicate version changes using release notes, and the topic of binary sharing in GitHub Releases. We'll explain GitHub Actions, which allows us to created CI/CD pipelines on open source projects that are hosted on GitHub. Finally, we will look at the source code analysis of open source projects. We'll do this using SonarCloud, which is used for static code analysis, and WhiteSource Bolt, which is used for analyzing package security vulnerabilities that are contained in an open source project.

In this chapter, we will cover the following topics:

- Storing source code in GitHub
- Contributing to open source projects using pull requests
- Managing the changelog file and release notes
- Sharing binaries in GitHub releases
- Getting started with GitHub Actions
- Analyzing code with SonarCloud
- Detecting security vulnerabilities with WhiteSource Bolt

Technical requirements

In this chapter, we will use GitHub as a Git repository platform to store our open source project. Therefore, you will need a GitHub account, which you can create for free at `https://github.com/`. To fully understand the DevOps practices that will be used in this chapter, you should be well-versed with the following chapters of this book:

- *Chapter 6, Managing Your Source Code with Git*
- *Chapter 7, Continuous Integration and Continuous Delivery*
- *Chapter 12, Static Code Analysis with SonarQube*

The complete code for this chapter can be found at `https://github.com/ PacktPublishing/Learning-DevOps-Second-Edition/tree/main/ CHAP16/`.

Check out the following video to see the code in action:

`https://bit.ly/3JJCb9V`.

Storing source code in GitHub

If we want to share one of our projects in an open source fashion, we must version its code in a Git platform that allows the following elements:

- Public repositories; that is, we need to have access to the source code contained in this repository, but without necessarily being authenticated on this Git platform.

- Features and tools for code collaboration between the different members of this platform.

Two main platforms allow us to host open source tools: **GitLab**, which we looked at in the *Using GitLab CI* section of *Chapter 7, Continuous Integration and Continuous Delivery,* and **GitHub**, which is now the most used platform for open source projects.

Let's learn how to use GitHub so that we can host our project or contribute to another project.

Creating a new repository on GitHub

If we want to host our project on GitHub, we need to create a repository. Follow these steps to do so:

1. First, log in to your GitHub account or create a new one if you are a new user by going to `https://github.com/`.

2. Once connected, go to the **Repositories** tab inside your account. Click on the **New** button, as shown in the following screenshot:

Figure 16.1 – Adding a repository

3. Create a new repository form that can be filled in, as shown in the following screenshot:

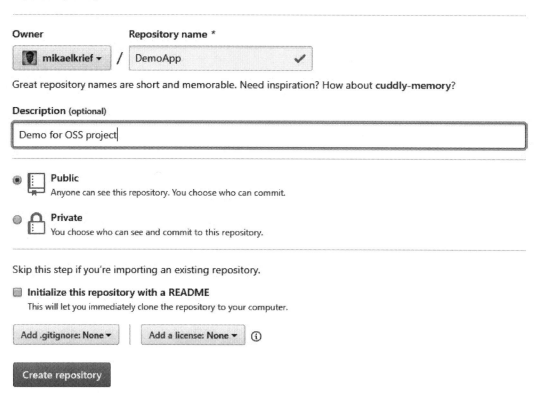

Figure 16.2 – GitHub repository details

The information that needs to be filled in to create a repository is as follows:

- The name of the repository.

- A description (which is optional).

- We need to specify whether the repository is **Public** (accessible by everyone, even if they're not authenticated) or **Private** (available only to the members we give it access to).

- We can also choose to initialize the repository with an empty README.md file, as well as a .gitignore file.

Then, validate the form by clicking on the **Create repository** button.

4. As soon as the repository is created, the home page will display the first Git instructions so that you can start archiving its code. The following screenshot shows part of the instruction page of a new GitHub repository:

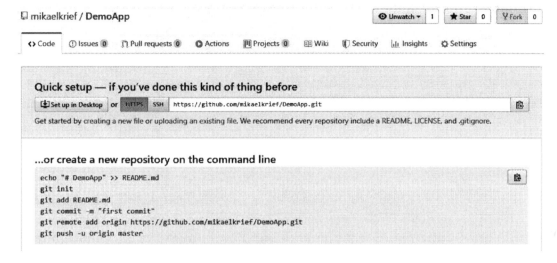

Figure 16.3 – GitHub repository – first Git instructions

Everything is ready for archiving the code in GitHub. Do this by using the workflow and Git commands we looked at in *Chapter 6, Managing Your Source Code with Git*.

This procedure is valid for creating a repository in GitHub. Now, let's learn how to contribute to GitHub by using a project from another repository.

Contributing to a GitHub project

We have just learned how to create a repository on GitHub. However, what we need to know is that, by default, only the owner of the repository is allowed to modify the code of this repository.

> **Note**
> We can add people as collaborators to this repository so that they can make changes to the code. For more information about this procedure, please go to https://help.github.com/en/articles/inviting-collaborators-to-a-personal-repository.

With the help of this principle, we don't have the right to modify the code of another repository.

To contribute to the code of another repository, we will need to create a **fork** of the initial repository that we want to contribute to. A fork is a duplication of the initial repository that is performed in our GitHub account, thus creating a new repository in our account.

Follow these steps to learn how to create a fork of a repository:

1. First, navigate to the initial repository that you want to contribute to. Then, click on the **Fork** button at the top of the page, as shown in the following screenshot:

Figure 16.4 – GitHub – forking a repository

2. After a few seconds, this repository will be forked and duplicated, along with all its content, in your account. By doing this, you get a new repository in your account that is linked to the initial repository, as shown in the following screenshot:

Figure 16.5 – GitHub fork link

3. Now, you have an exact copy of the repository that you want to contribute to in your GitHub account. You are free to modify the code and commit your changes, all of which will be archived in your repository.

However, even if there is a link between the initial repository and the fork, the code for each repository is completely uncorrelated and the code isn't synchronized automatically.

In this section, we learned how to create a GitHub repository or to make a fork of another repository so that we can contribute to it. Now, let's learn how to propose code changes and merge our code into another repository using a pull request.

Contributing to open source projects using pull requests

When we want to contribute to an open source project in GitHub, we need to make changes to the source code of the application that is in the repository of our GitHub account. To merge these code changes to the initial repository, we must perform a **merge** operation.

In GitHub, there is an element called a **pull request** that allows us to perform a merge operation between repositories. In addition to performing a simple and classic merge between code branches, a pull request also adds a whole new aspect of collaboration by providing features that allow different contributors to discuss code changes.

Let's learn how to carry out a pull request:

1. After making changes to the code source in the repository in your account, you must archive these changes by making a commit. The changes that have been made are now ready to be merged with the remote repository. To do this, go to your repository, go to the **Pull requests** tab, and click the **New pull request** button, as shown in the following screenshot:

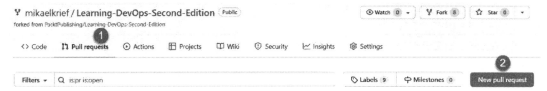

Figure 16.6 – GitHub – New pull request

2.   The page that appears specifies all of the information regarding the pull request that will be created, as shown in the following screenshot:

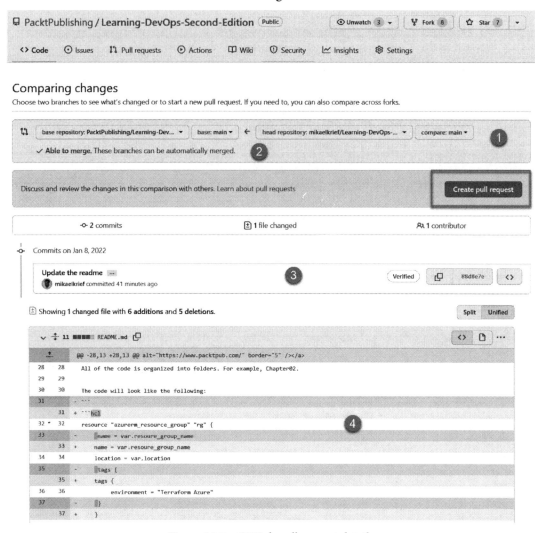

Figure 16.7 – GitHub pull request details

The following information is displayed on the screen:

- The source repository/branch and the target repository/branch

- An indicator that shows whether there are any code conflicts

- The list of commits that are included in this pull request

- The code differences of modified files

3. To validate the creation of the pull request, click on the **Create pull request** button.

4. Enter the name and description of the pull request in the form that appears, as shown in the following screenshot:

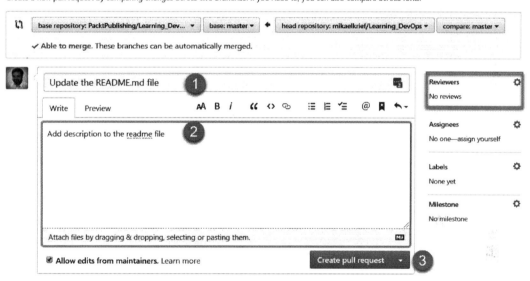

Figure 16.8 – GitHub pull request title and description

This information is important because it will help the repository's target owner quickly understand the objectives of the code changes included in this **pull request**. In addition, from the right-hand panel, it is possible to select reviewers who will be notified of the pull request by email. This will be done by the person who is in charge of reviewing the code changes and validating or rejecting them.

5. Finally, validate the creation of the pull request by clicking on the **Create pull request** button.

Once the pull request has been created, the owner of the original repository will see that a fresh pull request has been opened (with the title you provided) in the **Pull requests** tab of their repository. They can click on the **Pull requests** tab to access it and check all of its details.

Figure 16.9 – GitHub pull request list

In the following screenshot, we can see the different options that have been proposed for this pull request:

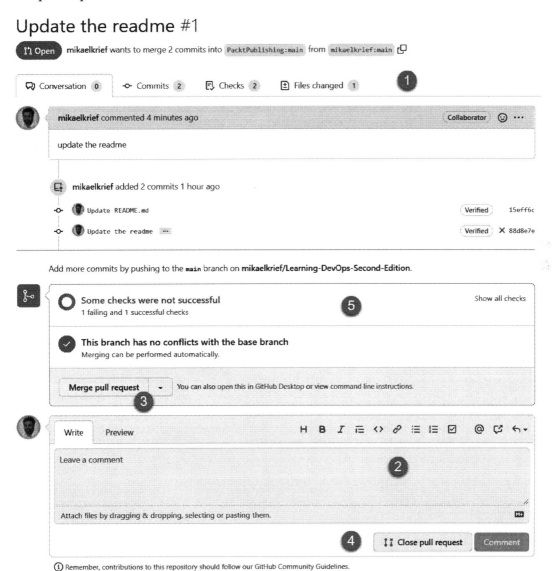

Figure 16.10 – GitHub pull request validation

The following are the different operations that the repository owner can perform on this pull request:

- By clicking on the **Files changed** tab, the reviewer can see the changes that have been made to the code and leave notes on each of the modified lines.

- The reviewer or repository owner can initiate a discussion on code changes and click on the **Comment** button to validate their comments.

- If the owner is satisfied with the code changes, they can click on the **Merge pull request** button to perform the merge.

- On the other hand, if the owner is not satisfied and refuses the pull request, they can click on the **Close pull request** button, where the request is then closed.

- We can also perform some automated checks.

Once merged, the pull request will have a **Merged** status and the code of the original repository will be updated with the code changes we have made.

In this section, we have seen that, with a pull request, we have a simple way of contributing to an open source project in GitHub by proposing code changes. Then, the project owner can either accept this pull request and merge the code or refuse the changes. In the next section, we will learn how to manage the changes that we've made to our project using the changelog file.

Managing the changelog file and release notes

When we host a project as open source, it is good practice to provide information to users about the changes that are being applied to it as they occur. This change logging system (also called **release notes**) is all the more important if, in addition to the source code, our repository also publicly provides a binary of the application since the use of this binary is dependent on its different versions and code changes.

Logically, we could find the history of code changes by navigating through the history of Git commits. However, this would be too tedious and time-consuming for Git novices. For these reasons, we will indicate the change in history with the code versions in a text file that can be read by everyone. This file has no fixed nomenclature or formalism, but for simplicity, we have decided to call it CHANGELOG.md.

So, this changelog file is a text file in markdown format, which is easy to edit with simple formatting and is placed at the root of the repository. In this file, the history of the changes is provided in a list and doesn't give away too many details about each change.

For better visibility, this history of the most recent changes will be ordered from newest to oldest so that we can quickly access the latest changes. To give you an idea of the shape of the changelog file, here is a screenshot that shows an extract from the changelog file of the Terraform provider for Azure:

1.30.1 (June 07, 2019)

BUG FIXES:

- Ensuring the authorization header is set for calls to the User Assigned Identity API's (#3613)

1.30.0 (June 07, 2019)

FEATURES:

- **New Data Source:** `azurerm_redis_cache` (#3481)
- **New Data Source:** `azurerm_sql_server` (#3513)
- **New Data Source:** `azurerm_virtual_network_gateway_connection` (#3571)

IMPROVEMENTS:

- dependencies: upgrading to Go 1.12 (#3525)
- dependencies: upgrading the `storage` SDK to `2019-04-01` (#3578)
- Data Source `azurerm_app_service` - support windows containers (#3566)
- Data Source `azurerm_app_service_plan` - support windows containers (#3566)
- `azurerm_api_management` - rename `disable_triple_des_chipers` to `disable_triple_des_ciphers` (#3539)
- `azurerm_application_gateway` - support for the value `General` in the `rule_group_name` field within the `disabled_rule_group` block (#3533)
- `azurerm_app_service` - support for windows containers (#3566)
- `azurerm_app_service_plan` - support for the `maximum_elastic_worker_count` property (#3547)
- `azurerm_managed_disk` - support for the `create_option` of `Restore` (#3598)
- `azurerm_app_service_plan` - support for windows containers (#3566)

Figure 16.11 – GitHub changelog sample

> **Note**
>
> The complete content of this file is available here: `https://github.com/terraform-providers/terraform-provider-azurerm/blob/master/CHANGELOG.md`.

The important information to mention in this file is the version history of the changes that have been delivered in this application. For each version, we write the list of new features, improvements, and bug fixes that were delivered.

For each change, there is a very short description, and the commit number is assigned as a link that allows us to view all the details of the changes by clicking on it.

> **Note**
>
> For full details on the format of the changelog file, take a look at the following documentation: `https://keepachangelog.com/en/1.1.0/`.

Finally, for integration into a DevOps process, it is also possible to automatically generate the changelog file using Git commits and tags.

Many scripts and tools allow this changelog to be generated, such as GitHub accounts (`https://github.com/conventional-changelog`). However, if you are unsure of whether you should write or generate this file, then here is a very interesting article explaining the pros and cons of these two methods: `https://depfu.com/blog/changelogs-to-write-or-to-generate`.

In this section, we learned how to inform users and contributors about the history of code changes that are made to open source projects using a changelog file. Then, we looked at the useful information we should mention in this changelog file so that users can find out exactly what changes the application is undergoing between each version.

In the next section, we will learn how to share binaries in an open source project in GitHub releases.

Sharing binaries in GitHub releases

The purpose of an open source project is not only to make the source code of a project visible, but also to share it with public users. For each new version of the project (called a **release**), this share contains a release note, as well as the binary resulting from the compilation of the project.

Thus, for a user who wishes to use this application, they don't need to retrieve the entire source code and compile it – they just have to retrieve the shared binary from the desired release and use it directly.

Note that a release is linked to a Git tag, which is used to position a label at a specific point in the source code's history. A tag is often used to provide a version number to the source code; for example, the tag could be v1.0.1.

> **Note**
>
> To learn more about tag handling in Git, read the following documentation: `https://git-scm.com/book/en/v2/Git-Basics-Tagging`.

In GitHub, in each repository, it is possible to publish releases from Git tags, which will have a version number (from the Git tag), a description specifying the list of changes, and the application binaries.

Following this introduction to releases in GitHub, let's learn how to create a release in GitHub using its web interface:

1. To create a GitHub release, go to the repository that contains the application code.

2. Click on the **Releases** link in the right panel, which can be found via the **Code** tab, as shown in the following screenshot:

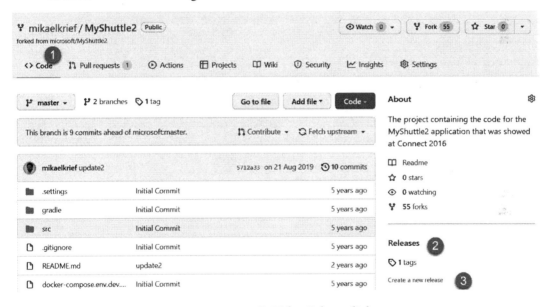

Figure 16.12 – GitHub – Releases link

3. On the next page that appears, click on the **Create a new release** button to create a new release. The release form is displayed and the release information is filled in, as shown in the following screenshot:

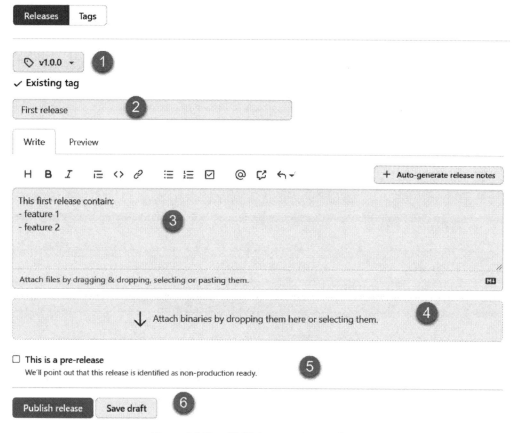

Figure 16.13 – GitHub – creating a release

In this form, we have entered the following information:

- The tag that's associated with the release.

- The title of the release.

- The description of the release, which may contain the list of changes (release notes).

- We upload the application binary in a ZIP file format that corresponds to this release.

- We also mark the checkbox regarding whether it's a pre-release.

Then, validate the new release by clicking on the **Publish release** button.

4. Finally, we are redirected to the list of releases for the project that we have just created, as shown in the following screenshot:

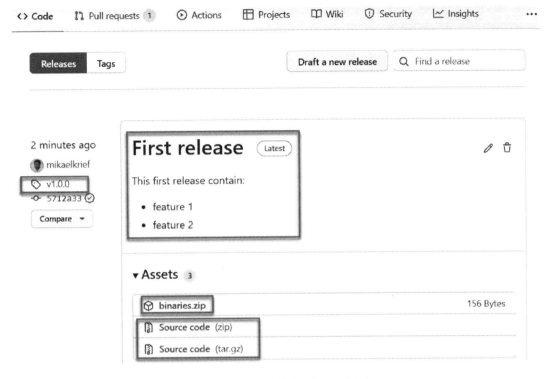

Figure 16.14 – GitHub release details

In the preceding screenshot, we can observe the tag (v1.0.0) that's associated with the release, the information we entered, and the `binaries.zip` file we uploaded. In addition, GitHub has been automatically added to the release of other assets; that is, the package (ZIP) that contains the source code of the application that's associated with this tag.

We have just seen that, via the GitHub web interface, we can create a GitHub release that allows us to share the release notes and binary files of a project with all users.

> **Note**
>
> It is also possible to integrate all of these steps into the CI/CD pipeline with an automatic script using various GitHub APIs. The documentation for this can be found at `https://developer.github.com/v3/repos/releases/`.

In the next section, we will create this same pipeline but in GitHub using GitHub Actions.

Getting started with GitHub Actions

GitHub has been integrating several other DevOps features into its repository source platform. This allows it to be fully integrated with the repository's code.

At the time of writing, these new features are as follows:

- A GitHub Package registry, a package manager whose presentation documentation can be found at `https://github.com/features/package-registry`

- GitHub Actions, a CI/CD pipeline manager whose presentation documentation can be found at `https://github.com/features/actions`

In this section, we will provide an overview of the use of GitHub Actions, which allows you to create CI/CD pipelines directly within GitHub. This will check and deploy the source code that is hosted in your GitHub repository.

For this demonstration, we will create a CI pipeline in GitHub that will compile and run the tests for our Node.js application. The resources for this can be found at `https://github.com/PacktPublishing/Learning-DevOps-Second-Edition/tree/main/CHAP16/appdemo`.

Follow these steps to create a CI pipeline with GitHub Actions:

1. Go to the repository that contains the source code to be deployed and click on the **Actions** tab, as shown in the following screenshot:

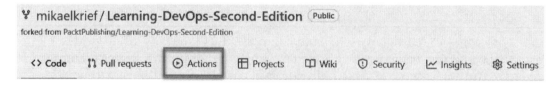

Figure 16.15 – GitHub – the Actions tab

2. At this point, the GitHub interface will propose pipeline templates, called **workflows**, according to the different development languages and target system, such as VM or Kubernetes. We can also create a custom workflow by starting with an empty template. The following screenshot shows the choices for creating a workflow:

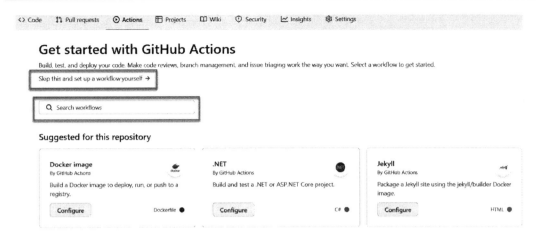

Figure 16.16 – GitHub Actions workflow templates

In the preceding screenshot, we can see the link called **set up a workflow yourself** for creating a custom workflow, as well as a textbox to search for workflow templates and suggested templates.

3. For this demonstration, let's create a workflow from the workflow template that's designed for Node.js applications by searching for node and clicking on **Configure** in the Node.js template box:

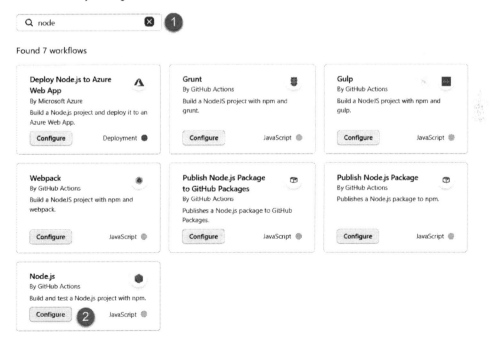

Figure 16.17 – GitHub Actions – selecting the Node.js template

4. GitHub will display the YAML code of the workflow that will be commuted in a node.js.yml file, which will be automatically created in the .github/ workflows folder tree. In this YAML code, which is also available at https:// github.com/PacktPublishing/Learning-DevOps-Second-Edition/ blob/main/.github/workflows/node.js.yml, we can see the following:

- The runs-on property, which specifies the Ubuntu agent of the pipeline that's provided by GitHub.

- A list of steps regarding the use of an action block (actions/checkout) so that we can retrieve the GitHub code, followed by a script block (npm) that will be executed on the Ubuntu agent.

Before archiving this file, add a small piece of code to it, indicating the execution path of the scripts, as shown in the following screenshot:

```
build:
  runs-on: ubuntu-latest
  strategy:
    matrix:
      node-version: [12.x, 14.x, 16.x]
      # See supported Node.js release schedule at https://nodejs.org/en/about/releases/
  steps:
  - uses: actions/checkout@v2
  - name: Use Node.js ${{ matrix.node-version }}
    uses: actions/setup-node@v2
    with:
      node-version: ${{ matrix.node-version }}
  - run: |
      cd CHAP16/appdemo
      npm ci
      npm run build --if-present
      npm test
```

Figure 16.18 – GitHub Actions workflow source code

The complete source code for this workflow is available at https://github. com/PacktPublishing/Learning-DevOps-Second-Edition/blob/ main/.github/workflows/node.js.yml.

5. Commit this file by clicking on the **Start commit** button at the top of the code editor. Once committed, the file will be present in the repository code and will trigger a new CI pipeline.

6. Finally, let's return to the **Actions** tab. We will see that a workflow has been triggered and completed:

Figure 16.19 – GitHub Actions workflow being run

Here, we can see the list of run executions for this workflow. By clicking on the run line, we can view the details of the execution. The following screenshot shows the details of the execution:

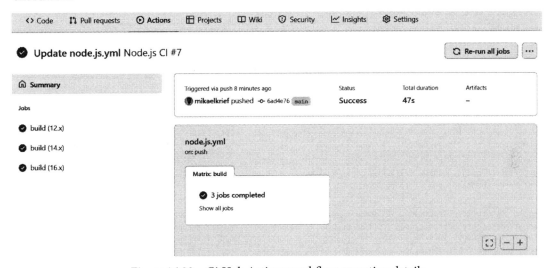

Figure 16.20 – GitHub Actions workflow execution details

The great advantage of GitHub Actions is that it natively provides a very extensive catalog of actions in its GitHub Marketplace (`https://github.com/marketplace?type=actions`) and that it can also develop and publish actions (`https://help.github.com/en/articles/development-tools-for-github-actions`).

In this section, we discussed implementing a CI pipeline in GitHub using the new GitHub Actions feature, which allows you to integrate DevOps for open source projects. So far in this chapter, we have focused on code management in GitHub and implementing CI/CD pipelines for open source projects using GitHub Actions.

In the upcoming sections, we will talk about open source code security. We will start by learning how to analyze code with SonarCloud.

Analyzing code with SonarCloud

In *Chapter 12, Static Code Analysis with SonarQube*, we explained the importance of implementing static code analysis practices. For open source projects, code analysis is more important because the source code and its binaries are published publicly.

One of the roles of open source is to provide code and components that can be used in enterprise applications, so this code must be written correctly and without any security issues.

Previously in this book, we have discussed the fact that SonarQube, with its installations and uses, is one of the major tools that allows code analysis to take place for enterprise applications. However, it requires an on-premises infrastructure to be installed, which is more expensive for a company.

For open source project code analysis, it is possible to use **SonarCloud** (`https://sonarcloud.io/`), which is the same product as SonarQube but comes in a cloud solution that requires no installation.

SonarCloud has a free plan that allows us to analyze the code of open source public repository projects from GitHub, BitBucket, or even Azure Repos. For more information on its price plans, go to `https://sonarcloud.io/pricing`.

Let's look at how quick it is to set up code analysis for an open source project that's hosted on GitHub. Before implementing the analysis itself, we will connect to our GitHub repository in SonarCloud. To do this, we need to access the `https://sonarcloud.io/` page by following these steps:

1. From the aforementioned home page, click on the **Log in** button:

Figure 16.21 – SonarCloud – Log in

2. Then, choose to log in with your GitHub account, as shown in the following screenshot:

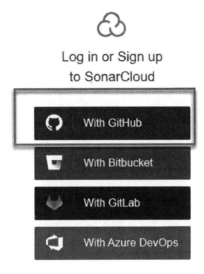

Figure 16.22 – SonarCloud – logging in with GitHub

Now, we must configure SonarCloud so that we can create a project that will contain the analysis of our GitHub project, which is available at `https://github.com/PacktPublishing/Learning-DevOps-Second-Edition/tree/main/CHAP16/appdemo`. To do this, follow these steps:

1. Once you've connected to SonarCloud with your GitHub account, click on the **Analyze new project** button on the home page:

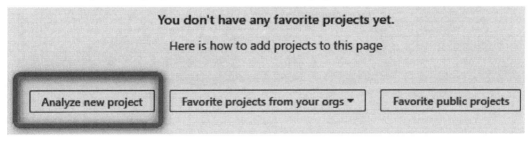

Figure 16.23 – SonarCloud – Analyze new project

2. SonarCloud proposes a few steps for selecting the target GitHub repository for analysis. First, choose to **Import an organization from GitHub**. Then, choose the **Only select repositories** option and select the target repository:

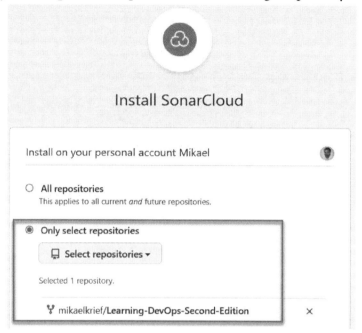

Figure 16.24 – SonarCloud – selecting a repository

3. Next, mark the checkbox of your repository and associate it with your organization by clicking on the **Set Up** button:

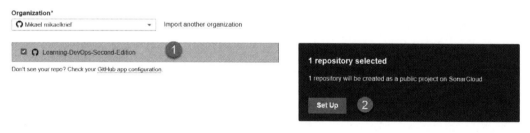

Figure 16.25 – SonarCloud – setting up a repository

4. The project analysis dashboard will be displayed and indicate that the code has not been analyzed yet.

With that, we have successfully configured the SonarCloud project. Now, let's analyze the project in the most basic way by following these steps:

1. In SonarCloud Project, under **Configure**, choose the recommended option, which is **With GitHub Actions** (as we learned in the previous section, *Getting started with GitHub Actions*):

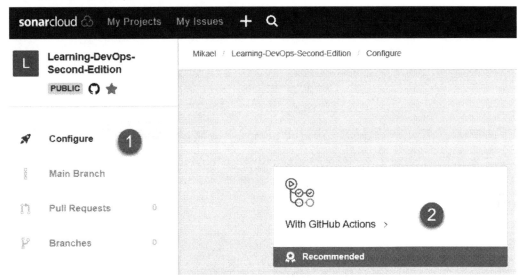

Figure 16.26 – SonarCloud – using a GitHub Actions template

2. Then, follow the indications provided by SonarCloud to create GitHub secrets (with the SONAR_TOKEN secret) inside the GitHub repository and add a new file with some Sonar configuration:

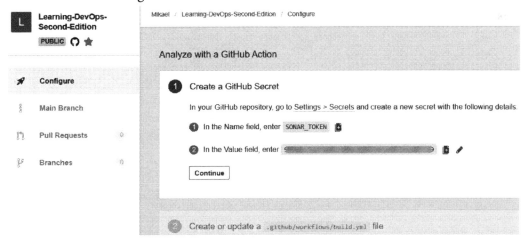

Figure 16.27 – SonarCloud GitHub Actions instructions

3. Then, commit this new GitHub Actions workflow file. This will automatically trigger the SonarCloud analysis of this project.

4. After a few minutes, you will see the result of two executions. First, you will see that the GitHub Actions workflow has succeeded:

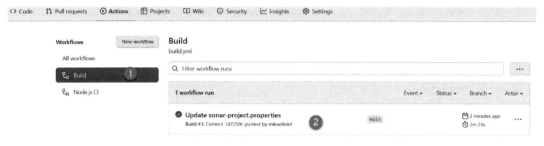

Figure 16.28 – GitHub Actions Sonar analyze

Then, you will see the analysis in the SonarCloud dashboard, as shown in the following screenshot:

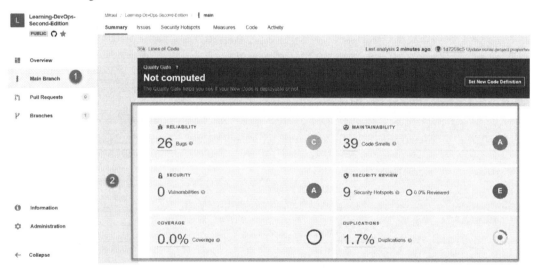

Figure 16.29 – SonarCloud analysis results

So, with each new code commit on this repository, either directly or via merging a pull request, code analysis will be triggered and the SonarCloud dashboard will be updated.

It is clear that our end goal is to integrate SonarCloud analysis into a CI/CD pipeline, so here are some resources to help us integrate it:

- If you're using Azure DevOps, here is a complete tutorial that will help you integrate SonarCloud into the pipeline: `https://docs.microsoft.com/en-us/labs/devops/sonarcloudlab/`.

- If you're using Travis CI, which we looked at in this chapter, take a look at the following documentation: `https://docs.travis-ci.com/user/sonarcloud/`.

In this section, we learned how to configure SonarCloud, a cloud platform that analyzes static code. We did this to analyze the source code of an open source project on GitHub via a continuous integration process. Then, we looked at the result of this analysis on the dashboard.

In the next section, we will look at another aspect of open source code security, which is analyzing code vulnerabilities using WhiteSource Bolt.

Detecting security vulnerabilities with WhiteSource Bolt

Due to their public visibility, open source projects or components are highly exposed to security vulnerabilities because it is easier to unintentionally inject a component (a package or one of its dependencies) containing a security vulnerability into them.

In addition to static source code analysis, it is also very important to continuously check the security of packages that are referenced or used in our open source projects.

Many tools are available that we can use to analyze the security of referenced packages in applications, such as SonaType AppScan (`https://www.sonatype.com/appscan`), Snyk (`https://snyk.io/`), and WhiteSource Bolt (`https://bolt.whitesourcesoftware.com/`).

> **Note**
>
> For more information on open source vulnerability scanning tools, take a look at the following article, which lists 13 tools that analyze the security of open source dependencies: `https://techbeacon.com/app-dev-testing/13-tools-checking-security-risk-open-source-dependencies`.

Among all these tools, we will look at **WhiteSource Bolt** (`https://bolt.whitesourcesoftware.com/`), which is available as a free plan, can analyze the package code of many development languages, and allows you to directly integrate with GitHub and Azure DevOps.

> **Note**
> The complete documentation on integrating White Source
> Bolt in GitHub is available at `https://whitesource.`
> `atlassian.net/wiki/spaces/WD/pages/556007950/`
> `WhiteSource+Bolt+for+GitHub`.

In our case, we will use it directly in GitHub to analyze the security of an application whose sources are available here: `https://github.com/PacktPublishing/` `Learning-DevOps-Second-Edition/tree/main/CHAP16/appdemo`.

To do this security analysis, we must install and configure WhiteSource Bolt on our GitHub account and trigger a code analysis. Follow these steps to learn how to do this:

1. In a web browser, go to `https://bolt.whitesourcesoftware.com/` `github/` and click on the **GitHub APP** button to install WhiteSource Bolt on your GitHub account.

2. You will be redirected to the WhiteSource Bolt application, which can be found on the GitHub Marketplace (`https://github.com/marketplace/` `whitesource-bolt`). To install it using the free plan, click on the **Install it for free** button at the very bottom of the page, as shown in the following screenshot:

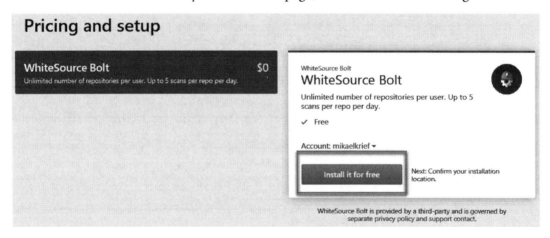

Figure 16.30 – Installing WhiteSource Bolt

3. Confirm that you're purchasing the application for $0 by clicking on the **Complete order and begin installation** button. Then, on the next page, confirm that WhiteSource Bolt has been installed on your GitHub account.

Once the installation has finished, you'll be redirected to the WhiteSource Bolt account creation page, where you must fill in your full name and country and then validate the form.

4. Now, activate the **Issues** features in GitHub by going to the **Settings** tab of the repository, which contains the code to scan, and checking the **Issues** checkbox, as shown in the following screenshot:

Features

Figure 16.31 – GitHub – activating issues

5. To configure the WhiteSource analysis on this repository, you must validate and merge the new pull request that was automatically created when you installed WhiteSource Bolt.

Figure 16.32 – WhiteSource Bolt issue configuration

This pull request adds a `.whitesource` file that is used for configuration at the root of the repository.

6. Finally, perform code analysis by committing the code of this application in the GitHub repository.

7. After a few minutes, you will see a list of security issues in the **Issues** tab of the repository.

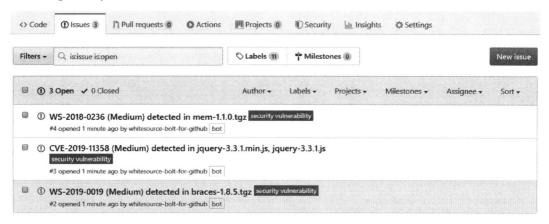

Figure 16.33 – WhiteSource analysis issues on GitHub

8. To uncover the full details of a security issue, simply click on the desired issue, read it, and take the information that's provided in the description of the issue into consideration.

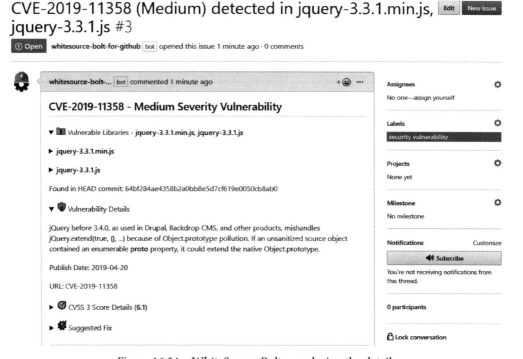

Figure 16.34 – WhiteSource Bolt – analyzing the details

We will have to fix all of these problems and redo code commits to trigger new WhiteSource Bolt scans and ensure that we have a secure application for those who will use it.

In this section, we learned how to analyze the code of open source projects using WhiteSource Bolt. We installed it and triggered a code analysis that revealed security issues in our demo application.

Summary

This chapter was dedicated to the DevOps best practices that can be applied to an open source project, especially on GitHub. In this chapter, we learned how to collaborate on open source code, starting with repository creation using GitHub and forks. Then, we learned how to use pull requests and how to share binaries in GitHub Releases.

After that, we implemented continuous integration processes with GitHub Actions, which is fully integrated with GitHub.

Finally, we learned how to analyze open source code for static code analysis with SonarCloud and security vulnerability analysis with WhiteSource Bolt.

In the next chapter, we will summarize every DevOps best practice we have talked about in this book.

Questions

1. In GitHub, can I modify the code of a repository of another user?
2. In GitHub, which element allows us to merge code changes between two repositories?
3. Which element allows us to simply display the history of code changes in an open source project?
4. In GitHub, which feature that was mentioned in this chapter allows us to share binaries?
5. What two tools that we have looked at in this chapter allow us to analyze the source code of an open source project?
6. In which GitHub tab are the security issues that have been detected by WhiteSource Bolt listed?

Further reading

If you want to learn more about using DevOps practices on open source projects, take a look at *GitHub Essentials,* by Achilleas Pipinellis, published by *Packt Publishing*: `https://www.packtpub.com/in/web-development/github-essentials-second-edition`.

17
DevOps Best Practices

We have reached the last chapter of this book and, finally, after reading everything, you are probably asking yourself: *What are the best practices to apply to effectively implement a development-operations (DevOps) culture?*

This chapter is a great overview of DevOps good practices that we have already seen and that will allow you to practice all the elements we have seen in this book.

We will discuss best practices in automation, tooling choice, **Infrastructure as Code (IaC)**, application architecture, and infrastructure design. We will also discuss good practices to be applied in project management to facilitate the implementation of a DevOps culture and practices. Then, we will review best practices for **continuous integration/continuous deployment (CI/CD)** pipelines, test automation, and the integration of security into your DevOps processes.

Finally, we will end this chapter with some best practices for monitoring in a DevOps culture.

This chapter covers the following topics:

- Automating everything
- Choosing the right tool
- Writing all your configuration in code
- Designing the system architecture
- Building a good CI/CD pipeline
- Integrating tests
- Shifting security left with **development-security-operations** (**DevSecOps**)
- Monitoring your system
- Evolving project management

Automating everything

When you want to implement DevOps practices within a company, it is important to remember the purpose of the DevOps culture: it delivers new releases of an application faster, in shorter cycles.

To do this, the first good practice to apply is to automate all tasks that deploy, test, and secure the application and its infrastructure. Indeed, when a task is done manually, there is a high risk of error in its execution. The fact that these tasks are performed manually increases the deployment cycles of applications.

In addition, once these tasks are automated in scripts, they can be easily integrated and executed in CI/CD pipelines. Another advantage of automation is that developers and the operational team can spend more time and focus their work on the functionality of their business.

It is also important to start the automation of the delivery process at the beginning of project development; this allows us to provide feedback faster and earlier.

Finally, automation makes it possible to improve the monitoring of deployments by putting traces on each action and allows you to make a backup and restore very quickly in case of a problem.

Automating deployments will, therefore, reduce deployment cycles, and teams can now afford to work in smaller iterations. Thus, the **time to market** (**TTM**) will be improved, with the added benefit of better-quality applications.

However, automation and orchestration require tools to be implemented, and the choice of these tools is an important element to consider in the implementation of a DevOps culture.

Choosing the right tool

One of the challenges a company faces when it wants to apply a DevOps culture is the choice of tools.

Indeed, many tools are either paid for or free and open source and allow you to version the source code of applications, process automation, implement CI/CD pipelines, and test and monitor applications.

Along with these tools, scripting languages are also added, such as PowerShell, Bash, and Python, which are also part of the DevOps suite of tools to integrate.

So, a question I'm often asked is: *How do I choose the right DevOps tools that are useful for my company and business?*

In fact, to answer this question, we must remember the definition of DevOps culture provided by Donovan Brown, which was mentioned in *Chapter 1, The DevOps Culture and Infrastructure as Code Practices*, and reproduced here:

> *"The DevOps culture is the union of people, processes, and products to enable continuous delivery of value to our end users."*

The important point of this definition is that a DevOps culture is the *union* of Dev, Ops, processes, and also *tools*. That is to say, the tools used must be shared and usable by both Dev and Ops and should be integrated into the same process. In other words, the choice of tools depends on the teams and the company model.

It is also necessary to take into account the financial system by choosing open source tools, which are often free of charge; it is easier to use them at the beginning of the DevOps transformation of the company. That is not the case with paid tools, which are certainly richer in features and support but require a significant investment.

Concerning scripting languages, I would say that the choice of language must be made according to the knowledge of the teams. For example, Ops teams that are more trained on Linux systems will be able to make automation scripts better with Bash than with PowerShell.

In this book, we have introduced you to several tools, some of which are open source and free—such as Terraform, Packer, Vault, and Ansible—and others that are paid for—such as Azure DevOps (for more than five users) or LaunchDarkly—and this is to help you choose the tools that best suit you.

After this reflection on the choice of tools in the implementation of a DevOps practice, we will look at another good practice, which is putting everything into code.

Writing all your configuration in code

We have seen throughout the book, especially with the first three chapters on IAC, that writing the desired infrastructure configuration in code offers many advantages for the productivity of both teams and the company.

It is, therefore, a very good practice to put everything related to infrastructure configuration in code. We have seen this in practice with Terraform, Ansible, and Packer, but many other tools exist that may be better suited to your needs and your organization. Among these tools, we are not only talking about the major editors, but also about the use of **JavaScript Object Notation** (**JSON**) files, Bash, PowerShell, and Python scripts that we'll apply to this configuration. The key is to have a description of your infrastructure in code that is easy for a human to read, and tools that are adapted to you, as discussed in the previous section.

Moreover, this practice continues to evolve in other fields, as we have seen in *Chapter 14*, *Security in the DevOps Process with DevSecOps*, with the use of InSpec, which allows us to describe the compliance rules of the infrastructure in code.

We have also seen this IaC practice in several chapters of this book with what is called **Pipeline as Code** (**PaC**), with GitLab CI, Travis CI, GitHub Actions, and also Azure Pipelines, which also allows a **YAML Ain't Markup Language** (**YAML**) pipeline mode (this mode has not been discussed in this book).

Putting any configuration into code is a key practice of the DevOps culture to take into account from the beginning of projects for both operational and development teams. For developers, there are also good practices for designing the application and infrastructure architecture, as we'll discuss in the next section.

Designing the system architecture

A few years ago, all services of the same application were *coded* in the same application block. This architecture design was legitimate since the application was managed in a waterfall model (`https://activecollab.com/blog/project-management/waterfall-project-management-methodology`), so new versions of the application were deployed in very long cycles. Since then, many changes have taken place in software engineering practices, starting with the adoption of the agile method and a DevOps culture, and then continuing with the arrival of the cloud.

This evolution has brought many improvements, not only in applications but also in their infrastructure.

However, in order to take advantage of an effective DevOps culture to deploy an application in the cloud, there are good practices to consider when designing software architecture and also when designing infrastructure.

First of all, cloud architects must work hand in hand with developers (or solution architects) to ensure that the application developed is in line with the different components of the architecture and that the architecture also takes into consideration the different constraints of the application.

In addition to this collaboration, security teams must also provide specifications that will be implemented by developers and cloud architects.

In order to be able to deploy a new version of the application more frequently without having to impact all of its features, it is a good practice to separate the different areas of the application into separate code at first, and then into different departments at a later stage. Thus, the separate code will be much more maintainable and scalable and can be deployed faster without having to redeploy everything.

> **Note**
> This method of separating code into several services is part of the architecture pattern called **microservices**; to learn more, read the following comprehensive article: `https://microservices.io/patterns/microservices.html`.

Once decoupled, however, there is still a need to control dependency in order to implement a CI/CD pipeline that takes into account all the dependencies of the application.

In *Chapter 15, Reducing Deployment Downtime*, we discussed another good practice that allows deployment in production more frequently, which consists of encapsulating the functionalities of the application in feature flags. These feature flags must also be taken into account when designing the application, as they allow the application to be deployed in the production stage, enabling/disabling its features dynamically without having to redeploy it.

Finally, the implementation of unit tests and the logging mechanism must be taken into account as soon as possible in the development of the application because these allow feedback on the state of the application to be shared very quickly in its deployment cycle.

A DevOps culture involves the implementation of CI/CD pipelines; as we have just seen, this requires changes in the design of applications, with the separation of functionalities to create less-monolithic applications, the implementation of tests, and the addition of a logging system.

After considering good practices for application design, we will explore some good practices for the implementation of CI/CD pipelines.

Building a good CI/CD pipeline

In this book, we have dedicated a complete chapter, *Chapter 7, Continuous Integration and Continuous Delivery*, to the creation of CI/CD pipelines using different tools such as GitLab CI, Jenkins, and Azure Pipelines, in which we have already mentioned the prerequisites for the implementation of CI/CD pipelines.

We also discussed the CI/CD process in *Chapter 16, DevOps for Open Source Projects*, with some examples of a CI pipeline for open source projects such as Travis CI and GitHub Actions.

Building a good CI/CD pipeline is indeed an essential practice in a DevOps culture and, together with the correct choice of tools, allows for faster deployment and better-quality applications.

One of the best practices for CI/CD pipelines is to set them up as early as the project launch stage. This is especially true for the CI pipeline, which will allow the code (at least the compilation step) to be verified when writing the first lines of code. Then, as soon as the first environment is provisioned, immediately create a deployment pipeline, which will allow the application to be deployed and tested in this environment. The rest of the CI/CD pipeline process's tasks, such as unit-test execution, can be performed as the project progresses.

In addition, it is also important to optimize the processes of the CI/CD pipeline by having pipelines that run quickly. These are used to provide quick feedback to team members (especially for CI) and also to avoid blocking the execution queue of other pipelines that may be in the queue.

Thus, if some pipelines take too long to run, such as integration tests (which can be long), it may be a good idea to schedule their execution for hours with less activity, such as at night.

Finally, it is also important to protect sensitive data embedded in CI/CD pipelines. So, if you use a configuration management tool in your pipelines, don't leave information such as passwords, connection strings, and tokens visible to all users.

To protect this data, use centralized secret management tools such as Vault, which we saw in *Chapter 14, Security in the DevOps Process with DevSecOps*, or use **Azure Key Vault (AKV)** if you have an Azure subscription.

These are some of the best practices for the implementation of CI/CD pipelines; we have mentioned other good practices for CI/CD pipelines that you can study in the different chapters of this book and in other books dedicated to DevOps cultures.

As a follow-up to the good practices for CI/CD pipelines, let's review good practices for the integration of tests into DevOps processes.

Integrating tests

Testing is, in today's world, a major part of the DevOps process, but also of development practices. Indeed, it is possible to have the best DevOps pipeline that automates all delivery phases, but without the integration of tests, it loses almost all its efficiency. For my part, I think that the minimum requirement for a DevOps process is to integrate at least the execution of unit tests of the application. In addition, these unit tests must be written from the first line of code of the application using testing practices such as **test-driven development (TDD)** (`https://hackernoon.com/introduction-to-test-driven-development-tdd-61a13bc92d92`) and **behavior-driven development (BDD)**, and in this way, the automatic execution of these tests can be integrated into the CI pipeline.

However, it is important to integrate other types of tests, such as functional tests or integration tests, that allow the application to be tested functionally from start to finish with the other components of its ecosystem.

It is certainly true that the execution of these tests can take time; in this case, it is possible to schedule their execution at night. But these integration tests are the ones that will guarantee the quality of the application's smooth operation during all stages of delivery, from deployment to production.

However, there is often a very bad practice of disabling the execution of tests in the CI pipeline in case their execution fails. This is often done to avoid the blocking of the complete CI process and thus deliver faster in production. But keep in mind that errors detected by the unit tests, including ones that would have been detected by tests that have been disabled, will be detected in the production stage at some point, and the correction of the failed code will cost more time than if the tests had been enabled during CI.

We have also learned about other types of tests in this book, such as code analysis tests or security tests, which are not to be ignored. The sooner they are integrated into CI/CD pipelines, the more value will be added for maintaining code and securing our application.

To summarize, you should not ignore the implementation of tests in your applications and their integration into CI/CD pipelines, as they guarantee the quality of your application.

After good practices for test integration, I suggest you see what good practices there are for the integration of security in your CI/CD processes.

Shifting security left with DevSecOps

As we discussed in *Chapter 14, Security in the DevOps Process with DevSecOps*, security and compliance analyses must be part of DevOps processes. However, in companies, there is often a lack of awareness among development teams about security rules, and this is why security is implemented too late in DevOps processes.

To integrate security into processes, it is, therefore, necessary to raise awareness among developers of aspects of application code security, but also of the protection of CI/CD pipeline configuration.

In addition, it is also necessary to eliminate the barrier between DevOps and security by integrating security teams more often into the various meetings that bring together Dev and Ops teams, thus ensuring better consistency between developers, operational teams, and also security. Regarding the choice of tools, don't use too many different tools, because the goal is for these tools to also be used by developers and be integrated into CI/CD pipelines. It is, therefore, necessary to select a few tools that are automated, do not require great knowledge of security, and provide reports for better analysis.

Finally, if you don't know where to start when it comes to analyzing the security of the application, work with simple security rules that are recognized by communities, such as the top 10 **Open Web Application Security Project (OWASP)** rules (`https://www.owasp.org/index.php/Category:OWASP_Top_Ten_Project`), which we saw in *Chapter 13, Security and Performance Tests*. You can use the **Zed Attack Proxy (ZAP)** tool, which uses these 10 rules, to perform security tests on a web application.

These are some good practices for integrating security into a DevOps culture in order to achieve a DevSecOps culture. We will now view some good practices for monitoring.

Monitoring your system

One of the main elements for the success of a DevOps culture is the implementation of tools that will continuously monitor the state of a system and applications. Monitoring must be implemented at all levels of the system by involving all teams, with the aim of having applications with real added value for the end user.

Indeed, the first component that can be monitored is the application itself, by implementing, as soon as possible, a logging or tracing system that will serve to gather information on the use of the application. Then, we will measure and monitor the state of the infrastructure, such as the **random-access memory (RAM)** and **central processing unit (CPU)** level of the **virtual machines (VMs)** or the network bandwidth. Finally, the last element that must be monitored is the status of DevOps processes. It is, therefore, important to have metrics on the execution of CI/CD pipelines, such as information on the execution time of pipelines, or the number of pipelines that have executed successfully or failed. With this data, for example, we can determine the deployment speed of an application.

There are many monitoring tools, such as Prometheus, Grafana, New Relic, Nagios, and others that are integrated into the various cloud providers, such as Azure Application Insights or Azure Monitor Logs.

Concerning good practices for monitoring, I would say that it is important to target the **key performance indicators (KPIs)** that are necessary for you and that are easy to analyze. It is useless to have a monitoring system that captures a lot of data or an application that writes a lot of logs, as it's too time-consuming when it comes to analyzing this information. In addition, on the volume of the captured data, we need to take care in ensuring its retention. The retention time of the data must be evaluated, and different teams should be consulted. Too much retention can cause capacity saturation on VMs or high costs for managed components in the cloud, and with too little retention, the log history is shorter, and therefore you can lose track of any problems.

Finally, when choosing a tool, you must make sure that it protects all the data that is captured, that the dashboards the tools present are understandable enough by all team members, and that it is integrated into a DevOps process.

We have explained that monitoring is a practice that must be integrated into a DevOps culture, taking into account some points of good practice that can improve communication between Dev and Ops and improve product quality for the end users.

After reviewing DevOps best practices with automation, CI/CD pipelines, and monitoring, we will take an overview of DevOps practices for project management and team organization.

Evolving project management

We have previously discussed some good DevOps practices to apply to projects, but all this can only be implemented and realized with a change in the way that projects are managed and teams are organized.

Here are some good practices that can facilitate the implementation of a DevOps culture in project management within companies.

First of all, it should be remembered that a DevOps culture only makes sense with the implementation of development and delivery practices that will allow applications to be delivered in short deployment cycles. Therefore, in order to be applicable, projects must also be managed with short cycles. To achieve this, one of the most suitable project management methods to apply a DevOps culture that has proven its worth in recent years is the agile method, which uses sprints (short cycles of 2 to 3 weeks) with incremental, iterative deployments and strong collaboration between developers.

A DevOps culture just extends the agile methodology by promoting collaboration between several domains (Dev/Ops/security/testers).

> **Note**
>
> To learn more about the agile method and its different frameworks (Scrum and **Extreme Programming** (**XP**), for example), I recommend http://agilemethodology.org/, which provides a lot of documentation.

In addition, for a better application of DevOps implementations, it is important to change your organization by no longer having teams organized by areas of expertise, such as having a team of developers, another team of operations, and a team of testers. The problem with this organizational model is that the teams are compartmentalized, resulting in a lack of communication (which we saw in *Chapter 1, The DevOps Culture and Infrastructure as Code Practices*, with the *wall of confusion*). This means that different teams have different objectives, which slams the brakes on applying good practices for a DevOps culture.

One of the models that allow for better communication is *feature team* organization with multidisciplinary project teams that are composed of people from all fields. In a team, we have developers, operational staff, and testers, and all these people work with the same objective.

If you want to know more about Microsoft's DevOps transformation, I suggest you watch the presentation by Donovan Brown at `https://www.agilealliance.org/resources/sessions/microsoft-devops-transformation-donovan-brown/`, which explains how Microsoft has changed its organization to adapt to a DevOps culture to continuously improve its products while taking into account user needs.

We have just seen that to implement a DevOps culture in companies, organizational changes are required, including agile project management and the composition of multidisciplinary teams.

Summary

In this final chapter, we have seen that the implementation of a DevOps culture within projects requires the use of best practices regarding the automation of all manual tasks, the proper choice of tools, a less-monolithic project architecture, and the implementation of monitoring.

On a large scale, for the organization of teams and the company as a whole, we have seen that the agile method, as well as multidisciplinary teams, contribute strongly to the implementation of a DevOps culture.

To finish this book, my advice to all you readers who are adopting DevOps practices is to implement and monitor them on small projects and to start by using the tools that are most familiar and accessible to you. Then, as soon as your DevOps process is working properly, you can extend this to larger projects.

Questions

1. What are the advantages of deployment automation?

2. Is it necessary to use Terraform to do IaC?

3. What needs to be done to improve security in DevOps processes?

4. Does monitoring only concern monitoring of the condition of the infrastructure?

5. Which good practice should be implemented in the application architecture?

6. In a DevOps organization, how are teams constituted?

Further reading

If you want to know more about DevOps best practices, here are some articles to aid you in this:

- *16 Best Practices Of CI/CD Pipeline To Speed Test Automation*: https://www.lambdatest.com/blog/16-best-practices-of-ci-cd-pipeline-to-speed-test-automation/

- *How To Implement Continuous Testing In DevOps Like A Pro?*: https://www.lambdatest.com/blog/how-to-implement-continuous-testing-in-devops-like-a-pro/

- *Secure DevOps*: https://www.microsoft.com/en-us/securityengineering/devsecops

- *9 Pillars of Continuous Security Best Practices*: https://devops.com/9-pillars-of-continuous-security-best-practices/

- *Top 5 Best Practices for DevOps Monitoring*: https://devops.com/top-5-best-practices-devops-monitoring/

- *10 Pitfalls to Avoid when Implementing DevOps*: https://opensource.com/article/19/9/pitfalls-avoid-devops

Assessments

Chapter 1: The DevOps Culture and Infrastructure as Code Practices

1. DevOps is a contraction that is formed from the words *Development* and *Operations*.

2. DevOps is a term that represents a culture.

3. The three axes of DevOps culture are collaboration, process, and tools.

4. The objective of continuous integration is to get quick feedback on the quality of the code archived by team members.

5. The difference between continuous delivery and continuous deployment is that the triggering of the deployment in production is done manually for continuous delivery, whereas it is automatic for continuous deployment.

6. Infrastructure as Code consists of writing the code of the resources that make up an infrastructure.

Chapter 2: Provisioning Cloud Infrastructure with Terraform

1. The language used by Terraform is HashiCorp Configuration Language (HCL).

2. Terraform's role is as an Infrastructure as Code tool.

3. No. Terraform is not a scripting tool.

4. The command that allows you to display the installed version is `terraform version`.

5. The name of the Azure object that connects Terraform to Azure is the Azure Service Principal.

6. The three main commands of Terraform are `terraform init`, `terraform plan`, and `terraform apply`.

7. The Terraform command that allows us to destroy resources is `terraform destroy`.

8. We add the `--auto-approve` option to the `terraform apply` command.

9. The purpose of the Terraform state file is to keep the resources and their properties throughout the execution of Terraform.

10. No, it is not a good practice to store a Terraform state file locally; it must be stored in a protected remote backend.

Chapter 3: Using Ansible for Configuring IaaS Infrastructure

1. The role of Ansible, as detailed in this chapter, is to automate the configuration of a VM.

2. No. We cannot install Ansible on a Windows OS.

3. The two artifacts studied in this chapter that Ansible needs to run are the inventory and the playbook.

4. The option is `--check`.

5. The name of the utility used to encrypt and decrypt Ansible data is Ansible Vault.

6. When using dynamic inventory in Azure, the script is based on VM tags that are used to return the list of VMs.

Chapter 4: Optimizing Infrastructure Deployment with Packer

1. The two ways to install Packer are manually or via a script.

2. The mandatory sections of a Packer template that are used to create a VM image in Azure are builders and provisioners.

3. The command used to validate a Packer template is `packer validate`.

4. The command that is used to generate a Packer image is `packer build`.

Chapter 5: Authoring the Development Environment with Vagrant

1. The role of Vagrant is to create a local development environment.
2. The Vagrant command to create a VM is `vagrant up`.
3. The Vagrant command to connect SSH to the VM is `vagrant ssh`.

Chapter 6: Managing Your Source Code with Git

1. Git is a distributed version control system (DVCS).
2. The command to initialize a repository is `git init`.
3. The artifact is the commit that consists of saving part of the code.
4. The command that allows you to save your code in the local repository is `git commit`.
5. The command that allows you to send your code to the remote repository is `git push`.
6. The command that allows you to update your local repository from the remote repository is `git pull`.
7. The branch is the mechanism that allows you to isolate the code.
8. GitFlow is a branch management model in Git.

Chapter 7: Continuous Integration and Continuous Delivery

1. The prerequisite for setting up a CI pipeline is to have its code in a source control manager.
2. The CI pipeline is triggered every time a team member commits/pushes code.
3. A package manager is a central repository used to centralize and share packages, development libraries, tools, or software.
4. The NuGet package manager allows you to store .NET libraries/frameworks.
5. Azure Artifacts is integrated into Azure DevOps.
6. No, it's an on-premises tool that you have to install on a server.
7. In Azure DevOps, the service that manages CI/CD pipelines is Azure Pipelines.

8. The GitLab services consist of a source code manager, a CI/CD pipeline manager, and a board for project management.

9. In GitLab CI, a CI pipeline is built with a YAML file named `.gitlab-ci.yml`.

Chapter 8: Deploying Infrastructure as Code with CI/CD Pipelines

1. The tool used is Azure Pipelines.

2. The provisioning order is Packer, then Terraform, and finally Ansible.

Chapter 9: Containerizing Your Application with Docker

1. Docker Hub is a public registry of Docker images.

2. The basic element is the Dockerfile.

3. The instruction is `FROM`.

4. The command to create a Docker image is `docker build`.

5. The instantiation command of a Docker container is `docker run`.

6. The Docker command to publish an image is `docker publish`.

Chapter 10: Managing Containers Effectively with Kubernetes

1. Kubernetes' role is to manage containers.

2. In Kubernetes, all objects are written in YAML specification files.

3. The Kubernetes CLI tool is called `kubectl`.

4. The command that applies a deployment in K8s is `kubectl apply`.

5. Helm is the package manager for Kubernetes.

6. Azure Kubernetes Services is a managed Kubernetes cluster in Azure.

Chapter 11: Testing APIs with Postman

1. Postman is a tool that allows you to perform API tests.

2. The first element to create is a collection.

3. In Postman, the API configuration is found in a request.

4. The collection runner allows you to execute all requests in a collection.

5. Newman is a command-line tool that performs Postman tests in a CI/CD pipeline.

Chapter 12: Static Code Analysis with SonarQube

1. SonarQube is developed in Java.

2. To install SonarQube, it is necessary to have Java installed.

3. SonarQube is a tool for static code analysis.

4. SonarLint allows developers to do code analysis while they write code.

Chapter 13: Security and Performance Tests

1. No. ZAP is not a tool to analyze the source code of an application.

2. In Postman, the performance metric is the execution time of each request.

Chapter 14: Security in the DevOps Process with DevSecOps

1. Its role is to test the compliance of a system or infrastructure.

2. The package manager is Gem.

3. The command is `inspec exec`.

4. Vault is edited by HashiCorp.

5. The command is `vault server -dev`.

6. No. When installed locally, it can only be used for development and testing.

7. In this mode, the data is stored in memory.

Chapter 15: Reducing Deployment Downtime

1. The Terraform option that reduces downtime is `create_before_destroy`.

2. A blue-green deployment infrastructure is composed of one blue and one green environment and a router or load balancer.

3. Both patterns are canary release and dark launch.

4. The Azure components that allow blue-green deployment are app service slots and Azure Traffic Manager.

5. The role of feature flags is to enable or disable features of an application without having to redeploy it.

6. The FeatureToggle is a simple feature flag, open source framework for .NET applications.

7. LaunchDarkly is an SaaS solution that frees you from any installation.

Chapter 16: DevOps for Open Source Projects

1. No, to modify the code of another repository, you will need to create a fork of this repository.

2. The element that allows the merge is the pull request.

3. The `CHANGELOG.md` file allows you to display the release notes.

4. A release is linked to a Git tag.

5. In Travis CI, the configuration of a job is written to a YAML file.

6. The two tools are SonarCloud and WhiteSource Bolt.

7. Security vulnerabilities are listed in the **Issues** tab.

Chapter 17: DevOps Best Practices

1. Deployment automation eliminates manual errors and reduces deployment cycles.

2. No. Any tool that allows you to script the configuration of an infrastructure can be used.

3. Security teams must be integrated with Dev and Ops.

4. No, monitoring is about applications, infrastructure, and IC/CD pipelines.

5. In the application, it is a good practice to separate the features or domains of the application to have code that can be easily deployed.

6. In the DevOps organizational structure, the teams are multidisciplinary.

Index

W

Y

Z

`Packt.com`

Subscribe to our online digital library for full access to over 7,000 books and videos, as well as industry leading tools to help you plan your personal development and advance your career. For more information, please visit our website.

Why subscribe?

- Spend less time learning and more time coding with practical eBooks and Videos from over 4,000 industry professionals
- Improve your learning with Skill Plans built especially for you
- Get a free eBook or video every month
- Fully searchable for easy access to vital information
- Copy and paste, print, and bookmark content

Did you know that Packt offers eBook versions of every book published, with PDF and ePub files available? You can upgrade to the eBook version at `packt.com` and as a print book customer, you are entitled to a discount on the eBook copy. Get in touch with us at `customercare@packtpub.com` for more details.

At `www.packt.com`, you can also read a collection of free technical articles, sign up for a range of free newsletters, and receive exclusive discounts and offers on Packt books and eBooks.

Other Books You May Enjoy

If you enjoyed this book, you may be interested in these other books by Packt:

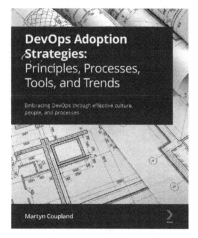

DevOps Adoption Strategies: Principles, Processes, Tools, and Trends

Martyn Coupland

ISBN: 9781801076326

- Understand the importance of culture in DevOps
- Build, foster, and develop a successful DevOps culture
- Discover how to implement a successful DevOps framework
- Measure and define the success of DevOps transformation
- Get to grips with techniques for continuous feedback and iterate process changes
- Discover the tooling used in different stages of the DevOps life cycle

Modern DevOps Practices

Gaurav Agarwal

ISBN: 9781800562387

- Become well-versed with AWS ECS, Google Cloud Run, and Knative
- Discover how to build and manage secure Docker images efficiently
- Understand continuous integration with Jenkins on Kubernetes and GitHub actions
- Get to grips with using Spinnaker for continuous deployment/delivery
- Manage immutable infrastructure on the cloud with Packer, Terraform, and Ansible
- Explore the world of GitOps with GitHub actions, Terraform, and Flux CD

Packt is searching for authors like you

If you're interested in becoming an author for Packt, please visit `authors.packtpub.com` and apply today. We have worked with thousands of developers and tech professionals, just like you, to help them share their insight with the global tech community. You can make a general application, apply for a specific hot topic that we are recruiting an author for, or submit your own idea.

Share Your Thoughts

Now you've finished *Learning DevOps - Second Edition*, we'd love to hear your thoughts! Scan the QR code below to go straight to the Amazon review page for this book and share your feedback or leave a review on the site that you purchased it from.

https://packt.link/r/1801818967

Your review is important to us and the tech community and will help us make sure we're delivering excellent quality content.

Printed in Poland
by Amazon Fulfillment
Poland Sp. z o.o., Wrocław

33962654R00316